Lecture Notes in Computer Science 11253

Commenced Publication in 1973
Founding and Former Series Editors:
Gerhard Goos, Juris Hartmanis, and Jan van Leeuwen

More information about this series at http://www.springer.com/series/7409

Andrzej M. J. Skulimowski · Zhengguo Sheng
Sondès Khemiri-Kallel · Christophe Cérin
Ching-Hsien Hsu (Eds.)

Internet of Vehicles

Technologies and Services Towards Smart City

5th International Conference, IOV 2018
Paris, France, November 20–22, 2018
Proceedings

 Springer

Editors
Andrzej M. J. Skulimowski 🆔
AGH University of Science and Technology
Krakow, Poland

Christophe Cérin
Université Paris 13
Villetaneuse, France

Zhengguo Sheng
University of Sussex
Brighton, UK

Ching-Hsien Hsu
National Chung Cheng University
Minxiong, Taiwan

Sondès Khemiri-Kallel
Université de Versailles St Quentin
Versailles, France

ISSN 0302-9743   ISSN 1611-3349 (electronic)
Lecture Notes in Computer Science
ISBN 978-3-030-05080-1   ISBN 978-3-030-05081-8 (eBook)
https://doi.org/10.1007/978-3-030-05081-8

Library of Congress Control Number: 2018962668

LNCS Sublibrary: SL3 – Information Systems and Applications, incl. Internet/Web, and HCI

This Springer imprint is published by the registered company Springer Nature Switzerland AG
The registered company address is: Gewerbestrasse 11, 6330 Cham, Switzerland

Preface

As the era of Internet of Things is arriving, the Internet of Vehicles (IOV) plays an important role for constructing smart cities as well as for establishing smart industrial environments according to the Industry 4.0 paradigm. Smart cities are complex integrated network systems, which connect different people within automotives, different automotives, and different environmental objects in cities. In the industrial environments, IOV focuses on providing new efficient solutions with digital intervehicular data transfer and overall communications. Yet, IOV is different from telematics, vehicle ad hoc networks, and intelligent transportation, in which vehicles like phones can run within the whole network, and obtain various services by swarm intelligent computing with people, vehicles, and environments.

This volume contains the proceedings of the 5th International Conference on Internet of Vehicles (IOV 2018), which was held in Paris, France during November 20–22, 2018. We accepted for publication a total of 21 high-quality papers selected from 41 submissions. The articles in this volume are grouped in 4 Parts, namely "IoV communications and networking" (5 papers), "IoV clouds and services" (6 papers), "Vehicular modelling and simulation" (5 papers), and "Vehicular security and privacy" (5 papers). The above Part titles correspond to the research areas traditionally covered by the IOV conference series. Like all previous conferences in this series, IOV 2018 was intended to play an important role for researchers and industry practitioners to exchange information regarding advancements in the state of art and practice of IOV architectures, protocols, services, and applications. It was also intended to identify emerging research topics and define the future directions of IOV and its related areas such as Internet-supported autonomous driving. We believe that this volume not only presents novel and interesting ideas but also will stimulate interesting discussions from the participants and inspire new ideas that will be submitted and presented at further conferences in this series.

The organization of conferences is hard work. This conference would not have been possible without the exceptional commitment of many expert volunteers. We would like to take this opportunity to extend our sincere thanks to all the authors, keynote speakers, Technical Program Committee members, and reviewers. Special thanks go to the entire local arrangements committee for their help in making this conference a success. We would also like to express our gratitude to all the organizations that supported our efforts to bring the conference to fruition. We are grateful to Springer for publishing the underlying proceedings.

Last, but not least, we hope that the participants not only enjoyed the technical program during this prestigious conference but also discovered many historical attractions in Paris, to make their stay unforgettable. Thanking you for your participation in this fruitful and enjoyable IOV 2018 Conference!

November 2018

Andrzej M. J. Skulimowski
Zhengguo Sheng
Sondès Khemiri-Kallel
Christophe Cérin
Ching-Hsien Hsu

Organization

General Chair

Mohamed-Cherif Rahal   VeDeCom, France

General Executive Chair

Christophe Cérin   Université Paris 13, France

Program Chairs

Andrzej M. J. Skulimowski   AGH University of Science and Technology, Poland
Zhengguo Sheng   The University of Sussex, UK

Publication Chair

Sondes Khemiri-Kallel   Université Versailles St Quentin, France

International Liaison and Publicity Chairs

Naercio Magaia   University of Sussex, UK
Benoît Parrein   Université de Nantes (Polytech Nantes), France

Steering Committee

Mohammed Atiquzzaman   University of Oklahoma, USA
Jiannong Cao   Hong Kong Polytechnic University, China
Ching-Hsien Hsu   Chung Hua University, Taiwan
Victor C. Leung   The University of British Columbia, Canada
Shangguang Wang   Beijing University of Posts and Telecommunications, China
Philip Yu   University of Illinois at Chicago, USA

Technical Program Committee

Witold Byrski   AGH University of Science and Technology, Poland
Carlos Calafate   Universitat Politècnica de València, Spain
Christophe Cerin   University of Paris XIII, France
Yao-Chung Chang   National Taiwan Technical University, Taiwan
Jyh-Biau Chang   National Taitung University, Taiwan
Rachid Chelouah   EISTI, France
Min-Xiou Chen   National Dong Hwa University, Taiwan

Additional Reviewers

Ferheen Ayaz	The University of Sussex, UK
Bastien Confais	CNRS, Polytech Nantes, France
Martin Lopez-Nores	University of Vigo, Spain
Andreas Pressas	The University of Sussex, UK
Przemyslaw Pukocz	AGH University of Science and Technology, Poland
Jianshan Zhou	Beihang University (BUAA), China

Contents

Vehicular Modelling and Simulation

Vehicular Security and Privacy

IoV Communications and Networking

Network Architectures in Internet of Vehicles (IoV): Review, Protocols Analysis, Challenges and Issues

Livinus Tuyisenge[1,2]([✉]), Marwane Ayaida[1], Samir Tohme[2], and Lissan-Eddine Afilal[1]

[1] CReSTIC, Reims University, 51100 Reims, France
{livinus.tuyisenge,marwane.ayaida,lissan.afilal}@univ-reims.fr
[2] VEDECOM Institute, 78 Rue des Chantiers, 78000 Versailles, France
samir.tohme@vedecom.fr
http://www.univ-reims.fr, http://www.vedecom.fr

Abstract. Since some decades ago, the evolution of the internet continues to revolutionize many aspects of human life. It started by connecting computers, then smartphones before it becomes generalized to connecting everything which gives birth to the Internet of Things (IoT) paradigm. Thanks to the telecommunication and technologies' advancements, vehicles are now able to have internet access and communications capabilities, thus, making communications networks called Vehicular Ad hoc Networks (VANETs). The Internet of Vehicles is, therefore, an evolution of VANETs where IoT is applied and in which the main component is the vehicle. Besides the many opportunities that IoV presents, there are still many challenges and issues that must be considered with great attention such as efficient and reliable network architectures that should provide an efficient IoV deployment. This is why, in this paper, we have made our contribution by establishing a review of existing novel IoV architecture solutions and we further propose a protocol stack analysis of these architectures.

Keywords: IoV · VANETs · D2D · Network architectures · C-ITS

1 Introduction

Similarly to the OSI model or TCP/IP model which are most used in the description of many processes involved in traditional network communications such as packets routing and packets delivering, communications between different Cooperative Intelligent Transportation System (C-ITS) components that form the IoV ecosystem are based on many mechanisms, and they always involve many different devices or infrastructures. Morever, being a particular MANETs network category, VANETs (vehicle-to-vehicle communications (V2V), Vehicle-to-Infrastructure (V2I) and Vehicle-to-Everything (V2X)) and consequently IoV

This work is supported by URCA in Partnership with VEDECOM Institute.

A. M. J. Skulimowski et al. (Eds.): IOV 2018, LNCS 11253, pp. 3–13, 2018.
https://doi.org/10.1007/978-3-030-05081-8_1

deployment is very complex and need a special effort and consideration due to their characteristics such as a high level of mobility and dynamic change in the topology, which generates scattered networks. In this way, Academia and Industries have made a special interest in this field and have proposed some architecture standardizations such as ETSI in Europe architecture described by Fig. 1 and Federal Communications Commission (FCC) in USA. As it can be seen in this Fig. 1, the main difference with the traditional TCP/IP or OSI model is:

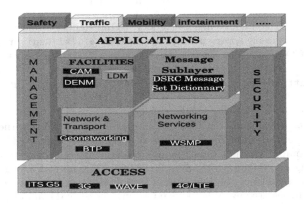

Fig. 1. ETSI architecture

- the presence of a facilities layer which is responsible for VANETs related applications (Cooperative Awareness Message (CAM), Decentralized Notification Message (DENM), Local Dynamic Map (LDM)) and communications process.
- The combination of Network and Transport layers in one layer
- Integration of two special layers: one for Management and another for Security.
- The presence of ITS dedicated stack which integrates the GeoNetworking addressing.

However, such architectures are only related to the internal structure and capabilities of one device involved in the communications without clarifying the interaction process in case of handover or other mechanisms that involve external devices interaction. The deployment of Internet of Things (IoT) in the VANETs context enabled promising solutions and applications (such as real-time applications for autonomous driving, road traffic management applications and comfort applications) which gave birth to the so-called Internet of Vehicles (IoV). The IoV ecosystem is basically composed by 4 components which are:

- End points: vehicles, smartphones, sensors and others connected devices,
- Infrastructure: Roadside units (RSUs), Wi-Fi hotspots, cellular networks (3G/LTE) base stations,

- Operations such as policy enforcement, flow-based management, security and pricing and
- Services such as public cloud for subscription-based services, private cloud, enterprise cloud for enterprise data, voice or video, etc.

Nowadays, some appropriate interaction architectures between these IoV components are proposed. This gives hope to the IoV deployment possibility despite the RSU deployment delay since its expensive implementation, which is estimated to €660 Millions from 2020 to 2026 [2].

As many specification and standardization activities in IoV domain are still in progress, we found that a review on network architecture in IoV might be of great importance and will help the researchers in this field to be aware and updated to what is already done in IoV. This motivates us to provide this work as a contribution to the IoV research community.

The remainder of this paper is organized as follows. In Sect. 2, we established an overview about advancements in IoV architectures, then we propose a protocols stack analysis in Sect. 3, followed by some challenges and issues in IoV that we present in Sect. 4 before concluding this paper in Sect. 5.

2   IoV Architectures Overview

Currently, many industries and academia researchers are paying great attention to novel network architectures that could efficiently allow the IoV deployment and related business market models. In [3], Bonomi from Cisco has proposed and described a 4 layers based architecture as shown in Fig. 2. He proposed to consider the 4 steps that every IoV communication always involves which are: Embedded systems and sensors, Multi service Edge, Core, Data center and Cloud, as it can be seen in this Fig. 2.

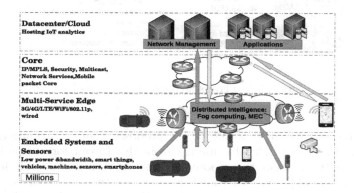

Fig. 2. IoV 4 layers architecture based on [3]

In [7], authors also proposed a 5 layered architecture, illustrated by Fig. 3, which is composed of the following layers:

- Perception: This layer represents the interaction between the vehicle and its environment. It uses the devices present inside the vehicles such as sensors, actuators, personal devices and those installed across the road such as RSU in order to gather relevant information to be used in vehicle's decisions.
- Coordination: this layer is mainly responsible of interoperability, routing and message transportation security.
- Artificial intelligence: This is the core layer where decisions component tasks have to be executed. This layer mainly focuses on big data analysis, data mining, cloud computing and expert systems based decision.
- Application: this layer concerns the kind of services and requirements available in the system.
- Business: it is the part that describes which kind of businesses the IoV market will offer to users.

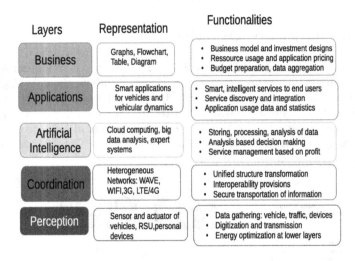

Fig. 3. IoV 5 layers architecture based on [7]

Other researchers such as [6,8,10,11] proposed their contribution in IoV architecture that we decided to summarize in the Table 1 for comparison and good readability. In order to propose a robust routing protocol for IoV environment, authors of [1] have extended these architectures presented in previous works, by integrating the Software Defined Networks (SDN) paradigm which consists in separating the network traffic control plane and the data transfer plane. Therefore, they proposed an architecture with 6 layers which are: Perception layer, communication layer, application layer, cost layer, security layer, and a layer for law, ethic, private life and legal use. Then, they applied the SDN paradigm in the communication layer in which they specify a SDN routing protocol (Control plane + Data plane) sub-layer and Radio Access Technologies (RAT) types (homogenous or heterogenous) sub-layer.

In [4], authors proposed a 7 layers based architecture, shown in Fig. 4. They designed this 7 layers architecture by reducing the layers functionalities' complexity and by grouping the very similar functions in a same and appropriate layers, thus, making easy its implementation.

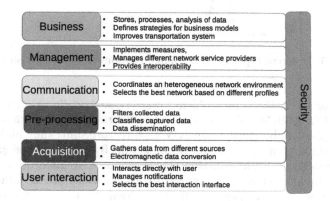

Fig. 4. IoV 7 layers architecture based on [4]

We must recall that the main objective of layered architecture is the optimization of the number of layers by enhancing the differentiability among layers. This optimization must be also deployed as more efficiently as possible in order to achieve the network characteristics and requirements which are mainly: interoperability, reliability, scalability, modularity, simplicity and integration flexibility with the internet, in other words, a service oriented architecture based on respect of QoS and QoE user preferences, and plug-and-play interfaces. Therefore, as illustrated in Fig. 4, they proposed a layer for user interaction which directly exchanges with the user interface, a layer for data acquisition, a preprocessing layer in which collected data must be pre-processed before being used in the communication layer, which coordinates the heterogenous network environment. After that, they include a layer for interoperability and network service providers which is called Management. Finally, they proposed a business layer and a security related layer.

They also introduce a device to device (D2D) communication approach which might be a promising and probably most used solution in the years to come in Machine to machine (M2M) communications context. A thoroughly and exhaustive review on the device to device communications can be found in [6]. The D2D architecture approach in IoV is illustrated by Fig. 5.

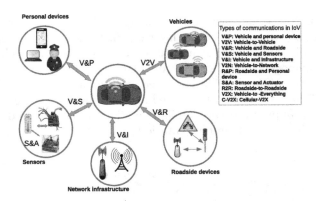

Fig. 5. Different types of D2D communications in IoV based on [4]

Considering the challenging problem towards resource allocation to guarantee Real-Time (RT) traffic in IoV and to enhance the resource utilization efficiency, authors of [8], not only specified an IOV architecture, but, they also proposed a model for resource allocation and optimization by following the supply and demand approach and utility function. Their proposed architecture is an hierarchical IoV architecture that consists of three layers which are: a data-gathering cloud, an internet-access cloud, application cloud. In their architecture, they also considered four networks which are: the On-Vehicle-Sensor (OVS) network, Vehicle-to-Vehicle (V2V) network, Vehicle-to-Infrastructure beside road (V2I) network and a Vehicle-to-People (V2P) network. In the same direction of real-time challenges, Authors of [5] proposed a fog computing Real-time Based ITS Big Data Analytics (RITS-BDA) architecture in the IoV environments, which is composed of a three dimension system architecture including the dimensions of IoV, intelligent computing and real-time big data analytics. RITS-BDA is then a multi-dimensional layered architecture which is made of the following layers: 4 layers in the intelligent computing dimension (3 hierachical Fog computing layers, cloud computing layer), 3 layers for the real-time big data analytics dimension (serving layer, batch layer, speed layer) and 6 layers for the IoV dimension (Perception layer, Infrastructure network layer, Communication layer, Application layer, Business layer). Their architecture aims to serve the real implementation of real-time ITS big data applications and is extended from a generic real-time big data processing architecture called lambda architecture that was introduced in [9]. For more information on these big-data and analytics based architectures, readers are referred to their respective articles: [5,9]

Therefore, we summarized the existing IoV novel architecture solutions that we found in the literature in the Table 1.

Table 1. Summary of IoV layers architecture solutions

Proposed IoV architectures based on numbers of layers	Names of layers	Communication models supported	Security	References
3 layers	Client, connection, cloud	V2V, V&R, V&P, V&I	Security as a service	[10]
3 layers	Vehicle, location, cloud	V2V, V&R	Cross-layered	[11]
3 layers	A data-gathering cloud, an internet-access cloud, application cloud	OVS, V2V, V2I, V2P	Not specified	[8]
3 layers	D2D area network, network management, D2D applications	D2D-B, D2D-C, D2D-D, M2M-D and D2D-N	Not specified	[6]
4 layers	Services, operation, infrastructure, end points	V2V, V&I	Cross-layered	[3]
5 layers	Perception, coordination, artificial intelligence (AI), application, business	V&I, V2V, V&S, V&P, V&R	Security plane	[7]
6 layers	Perception, communication, application, Cost, Security, legal, ethical use	V2V, V&I, V2X	Security plane	[1]
7 layers	User interaction, Acquisition, pre-processing, communication, management, Business, security	V&I, V2V, V&S, V&P, V&R, R&P, R2R, S&A	Cross-layered	[4]
Multi-dimensional: 13 layers	Perception, Fog computing (3 tiers), cloud computing, serving, batch, speed, Infrastructure network, AI, Communication, Application, Business	V&I, V2V, V&S, V&P, V&R, R&P, R2R, S&A, V2X	Cross-layered	[5]

where: D2D-B represents Backhaul applications, D2D-C is for critical application, D2D-D stands for direct D2D, M2M-D: direct M2M and D2D-N represents the non-critical applications.

Thus, in the following section, we made a protocols stack analysis of this IoV network architectures, in order to show some advancements that need to be taken into account in the IoV standardization activities.

3   IoV Protocols Stack and Architecture Analysis

For each architecture, a protocol stack is proposed. It consists of specification of the functional requirements of each architecture layer by organizing the appropriate existing protocols such as VANETs standards, IEEE, ETSI, 3GPP standards, etc. For the 5 layers architecture in [7], authors proposed a protocol stack (illustrated by Fig. 6) composed by 4 planes which are : management plane, operation plane, security plane and layer plane. However, Authors of [4] proposed a protocol stack of two plane: an operational plane and a security plane as illustrated by Fig. 7 where:

- CALM-SL = CALM Service Layer
- OMA-DM = Open Mobile Alliance Device Management

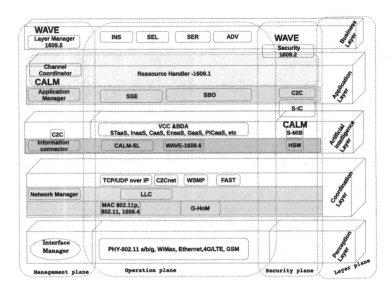

Fig. 6. Protocol stack of the IoV architecture with 5 layers based on [7]

- 6LoWPAN = IPv6 over Low Power Wireless Personal Area Network
- RPL = Routing Protocol Low Power and Lossy Networks
- μIP = Micro Internet Protocol
- ROLL = Routing overlow Power and Lossy Networks
- XMPP = eXtensible Messaging and Presents Protocol
- CoAP = Constraint Application Protocol
- HTTP REST = HyperText Transfer Protocol Representational State Transfer
- MQTT = Message Queuing Telemetric Transport
- LLAP = Lightweight Local Automation Protocol
- LoRaWAN = Low Power WAN
- OTrP = Open Trust Protocol
- S-MIB = Security Management Information Base
- HSM = Hardware Security Management
- S-IC = Security Information Connector.

It is to be noticed that each plane interacts with all the layers in its respective architecture. For more details about protocol stack functionalities and description, readers are encouraged to refer to the corresponding articles in [4,7].

By analyzing these aforementioned proposed architectures in IoV domain, we found many aspects that proved that the IoV is still in its early stage of standardization and presents many opportunities and challenges for both academia and industries researchers, IT engineers, internet services providers, etc. This is remarkable especially when considering the IoV perception from different studies, whether it is from industrial or academic researchers. The considered point of view used to propose and design these architectures are completely different and sometimes there is interchangeability between layers. For examples:

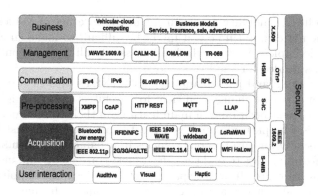

Fig. 7. IoV protocol stack with 7 layers based on [4]

- In Fig. 3, the perception layer (L1) functionalities corresponds to the function-
  nalities presented in embedded systems and sensors layer (L1) in Fig. 2. The
  same layer is split into two layers (i.e. user interaction (L1) and acquisition
  (L2)) in Fig. 4.
- coordination layer (L2) in Fig. 3 is called multi-service edge (L2) in Fig. 2
  whereas it is called communication layer (L4) in Fig. 4.
- data center/cloud layer (L4) in Fig. 2 is divided into 3 layers (artificial intelligence layer (L3), application layer (L4), business layer (L5)) in Fig. 3 while
  it is divided into 2 layers (Management layer (L5) and Business layer (L6))
  in Fig. 4.

We can also remark a problem in layer's order between Figs. 4 and 3. In
Fig. 4, there is a pre-processing layer, which corresponds to artificial intelligence
in Fig. 3, before the communication layer. However, in Fig. 3, the processing
which takes place in the artificial intelligence layer comes after the coordination
layer.

Another aspect to be considered is the presence of a security dedicated layer
in Fig. 2 which was not available in the 5 layers based architecture in figure 3.

The comparison may be long when comparing these architectures one by one,
from a 3 layers based architecture to a 13 layers based architecture. It is why we
preferred to make it briefly by establishing the Table 1. All those aforementioned
aspects show the earlyness stage of the IoV standardization which means that
there still be a lot of challenges and research' opportunities in this field. Details
of some challenges in IoV deployment are given in the following section.

4   Challenges and Issues in IoV

Some of many challenges and issues that need to be resolved in IoV are:

- Interoperability of network architectures: there is a great need for enhanced
  communications protocols and algorithms which might be able to facilitate

and to handle the mobility management in the Internet of Vehicles domain. As it can be noticed, untill now, it might be difficult to make an efficient and interoperable implementation which might satisfy all the IoV constraints and requirements needed for the IoV deployment.

- Intelligent routing and path planning : as VANETs present a high mobility and frequent topology changes, efficient IoV architecture must highly consider the predictive next position as a main features in their communication's layer decision. It is why path planning is a great challenges that must be resolved in IoV, especially for autonomous vehicles in urban environments, because it enables self-driving cars to find the safest, most convenient, and most economically beneficial routes from a depart point to a destination point. Effective path planning algorithms are what make autonomous driving genuinely feasible, safe, and fast[1] which leads to an efficient IoV deployment.
- Sensors & artificial intelligence : vehicle continuously interacts with its environnement through a certain amount of sensors data. These data sensed from different sensors need to be fused before being used in making vehicles'decision. Currently, the artificial intelligence is a great core technology that is used in this field and needs to be well tested in different real scenario before vehicle passengers can confidently use full self-driving cars.
- Real time massive data processing: a good combination of parallel and sequential data processing is needed in scenarios where only parallel data processing is not sufficient. A parallel data acquisition, data processing and big data analytics are needed and are essential in IoV.

5   Conclusions

The IoV has many promising market's opportunities especially in the field of smart transportation system through the Cooperative Intelligent Transportation Systems (C-ITS), the IT equipment manufacture sectors, software industry and Internet service providers. However, it is still facing many challenges and issues such as commercialization, growing traffic casualities like accidents, safety issues, efficiency, pollution, etc. It is predicted and also evident that IoV components will produce big data in high speeds and many IoV applications are realtime, highly sensitive to latency and require fast big data processing and reliable fast feedbacks [5]. Therefore, efficient and reliable network architectures that should provide an efficient IoV deployment are needed.

An effective and efficient integration of existing and different networks types standards are very important in the IoV ecosystem. Furthermore, the integration of cloud computing, fog computing, mobile edge computing, artificial intelligence and big data analysis are essential for an efficient IoV deployment. In this paper, we have made our contribution to the IoV advancements' literature by establishing a review of existing novel IoV architecture solutions and we also propose a protocols' stack analysis of these architectures. In our future works, we are going

---

[1] https://www.intellias.com/path-planning-for-autonomous-vehicles-with-hyperloop-option/

to focus our attention to the communication's layer and related mechanisms in IoV, especially the interoperability between different networks that might be available in the vehicles in the IoV ecosystem. We will also highly consider the use of D2D communications between vehicles.

References

1. Alouache, L., Nguyen, N., Aliouat, M., Chelouah, R.: Toward a hybrid SDN architecture for V2V communication in IoV environment. In: 2018 Fifth International Conference on Software Defined Systems (SDS), pp. 93–99, April 2018. https://doi.org/10.1109/SDS.2018.8370428
2. Asselin-Miler, N., et al.: Study on the deployment of C-ITS in Europe: final report. Technical report, February 2016. https://ec.europa.eu/transport/sites/transport/files/2016-c-its-deployment-study-final-report.pdf
3. Bonomi, F.: The smart and connected vehicle and the Internet of Things. In: Seminars, Cisco Systems: Advanced Architectures and Research, WSTS, San Jose (2013). http://tf.nist.gov/seminars/WSTS/PDFs/1-0_Cisco_FBonomi_ConnectedVehicles.pdf
4. Contreras-Castillo, J., Zeadally, S., Ibez, J.A.G.: A seven-layered model architecture for internet of vehicles. J. Inf. Telecommun. 1(1), 4–22 (2017). http://dx.doi.org/10.1080/24751839.2017.1295601, http://www.tandfonline.com/doi/pdf/10.1080/24751839.2017.1295601
5. Darwish, T.S.J., Bakar, K.A.: Fog based intelligent transportation big data analytics in the internet of vehicles environment: motivations, architecture, challenges, and critical issues. IEEE Access 6, 15679–15701 (2018). https://doi.org/10.1109/ACCESS.2018.2815989
6. Gandotra, P., Jha, R.K., Jain, S.: A survey on device-to-device (D2D) communication: architecture and security issues. J. Netw. Comput. Appl. 78, 9–29 (2017). https://doi.org/10.1016/j.jnca.2016.11.002, http://www.sciencedirect.com/science/article/pii/S1084804516302727
7. Kaiwartya, O., et al.: Internet of vehicles: motivation, layered architecture, network model, challenges, and future aspects. IEEE Access 4, 5356–5373 (2016). https://doi.org/10.1109/ACCESS.2016.2603219
8. Kang, L., Li, J., Li, X., W.Wang, Zhang, Y., Poslad, S.: A traffic-aware resource allocation scheme for internet of vehicles: a supply and demand function approach. J. Comput. Inf. Syst. 11(3), 987–994 (2015). https://doi.org/10.12733/jcis13115, https://www.researchgate.net/publication/281704933_A_traffic-aware_resource_allocation_scheme_for_internet_of_vehicles_A_supply_and_demand_function_approach/citations
9. Marz, N., Warren, J.: Big Data: Principles and Best Practices of Scalable Realtime Data Systems. Manning Publications, Shelter Island (2015)
10. Nanjie, L.: Internet of vehicles: your next connection (2011). http://www1.huawei.com/enapp/28/hw-110836.htm
11. Wan, J., Zhang, D., Zhao, S., Yang, L.T., Lloret, J.: Context-aware vehicular cyber-physical systems with cloud support: architecture, challenges, and solutions. IEEE Commun. Mag. 52(8), 106–113 (2014). https://doi.org/10.1109/MCOM.2014.6871677

Improved Latency of CAN Vehicle Data Extraction Method

Kavian Khosravinia[1](✉) ⓘ, Mohd Khair Hassan[1] ⓘ,
Ribhan Zafira Abdul Rahman[1] ⓘ,
and Syed Abdul Rahman Al-Haddad[2] ⓘ

[1] Department of Electrical and Electronic Engineering,
University Putra Malaysia, UPM, 43400 Serdang, Selangor, Malaysia
Kavian.khn@gmail.com, {Khair,ribhan}@upm.edu.my
[2] Department of Computer and Communication Systems Engineering,
University Putra Malaysia, UPM, 43400 Serdang, Selangor, Malaysia
sar@upm.edu.my

Abstract. Road vehicle-related data can be classified into multiple types. The technical data generated through the controller area network (CAN) bus technology provide real-time information on the vehicle. This is one of the important data that can support vast range of services for various applications like in intelligent transportation systems. OBD system is a wide-spread solution for extracting these data from the vehicles. Unfortunately, most of the past researches don't consider the accuracy and reliability of their input data extracted from OBD. Most of the current systems for vehicle data extraction are based on the integration of microcontroller boards and smartphones. These systems do not have a high modularity and flexibility, due to their limitations in terms of both hardware and software. This study aims to present a real-time system for communicating with the CAN bus, which could work as the system server-side for improving vehicle data extraction with higher data frequency rates than existing systems. Digital data accuracy could vary based upon different logging methods. Multiple hardware and software solutions exist for collecting vehicle data. Desired data was collected from the vehicles utilizing Raspberry Pi3 as computing and processing unit as data acquisition solutions to quantify differences among collection methods. Two types of data were observed for this study. The first CAN bus frame data that illustrates data collected for each line of hex data sent from an electronic control unit. The second, OBD data that represents some limited data that is requested from the electronic control unit under standard condition. Data log by the proposed system is a flexible (i.e. communicate with multiple electronic control units), modifiable (i.e. multiple input data simultaneously), multi-task, data dominant, latency sensitive, and a configurable device that can be fitted into any vehicle with minimum effort and minimum time lag in the data extraction process.

Keywords: Controller area network · Raspberry Pi3
On board diagnostic (OBD) · Data accuracy · Vehicle data extraction

© Springer Nature Switzerland AG 2018
A. M. J. Skulimowski et al. (Eds.): IOV 2018, LNCS 11253, pp. 14–26, 2018.
https://doi.org/10.1007/978-3-030-05081-8_2

1 Introduction

Modern vehicles are no longer mere mechanical devices, they are completely controlled and monitored by dozens of electronic control units coordinated via internal vehicular networks. A vehicle produces different macro-categories of data and this could enable a wide range of services such as telemetry applications, fleet management, driving analysis, and fault detection to provide benefits for the driver, passenger, and other road users [1].

With the development of information technology (IT) in many industries, and now appears poised to transform countries transportation system. One of the applications that described was intelligent transportation system (ITS), that to deploy communications, control, electronics, and computer technologies to improve the performance of traffic congestion, traffic safety, reduce fuel consumption, through transmitting real-time information. ITS include a wide and growing suite of technologies and applications such as real-time traffic information systems, in-car navigation and CAN data acquisition (telematics) systems, vehicle-to-infrastructure integration (VII), vehicle-to-vehicle integration (V2V), and etc. ITS applications are based on the technical data that obtained from the vehicle network using the in-vehicle embedded system Indeed, most of these services and applications must be access to the real-time in-vehicle data [2]. Figure 1 shows an in-vehicle interface (telematics hardware) which is connected to the internal network (CAN) of the vehicle to extract some specific set of data. For transmitting this data to authorized devices via Wi-Fi or to cloud applications via UMTS (Universal Mobile Telecommunications Service). On-board diagnostic (OBD) system is a wide-spread solution for extracting sensor information on vehicles. Detecting an OBD event includes several phases, requesting information from the electronic control unit, replaying the demand from the electronic control units, and reading the response. Every phase of this event chain has a time frame that can be varied and cause a delay in an event detecting (e.g., ELM327 uses as a data gathering device). Unfortunately, most of the past researches do not consider accuracy and reliability of their input data extracted from OBD [3]. Using the well-known request-response model, the maximum feasible scan rate is only 9 queries per second which significantly reduces the accuracy of measured data, lacking to provide high precision requirements for many real-time automotive applications such as autonomous vehicles and intelligent transportation systems [4].

Furthermore, most of current systems for vehicle data extraction are based on integration of microcontroller boards and smartphones. These systems do not have a high modularity and flexibility, due to their limitations in terms of both hardware and software. In fact, such systems are based on very low capacity microcontroller hardware which can run only a single process for the server-side [5–9].

Moreover, using request-response with OBD will force the ECU to enter a diagnostic session, resulting to suspend other ECU's processes. This might be tolerable for a vehicle's non-safety processes. However, ECU provides priority to the latency-sensitive, safety-operations and stops OBD's request-response queries. As the results, the overall query response time will be increased (due to query failures), leading to decrease the scan rate for the data extraction [10].

All of these factors have resulted in the extraction of inaccurate values, which might have affected the results in the analysis, algorithms, and driver application. Therefore, it is necessary to develop a new system to overcome these obstacles. This study aims to provide a real-time system with a high level of modularity and flexibility which considerably improves the accuracy and reliability of vehicle data extraction with higher data frequency rates than existing systems.

This paper is structured as follow: in Sect. 2 reviews the related works that were investigated and considered important to this project. In Sect. 3 explains the design and integration network test bench. Section 4 provides a brief overview of the modules of the system. Section 5 describes the design and implementation of the system. The observations and results are discussed in Sect. 6, and finally, the paper concludes with Sect. 7.

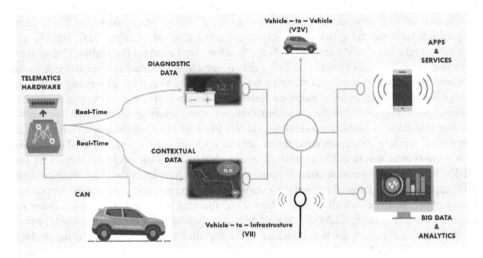

Fig. 1. Telematics control unit serve as an information gateway in vehicle

2   Related Work

Different sources were studied to know more about different techniques, methods, and hardware used to retrieve vehicle data. In the following section, the related works that were investigated and considered relevant to this research are reviewed.

A platform was designed by Meseguer et al. to have a safe and economical driving style [11]. The goal of this study was to create an Android application, which can communicate with ELM327 for extracting data such as acceleration, vehicle speed, and throttle position. Once accessed, this data was stored in XML file for uploading on the web platform. The system used off-line analysis, and the XML format file occupied a large storage space.

An Android mobile application was developed to communicate with ELM327 to collect vehicle information [12]. The data transmission between the mobile and

ELM327 was done via Wi-Fi. This platform only prepares the data for the user after the user initializes it.

A system for monitoring real-time parameters through the CAN-bus of a hybrid electric vehicle has been developed in [13]. The ELM327 has been equipped with Bluetooth module for extracting the vehicle data from the CAN bus. ELM327 then transferred the acquired data to the Android mobile via Bluetooth. Then Android mobile transfer the data via GPRS technology to a web server. The Android and web server are both programmed in Java, and HTTP was utilized to transmit information between the client and server.

In most of the studies above, ELM327 or other development boards are OBD readers that act as an interface between engine control unit and a mobile device. This type of design is suitable for monitoring and diagnostic purposes hence the polling rate is not necessary. However, in all studies, the researchers did not have any consideration for data latency and data scanning rates. It was also observed from the studies that ELM327 has a lot of limitation in extracting vehicle data from all the electronic control units.

3 Experimental Environment

In order to do an experimental test on the vehicle network, it was necessary to buy or rent a vehicle. But buying or renting a modern vehicle for research purposes is not practical and also poses some risk. The inspection process of an on-vehicle network may cause severe damages to the expensive electronic control units of the vehicle. Thus, to address this research barrier, a vehicle network test bench was designed instead of buying a vehicle. The vehicle network test bench aimed to decrease the risk of vehicle bus damaging [14].

3.1 Design Automotive Network Test Bench

In order to build an advanced vehicle network test bench, some necessary components are needed. The test bench consists of at least two electronic control units which were

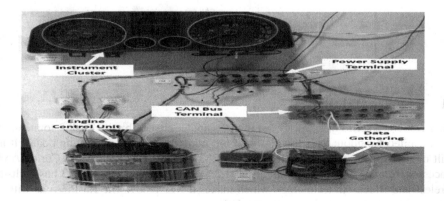

Fig. 2. Test bench

physically extracted from the vehicle. For generating sensor signals such as engine temperature, and speed variable resistor and microcontroller were used to simulate crankshaft signals and engine temperatures of the engine control unit. Figure 2 shows an example setup, with the engine control unit, instrument cluster hooked up to a power supply, proposed system, CAN bus terminal, and simulator sensors were installed on the plywood for further analysis and observation in the laboratory.

4   System Overview

A basic overview of the system is shown in Fig. 3. The proposed system is designed to communicate with the vehicle bus and act as an interface between the user and OBD-II port. This data gathering unit was developed to log OBD and direct CAN data at the same time. To expand the data gathering unit, research into wireless communications protocols was also required. By using this data gathering unit, it became possible to construct the required dataset. The proposed system consists of two main elements.

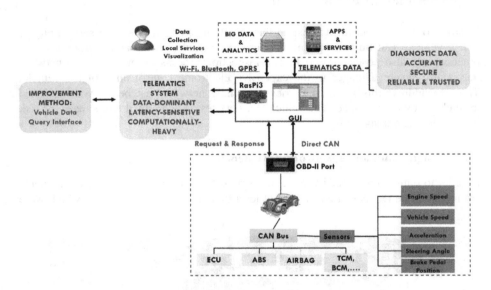

Fig. 3. System overview

4.1   Raspberry Pi3 (RasPi3)

The RasPi3 is a series of single-board mini-computer created by the RasPi3 foundation in the United Kingdom. It is low cost and has a highly capable computing board. It is built on a powerful new generation of BCM2837 64-bit quad-core ARM Cortex-A53 processor from Broadcom and that runs at 1.2 GHz frequency. The RasPi3 has built-in wireless and Bluetooth technology which makes it IOT ready. The RasPi3 runs with a 5 V power supply and at least 300 mA [15].

4.2   CAN Connectivity

SK Pang electronics provided a CAN shield that was installed on Raspberry Pi3 board. In order to interface with the physical CAN bus pins of the vehicle, a hardware shield was connected via a serial peripheral interface (SPI). This hardware shield consisted of a CAN controller (MCP2515) with the SPI for communicating with GPIO interface and a CAN transceiver (MCP2551) acted as an interface between the CAN controller and the physical CAN bus [16].

4.3   Prototype Development

The development of the prototype is shown on Fig. 4. RasPi3 is built into a custom-made plastic housing which is developed using a 3D-printer. The prototype is sufficiently small to be non-meddling and can be put beneath the driver's seat.

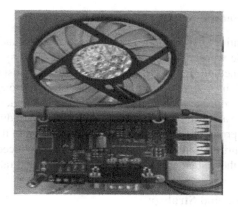

Fig. 4. Prototype

5   System Design

5.1   CAN Structure

The CAN protocol is a kind of bus protocol that is widely used in in-vehicle networks. CAN is a broadcast digital bus that is designed to operate at various speeds in the vehicle for different purposes. There are two different frame formats which follow the requirements of manufacturers of CAN controllers. Furthermore, a message frame is designed to transfer data on the bus. It means the ECUs need to talk each other with using one type of message frames [17]. All the vehicle data (sensor information) in the CAN bus protocol is transmitted with the data frame format. Figure 5 shows a typical CAN network which consists of high-speed CAN bus and low-speed CAN bus and a data frame structure wherein the size of the field is described in bits [18].

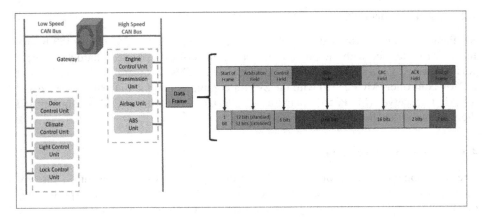

Fig. 5. Vehicle CAN structure and data frame format

5.2   On Board Diagnostic (OBD)

The purpose of the entire OBD system in the vehicle is to create a link between the vehicle and the outside world. The work structure of the OBD system is based on the request and response method. In the OBD system, the user, by using a scan tool, sends a request to the ECU in a specific format and the ECU responds with the specific information in the appropriate diagnostic format. The CARB describes five different OBD-II protocols: variable plus-width (VPW), plus-width modulation (PWM), ISO 9141-2, and keyword protocol (KWP) ISO 14230-4 [19]. Due to the usage of the CAN bus as the vehicle's' primary network, ISO 15765 was introduced for diagnosis over the CAN bus. In fact, these standards define the data flow, baud rates, and timing rates.

5.3   New Data Extraction Strategy

Figure 6 illustrates the two data extraction methods. The first method creates a physical connection to the vehicle CAN bus network by using the OBD-II port. It means the proposed system act as an interface between the user and electronic control units. In the second method, it is possible to read vehicle sensor data via direct CAN bus, without requiring any queries on the CAN bus. In this method, the data extracted are more reliable, accurate, and, of course, has higher measurement point than the OBD-II data.

In order to facilitate access to the application, a graphical user interface (GUI) was created. GUI is shown in Fig. 7. Python language recommends several libraries for writing GUI applications, such as Tkinter, PyGTK, and PyQt among others [20]. The developed GUI has several panels with different functions. The first panel was designed to initialize the CAN device for RasPi3, to select the proper bus bit rate, and to enable the listen mode to traffic the bus. The second panel of GUI is responsible for displaying the normal CAN packets. This part includes a timestamp which indicates the time the message was received. The ID is the identifier of each received packet. The DLC shows the length of each packet, and the last item shows the information about each packet in hex format. The third panel is responsible for extracting vehicle data via OBD

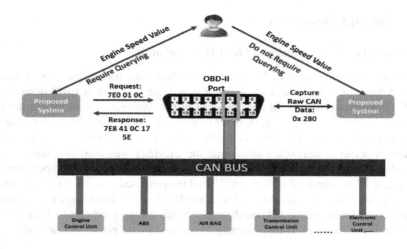

Fig. 6. New data extraction model

technique (request and response method) and displaying the desired value into actual value. The third part of the GUI can also extract the normal CAN packets from the bus and convert it to the actual value. The second version of the GUI has similar Panels 1 and 2. But the third panel uses a different method to collect the vehicle data. The purpose of this design is to extract vehicle data with the direct CAN and request-response method simultaneously.

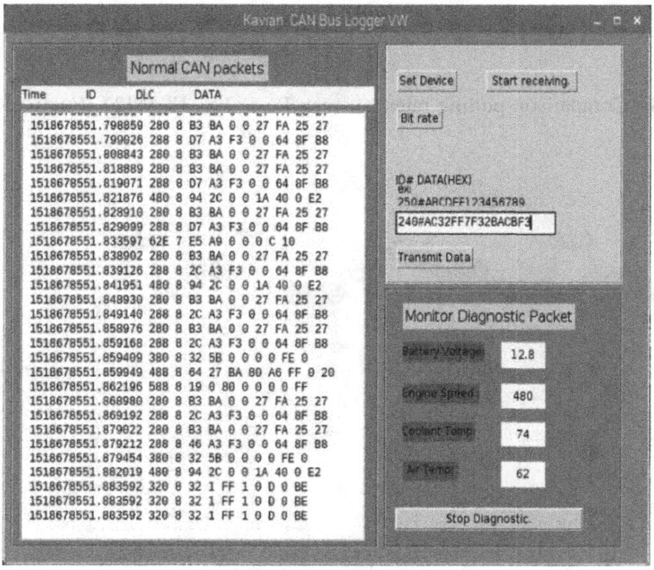

Fig. 7. The graphical user interface

6 Results and Discussion

6.1 Evaluation Data Latency in OBD-II Commands

The majority of studies used ELM327 as OBD reader that uses request and response method. A few tests were conducted in order to provide real data that will demonstrate the differences between external devices used in the previous system and in the proposed system. The first test was performed to measure the average data points that can be extracted by ELM327. The network packet sniffer program, Wireshark, was utilized to monitor and record network traffic while the ELM327 was used to request engine speed value. Figures 8 and 9 shows the comparison of the coolant temperature and engine speed values obtained with ELM327 and the proposed system. It is clear that the fastest scan rate that can be obtained while using ELM327 as data logger is nine points. The main core system of RasPi3, on the other hand, can be modified to have a much higher data processing speed that can acquire up to 15 data points per second.

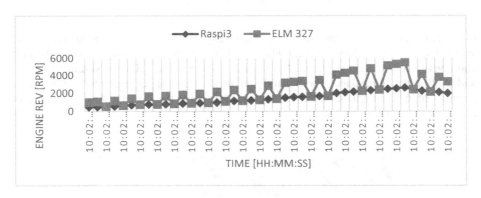

Fig. 8. Comparison polling rates between RasPi3 vs ELM327 (Engine Rev)

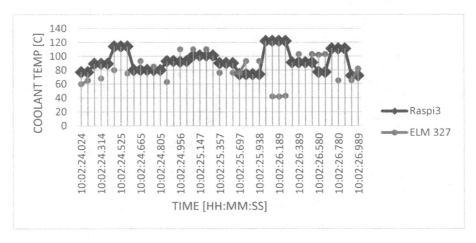

Fig. 9. Comparison polling rates between RasPi3 vs ELM327 (Coolant Temp)

6.2   Comparison CAN Vs OBD-II Data

Figure 10 shows a normal CAN packet which is responsible for transferring the engine speed and coolant temperature information from the engine control unit to the vehicle bus. Since the normal CAN packets are both physically and logically broadcast to all nodes, the proposed system can easily snoop on all communications or send packets to any other ECU on the network. So in order to relate the data gathered between various sensors and methods, the timestamp was used. It is important to validate the data obtained from the direct CAN bus and OBD data. To validate the data obtained from direct CAN, the direct CAN and OBD data were plotted against time.

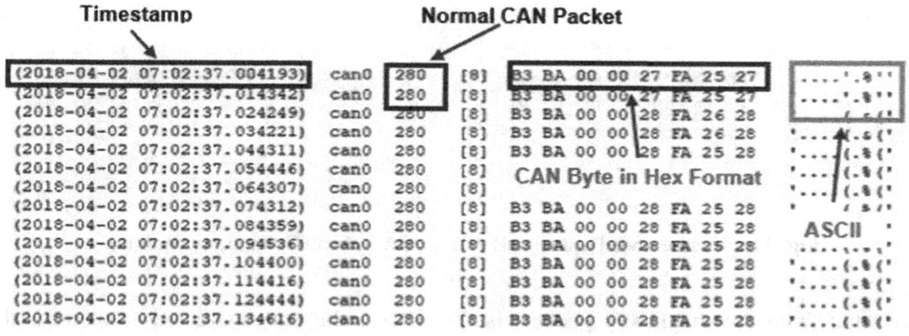

Fig. 10. Timestamp and normal CAN packet for carrying engine speed and coolant temp value

Figure 11 shows three different types of data points normal packet rates, diagnostic packets, and RPM values and the engine speed value plotted on the y-axis. In this test, two ways of obtaining information can be compared to each other. Each blue point represents a normal CAN packet that was extracted by the proposed system, and it includes the engine speed value that repeats every 10 ms. These normal CAN packets are in the hex format. CAN packet with an ID 0x280 is repeated 99 times per second and, this rate is specified according to the bus speed and the importance of the information that has been scheduled in the CAN controller. As mentioned in the previous section, in order to facilitate the experimental analysis, a GUI was created. This GUI can turn the normal CAN packet into meaningful information. This happens at the core of RasPi3, and it takes 40 ms for each data point. The green points show the measuring points achieved from the conversion of normal CAN packets. This means the proposed system can obtain 25 data points for engine speed value in one second. In addition, the red points represent the data points that are acquired by diagnostic packets through the proposed system's request and response technique.

The deficiency of the diagnostic packets in the first and second tests is clear. If the data is extracted from these sensors through normal CAN packets, the accuracy of applications and algorithms will increase, and the latency in the data transmission process will decrease. To illustrate further, take the engine speed value. It is one of the significant parameters used to discover the driver behavior. The number of data

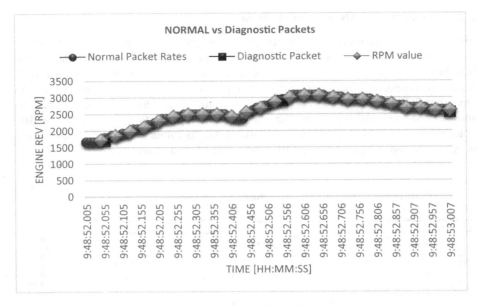

Fig. 11. Engine speed value: OBD-II vs CAN data (Color figure online)

extracted from the diagnostic packets is fewer than the data extracted from normal packets. In this case, the quality of analysis can be improved by having more information. The proposed system successfully gathered data using both methods from various vehicular sensors such as accelerator pedal position and vehicle speed, among others.

7 Conclusion

The open telematics data acquisition platform is a network device that was developed to overcome the limitations of the in-vehicle data logging process. In this research, a system was designed and developed for connecting to the internal network (CAN) and a GUI for end-users to retrieve the desired data by using two different methods at the same time. The proposed system utilizes a RasPi3 device to manage and process the system operation. With regard to the milestones of the study, that based on extraction some specific data a GUI was designed with using Python language to facilitate the data logging process. The GUI is capable of extracting and displaying the normal CAN packet in the hex format. Also, the in-vehicle interface based on two methods for data extraction which can improve the data accuracy and consistency as compared to the previous existing systems. This is due to higher polling rate of normal packet available from the CAN and also due to processing speed of the RasPi3 to collect the specific data. Furthermore, the system that presented is modifiable and multitask. It means it applies to communicate with different control units and extract diagnostic and normal packet at the same time. Moreover, the system is based on the wireless network, and it is capable of transferring to the user device via Wi-Fi network. Lastly, the point of attention is the quality of available data. Because these data are utilized for research purposes, such as driving behavior, traffic management, collision avoidance algorithms, etc. If the data does not have enough quality, it will be shown more inconclusive results and cause to create an inaccurate application.

Acknowledgments. The authors would like to thank the Faculty of Engineering, Universiti Putra Malaysia (UPM) for providing the facilities and conductive learning environment in conducting the research. The research is supported by the research grant of GP-2018/9591900 with vot. No. 9591900.

References

1. Wang, P.W., Yu, H.B., Xiao, L., Wang, L.: Online traffic condition evaluation method for connected vehicles based on multisource data fusion. J. Sensors **2017** (2017). https://doi.org/10.1155/2017/7248189
2. Ezell, S.: Intelligent transportation systems. Inf. Technol. Innov. Found. **58** (2010). https://doi.org/10.1109/mcs.1995.471004
3. Engelbrecht, J., Booysen, M.J., Bruwer, F.J., van Rooyen, G.-J.: Survey of smartphone-based sensing in vehicles for intelligent transportation system applications. IET Intell. Transp. Syst. **9**, 924–935 (2015). https://doi.org/10.1049/iet-its.2014.0248
4. Türker, G.F., Kutlu, A.: Survey of smartphone applications based on OBD-II for intelligent transportation systems. Int. J. Eng. Res. Appl. **6**, 69–73 (2016)
5. Jhou, J.-S., Chen, S.-H.: The implementation of OBD-II vehicle diagnosis system integrated with cloud computation technology. In: Pan, J.-S., Snasel, V., Corchado, Emilio S., Abraham, A., Wang, S.-L. (eds.) Intelligent Data analysis and its Applications, Volume I. AISC, vol. 297, pp. 413–420. Springer, Cham (2014). https://doi.org/10.1007/978-3-319-07776-5_43
6. Ceuca, E., Tulbure, A., Taut, A., et al.: Embedded system for remote monitoring of OBD bus. In: Proceedings International Spring Seminar on Electronics Technology, pp. 305–308 (2013). https://doi.org/10.1109/isse.2013.6648262
7. Iqbal, M.N., Xin, L.Y., Rehman, W.U., et al.: Diagnostic tool and remote online diagnostic system for Euro standard vehicles. In: 2017 IEEE 3rd Information Technology and Mechatronics Engineering Conference, pp. 415–419 (2017). https://doi.org/10.1109/itoec.2017.8122328
8. Pacheco, J.E., Lopez, E.: Monitoring driving habits through an automotive CAN network. In: 23rd International Conference on Electronics, Communications and Computing, CONIELECOMP 2013, pp. 138–143 (2013). https://doi.org/10.1109/conielecomp.2013.6525774
9. Malekian, R., Moloisane, N.R., Nair, L., et al.: Design and implementation of a wireless OBD II fleet management system. IEEE Sens. J. **17**, 1154–1164 (2017). https://doi.org/10.1109/JSEN.2016.2631542
10. Valasek, C., Miller, C.: Adventures in automotive networks and control units. In: Technical White Paper, p. 99 (2013)
11. Meseguer, J.E., Calafate, C.T., Cano, J.C., Manzoni, P.: DrivingStyles: a smartphone application to assess driver behavior. In: Proceedings of the International Symposium on Computers and Communications, pp. 535–540 (2013). https://doi.org/10.1109/iscc.2013.6755001

12. Reininger, M., Miller, S., Zhuang, Y., Cappos, J.: A first look at vehicle data collection via smartphone sensors. In: SAS 2015 - 2015 Proceedings of IEEE Sensors Applications Symposium (2015). https://doi.org/10.1109/sas.2015.7133607
13. Yang, Y., Chen, B., Su, L., Qin, D.: Research and development of hybrid electric vehicles CAN-bus data monitor and diagnostic system through OBD-II and android-based smartphones. Adv. Mech. Eng. **2013**, 1–9 (2013). https://doi.org/10.1155/2013/741240
14. Koscher, K., Czeskis, A., Roesner, F., et al.: Experimental security analysis of a modern automobile. In: Proceedings of the IEEE Symposium on Security and Privacy, pp. 447–462 (2010). https://doi.org/10.1109/sp.2010.34
15. FrontPage - Raspbian. https://www.raspbian.org/. Accessed 26 Jan 2018
16. Electronics SP PiCAN board. http://skpang.co.uk/catalog/pican2-canbus-board-for-raspberry-pi-23-p-1475.html. Accessed 22 Jan 2018
17. Lawrenz, W.: CAN System Engineering, 2nd edn. Springer, London (2013). https://doi.org/10.1007/978-1-4471-5613-0
18. Di Natale, M., Zeng, H., Giusto, P., Ghosal, A.: Understanding and Using the Controller Area Network Communication Protocol - Theory and Practice. Springer, New York (2012). https://doi.org/10.1007/978-1-4614-0314-2
19. Khorsravinia, K., Hassan, M.K., Zafira, R., et al.: Integrated OBD-II and mobile application for electric vehicle (EV) monitoring system, pp. 202–206 (2017)
20. Romano, F.: Learning Python, vol. 1. Packt Publishing, Birmingham (2015)

GeoDTC: A New Geographic Routing Protocol Based on Distance, Time and Custody Transfer

Arslane Hamza-Cherif[1]([✉]), Khaled Boussetta[2,3], Gladys Diaz[2],
and Fedoua Lahfa[1]

[1] Department Computer sciences, University of Tlemcen, Tlemcen, Algeria
`arslane.hamzacherif@gmail.com, f_didi@mail.univ-tlemcen.dz`
[2] L2TI, Institut Galilée, Université Paris 13, Sorbonne Paris Cité,
Villetaneuse, France
`{khaled.boussetta,gladys.diaz}@univ-paris13.fr`
[3] Agora, INRIA, Lyon, France

Abstract. This paper fits into the continuous efforts of researchers to propose a routing protocol able to successfully deliver data at an affordable cost under the challenging networks that are Vehicular Delay Tolerant Networks. Through the literature, several routing protocols based on various approaches have been proposed. However, during the last decade, the geographical approach emerged as the most natural to apply, due mainly to the popularisation of embedded GPS navigation systems. Despite this, and the proposal of different geographic based routing protocols for VDTNs, researchers are still looking for an ideal one, because of hard assumptions, limited performances or small and idealistic evaluation scenarios compared to real word environments. In this paper, we propose GeoDTC, a new geographic routing protocol dedicated to VDTNs, based on two distinct metrics namely: Distance and Time; jointly to the recurrent use of Custody Transfer. We conduct an extensive study to compare our proposal against well-knows protocols namely: Epidemic, Direct Delivery, GeoSpray and Prophet, under realistic simulation environment and scenario by using the large-scale dataset TAPAS Cologne. Simulations results reveal better performances for our proposal. Moreover, they demonstrate the potential benefits of intensive usage of the Custody Transfer and the introduction of various mechanisms.

Keywords: Vehicular Delay Tolerant Networks · Routing protocol
Geographic routing protocol · Vehicle to infrastructure
Custody transfer

1 Introduction

In nowadays, Vehicular Delay Tolerant Networks (VDTNs) have emerged as a hot research topic on the global context of an increasing adoption of Intelligent

© Springer Nature Switzerland AG 2018
A. M. J. Skulimowski et al. (Eds.): IOV 2018, LNCS 11253, pp. 27–45, 2018.
https://doi.org/10.1007/978-3-030-05081-8_3

Transportation Systems (ITS), fostered by public policies and national projects that aim to increase the safety of road passengers, and to minimize the various sides effects of traffic congestions. Nevertheless, one of the remaining issues that delay the adoption of VDTNs consists in the routing protocol that must route data of applications envisioned to operate over such networks. In fact, researchers have already proposed different VDTN routing protocols, which vary considerably regarding the advocated forwarding approach and replication strategy, or the nature of the information involved in the forwarding decision. However, some of these protocols achieve a high delivery ratio at the price of a no-affordable overhead, whereas the performances of others cannot be truly evaluated due to various factors. The latter can vary greatly and may include for instance the degree of realism of the considered scenario, the lake of base implementation of compared routing protocols, or more tragically the use of unrealistic simulators and radio propagation models.

Despite this, researchers assume in general that these protocols can be classified accordingly to the nature of the information involved in the forwarding decision. Therefore, several VDTN routing families emerge based on different approaches, ranging from the zero-knowledge based to the predictive/social-based family and the geographic-based family. These routing approaches are competing between them, especially the predictive/social-based and the geographic-based, to provide the best routing approach and consequently the routing protocol with the best trade-off between a high delivery ratio and an acceptable overhead. For instance authors in [24] and [21] presented two well-known routing protocols belonging to the zero-knowledge family, namely the flooding based Epidemic protocol and the Direct Delivery protocol, which force the sender to carry its data until meeting the final recipient. Regarding the predictive/social-based family, Prophet [8] is one of its main-flag carriers. It routes data by predicting future contacts between vehicles based on their history. Lastly, GeoSpray [16] is one the most promising protocol among the geographic-based family, it achieves an acceptable delivery ratio at the price of a limited overhead, by relying on the limited replication scheme of the Spray & Wait protocol (abbreviated S&W) [22], and the geographical approach of the GeOpps protocol [14].

In this work, we deliberately propose a new routing protocol able to provide an ideal trade-off between a high delivery ratio, like the Epidemic protocol, and an affordable generated overhead similar to the one of GeoSpray for instance. Furthermore, it should be noted that the proposal is based on the geographical approach instead of another one, due to two main factors. In fact, by now many studies have proved that routing protocol based on this approach generally outperforms those based on the predictive/social-based approach [9]. Moreover, a steadily increasing popularisation of GPS navigations systems, facilitate the adoption of geographic-based routing protocols. Therefore, the rest of the paper is organised as follow. Section 2 presents already proposed geographic-based VDTN routing protocols. In Sect. 3, the proposed protocol GeoDTC is detailed, in addition to its mechanisms and features, while Sect. 4 deals with the performance evaluations of GeoDTC and compares its performances against well-known routing protocols. Finally, Sect. 5 concludes this work and presents the key facts that can be drawn from the realistic evaluation of GeoDTC.

Table 1. Geographic-based VDTN routing protocols proposed during the last decade.

Protocol	Year	Protocol Design		Simulation		Evaluation				
		Replication Scheme	#Replica Sent[1]	Simulation Tool	Medium Access	Mobility Dataset	RoadMap (Size)	Duration	#Nodes	#Compared Protocols
GeOpps [14]	2007	Single	0	Omnet++ (MF)[2]	802.11b	ETH Zurich	Zurich (15x15km)	24h	21500	2
DAER [10]	2007	Multiple Unlimited	0,1	ND	802.11g+n	SUVNet	Shanghai (10x10km)	1200s	1000	1, Including: - Epidemic
VADD [26]	2007	Single	0	NS-2[3]	802.11 with DCF	Tiger	ND (4x3,2km)	ND	210	2, Including: - Epidemic
GeoDtn + Nav[6]	2010	Single	0	QualNet[2] Vanet-Mobisim[3]	802.11b	Tiger	Oakland (1,5x4km)	ND	90	2
CMGR [15]	2010	Single	0	NS-2[2] Move[4] SUMO[3]	802.11 with DCF	Tiger	ND (2,5x2,5km)	20000s	400	2, Including: - VADD
GeoSpray [16]	2011	Multiple Limited	0,N	ONE (VDTN-Sim)[2]	No	No	Helsinky (4,5x3,4km)	6h	115	4, Including: - Epidemic - S&W - Prophet - GeOpps
GSAR [4]	2014	Multiple Limited	0,1,N	ONE[2]	No	No	Helsinky (4,5x3,4km)	9h	100	4, Including: - Prophet
TBHGR [5]	2016	Multiple Limited	0,N	ONE[2]	No	No	Helsinky (4,5x3,4km)	12h	100	4, Including: - GeoSpray - S&W
TDOR [3]	2018	Multiple Unlimited	0,1	ONE[2]	No	No	Helsinky (4,5x3,4km)	6h	120	3, Including: - Epidemic - TBHGR

[1] Replica Sent & Replication Type:
  0: No replica is sent,instead the same copy is forwarded.
  1: One replica is sent only.
  N: N copies are sent, following the replication scheme of the S&W protocol.
[2] Network Simulator + (optionally an Extension or a dedicated Library).
[3] VANET Simulation Framework.
[4] Road Traffic Simulator.
[*] ND: Not Defined.

2 Geographic Routing Protocol for VDTNs

Through the last decade, researchers proposed numerous geographic routing protocols dedicated to VDTNs, that differ sensibly regarding the considered replication strategy or the forwarding metric, as highlighted in Table 1.

For instance, authors of [14] proposed the single copy routing protocol GeOpps, which forwards data based on the vehicle trajectory and the computed forwarding time metric $METD$ (which stands for Minimum Estimated Time of Delivery). The proposal was evaluated via a realistic network simulator and real-world traffic traces, extracted from the canton of Zurich, Switzerland. While the first results showed good performances and confirmed the applicability of the advocated protocol design, further works highlighted the limited performances due to the use of the single replication scheme. In [10], the authors proposed an enhanced Epidemic routing protocol, called DAER. This protocol is characterised by the newly introduced geographic information, like the moving direction and the distance which are used to limit the bundle replication and consequently the generated overhead too. DAER protocol showed good performances when evaluated against Epidemic, under a large scale scenario, based on real-world traffic traces extracted from taxi mobility of Shanghai city, China. Regarding the VADD protocol [26], it first calculates the shortest path to the destination accordingly to the Dijkstra Algorithm; then it routes data by selecting each time the next intersection by which data must be routed. To correctly select the next junction, it continuously alternates between two modes, based on different geographic information as the current location, or the heading direction of vehicles.

Besides, some works are highly inspired by non-tolerant to delay MANETs & VANETs routing protocols like the GPSR protocol [11]. For instance, work presented in [6] is one of them, and to correctly perform under sparse networks, it relies on a new DTN forwarding mode if the greedy and the perimeter modes successively fail to deliver data. Whereas other works propose novel approaches, like the CMGR protocol [15] which use a novel route selection logic, aware and adaptive to vehicle density in the network; Consequently, data delivery goes through an on-demand process of route discovery and selection, triggered each time a bundle is sent, and by relying on multiple intermediate nodes.

In parallel to works cited above, many protocols as those presented in [4,16] and [5], follow a hybrid approach, based on the limited replication scheme advocated by S&W [22]. For instance, GeoSpray relies jointly on GeOpps [14] and its forwarding metric $METD$, and on the binary version of S&W to diffuse and deliver remaining bundle replicas. When only one replica remains, it stops its replication and switches instead to its transfer whenever encountering a better forwarder. This behaviour is justified by the need to comply with the limited replication scheme. Regarding GSAR, it aims to deliver data to both fixed and mobile destination, by diffusing replicas to the broadest extent possible during the spray phase, until only a single replica remains. Then, it switches to a second phase, where it focuses solely on the delivery of its unique replica, based on historical records of nodes mobility, and their best potential moves towards the estimated movement range of the final destination. TBHGR protocol delivers data also through two distinct steps. However, it makes the forwarding decision by computing a newly introduced metric, based on various geographic information of the current vehicle, like direction, speed, distance and time towards the destination.

Last but not least, the authors of [3] present a unique trajectory driven protocol called TDOR. This work differs sensibly from other works because it considers the trajectory of bundles rather than vehicles as the critical factor to successfully deliver data. Consequently, it computes and embeds an optimal delivery path into the bundle, then it tries to deliver the bundle accordingly to the computed path.

Finally, readers should be aware that one of the major concerns regarding routing protocol like those presented above, is the realism of their evaluation scenario. In fact, only some works as those presented in [14] (GeOpps), [26] (VADD) or [6] (GeoDtn+Nav), are evaluated through the use of realistic simulation tools. Moreover, in 2010, a Wi-Fi radio standard dedicated to vehicular networking was introduced, namely the 802.11p standard [7], and by now, it is considered as the de-facto standard. However, all presented works avoided the use of this standard. Finally, some parameters regarding protocols evaluation are frequently missing like the simulation duration in [26] and [6], or set to minimalist values like the number of simulated vehicles. All these factors limit the reproducibility and the degree of confidence in results greatly.

3   GeoDTC: A Geographic Routing Protocol Based on Distance, Time and Custody Transfer

3.1   Assumption and Overview

GeoDTC is a new geographic routing protocol based on two distinct forwarding metrics, and intensive use of the Custody transfer (or simply Custody) mechanism. Furthermore, it follows an unlimited multiple-copy replication scheme, while being highly inspired by the general guidelines of well-known geographic VDTN routing protocols, namely GeOpps [14] & GeoSpray [16]. Consequently, this protocol assumes that vehicles which are at the core of the networks, embed a GPS navigation system able to provide a set of basic functionalities like geographic awareness, geo-localisation, or shortest route calculation between two map points. Such assumptions are largely acceptable by now, due to the broad democratisation and continuously increasing adoption of GPS navigation systems. Moreover, readers should note that GeoDTC focuses mainly on Vehicle-To-Infrastructure communication denoted V2I, from mobile sender nodes to fixed receiver ones, which corresponds respectively to vehicles and Road Side Units (RSUs), while bundles can be addressed to a single RSU (Unicast) or any RSU (Anycast). Therefore, the protocol assumes that vehicles are aware of their current route, whereas the positions of the terminal nodes (RSUs) are known and already loaded in their digital map. Regarding targeted applications, GeoDTC is intended to deliver data for applications able to be deployed over networks prone to frequent disconnections & reconnections and long delays, like VDTNs. Such applications range from road traffic information to third-party services, including email service, web access, multimedia content download or geographic services discovery. Thus, this routing protocol is not adapted to the hard deadlines of road safety applications.

3.2   Main Characteristics and Keys Features

Forwarding Metrics: Based on its GPS navigation system, a vehicle carrying a message M_D that must be delivered to the destination D, can determine along its suggested route, the nearest point to the location of the same destination D, denoted NP. Such concept that has been first defined by GeOpps then taken up by GeoSpray, allows the computing of the time based metric $METD$, already used by GeOpps and GeoSpray, in addition to the alternative, newly introduced, distance-based metric $Dist$. Therefore, these two metrics are at the base of the forwarding decision made by GeoDTC.

In practical terms, a vehicle can estimate the required travel time from its current position to its NP, denoted $ETA_{to\ NP}$ (for Estimated Time of Arrival to NP), and moreover the required travel time of the message between the NP and the position of the final destination D, denoted $ETA_{from\ NP\ to\ D}$, based on the topological shortest path between these two geographic positions and by considering the maximum allowed speed on streets. Thus, and accordingly to Eq. 1, the sum of these two measurements constitute the Minimum Estimated Time of Delivery metric, denoted $METD$.

$$METD = ETA_{to\ NP} + ETA_{from\ NP\ to\ D} \tag{1}$$

However, one of the major drawbacks of the $METD$ metric is its incapacity to determine if a candidate vehicle will pass by the destination, which can substantially increase the likelihood of successfully delivering the message M_D. In fact, this time-based metric don't distinguish between a vehicle that is converging quicker or closer to the final destination, while sometimes it might be interesting to choose one that is moving slowly but will get close, or even better pass-by the destination D, and consequently deliver M_D directly under acceptable network conditions (No storm broadcast or similar phenomena). To address this issue, GeoDTC introduces the topological distance of the shortest path between the NP and the destination D as a second metric denoted $Dist$. Therefore, the protocol can determine if the candidate vehicle will pass-by the destination D (if $Dist = 0$), which makes it an ideal forwarder while potentially limiting the induced overhead, as it will be highlighted later.

$$Dist = Distance_{from\ NP\ to\ D} \tag{2}$$

Custody Transfer and BRAC Mechanism: Under a DTN environment, each node is intrinsically a custodian node, because it is responsible for its carried bundles until their delivery or forwarding. Therefore, the Custody transfer referees to the transfer of responsibility from one node to another over the management, the replication and the deletion of a single or a set of bundles, called also custodian bundles. In practical terms, this interesting mechanism allows a protocol to differentiate custodian bundles from others, or to assign them to specific nodes; like for instance delegating a bundle and its final delivery to a node which is supposed to increase the likelihood of successfully delivering the bundle, since its current carrier is no longer a suitable forwarder. Regarding GeoDTC, if a carrier vehicle will not pass-by the destination D (if $Dist_{carrier} \neq 0$), and it meets a candidate vehicle that will (if $Dist_{candidate} = 0$), then this vehicle must proceed to a Custody transfer of M_D, by transferring it to the candidate node which is now in charge of the bundle delivery instead of replicating it. By doing so, the protocol achieves a twofold goal, by first increasing the likelihood of successfully delivering M_D, and secondly preventing any further and unnecessary replication of M_D by the initial carrier, which limits the protocol overhead. Lastly, it should be noted that the Custody as employed by GeoDTC also implies an acknowledgement (ACK) upon a successful Custody transfer, sent to the previous custodian vehicle by the new one. It is done to avoid the deletion of a custodian bundle that has not yet been transferred to the new custodian vehicle.

In parallel to the Custody transfer, GeoDTC introduces the Bundle Replication Avoidance based on Custody (BRAC) mechanism. The basic idea here lies on whether or not use the Custody and more interestingly how to use it. Indeed, instead of simply processing to a Custody transfer whenever needed, it is possible to notify the existence of custodian bundles and diffuse the list of these bundles among other vehicles, to prevent any further replication. Moreover, it is possible to take a specific action upon the receipt of such list, like deleting custodian bundles from any no-custodian vehicles. Therefore, the BRAC mechanism can be viewed as a set of strategies regarding the usage and the implementation of the Custody transfer, with the goal of preventing the replication of custodian bundles, and that range from the laziest and the most reactive strategy to the most restrictive and proactive one, as highlighted in Table 2.

Table 2. Strategies for the BRAC mechanism of the GeoDTC protocol.

Strategy N	Strategy Name	Make use of Custody transfer?	Diffuse list of custodian bundles?	Required action upon the receipt of the list
0	$BRAC_0$	No	No	None
1	$BRAC_1$	Yes	No	None
2	$BRAC_2$	Yes	Yes	None
3	$BRAC_3$	Yes	Yes	Delete Custodian Bundles

Time to Live for Control Messages. It is well established by now that the use of acknowledgements (ACKs) upon a successful bundle delivery, enhance the overall performances of any considered protocol. Indeed, the usages of ACKs have many benefits like avoiding unnecessary replication of delivered bundles, which in turn free-up buffers and network resources for remaining bundles, and therefore increase their likelihood to be successfully delivered. Furthermore, by nowadays many routing protocols like Epidemic, Prophet, and GeoSpray advocate a proactive strategy to take the most from acknowledgements, by diffusing for instance lists of ACKs among other nodes to purge the whole network from delivered bundles. However, such a strategy has a significant drawback. Indeed, while it is commonly assumed that bundles will be deleted upon the expiry of their assigned Time To Live (TTL), there is no such TTL for Control Messages as for ACKs. Consequently, the use of an ACK list can be even harmful if its size continues to grow until reaching its maximum, which results in increased usage of bandwidth to diffuse ACKs rather than deliver bundles.

To address this drawback, GeoDTC introduces a TTL for Control Messages denoted TCM, which includes lists of ACKs and Custodians Bundles like those used by the BRAC mechanism, denoted respectively TCM_{Ack} and $TCM_{Custody}$. Moreover, it introduces two types of TCM, namely Fixed and Adaptive denoted respectively $FTCM$ and $ATCM$. The $FTCM$ aims to reduce the size of control messages lists, based on a fixed value, aligned with the current bundle TTL. The $ATCM$ is based on a more evolved approach, where the computed value of the TCM depends on the type of control messages (ACKs vs Custodian Bundles) and the purpose of using it. For instance, a $ATCM_{Ack}$ must expire at the same time as bundle expiry. Regarding a $ATCM_{Custody}$, it must last only during the short period needed by the custodian vehicle to deliver the carried custodian bundles, majored by a regular guard interval of 10%. If it lasts more, it can be harmful because it will prevent the replication of any undelivered custodian bundles by custodian vehicles, which may happen in real conditions. Therefore, TCM_{Ack} and $TCM_{Custody}$ are computed accordingly to Eqs. 3 and 4.

$$TCM_{ACK} = \begin{cases} FTCM_{ACK} = TTL_{BundleM_D} \\ ATCM_{ACK} = TTL_{BundleM_D} - Delay\ Of\ Delivery_{BundleM_D} \end{cases}$$
(3)

$$TCM_{Custody} = \begin{cases} FTCM_{Custody} = TTL_{BundleM_D} \\ ATCM_{Custody} = METD_{BundleM_D} + Guard\ Interval \end{cases}$$
(4)

3.3   Protocol Operations

The GeoDTC protocol forward a bundle M_D from a carrier vehicle X to a candidate vehicle Y, through a three-step process. The vehicle Y starts the exchange of informations by sending to X, its current $METD$ and $Dist$ metrics, in addition to the list of ACKs and Custodian Bundles, accordingly to the considered BRAC strategy (For instance, If the current strategy is $BRAC_0$, then there is no Custody and therefore no need for a list of Custodian Bundles, which contrasts with other BRAC strategies). Following to this first step, X updates its own lists of ACKs and Custodians Bundles, deletes any unnecessary bundles identified by those lists, according to the considered BRAC strategy (For instance, if the current strategy is $BRAC_2$, and X is not a Custodian Vehicle, then it must deletes any possessed Custodian Bundles), and lastly computes and compares its metrics to those of Y, and if Y enhances one of them (If $METD_X \geq METD_Y$ or $Dist_X \geq Dist_Y$) then X must sent a replica of M_D to Y. Except if Y will encounter the destination D (if $Dist_Y = 0$) then X must proceed to a Custody

Transfer of M_D, instead of its replication. Finally, Y receive the bundle and process to its storage, and if it is the final recipient of M_D or X requested a Custody Transfer, then it must reply to X, by sending respectively the generated ACK upon the receipt of M_D or an acknowledgement for a successful Custody Transfer, which in both cases allows X to delete M_D from its storage. The overall process is described through the UML activity diagram illustrated in Fig. 1

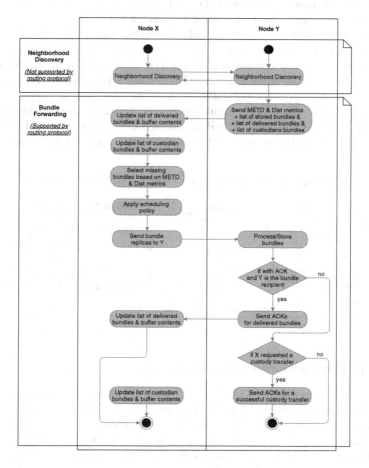

Fig. 1. UML activity diagram describing the sequence of main operations executed by GeoDTC protocol to route data at each node encountering.

4   Evaluation and Simulation Results

4.1   Simulation Environment

To correctly assess the performance of GeoDTC, a quantitative evaluation of the protocol against well-known routing protocols, namely Epidemic, Direct Delivery, Prophet and GeoSpray is performed. The choice of these routing proto-cols obeys to different criteria. Indeed, Epidemic offers a high delivery ratio at the price of high overhead and greedy approach. Conversely, Direct Delivery is a lightweight protocol with poor performances. Prophet is the main proto-col among the predictive/social-based major routing family. Lastly, GeoSpray is one of the greatest routing protocol among those advocating a geographic-based approach. Furthermore, since GeoDTC is inspired in the general guidelines of GeOpps and GeoSpray, this latter must be considered.

Regarding the working environment, the Veins simulation framework [18] was selected for the implementation of all considered protocols, including the proposal, since no reference implementation is available for them. Veins is a well established by now since it is one of the most advanced simulation frame-work dedicated to vehicular networks. It is built upon the network simulator Omnet++ [25] and the traffic simulator Sumo, which is responsible for vehi-cle mobility [13]. Finally, the High-Performance Computing Grid MAGI of the University of Paris XIII [20] was used to simulate this large scenario successfully.

Table 3. Global simulation parameters for the large-scale evaluation of protocols.

Global Parameters		Values	Global Parameters		Values
Simulation	Duration	3600s	**Bundle**	Size	1Kbit
	# Runs	20		Generation Period	150s
Wi-Fi	Technology & Mode	802.11p Broadcast		Bundle TTL	600s
	Transmission Rate	18Mbits/s	**Transmission**	# Vehicles	9920
	Maximum Range	127m		# RSUs	957
	Propagation Model	Two Ray Interference & Simple Obstacle Shadowing		Mode	From Vehicles To RSUs only

4.2   Simulation Scenario and Parameters

To evaluate the performances of GeoDTC without any overestimation, a large-scale scenario based on the TAPAS Cologne dataset [23] is considered. The dataset which is known to be the largest freely available to researchers, includes mobility traces of 38 592 vehicles during 2 h, from 6h00 to 8h00 AM (due to computational constraints, the road traffic is limited to 1 h and 9920 vehicles only), from the town of Cologne-Germany and its peripheral zone, for a total roadmap size of 29 km × 33 km. Over this map, 957 Road Side Units (RSUs) are deployed over 957 sectors of 1 km^2 area.

Regarding the considered radio specifications, Veins implements the de facto Wi-Fi standard for vehicular networks, namely, the IEEE 802.11p, limited to broadcast mode only, since recent research works highlighted the unsuitability of Unicast transmissions due mainly to head of line blocking effects [12]. More-over, the framework implements various radio propagations models, including the Two Ray Interference model [19] and the Simple Obstacle Shadowing [17] whose uses are highly advised by the authors. For data traffic modelling, since GeoDTC is envisioned to provide a routing service from mobile vehicles to fixed RSUs, this communication scheme is the only one considered, and vehicles generate periodically bundles addressed to the RSU of the current sector, through a unicast communication. Remaining simulation parameters can be reviewed in Table 3.

Table 4. Protocol parameters for ProphetV2 and considered configurations of GeoDTC & GeoSpray.

Configuration Name	Configuration Parameters	Configuration Name	Configuration Parameters
GeoDTC-A1	$BRAC_0 + FTCM$	GeoDTC-A2	$BRAC_0 + ATCM$
GeoDTC-B1	$BRAC_1 + FTCM$	GeoDTC-B2	$BRAC_1 + ATCM$
GeoDTC-C1	$BRAC_2 + FTCM$	GeoDTC-C2	$BRAC_2 + ATCM$
GeoDTC-D1	$BRAC_3 + FTCM$	GeoDTC-D2	$BRAC_3 + ATCM$
GeoSpray-E	Parameters: R=20	GeoSpray-F	Parameters: R=60
ProphetV2	Parameters: P_{max}=0.7; $P_{first_contact}$=0.5; I_{typ}=1800; β=0.9; T_{unit}=30; γ=0.999		

Finally, three (03) performances metrics are considered. They are described below and arranged in decreasing order of importance:

- Delivery Ratio (DR): since the main target of this work is VDTN routing protocol, this metric is considered as being the main performance metric. It is the ratio between the unique received bundles and the whole unique emitted bundles.
- Overhead (O): it corresponds to the total number of bundle replica divided by the total number of emitted bundles.
- Average Delay (AD): this metric is less important than those cited before. It is the average delay needed to deliver the first replica of any bundle.

4.3   Global Performance Evaluation for All Protocols

The main goal of this study is to provide researchers with a first overview regarding the performance evaluation of the proposal GeoDTC under its basic configuration when ran against DirectDelivery, Epidemic, ProphetV2 and GeoSpray. More significantly, this first study attempts to addresses the recurrent answer that rises when a proposal of a new VDTN routing protocol is made, namely:

- Is the proposal able to achieve an ideal trade-off between a high delivery ratio similar to Epidemic, and a low or at least an affordable overhead like those generated by GeoSpray or Prophet?

Indeed, due to the inherent constraints and specificities of the vehicular environment, the loss of a packet or bundle is frequent which implies addressing such phenomena by designing routing protocol that maximises first the delivery ratio, and after that the generated overhead or the average delivery delay. Therefore,

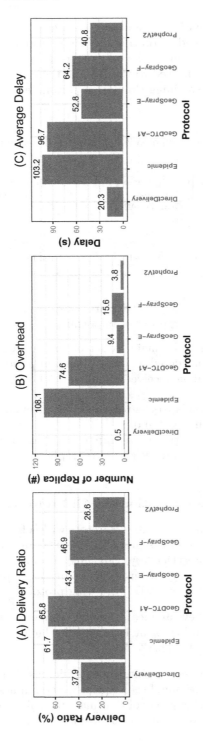

Fig. 2. Simulation results for DirectDelivery, Epidemic, ProphetV2, GeoSpray and GeoDTC protocols under the large-scale scenario based on TAPASCologne.

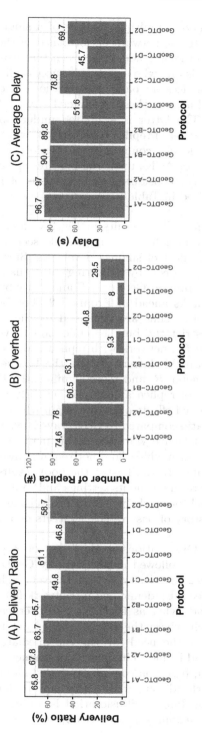

Fig. 3. Simulation results for all considered configurations of GeoDTC under the large-scale scenario based on TAPASCologne.

such protocols tend to generate multiple replicas of a single bundle, which in turn can severely deteriorate the network performances if the replication is not controlled. Consequently, an ideal trade-off between the two is sought, whereas a suitable routing protocol is one who achieves it successfully.

To this end, the performances of a basic configuration of GeoDTC, denoted by GeoDTC-A1 are compared against those of Direct Delivery, Epidemic, Prophet and GeoSpray protocols. The latter is evaluated under two distinct settings regarding the maximum number of replica parameter R, whereas other protocols are evaluated under their default configurations. Besides, readers should note that all protocols make use of ACKs upon the final receipt of bundles. Finally, the parameters related to the considered configurations of Prophet, GeoSpray and GeoDTC are summarised in Table 4.

Evaluation of Delivery Ratio: The results in Fig. 2A show acceptable performances for all protocols, especially for a large-scale scenario with an unicast communication and a large fleet of simulated vehicles. Surprisingly, GeoDTC-A1 outperforms all other protocols by delivering more than 65.8% of bundles, followed by Epidemic, GeoSpray-F, GeoSpray-E and lastly by an unusual Direct Delivery protocol which ranks ahead of ProphetV2. The better performances of GeoDTC compared to Epidemic are explained by the use of accurate forwarding metrics which restrict the bundle replication to vehicles with better metrics, instead of flooding the network with replicas. Moreover, GeoDTC outperforms GeoSpray, because this latter restricts the bundle replication to the current value of the parameter R, and more significantly, the binary spray in use leads to slow diffusion of replica among the network and a lower delivery ratio. Therefore, the combined effects of both explain why GeoSpray-F achieves a slightly higher delivery ratio compared to GeoSpray-E, even if the parameter R is tripled. Regarding Direct Delivery, its acceptable performances are due to its zero-overhead, and its approach which does not require any control information jointly to proper placement of RSUs. Lastly, the poor results of ProphetV2 are explained by the difficulty to fine-tune its settings and to its inadequate routing approach, especially in such networks where future vehicle contacts cannot be predicted based on the history of past vehicle contacts and patterns.

Evaluation of Overhead: Observations made based on Fig. 2B reveal a very high overhead for Epidemic, followed respectively by GeoDTC-A1, GeoSpray-F, GeoSpray-E, ProphetV2 and lastly Direct Delivery. These overall results were widely expected. Indeed, Epidemic and its network flooding approach generate a very high overhead, whereas the near-zero overhead of Direct Delivery is due to its approach where the sender carries a bundle until meeting the final recipient, without the need for any intermediate relays. Regarding ProphetV2, its low overhead is due to its poor performances and the unsuitability of its routing approach, based on community-based mobility. For GeoSpray, the low and affordable overhead compared to its overall performance is due to its limited replication and slow bundle diffusion that is confirmed by the relatively small difference between GeoSpray-E and GeoSpray-F even if the parameter

R has tripled. Finally, GeoDTC generates a significant overhead compared to GeoSpray, but it is still lower than the one of Epidemic. A less restrictive approach explains such results compared to GeoSpray, which generates more replicas in order to achieve higher performances, and ultimately can be acceptable since the primary goal is to maximise the bundle delivery while achieving a trade-off between the high delivery rate of Epidemic and the low overhead of GeoSpray.

Evaluation of Average Delay: Surprisingly, the results in Fig. 2C highlight the higher average delay (for the delivery of the 1st copy) for Epidemic, compared to all other protocols, followed by GeoDTC-A1, GeoSpray-F, GeoSpray-E, Prophet and Direct Delivery. Far from being expected, the high delay of Epidemic is due to the network congestion that arises due to the excessive use of bandwidth by the uncontrolled bundle replication, additionally to an increasing competition between vehicles to access the communication channel. A similar phenomenon is also observed for GeoDTC-A1 but with a limited extent due to a higher but controlled bundle replication. Meanwhile, GeoSpray achieves an average delay that confirms the slow diffusion of bundles in the network, due to the binary S&W adopted by the protocol, whereas Prophet achieves a low delay that comes to the expense of poor performances. Lastly, Direct Delivery can deliver bundles in a very short delay, which confirms the good placement of a fringe of RSUs, and the possibility to relay some bundles through a simple and straightforward protocol as Direct Delivery.

4.4   Performance Evaluation of All GeoDTC Protocol Configurations

After revealing the potential benefits of using the proposal GeoDTC protocol to route data from vehicles to RSUs, and showing encouraging results toward an ideal trade-off between a high delivery ratio and a low overhead; the following study aims to improve the overall performances of GeoDTC, by evaluating different configurations of the proposal based on the four BRAC strategies and the two distinct TCM detailed in Sect. 3.2 respectively. Therefore, eight configurations of GeoDTC are considered, the first one is $GeoDTC - A1$, whereas other configurations can be reviewed in Table 4. Finally, regarding the considered simulation parameters and scenario, they are similar in all respects to those of the previous study.

Evaluation of Delivery Ratio: The results in Fig. 3A show a clear hierarchy among the different configurations of GeoDTC with, GeoDTC-A2 outperforming all considered configurations followed respectively by A1, B2, B1, C2, D2, C1 and lastly D1. Such hierarchy highlights the existence of several trends. At first, this stresses the benefit of using an Adaptive TCM ($ATCM$) like in A2, B2, C2 & D2 instead of a fixed one ($FTCM$) like in A1, B1, C1 & D1, which increases the delivery ratio, due to a more adapted expiry delay for control messages that frees the bandwidth and ultimately allows the delivery of more bundles. This applies even more for configurations C & D, because these latter send list of custodian bundles, and therefore correctly adapting the $TCM_{Custody}$

increases the likelihood of successfully delivering undelivered custodian bundles, whereas a long and fixed $TCM_{Custody}$ prevents their replication. Regarding the BRAC strategies, observations show that a basic one increases the delivery ratio, whereas a more intelligent and complex one slightly lowers it. This is explained by the fact that the latter tends to prevent the bundle replication by exchanging a list of custodian bundles (e.g. $BRAC_2$) or deleting them from non-custodian vehicles upon the receipt of such list (e.g. $BRAC_3$), which in turn translates in a lower delivery ratio.

Evaluation of Overhead: As shown in Fig. 3B, GeoDTC-A2 generates the highest overhead followed respectively by A1, B2, B1, C2, D2, C1 and lastly D1. In general terms, these reflect the good performances observed previously, which explain why the best configuration in term of delivery ratio achieves the highest overhead and vice versa. Furthermore, through results, it is clear that the Adaptive TCM ($ATCM$) generates a higher overhead compared to the fixed one ($FTCM$) which is directly related to its capacity to release more bandwidth by correctly adapting the expiry of entries included in the lists of ACKs and custodian bundles. Regarding the considered BRAC strategies, it is interesting to note that the Custody transfer can reduce the overhead on its own, by up to 20% (e.g. when comparing A1 with B1 and A2 with B2), while offering near comparable overall performances. Moreover, further strategies like $BRAC_2$ reduces more the overhead, by up to 45% (e.g. when comparing A2 with C2) which comes with a reduced but still good overall performances, whereas $BRAC_3$ reduces the overhead sensibly but at the price of lower performances. Therefore, the results of the eight considered configurations of GeoDTC highlight the positive impact of the often neglected use of the Custody transfer, additionally to the more evolved BRAC strategies that can sensibly reduce the overhead.

Evaluation of Average Delay: the high average delay depicted in Fig. 3C was partially expected. Indeed, the overall good performances of the different configurations of GeoDTC are made at the price of a longer delivery delay which is two main factors: the existence of a great number of replicas and the use of the Custody transfer. These statements are supported by the high average delay observed for configurations based on $BRAC_0$ & $BRAC_1$, which are known to generate a great number of replicas; whereas remaining configurations rely intensively on Custody transfer which slows the delivery process but offers a more robust delivery solution. However, the side effect of Custody transfer is counterbalanced by the better usage of the bandwidth thanks to the list of ACKs and custodian bundles that avoid unnecessary bundle replication and forwarding. Therefore, even if the average delay is high, it is sensibly reduced compared to former BRAC strategies.

5   Conclusion and Perspectives

This paper presents an unlimited multiple-copy and geographic-based routing protocol dedicated to VDTNs, inspired by the general guidelines of previous major works like GeOpps and GeoSpray, called GeoDTC. To route data, GeoDTC relies on the joint use of two (02) forwarding metrics, namely the Distance-based metric $Dist$ and the Time based metric $METD$. Moreover, to the best of authors knowledge, GeoDTC is the first routing protocol to extend the application scope of the Custody transfer mechanism, by introducing the Bundle Replication Avoidance based on Custody (BRAC) mechanism with the goal of limiting the overhead induced by the protocol replication strategy. Furthermore, GeoDTC introduces the Time To Live For Control messages (TCM), for ACKs and list of Custody Bundles to optimise the usage of the network bandwidth. Lastly, readers should note that GeoDTC can operate with a single forwarding metric ($Dist$ or $METD$), however preliminary studies showed better results when combining the use of both metrics.

Regarding the performance evaluation of GeoDTC, it was conducted against well-known VDTN routing protocols, namely, Direct Delivery, Epidemic, Prophet and GeoSpray; under a large-scale and realistic scenario based on the TAPAS Cologne dataset. Moreover, multiple configurations of GeoDTC were considered with the sole purpose of improving its performance. The overall results reveal the capacity of GeoDTC to achieve an honourable trade-off between a high delivery ratio and an acceptable overhead or average delay, mainly by extending the usage scope of the Custody transfer, which contrasts with the performances of the flooding based Epidemic and the geographic-based GeoSpray protocols. Moreover, the various evaluated configurations of GeoDTC demonstrate the ability of the protocol to cope with different needs as maximising the delivery ratio (e.g. GeoDTC-A2), minimising the overhead and average delay (e.g. GeoDTC-D1), or achieving an ideal trade-off between the formers (e.g. GeoDTC-B2 or GeoDTC-C2). Therefore, the recommended configuration may depend heavily on the intended objective, even if authors recommend the use of GeoDTC-B2 or GeoDTC-C2 because they offer similar or better delivery ratio than Epidemic while drastically reducing the overhead of the average delay. Besides, the results demonstrate also the potential benefits of adopting a $ATCM$, which increase the delivery ratio at the expense of a slight increase of overhead and average delay, which ultimately must not prevent its use.

Finally, to contribute and enrich the research community, the base implementation codes related to considered routing protocols in this work, are made publicly available by authors on the software development platform GitHub [1,2].

References

1. Arslane HAMZA CHERIF: Arslan90/mixim: DTN architecture for veins - omnet++code (2018). https://doi.org/10.5281/zenodo.1323150
2. Arslane HAMZA CHERIF: Arslan90/pyservergeneric: Dtn architecture for veins - pythonserver (2018). https://doi.org/10.5281/zenodo.1323149
3. Cao, Y., et al.: A trajectory-driven opportunistic routing protocol for VCPS. IEEE Trans. Aerospace Electron. Syst., 1 (2018). https://ieeexplore.ieee.org/document/8338142

4. Cao, Y., Sun, Z., Wang, N., Riaz, M., Cruickshank, H., Liu, X.: Geographic-based spray-and-relay (GSaR): an efficient routing scheme for DTNs. IEEE Trans. Veh. Technol. **64**(4), 1548–1564 (2015)
5. Cao, Y., Wei, K., Min, G., Weng, J., Yang, X., Sun, Z.: A geographic multicopy routing scheme for DTNs with heterogeneous mobility. IEEE Syst. J. **12**(1), 790–801 (2018). https://doi.org/10.1109/jsyst.2016.2563519
6. Cheng, P.C., Lee, K.C., Gerla, M., Härri, J.: GeoDTN+Nav: geographic dtn routing with navigator prediction for urban vehicular environments. Mob. Netw. Appl. **15**(1), 61–82 (2010)
7. Institute of Electrical and Electronics Engineers: IEEE standard for information technology- telecommunications and information exchange between systems- local and metropolitan area networks- specific requirements: part 11: wireless LAN medium access control (MAC) and physical layer (PHY) specifications: amendment 6: wireless access in vehicular environments. Institute of Electrical and Electronics Engineers, New York (2010)
8. Grasic, S., Davies, E., Lindgren, A., Doria, A.: The evolution of a DTN routing protocol - PRoPHETv2. In: Proceedings of the 6th ACM Workshop on Challenged Networks, no. 2, pp. 27–30 (2011)
9. Hamza-Cherif, A., Boussetta, K., Diaz, G., Lahfa, F.: Performance evaluation and comparative study of main VDTN routing protocols under small- and large-scale scenarios. Ad Hoc Netw. (2018). https://doi.org/10.1016/j.adhoc.2018.07.008
10. Huang, H.Y., et al.: Performance evaluation of SUVnet with real-time traffic data. IEEE Trans. Veh. Technol. **56**(6), 3381–3396 (2007). https://doi.org/10.1109/tvt.2007.907273
11. Karp, B., Kung, H.T.: GPSR: greedy perimeter stateless routing for wireless networks. In: Proceedings of the 6th Annual International Conference on Mobile Computing and Networking - MobiCom, pp. 243–254. ACM, ACM Press (2000). https://doi.org/10.1145/345910.345953
12. Klingler, F., Dressler, F., Sommer, C.: IEEE 802.11p unicast considered harmful. In: 2015 IEEE Vehicular Networking Conference (VNC), pp. 76–83. IEEE (2015)
13. Krajzewicz, D., Erdmann, J., Behrisch, M., Bieker, L.: Recent development and applications of SUMO - Simulation of Urban MObility. Int. J. Adv. Syst. Meas. **5**(3&4), 128–138 (2012)
14. Leontiadis, I., Mascolo, C.: GeOpps: geographical opportunistic routing for vehicular networks. In: 2007 IEEE International Symposium on a World of Wireless, Mobile and Multimedia Networks. IEEE, June 2007
15. Shafiee, K., Leung, V.C.: Connectivity-aware minimum-delay geographic routing with vehicle tracking in VANETs. Ad Hoc Netw. **9**(2), 131–141 (2011). https://doi.org/10.1016/j.adhoc.2010.06.003
16. Soares, V.N., Rodrigues, J.J., Farahmand, F.: GeoSpray: a geographic routing protocol for vehicular delay-tolerant networks. Inf. Fusion **15**, 102–113 (2014). https://doi.org/10.1016/j.inffus.2011.11.003
17. Sommer, C., Eckhoff, D., German, R., Dressler, F.: A computationally inexpensive empirical model of IEEE 802.11p radio shadowing in urban environments. In: 8th IEEE/IFIP Conference on Wireless On demand Network Systems and Services (WONS 2011), pp. 84–90. IEEE, Bardonecchia, January 2011
18. Sommer, C., German, R., Dressler, F.: Bidirectionally coupled network and road traffic simulation for improved IVC analysis. IEEE Trans. Mob. Comput. **10**(1), 3–15 (2011). https://doi.org/10.1109/TMC.2010.133

19. Sommer, C., Joerer, S., Dressler, F.: On the applicability of two-ray path loss models for vehicular network simulation. In: 4th IEEE Vehicular Networking Conference (VNC 2012), pp. 64–69. IEEE, Seoul, November 2012. https://doi.org/10.1109/VNC.2012.6407446
20. Sorbonne Paris Cité University (USPC): Magi computing cluster. https://magi.univ-paris13.fr/intranet/
21. Spyropoulos, T., Psounis, K., Raghavendra, C.S.: Single-copy routing in intermittently connected mobile networks. In: 2004 First Annual IEEE Communications Society Conference on Sensor and Ad Hoc Communications and Networks, SECON 2004, pp. 235–244. IEEE (2004)
22. Spyropoulos, T., Psounis, K., Raghavendra, C.S.: Spray and wait: an efficient routing scheme for intermittently connected mobile networks. In: Proceedings of the 2005 ACM SIGCOMM Workshop on Delay-Tolerant Networking, WDTN 2005, pp. 252–259. ACM, New York (2005). https://doi.org/10.1145/1080139.1080143
23. Uppoor, S., Fiore, M.: Large-scale urban vehicular mobility for networking research. In: IEEE Vehicular Networking Conference, VNC, pp. 62–69 (2011). https://doi.org/10.1109/VNC.2011.6117125
24. Vahdat, A., Becker, D.: Epidemic routing for partially-connected ad hoc networks. Technical report, Internet Systems and Storage Group - Duke Computer Science (2000)
25. Varga, A., Hornig, R.: An overview of the OMNeT++ simulation environment. In: Proceedings of the 1st International Conference on Simulation Tools and Techniques for Communications, Networks and Systems & Workshops, pp. 60:1–60:10 (2008)
26. Zhao, J., Cao, G.: VADD: vehicle-assisted data delivery in vehicular ad hoc networks. IEEE Trans. Veh. Technol. 57(3), 1910–1922 (2008)

User-Centric vs Network-Centric Vertical Handover Algorithms in 5G Vehicular Networks

Nadia Mouawad[1,2]([⊠]), Rola Naja[1,2], and Samir Tohme[2]

[1] Doctoral School of Science and Technology, Lebanese University, Beirut, Lebanon
mouawad.nadia@gmail.com,rola.naja@ul.edu.lb
[2] Li-Parad Laboratory, University of Versailles Saint Quentin, Versailles, France
samir.tohme@uvsq.fr

Abstract. 5G vehicular networks are designed to provide a guaranteed Quality-of-Service (QoS) in a heterogeneous wireless access technologies environment. In this case, the mobility management problem especially vertical handover decision should be carefully studied. In this paper, we work in a Software Defined Networking (SDN) environment. We propose two vertical handover decision schemes: user-centric where the handover decision is processed in the vehicles and network-centric where the handover decision is centralized in the network side. For both schemes, we use the Media Independent Handover for handover signaling and integrate the utility theory in the network selection calculation. Finally, we run several simulation scenarios in order to formalize a comparative conclusion about the proposed schemes.

Keywords: Software Defined Networking · Utility theory
Vertical handover · Media independent handover · User-centric
Network-centric

1 Introduction

5G mobile networks are expected to provide high data rate, offer a variety of applications and allow users to roam across heterogeneous technologies. In this environment, intelligent vehicles with multiple interfaces will be able to choose the best technology that satisfies their QoS requirements. In fact, the Always Best Connected (ABC) concept [10] is a primordial issue. Therefore, in order to answer ABC requirements, a vertical handover (VHO) strategy and a network selection algorithm should be derived.

Handover is an event where a mobile node (MN) disconnects from its current Point of Attachment (PoA) and connects to a new Access Point (AP). When this procedure occurs within the same wireless technology, the process is known as horizontal handover. In this case, the signal strength is the only criteria to choose the target AP. Contrarily, vertical handover takes place when the handover occurs among heterogeneous wireless access technologies. In this

© Springer Nature Switzerland AG 2018
A. M. J. Skulimowski et al. (Eds.): IOV 2018, LNCS 11253, pp. 46–59, 2018.
https://doi.org/10.1007/978-3-030-05081-8_4

case, several criterion are considered and a decision algorithm is derived in order to select the best technology to deploy.

SDN [17] is a new paradigm that defines network structures in a simpler way by providing programmable devices and a centralized control logic. Open Networking Foundation (ONF) [13] defines the SDN architecture by three main planes: control plane that consists of SDN controllers, data planes that comprises SDN switches and application plane that includes networks applications. An interface between the control and data planes is defined and implemented using the openflow protocol [11]. The latter describes the interaction between SDN controllers and switches.

The emergence of SDN in 5G vehicular networks helps in handling handover procedure efficiently. Therefore, we study in this paper the VHO decision in a heterogeneous SDN based 5G vehicular environment.

Moreover, in order to enhance the VHO procedure and optimize handover between heterogeneous technologies, we utilize Media Independent Handover (MIH) [9]. The MIH defines 3 main services: MIH event services (MIES), MIH command services (MICS) and MIH information services (MIIS). In addition, MIH defines an MIH Function (MIHF) that realizes these services listed as follows:

1. **MIES**: provides event reporting corresponding to the dynamic changes in link characteristics.
2. **MICS**: sends commands related to mobility and connectivity decisions.
3. **MIIS**: provides a framework to discover available neighboring network information within a geographical area to facilitate the handover process.

Our work presents two network selection schemes: (1) user-centric approach where the network selection is executed in the vehicles considered as intelligent network nodes, (2) network-centric approach where network selection computation is centralized in the SDN controllers. In both approaches, the network selection calculation is based on utility theory.

Figure 1 depicts the overall algorithm.

This paper is structured as follows: in Sect. 2, we give a review about literature works related to VHO decision problem. We present our proposed work in Sect. 3. In Sect. 4, we evaluate our proposed algorithms. Finally, we conclude our paper in Sect. 5.

2   Literature Review

In this section, we survey the most significant proposals found in the literature concerning VHO schemes. We classify the VHO algorithms into three categories according to the methods, techniques and technologies used in each algorithm. These categories are listed as follows: Multiple Attribute Decision Making (MADM) based solutions, MIH based solutions and SDN network selection solutions. In the following, we elaborate related works for each category and analyze their advantages and drawbacks.

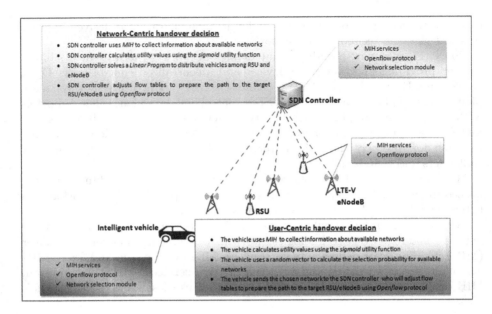

Fig. 1. Overall vertical handover algorithm

2.1 Multiple Attribute Decision Making Based Solutions

MADM schemes make selection among limited number of candidate networks from various service providers and technologies with respect to different criteria. The most popular classical MADM techniques for the computation of network selection result are: SAW (Simple Additive Weighting) [1], TOPSIS (Technique for Order Preference by Similarity to Ideal Solution) [21] and GRA (Grey Relational Analysis) [14].

However, the classical MADM-based schemes mainly have the following drawbacks:

– These schemes lack of the combination between network side attributes and user profile specification. This make the users pay a high cost for a slight QoS degree improvement.
– MADM-based schemes do not consider user distribution among networks and the Ping Pong effect caused by handover procedure.

2.2 MIH Based Handover Management

In [18], authors proposed an intelligent VHO scheme that takes into account multiple requirements and various context information in order to reduce handover delays and guarantee session continuity. The solution is based on MIH which can decrease exchanged messages through IEEE 802.21 standard to select the best network.

In [19], authors assume that VHO service runs in the MN. The proposed MIH based QoS aware VHO algorithm (QAVHA) does a priority based ranking that estimates the Signal to Noise Ratio (SINR), bandwidth and QoS delay of different Access Categories (AC) running in each AP. After the algorithm estimates the different handover metrics in each AP, the MN can select the AP with highest SINR, bandwidth and minimum QoS delay according to the application running on it.

These solutions help in accelerating the VHO procedure by using MIH. However, they only considered user-centric approach. In addition, calculation is based on a strategic ranking rather than the combination of all handover criteria. Moreover, user distribution among access networks is not considered.

2.3 Network Selection in SDN

The before mentioned works share a common limitation: the lack of global network view. The emergence of the SDN makes it possible to overcome this limitation. In fact, SDN controllers have an abstracted centralized control of network devices. In consequence, several literature works tailored SDN in the network selection and vertical handover decision.

In [4], QoS values of available networks are calculated and sent to SDN controllers. Network selection process is formulated as an 0–1 integer programming problem, with the objective of maximizing overall QoS and avoiding network congestion. After the network selection process is finished, mobiles have to wait for a stability period, then calculate the QoS values of their current networks and selected networks again. Only if the selected networks are consistently more appropriate than the current networks, mobiles transfer their inter-network connections to the selected networks. This solution is prone of a handover decision delay since it imposes two stages of VHO selection and decision computation.

In [20], Linear Programming is a problem-solving method that optimizes the objective function while satisfying linear constraints. In this paper, a handover method is proposed where the SDN controller performs channel pre-allocation for next cell after selection, so the overall handover delay is reduced. However, this work did not considered important selection attributes such as delay and data rate.

The previously mentioned literature papers proposed a VHO solution centralized either in vehicles or in SDN controllers. The majority of these works focused on the user satisfaction as a primary objective while a few of them considered user distribution and network load.

In this paper, we propose two solutions for VHO decision in a SDN environment. Our contributions are listed as follow:

- We solve the VHO decision problem following two approaches: user-centric and network-centric. In addition, we give a comparative synthesis of both proposed schemes.
- We use MIH signaling in order to accelerate the VHO procedure.

- We consider the utility theory [6] in network selection calculation. Network attributes, used in classical MADM schemes, are transferred to utility values by a sigmoid function.
- We consider network load and user distribution in the network selection procedure. Therefore, we proposed a method to avoid network overload and congestion in each proposed approach.
- We consider important criteria for the network selection such as the delay and data rate.

In the following, we present our proposed work.

3   Vertical Handover Decision Algorithms

In this section, we proceed in three steps to explain our proposed VHO schemes. First, since we are working in a SDN environment, we find it crucial to the define the adopted SDN architecture. Second, we explain the sigmoid utility function used for network selection calculation. Finally, we present our proposed MIH based VHO solutions.

3.1   Network Architecture

Our network SDN architecture depicted in Fig. (1) is structured as follows:

- SDN controllers that are control plane elements responsible of the network management.
- Road Side Units (RSU) and eNodeB for different wireless access technologies mainly (IEEE802.11p [8] and LTE-V [5]) that implement openflow switches (SDN data plane elements) and MIH services.
- Intelligent Vehicles that implement openflow switches (SDN data plane elements) and MIH services.

We present the SDN based logical structure as follows:

1. The application plane consists of the following modules:
    - Path Computation Module (PCM): PCM computes the shortest paths between nodes and sends them to the control plane to install flow tables in the switches according to the openflow protocol specification.
    - Network Selection Module (NSM): NSM calculates the best technology to deploy for each user in case of network-centric approach.
2. The control plane comprises the following modules:
    - Topology manager helps the controller to maintain network topology information.
    - MIH Module (MIHM) that provides MIH services to the control plane.
3. The data plane consists of the following element:
    - MN MIHM responsible of providing MIH services to vehicles. This module consists of MIHF and all MIH services (i,e. MIIS, MIES and MICS).

- MN Network selection Module (MN-NSM): MN-NSM takes in charge the VHO decision in case of user-centric approach.
- RSU/eNodeB MIH module responsible of providing MIH services to Access Points.

In the following, we explain the integration of the utility theory in the network selection calculation.

3.2   Utility Theory in Network Selection

In economy, utility refers to a level of satisfaction that a user derives from a given product. In the network selection, it measures the user satisfaction level corresponding to a set of characteristics offered by an access network.

One of the proposed utility functions is the step function, however it is not appropriate for the network selection in a wireless environment due to the fluctuating nature of these networks.

Authors in [2,16] demonstrated that the sigmoid form is the most suitable to model the utility for each network selection criterion. The sigmoid utility function was proposed as follows:

$$
u(x) = \begin{cases}
0 & \text{if } x < x_\alpha \\
\dfrac{(\frac{x-x_\alpha}{x_m-x_\alpha})^\xi}{1+(\frac{x-x_\alpha}{x_m-x_\alpha})^\xi} & \text{if } x_\alpha \leq x \leq x_m \\
1 - \dfrac{(\frac{x_\beta-x}{x_\beta-x_m})^\gamma}{1+(\frac{x_\beta-x}{x_\beta-x_m})^\gamma} & \text{if } x_m < x \leq x_\beta \\
1 & \text{if } x > x_\beta
\end{cases}
$$

Where: $\gamma = \frac{\xi(x_\beta-x_m)}{x_m-x_\alpha}$ and $\xi \geq max(\frac{2(x_m-x_\alpha)}{x_\beta-x_m}, 2)$

u is the utility of network criterion x. x_α and x_β are respectively lower bound and upper bound user constraints for each criterion x. The value x_m corresponds to the threshold between the satisfied and unsatisfied areas of a specific parameter. The γ and ξ values determine the steepness of the utility curve and make it possible to model the user sensitivity to access network characteristic variation.

Network Selection Criteria

In the network selection, when evaluating the utility of an access network, we distinguish between the upward and downward criteria associated with a network. Upward criteria are for example the bandwidth, and throughput. Conversely, the downward criteria encompass parameters such as network usage cost, energy consumption and transfer delay. Indeed, users prefer the higher values of upward criteria and lower values of downward criteria. And therefore, we consider that $u(x)$ is calculated for upward criteria. However, for the downward criteria, we use the form of $v(x)$ as $v(x) = 1-u(x)$.

Our VHO decision algorithm considers that the attributes used for network selection are inputted into the sigmoid utility function and transformed into utility values.

We consider a set of M vehicles where each user $i \in \{1, 2, 3.., M\}$ wants to perform handover, and a set of J available access network. Each access network

$j \in \{1, 2, 3.., J\}$ presents K attributes. We note $u_i(x_{kj})$ the calculated user i utility for attribute x_k given by access network j.

Global Utility Calculation

Authors in [2] proved mathematically that global utility should be calculated as follows:

$$U_{ij} = \prod u_i(x_{kj})^{w_{ik}} \tag{1}$$

where w_{ik} is user i weighting factor for each criterion parameter x_k for user i and U_{ij} user i global utility for network j. We note that w_{ik} should follow the following constraint: $(\sum_k w_{ik} = 1 \quad \forall i)$.

In this section, we presented the utility function integration in the VHO network selection algorithm. Next, we explain our proposed VHO decision with a user-centric scheme.

3.3   User-Centric VHO Decision

In this section, we consider that the handover initiation and decision are computed in the vehicles. The final decision is sent to the SDN controller.

We proceed first by explaining the handover initiation and decision, next we explain the handover execution.

Handover Initiation and Decision. The handover initiation and decision are done according to the following steps. First, we consider that the vehicle $i \in \{1, 2, 3.., M\}$ (i,e. MN) is moving during its communication with a Corresponding Node (CN). When the MN senses a signal degradation, it sends MIH_MN_Candidate_Query.Request to MN MIH module. After receiving MIH_MN_Candidate_Query.Response, the MN retrieves information about the available access technologies. These information are sent to the MN-NSM to calculate the utility given by each available access network attributes.

MN-NSM of each user i calculates the utility values where $u_i(x_{kj})$, and gives a global utility vector $U_i = [U_{i1}, U_{i2}, ..., U_{iJ}]$ where U_{ij} is user i global utility for network j (the utility values are calculated as explained in the previous section).

According to the traditional MADM decision making algorithms, network with the highest ranking value is selected. However, this method may have negative impacts on network performance especially in terms of load. In fact, if we consider that we have 3 available access networks and 3 users that want to perform handover. Each user i calculates the global utility vector $U_i = [U_{i1}, U_{i2}, U_{i3}]$. Traditional MADM scheme consists of ranking vector U_i and choosing network j with the highest utility. We consider that $network_1$ will give the highest utility for the 3 users. Therefore, the 3 users will be select $network_1$ as a target network. This may cause network congestion since the user distribution is not considered. As a result, we propose a random VHO decision algorithm explained as follows:

Algorithm 1. User-centric VHO decision algorithm

Each user $i \in M$ run this algorithm:
for $U_{ij} \in U_i$ **do**
   if $(U_{ij} \geq U_{ith})$ **then**
      U_{temp}.append (U_{ij})
   end if
end for
J_1=len(U_{temp})
Generate a random vector $R_i(1xJ_1)$ *where* $r_{ij} \in [0,1]$
for networks $j \in J_1$ **do**
   $P_{ij} = \frac{r_{ij}*U_{temp}(j)}{\sum_{j=1}^{J_1} r_{ij}}$
end for
User i chooses the network j with the highest P_{ij}

The algorithm considers the global utility U_i vector for each user i. It specifies U_{th} as a threshold value for the global utility and omit the networks that give a utility $\leq U_{th}$. This aims at avoiding the MN from choosing a network that gives unfavorable conditions. A random vector R_i is generated where r_{i_j} is a random value $\in [0,1]$. Each vehicle i calculates a selection probability P_{ij} for each remaining access networks j. Finally, the vehicle chooses network j with the highest selection probability value. This method aims at avoiding network congestion and considers the user distribution among several access technologies while taking into account the users utility.

Handover Execution. The calculated target network is sent to the controller via MIH_MN_commit_Query.Request who will prepare the new path from the CN to the target network using the openflow protocol. When the vehicle connects to the new access network it sends MIH_MN_HO_complete.Request to the controller and receives a corresponding response.

In this section, we explained the user-centric VHO scheme. The latter focuses on the user utility as a primary objective and considers the user distribution among available access technologies. However, in order to obtain a global solution, the computation tasks should be migrated to a higher level i.e. the SDN controller. To this end, we study the network-centric VHO approach.

3.4   Network-Centric Approach

SDN controller is a centralized control plane element that has the ability to monitor the data plane and collects information related to network load and signaling. Therefore, SDN controller plays an important role in the VHO decision.

We explain the network centric VHO in details. We proceed by explaining the handover initiation, decision and execution.

Handover Initiation and Decision. The handover initiation and decision are done according to the following steps:

1. We consider that we have J available access networks and M users want to perform handover.
2. The vehicle (or MN) moves while communicating with the CN.
3. The MN senses a signal degradation.
4. The MN sends a notification to the controller via MIH_Link_Going_Down.Indication.
5. The controller sends MIH_Net_HO_Candidate_Query.Request to the MN and receives MIH_Net_HO_Candidate_Query.Response to form a list of available access networks.
   In addition, it sends MIH_N2N_HO_Query_Resources.Request to the available access networks to get their current number of resources via MIH_N2N_HO_Query_Resources.Response.
6. After receiving the requirements of the running application of each MN, the controller calculates the global utility of each MN.
7. The controller solves a linear program to associate each MN with the corresponding technology.

The linear program has the following inputs:

- M users wants to perform handover and J access networks are available.
- $U_i(MxJ)$ matrix where U_{ij} is the calculated global utility for user i from network j. We note that if network j is not available for user i then $U_{ij} = 0$.
- $B(1xJ)$ matrix where b_j is the load of network j (number of users).
- $B_{max}(1xJ)$ matrix where b_{maxj} is the maximal load of network j (maximal number of users).

The linear program will give as output:

- $X(MxJ)$ matrix where $x_{ij} = 1$ when user i should connect to network j and 0 otherwise.

The linear program is formulated as follows:

$$\max \quad \sum_i \sum_j (U_{ij}) * x_{ij} \tag{2}$$

$$\text{s.t.} \quad \sum_{j \in N} x_{ij} = 1 \qquad \forall i \in M \tag{3}$$

$$\sum_{i \in M} x_{ij} + b_j \leq b_{maxj} \quad \forall j \in J \tag{4}$$

$$x_{ij} \in \{0, 1\} \qquad \forall j \in J; \forall i \in M \tag{5}$$

This problem maximizes the objective function formulated as the user global utility. The first constraint makes sure that each user i will connect to 1 access technology j. In addition, the second constraint takes into account the number of resources in each network j.

Handover Execution. After solving the linear program, the controller sends the calculated access technology to the users via MIH_Net_HO_Candidate_ Commit.Request and prepares the new path from the CN to the target network using the openflow protocol.

When the handover is completed the chosen network sends MIH_N2N_HO_Complete.Request to the controller indicating the completion of the handover and receives MIH_N2N_HO_Complete.Response.

In this section, we explained the network-centric VHO scheme. The latter integrates the SDN controller in the network selection procedure. The global view brought by this controller results in an optimal users distribution among available access networks.

In the next section, we present a performance analysis for each proposed scheme by studying several parameters.

4 Performance Analysis

In order to evaluate and compare the performance of the proposed approaches, we conducted a set of simulation batches. We implemented the network elements using mininet-wifi [7] and the controller using Ryu controller program [12].

In the following, we describe our simulation environment:

We consider 2 available technologies: IEEE 802.11p and LTE-V. We consider 2 selection attributes for each access network j:

- x_{1j}: the data rate for each access network j (upward criteria)
- x_{2j}: the delay of each access network j (downward criteria)

The attribute values for each technologies, weighting factors are represented in Table 1. In addition to the limit values [15] for utility calculation considering a road safety application

Table 1. Network selection parameters values

	IEEE 802.11p	LTE-V	Weighting factors	x_α	x_m	x_β
Delay (ms)	$x_{11}:50$	$x_{12}:20$	w_1=0.6	0	20	100
Data rate (Mbps)	$x_{21}:27$	$x_{22}:50$	w_2=0.4	0.02	5	25

We study several performance parameters in order to show the enhancement brought by our proposal and to compare between the network and user centric approaches. To this end, we consider the traditional MADM scheme proposed in the literature and give it the name: max-approach since it chooses the network with the maximal attributes value. In addition, we name our user-centric scheme rand-approach since it integrates a random selection probability. Finally, the network-centric scheme is named net-approach. We compare the following performance parameters:

User Satisfaction. In order to analyze whether a user is convinced with the chosen network, a concept is introduced in [3] based user satisfaction degree.
In case of road safety application, the delay is very critical criteria and therefore we measured the satisfaction in terms of global utility and delay utility as follows:
$A(U_i, delay) = 1 - exp(-KU_i^{\mu} u(delay)^{-\epsilon})$

Where $\mu \geq 0$ and $\epsilon \geq 0$ control the sensitivity to utility and delay respectively and K is a positive constant representing the satisfaction reference value. The values of μ, ϵ and K are respectively 2, 0.2 and 0.5.

Figure 2 represents the users satisfaction for the delay attribute. It was expected to obtain the highest user satisfaction with the max-approach since it focuses only on maximizing user utility. However, this approach do not take in consideration network load. Therefore, this will lead to network congestion and delays. This justifies the results obtained in this figure, where user satisfaction decreases with higher handover rate. In addition, we can see that the net-approach gives the best values with higher handover rate since it optimally distribute users among available networks.

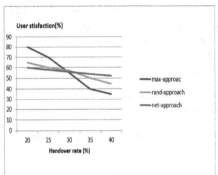
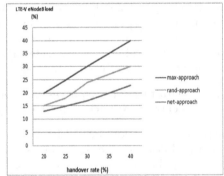

Fig. 2. User satisfaction   **Fig. 3.** LTE-V eNodeB load

Network Load. Figure 3 depicts the variation of LTE-V eNodeB load. In this figure, we can see that the max-approach induces the highest load since it does not consider the user distribution in the VHO decision. The rand-approach brings lower values due to the proposed random selection scheme. Finally, the net-approach leads to more balanced load since it considers user utility and distribution simultaneously.

Number of Re-selection. Figure 4 presents the number of re-selection in terms of handover rate. We mean by re-selection the trigger of a second handover directly after the first one due to unfavorable network conditions or congestion. This figure shows that the net-approach leads to a null re-selection value, because it brings an optimal network selection solution and a global network view for the computation and decision. The rand-approach results in a lower number of re-selection, this number varies according to the random values obtained for the selection probability calculation. Concerning the max-approach, the number of re-selection increases with the handover rate because this approach do not consider the network load and user distribution among AP.

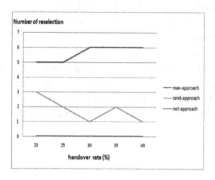

Fig. 4. Number of re-selection

4.1 Discussion

In the following, we present a discussion about our proposed schemes.

First, we proceed by discussing the reasons why our proposed work surpasses the literature studies mentioned in Sect. 2. In fact, mobility management is a challenging issue in 5G vehicular networks. Critical messages such as road safety and traffic monitoring messages should be delivered in a critical time window. In this case, network selection procedure should wisely select the technology that guarantees QoS requirements specially in term of latency. Unlike our proposed approaches, this important issue was missed in the majority of the literature papers who ignored crucial metrics such as latency and network congestion.

Second, we compare in the following the proposed approaches:

Simulation results showed that each approach presents some advantages to the network selection procedure. Therefore, we discuss the case where each approach could be used.

The user-centric approach could be used in case of highly congested networks in order to migrate some computational tasks to the data plane and to reduce signaling exchanges.

However, network-centric approach could be used in case of normal network state, since it induces some additional computation tasks in the controller.

5 Conclusion

In this paper, we studied VHO decision and network selection problem in 5G SDN based vehicular networks. We proposed two VHO network selection schemes: the first is user-centric approach where the decision and calculation are centralized in vehicles. The second is network-centric approach where all VHO decision and computation are migrated to the SDN controller. In both approaches, handover signalization is based on MIH protocol in order to accelerate the handover procedure. In addition, we integrated the utility theory in the network selection calculation.

We conducted several simulation batches in order to retrieve performance parameters of the proposed schemes. Simulation results showed that our approach outperforms the classical MADM schemes proposed in the literature specially in terms of network load. In addition, a comparative study was derived to compare the impact of the user-centric and network-centric schemes on the network.

References

1. Afshari, A., Mojahed, M., Yusuff, R.M.: Simple additive weighting approach to personnel selection problem. Int. J. Innov. Manag. Technol. **1**(5), 511 (2010)
2. Amali, C., Jayaprakash, D., Ramachandran, B.: Optimized network selection using aggregate utility function in heterogeneous wireless networks. Comput. Softw. 1293 (2014)
3. Bai, X., Bölöni, L., Marinescu, D., Siegel, H.J., Daley, R.A., Wang, I.J.: Are utility, price, and satisfaction based resource allocation models suitable for large-scale distributed systems? In: Proceedings of the Third International Workshop on Grid Economics and Business Models (GECON), Singapore (2006)
4. Qiang, L., Li, J., Huang, C.: A software-defined network based vertical handoff scheme for heterogeneous wireless networks. In: Proceeding Global Communications Conference (GLOBECOM), pp. 4671–4676. IEEE (2014)
5. ETSI: Evolved universal terrestrial radio access (E-UTRA) and evolved universal terrestrial radio access network (E-UTRAN); overall description; stage 2 (2011)
6. Fishburn, P.C.: Utility theory for decision making. Technical report, Research analysis corp McLean VA (1970)
7. Fontes, R.R., Afzal, S., Brito, S.H., Santos, M.A., Rothenberg, C.E.: Mininet-WiFi: emulating software-defined wireless networks. In: Proceeding of the 11th International Conference on Network and Service Management (CNSM), pp. 384–389 (2015)
8. Group, I.W., et al.: IEEE standard for information technology-telecommunications and information exchange between systems-local and metropolitan area networks-specific requirements-part 11: Wireless LAN medium access control (MAC) and physical layer (PHY) specifications amendment 6: Wireless access in vehicular environments. IEEE Std 802(11) (2010)
9. Group, I.W., et al.: Draft IEEE standard for local and metropolitan area networks: media independent handover services. IEEE P802. 21/D00. 05 (2007)
10. Gustafsson, E., Jonsson, A., et al.: Always best connected. IEEE Wirel. Commun. **10**(1), 49–55 (2003)

11. Heller, B.: Openflow switch specification v1.5 (2014)
12. https://osrg.github.io/ryu/: Ryu SDN framework
13. https://www.opennetworking.org/: Open networking foundation (2013)
14. Kuo, Y., Yang, T., Huang, G.W.: The use of grey relational analysis in solving multiple attribute decision-making problems. Comput. Ind. Eng. **55**(1), 80–93 (2008)
15. Masini, B., Bazzi, A., Zanella, A.: A survey on the roadmap to mandate on board connectivity and enable V2V-based vehicular sensor networks. Sensors **18**(7), 2207 (2018)
16. Nguyen-Vuong, Q.T., Ghamri-Doudane, Y., Agoulmine, N.: On utility models for access network selection in wireless heterogeneous networks. In: Network Operations and Management Symposium NOMS, pp. 144–151. IEEE (2008)
17. Nunes, B.A.A., Mendonca, M., Nguyen, X.N., Obraczka, K., Turletti, T.: A survey of software-defined networking: past, present, and future of programmable networks. IEEE Commun. Surv. Tutor. **16**(3), 1617–1634 (2014)
18. Maaloul, S., Afif, M., Tabbane, S.: A new vertical handover decision based context awareness for ubiquitous access. In: Proceeding of International Conference on Communications and Information Technology (ICCIT), pp. 231–236. IEEE (2012)
19. Edward, E.P., Sumathy, V.: MIH based QOS-aware algorithm for efficient handoff in Wifi/Wimax integrated networks. J. Theor. Appl. Inf. Technol. 61(2) (2014)
20. Lee, J., Yoo, Y.: Handover cell selection using user mobility information in a 5G SDN-based network. In: Proceedings of Ninth International Conference on Ubiquitous and Future Networks (ICUFN), pp. 697–702. IEEE (2017)
21. Zhang, W.: Handover decision using fuzzy MADM in heterogeneous networks. In: Wireless Communications and Networking Conference WCNC, vol. 2, pp. 653–658. IEEE (2004)

Dependability Aware Protocol for Urgency Messages Delivery in Internet of Vehicles

Zibouda Aliouat[1,2](✉), Makhlouf Aliouat[1,2], and Mourad Gueroui[3]

[1] Computer Science Department Faculty of Sciences
University Ferhat Abbas Sétif 1, Sétif, Algeria
{zaliouat,maliouat}@univ-setif.dz
[2] Networks and Distributed Systems Laboratory, Darmstadt, Germany
[3] LI-PaRAD Laboratory, University Paris Saclay, University of Versailles,
Saint Quentin, Yvelines, France
mourad.gueroui@uvsq.fr

Abstract. Over just one decade and due to their promising potential in greatly improving transportation usage, Vehicular Ad hoc NETworks (VANETs) have increasingly gained researcher attention in order to ensure them an expected and merited maturity. So, VANETs have been predicted to revolutionize transportation system domain giving them new dimension via Intelligent Transportation Systems (ITS) paradigm. ITSs suggest providing user vehicles with more safety, comfort, rapidity of moving, infotainment, etc.. This undeniable advantage allows saving human lives, money, power consumption, time and making use of vehicles more attractive for passengers. This paper is dealing with dependable alert and urgent messages. So, when an alert is sent, we rely on that message to surely reach its destination in order that appropriate actions will be taken. Therefore, we devised a communication protocol ensuring emergency messages to be correctly delivered to their recipients in a way complying with real time requirements. The protocol is tested with repairing messages issued by failed vehicles and the simulation results provided by NS2-VanetMobiSim simulators are convincing.

Keywords: Emergency messages · Dependable delivery
Minimum network latency · Vanets · IoV

1 Introduction

Vehicular Ad Hoc NETworks (VANETs) [3, 13], as a practical aspect of Mobile Ad hoc NETworks (MANETs) have been introduced to provide efficient solutions to some problems caused by road traffics notably the issue of roads safety. The main goal was to reduce vehicles crashes responsible for an unbearable human life costs and injured people. After this, are included issues related to the comfort of vehicle drivers and passengers. Nevertheless, safety issue is the most important problem to be addressed in order to save human lives and decrease injuries by reducing the number of road accidents. This may be done through accident prevention by signaling in advance any event which may be the cause like pointing out a dangerous obstacle on the road, for example: a vehicle moving in opposite direction in a highway or a truck spilled in a road critical

© Springer Nature Switzerland AG 2018
A. M. J. Skulimowski et al. (Eds.): IOV 2018, LNCS 11253, pp. 60–73, 2018.
https://doi.org/10.1007/978-3-030-05081-8_5

location etc. Any signaling critical event, like accident occurrence, dangerous obstacle or a simply a failed vehicle requiring troubleshooting has to be achieved through an alert message transmitted via a communication broadcast to reach the maximum number of nodes (acting as routers between source and destination) in order to arrive at the targeted destination equally reliably and fast as possible. In fact, alert or urgency messages are not only important in case of accident occurrences but also in any other situations requiring rapid reaction or intervention. One way to send surely an important message, such that it reaches its destination is to make a broadcast [10]. However a classical broadcast, in a VANET environment, has a serious drawback of producing a network congestion which creates many collisions, in turn, provokes lot of message losses which induces time wasting and delays alert messages to reach their recipients. Delivery delays are unfitted to emergency messages. So, criteria to appropriate emergency broadcast messages are: Real time, dependability (Ensuring that urgency messages surely reaching their recipients), and overhead and security requirements. The security area does not concern us here, but the trilogy: real time respect, dependability and low time overhead have to be taken into account as strictly as possible in the design of efficient VANET alert message protocols and consequently in Intelligent Transportation Systems (ITS) or more generally in Internet of Vehicles (IoV).

Our proposal is dedicated to deal with the emergency message communications in vehicle network environments. Thereby, when issued from a sender node, alerting a crucial event occurring in the road requiring informing the concerned parts, the alert message will be dependably delivered to its recipient(s) with an acceptable time overhead induced by the network latency. The proposal has been applied in the event of failed vehicle on road requesting troubleshooting by means of urgent messages.

The paper is organized as follows: Sect. 2 deals with related work while Sect. 3 describes the proposal and its performance evaluation. We conclude our work with a conclusion and a prospective future work.

2 Related Works

In [8], the authors have proposed EMDV: Emergency message dissemination for vehicular by allowing the vehicle the more distant within the scope of transmission to retransmit the urgent message. The choice of a single median node is not appropriate in a network of high mobility as VANET, because the position is always in change, and the receiver vehicle can become out of reach at the time of the sending of the message or simply the receiver may not receive the message because of channel problems as the denial of service.

In [6], the authors have proposed UMB (Urban Multi hop Broadcast Protocol), a routing protocol which is an effective protocol for the 802.11 standard, based on a multi-hop diffusion algorithm in vehicular Networks with infrastructure support. The purpose of the protocol is to maximize the progress of messages, avoiding the problems of broadcast storm, the hidden node, and the problems of reliability.

Contention-Based Broadcasting protocol (CBB), is a protocol proposed in [9]. It is based on the dissemination of the urgency messages in a multi-hop way, and according to the authors, it outperforms the performance of the Protocol EMDV, because it defines all vehicles located in the not empty last segment as median nodes, but the choice of several median nodes can pose a problem of collusions if the segment includes a large density of vehicles.

In [4], the authors proposed EEMB: Efficient Emergency Message Broadcasting, a protocol working with two main phases: the normal phase in which Beacon safety messages are transmitted and the emergency phase in which emergency messages are transmitted. The selection of the relay passes through three scenarios depending on the direction of the vehicles.

The protocol entitled "Time critical emergency message dissemination in VANETs" is proposed in [1]. The direct communication (V2 V) is sensitive to interference and can be blocked by physical obstacles such as large buildings and mountains. If the density of the network is small, the protocol proposes to use the V2i communication to allow dissemination of emergency messages faster and more reliable by reducing the time to access to the canal and the contention period. However, the use of the infrastructure is very costly and may not be always deployed along all the roads.

In [11] the authors proposed Black-burst and Multi-channel based Multihop Broadcast (BMMB) protocol using multiple antennas aiming to efficiently disseminating emergency messages in VANETs. BMMB enables alternatively unidirectional broadcast and multi-directional broadcast for straight roads and intersections respectively. Performance evaluation of BMMB carried out throw mathematical analysis and simulation exhibited results showing that BMMB performs better in terms of average one-hop delay and propagation speed. However, the protocol lacks generally since the end to end delay related to urgent events besides collisions avoidance has not been considered.

Bae proposed in [2] EW-ICAST: Early Warning Intelligent BroadCASTing protocol for safety messages dissemination for VANETs using fuzzy logic to cope with the broadcast storm issue and to respect the time criticality constraint in the context of vehicle collision avoidance. The performance of the proposal has been evaluated via MATLAB simulator and the results have been compared to those of some existing not recent protocols dedicated to the same issue.

3   Proposed Protocol

In this section we present a data communication approach in VANETs, combining both high reliability safety and minimum latency delay. This approach, a broadcast protocol, is based on the idea of selecting a single relay, to get the emergency message across until its destination, with integrating of fault-tolerance capability. The idea is implemented as a reliable routing protocol for emergency messages transmission. For the performance evaluation of this approach, we started by implementing the broadcast protocol, in which each node rebroadcasts the emergency message to its neighborhood up to its destination. We used the NS2 simulator and the Vanet- MobiSim mobility generator.

The simulation of VANETs is slightly different from the simulation of ad hoc networks because the environment of vehicles imposes new requirements such as route topology constraints, mobility model, the obstacles of the environment, and the high speed of vehicles. In order, for the results to be useful, it is important that the simulation model should remain faithful as possible to the reality. For that, we used the combination of the two known simulators: VanetMobiSim for generating realistic vehicles movements and NS2 for network aspects.

3.1 Protocol Ensuring Dependable Broadcast of Emergency Messages

As a first step in our approach, we introduced a broadcast protocol applied to troubleshoot failed vehicles. So, after the disadvantages observed during the realization of this Protocol, we proposed an approach to avoid some problems raised by the broadcast protocol, and ensure a high dependability with a minimum response time. To save time, we started from a well-known protocol already existing, the LEACH protocol [5]. This last is a hierarchical protocol; in our case we have kept the election method of Cluster Heads (CH). We have considered these CHs as falling nodes by integrating the scenario of mobility we previously obtained from the mobility generator VanetMobiSim. The reliability of our approach will be ensured by the troubleshooting of a maximum number of failing vehicles taking into account the latency delay factor.

Broadcast Protocol Principle. The algorithm of this protocol takes place in two phases.

- The phase of warning: when a node fails (vehicle), it broadcasts a message of type ADV_help for requesting the assistance of its direct neighbors.
- The rebroadcast phase: Each neighboring node of a failed one, receiving the message ADV_help, will rebroadcast the same message to its neighbor nodes but with a type of FWRD_help. Upon the reception of the FWRD_help message, the receiving node rebroadcasts the message if the source node is still failed, otherwise the broadcast of the message is stopped.

Upon message reception of type ADV_help or FWRD_help, the base station broadcasts a message help_ok. Upon the reception of the help_ok message from the base station, if the receiving node is the failed one, it will change its state, otherwise it will stop rebroadcasting the request "repaired node".

Simulation Results. Figure 1 represents the simulation results of the rebroadcasting protocol, with 100 vehicles moving with a mobility model created by VanetMobiSim generator. The mobility model follows the Intelligent Driver Model with Lane Changing (IDM_LC) of VANET Mobility Simulator (VANETMobiSim), in which, vehicles regulate their velocity according to neighboring vehicle movements. This model also supports smart intersection and lane changing management.

We note in the Fig. 1 and with a simulation time equal to 30 s (3 rounds = 3 simulation periods) only, among 21 vehicles get failed only 3 vehicles have received the message of troubleshooting sent by the base station. This is due to the significant number of messages circulating over the network which also introduce a significant number of collisions. Figure 2 shows vehicles getting failed with latency time difference between the two first and the third one very important. Therefore, the problems generated by a simple broadcast of emergency messages may be costly and unfavorable for reacting in time to critical event occurrences. This drawback may come from the following inconvenient situations:

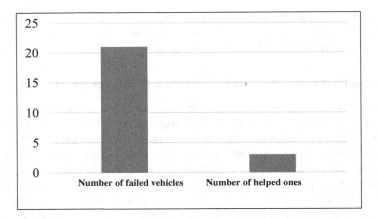

Fig. 1. Number of failed vehicles vs. helped ones.

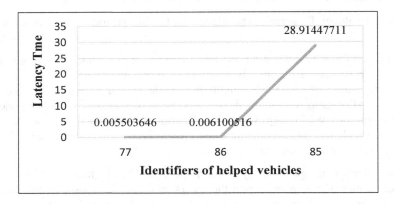

Fig. 2. Latency delay of helped vehicles in classical broadcast protocol

- Increase of network load especially in case of multiple failed nodes.
- Message flooding which generates the problem of collisions, which in turn causes loss of messages which leads to certain nodes having no chance to be helped.
- Loop problem caused by the partitioning of the network such that a message may not reach its destination.

3.2 Communication Protocol Improving Data Delivery Delays

In order to eliminate or at least reduce the negative aspects of the broadcast protocol presented in the previous section, we propose RRPML (Reliable Routing Protocol with Minimum Latency), which leads to several modifications to broadcast protocol taking into account the following improvements: Each node has an OPR (One Point Relay like MPR in the well known OLSR routing protocol [7] or the improved MPR proposed in [12]) which is determined in advance, and which will change according to the topology change.

- Only the OPR node assigned to the sending node retransmits the urgent message.
- If the message is redundant (already sent by OPR), the message will be sent to the infrastructure to avoid the looping problem.

Select_OPR Procedure. This procedure is performed by all nodes of the network; it is launched after each update of the neighbors table, exactly after 0.1 s in order to select its next hop. The value 0.1 is not chosen randomly, but after a few tests we have concluded that this period is sufficient to update all neighbor tables in order to select a recent OPR. The OPR choice criterion is that the latter is a neighboring node in the direction of the base station. This procedure consists of two parts. The first part is to calculate the distance of the node from each neighbor plus the distance that separates this neighbor to the base station. That is, the calculated number of neighbors covered by each neighbor and not covered by the current node (fills the list num_neigbour_).

Pseudocode of the first phase

    Variables: Neigbour_list_ : list of direct neighbors of nodeID

dist_neigbour_ : list holding distances (dist)

v2bs : distance from neighbor to base station

d2v : distance from nodeID to neighbor

Num_neighbor_ : list holding neighbors to 2 hops not covered by nodeID

Num : number of neighbors of a neighbor absent in neigbour_list_

Begin

    For any neigbour in Neigbour_list_ **Do**

      Begin

        Compute the distance (d2v), Compute the distance (v2bs)

        dist = v2bs + d2v, Add (dist_neigbour, dist)

        Compute Num, Add (Num_neigbour, Num)

      End

    EnFor End

The second part consists in selecting the OPR according to the calculated distance in first phase; if there is more than one node with the same minimum distance, we then consider the candidate node with the maximum number of neighbors at two hops (see Fig. 3).

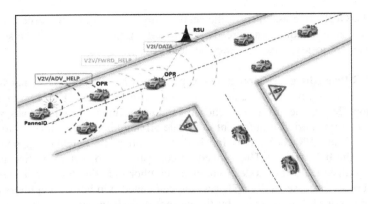

Fig. 3. Vehicle behaviors during node failure.

Pseudocode of the second phase

    Variable: OPR :   */ The next hop which enables to select nodeID

Begin

         min_dist = first element of dist_neigbor   /* dist-neigbor: table containing
                                                    neighbor distances

      For any   dist in dist_neigbour do

      If (dist < min_dist) then

       Begin   min_dist = dist,

              opr = Node /*corresponding to   min_dist

      End

      ElseIf (dist = min_dist)   then

       Begin   N = number of neighbors corresponding to min_dist

              NN = number of neighbors corresponding to dist

         If (NN>N)   then

          begin min_dist = dist OPR =   node corresponding to min_dist) **end**

         Endif

       End

      Endif

     End For

    OPR = opr

End

Principle of RRPML

- Each node checks its state periodically, the state may be in fault or not.
- If the node is failed, it sets the variable *Fault* to 1 to indicate to its neighbors that it is in failure, and calls the procedure {*advertisefailure*} to disseminate the message of help request (ADV_HELP).
- A node that fails makes a call to the procedure {*re_broad_fail*} at the moment (now + 1), to rebroadcast its help request if it stills in failure.

The Procedure {Advertisefailure}. This procedure is executed only by the failed nodes in two different cases, the first is at its failure time, the node records the time of failure (To compute latency time), and broadcasts a message of type ADV_help. In the second case, the procedure is called by the procedure {*re_broad_fail*}, if the node is still in failure (Fault = 2). If the next hop is the base station or the message is already passed by OPR, the message will be transmitted directly to the base station (communication V2I). The node executing the procedure {*re_broad_fail*} tests its variable Fault if it is equal to 1, it calls the procedure {*advertisefailure*} with Fault = 2.

Upon message reception of type ADV_help, if the receiving node is OPR of the sending node, it will call the procedure {*Foward_help*}, otherwise the node has nothing to do.

The Procedure Forward_Help. The principle of this procedure is similar to that of the procedure {*advertisefailure*}, with the difference that this procedure is only performed by the OPRs, and not by the failed nodes, and does not record the time of failure; it simply forwards the alert message with a type FWRD_help with the avoidance mechanism of loops.

Upon the reception of a message of type FWRD_help if the receiving node is OPR of the sending node, it will call the procedure {*Foward_help*}, otherwise the node has nothing to do.

Behavior of the Base Station (Infrastructure Station: RSU). The mission of the base station is to deliver a troubleshooting to vehicles that failed. Therefore, when the base station receives a message of type HELP, its delivers a message of type HELP_OK in broadcast. When a node receives from the base station the message HELP_ok, it changes its status (Fault = 1 or Fault = , 2) by (Fault = 0).

4   Simulation Results and Discussion

In order to evaluate the proposal performance, we carried out some simulation scenarios to estimate some relevant metrics complying with the context of VANETs area and time criticality.

4.1   Simulation Parameters and Evaluation Metrics

The simulation environment is depicted in Table 1 and the used performance evaluation metrics are:

Table 1. Simulation parameters

Parameter	Value
Network area size	1000 m * 1000 m
Number of vehicles	100
Velocity	50, 75, 100 km/h
Simulation time	500 s
Traffic Light	6
Number de Lanes	2
Mobility model	Random according to IDM_LC

- Number of messages sent out and received by destination enabling to calculate packets loss.
- Latency time = Response reception time – Time of fault occurrence to estimate message propagation delays in an environment often perturbed by frequent packet collisions.

4.2   Impact of the Variation of the Vehicles Velocity

In this part, we have fixed all the simulation parameters, but also, we varied the nodes velocity to 50 km/h, 75 km/h and 100 km/h.

Simulation Results with Speed = 50 km/h. According to the graph shown in Fig. 4, we note that the number of messages sent and received (during 50 rounds) increased almost in parallel as a function of the round, which affects the number of vehicles serviced. The graph shows that the proposed approach reduces the network load compared to the protocol of rebroadcasting. The difference between the messages sent and received is that messages are lost due to the problem of network partitioning.

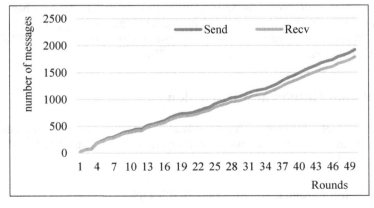

Fig. 4. Packets sent/received number (speed 50 km/h).

The latency time (Fig. 5) varies depending on the characteristics of the vehicles such that: their locations in relation to the base station and how many hops are necessary to ensure that the message reaches its destination (the base station). We found that the latency times which exceed 1 s are due to a loss and a rebroadcast of the emergency message of failed vehicles. We note that our approach is tolerant to message losses but with a quality of service a bit degraded (latency time).

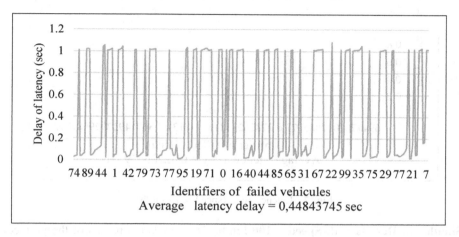

Fig. 5. Latency time (velocity = 50 km/h)

Simulation Results with Velocity v = 75 km/h. Figure 6 shows simulation result for the protocol RRPML with a scenario of nodes moving at speed of 75 km/h. This graph shows the evolution of the number of packets sent (Help request) and received as a function of time, with an acceptable loss which is due to the vehicles mobility with speed of 75 km/h. This loss of messages influence the number of vehicles serviced.

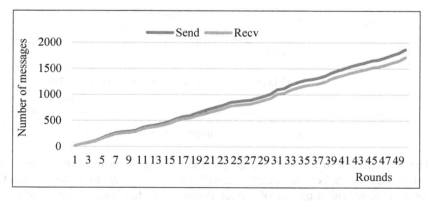

Fig. 6. Number of packets sent/received (velocity = 75 km/h).

The simulation of the protocol RRPML with the scenario of speed = 75 km/h, gives us the graph of Fig. 7, we note in the latter that the latency time varies from one vehicle to another all depends on the distance that separates it from the base station which has an impact on the number of hops and increases the latency time.

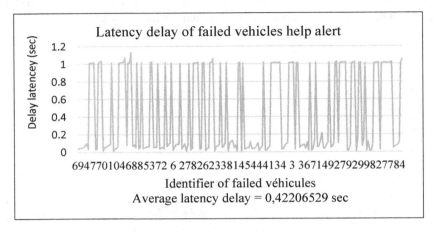

Fig. 7. Latency time (speed = 75 km/h).

Simulation Results with Speed = 100 km/h. The simulation results of the protocol RRPML with the scenario of speed equals to 100 km/h are presented in Figs. 8, 9 successively, according to the number of messages sent/received and the latency time.

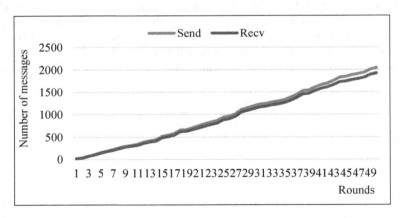

Fig. 8. Packets sent/received number (Speed 100 km/h).

The simulation with this scenario gives almost the same results with the first two scenarios: That is a packet loss acceptable, with the continuation of operation when the loss of a message with a quality of service degrades (higher latency compared to the latency of messages well received during the first dissemination, which is the consequence of rebroadcast).

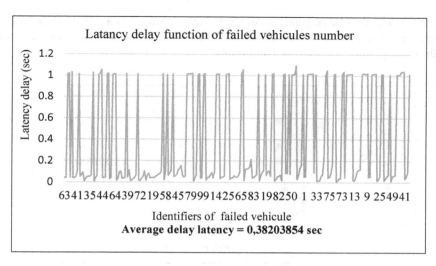

Fig. 9. Latency time (Speed 100 km/h).

Comparison. The Fig. 10 shows that the speed of vehicles does not influence much the performance of our protocol because of the updating of neighbor tables as well as the relay node (OPR) to each topology change.

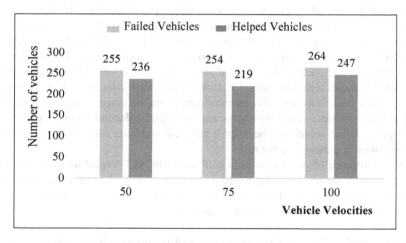

Fig. 10. Number of failed/helped vehicles function of speed.

$$\text{Average latency Time} = \sum \text{Latency Times} / \text{number of helped vehicles}.$$

Figure 11 shows the computation of the average of latency times of each scenario, we inferred that the speed is an important factor in the vehicular networks, because it fosters the delivery of emergency messages to the base station in a minimum time limit, which reduces the latency time, but it should not exceed the limits otherwise it will produce the problem of network partitioning.

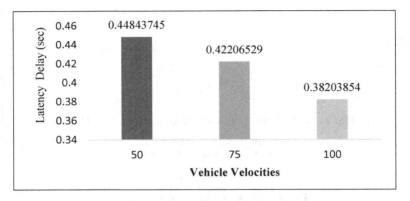

Fig. 11. Average latency time function of vehicle Speeds.

5 Conclusion

The initial paradigm of VANETs has paved the way to the field of Intelligent Transport Systems and Internet of Vehicles. So, overcoming VANETs obstacles involves contributing to ITS and IoV mature development. This is what is devoted to this paper in which an efficient emergency messages communication protocol for vehicular networks has presented. The main advantage of this protocol is to minimize the latency time, and tolerate disturbances such as the loss of messages due to several problems, by re-broadcasting the message lost, which ensures dependable communication of urgency messages. This dependability (Having confidence that messages will reach their destinations) is crucial since response to urgency messages is depending on. We have used the example of failed vehicles to be helped, but we could have used collided vehicles to rescue the injured persons on board.

The performance of our proposal is evaluated via NS2-VanetMobiSim simulators according to relevant scenarios by modifying nodes mobility speed which is the main characteristic and obstacle of the vehicular networks. We note that the simulation results obtained are convincing and our proposal is reliable.

Acknowledgement. This research work is supported in part by PHC-Tassili Grant Number 18MDU114.

References

1. Anees, A.S., Kurien, B.V.: Time critical emergency message dissemination in VANETs. Int. J. Eng. Res. Gen. Sci. **3**(4), 22–28 (2015). Part-2
2. Bae, I.H.: An intelligent broadcasting algorithm for early warning message dissemination in VANETs. Mathematical Problems in Engineering **2015**, 8 (2015). Article ID 848915
3. Chaqfeh, M., Lakas, A., Jawhar, I.: A survey on data dissemination in vehicular ad hoc networks. Veh. Commun. **1**(4), 214–225 (2014)
4. Dawood, H.S., Wang, Y.: An efficient emergency message broadcasting scheme in vehicular ad hoc networks. Int. J. Distrib. Sens. Netw. **9**(11), 232916 (2013). https://doi.org/10.1155/2013/232916
5. Heinzelman, W.R., Chandrakasan, A., Balakrishnan, H.: Energy-efficient communication protocol for wireless microsensor networks. In: 2000 System sciences,. Proceedings of the 33rd Annual Hawaii International Conference on Maui, HI, IEEE (2000)
6. Korkmaz, G., Ekici, E., Özgüner, F., Özgüner, Ü.: Urban multi-hop broadcast protocol for inter-vehicle communication systems. In: Proceedings of the 1st ACM International Workshop on Vehicular Adhoc Networks, pp. 76–85. ACM, Philadelphia, USA (2004)
7. Priyadharshini, A., Sundarambal, M.: OLSR protocol for vehicular sensor network in cognitive radio. Int. J. Mobile Netw. Des. Innov. **8**(3), 168–178 (2018)
8. Samara, G., Alhmiedat, T.: Intelligent emergency message broadcasting in VANET using PSO. arXiv preprint arXiv:1406.7399 (2014)
9. Samara, G., Al-Salihy, W.A.H., Ramadass, S.: Increasing network visibility using coded repetition beacon piggybacking. World Appl. Sci. J. **13**(1), 100–108 (2011).arXiv preprint arXiv:1301.7170 (2013)
10. Sanguesa, J.A., Fogue, M., Garrido, P., Martinez, F.J., Cano, J.C., Calafate, C.T.: A survey and comparative study of broadcast warning message dissemination schemes for VANETs. Mob. Inf. Syst. 1–18 (2016). https://dx.doi.org/10.1155/2016/8714142
11. Wu, L., Nie, L., Fan, J., He, Y., Liu, Q., Wu, D.: An efficient multi-hop broadcast protocol for emergency messages dissemination in VANETs. Chin. J. Electron. **26**(3), 614–623 (2017)
12. Wu, Y., Xu, L., Lin, X., Fang, J.: A new routing protocol based on OLSR designed for UANET maritime search and rescue. In: Peng, S.-L., Lee, G.-L., Klette, R., Hsu, C.-H. (eds.) IOV 2017. LNCS, vol. 10689, pp. 79–91. Springer, Cham (2017). https://doi.org/10.1007/978-3-319-72329-7_8
13. Zeadally, S., Hunt, R., Chen, Y.S., Irwin, A., Hassan, A.: Vehicular adhoc networks (VANETS): status, results, and challenges. Telecommun. Syst. **50**(4), 217–241 (2012)

IoV Clouds and Services

Vehicular Fog Computing on Top of a Virtualization Layer

Esteban F. Ordóñez-Morales[1], Martín López-Nores[2(✉)],
Yolanda Blanco-Fernández[2], Efrén P. Reinoso-Mendoza[1],
Jack F. Bravo-Torres[1], and José J. Pazos-Arias[2]

[1] Universidad Politécnica Salesiana, Calle Vieja 12-30 y Elia Liut, Cuenca, Ecuador
{eordonez,preinoso,jbravo}@ups.edu.ec
[2] AtlantTIC Research Center for Information and Communication Technologies,
Departamento de Ingeniería Telemática, Universidade de Vigo, EE Telecomunicación,
Campus Universitario s/n, 36310 Vigo, Spain
{mlnores,yolanda,jose}@det.uvigo.es

Abstract. This paper presents a networking architecture that brings
the principles of fog computing to the realm of vehicular ad-hoc networks (VANETs), by systematizing the use of one or more end-user
clients or near-user edge devices to carry out tasks on behalf of others.
The proposal is grounded on a virtualization layer and specific routing algorithms, adding new constructs and protocols to orchestrate the
allocation of tasks and the sharing of resources. This proposal solves
persistent problems of previous approaches to mobile augmentation in
VANETs, which require the nodes offering their resources to stay close
to the ones that would use them transiently. The advantages are proved
by simulations of an application of collaborative mapping and navigation,
in which the vehicles in a city share storage, computing and communication resources to distribute the tasks of (i) downloading, storing and
sharing chunks of maps from a server, and (ii) computing routes to the
intended destinations.

1 Introduction

The term *fog computing* refers to an architecture that uses one or more collaborative end-user clients or near-user edge devices (hereafter, *collaborator nodes*
or CNs) to carry out a substantial amount of work in a given service on behalf
of other devices (the so-called *application nodes* or AppNs). That work may
involve storage (in the CNs rather than primarily in remote servers or cloud
datacenters), communication (involving only proximal links rather than routes
over the Internet backbone) and computing (doing with local information and
resources as far as possible), as well as control, configuration, measurement and
management [1,2].

In this paper, we present an approach to enable fog computing in vehicular
ad-hoc networks, aiming to provide convenient foundations for intelligent transportation systems [3,4] and infotainment services [5,6]. This approach, named

© Springer Nature Switzerland AG 2018
A. M. J. Skulimowski et al. (Eds.): IOV 2018, LNCS 11253, pp. 77–91, 2018.
https://doi.org/10.1007/978-3-030-05081-8_6

ViVeFog (*Virtualization under the Vehicular Fog*) systematizes the use of on-board and roadside devices to carry out tasks on behalf of others. ViVeFog is grounded on a virtualization layer and specific routing algorithms presented in [7,8], adding new constructs and protocols to orchestrate the allocation of tasks and the sharing of resources among vehicles. This proposal overcomes persistent problems of previous approaches to cloud-based mobile augmentation in VANETs, which, according to the taxonomy presented in [9], can be categorized into four main types:

- *Distant immobile clouds* comprise a potentially large number of stationary remote servers that are located far from the vehicles [10,11]. The distance between lenders and borrowers of resources causes relatively high latencies in the communications, hampering the deployment of non-delay-tolerant information services.
- *Proximate immobile clouds* exploit the underutilized resources of the vehicles left in parking lots, malls, airports and the like, which are brought together into *cloudlets* [12]. Typically, the augmentation facilities are available only in the areas around the cloudlets.
- *Proximate mobile clouds* allow moving vehicles to lend resources to other moving vehicles [13–16], though most often restricting the movements of both AppNs and CNs to ensure that they remain within communication range during the entire augmentation processes [17–19].
- *Hybrid approaches* offer different combinations of the previous models [20,21].

The advantages of ViVeFog (a hybrid approach itself) arise from the fact that the resource-sharing facilities can be implemented seamlessly on top of the collaboration processes that take place already at the virtualization and routing layers (see our stack of protocols in Fig. 1). Therefore, an AppN can start using the resources of a CN when they are close to one another, and the communication channel between them persists as a multi-hop route if they move apart, if necessary. The benefits attained at the applications layer show up as if the AppNs were more resourceful than they are, e.g. saving computing time or enjoying greater effective bandwidth. In this paper, we present the results of simulations of an application of collaborative mapping and navigation, in which the vehicles in a city share resources to distribute the tasks of (i) downloading, storing and sharing chunks of maps from a server, and (ii) computing routes to the intended destinations.

The paper is organized as follows. Section 2 provides an overview of the virtualization layer (VaNetLayer [7]) and the routing protocol (VNIBR [8]) that provide the foundations for ViVeFog. The resource sharing and task allocation mechanisms of the latter are presented in Sect. 3. The experiments carried out to assess the advantages of our proposal are detailed in Sect. 4, following a review of the state-of-the-art in resource-sharing mechanisms applied to similar applications. Conclusions and future work are given in Sect. 5.

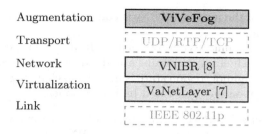

Fig. 1. The protocol stack of our approach.

2 Background on the Supporting Protocols

VANETs are a particularly challenging environment because the mobility of the vehicles causes changes in network topology, leading to route breakages, packet losses, significant routing overhead and, ultimately, low throughput and unreliability as seen from the protocols above. Next, we summarize the mechanisms than underpin the fog computing features of ViVeFog from the virtualization layer (Subsect. 2.1) and the network layer (Subsect. 2.2). Further details and experimental assessments can be found at [7,8], showing that these underlying protocols can attain good performance in urban scenarios of vehicle-to-vehicle (V2V) and vehicle-to-infrastructure (V2I) communications. It was also shown that they entail lower computational cost than other existing protocols, working reasonably within the resources of commercially-available on-board computers.

2.1 The Virtualization Layer: VaNetLayer

The VaNetLayer defines procedures for the mobile *physical nodes* (PNs) to collaborate in emulating *virtual nodes* (VNs) that can be addressed as static and proximal server devices, and that can be used to store *persistent state information* (PSI). The VNs cover non-overlapping *regions*, whose boundaries are computed automatically from the street maps.

The basic task in the operation of a VN is to distribute roles of *leaders* and *backups* among the PNs. The leader of a region takes charge of packet reception, buffering and forwarding in the communication with other VNs, whereas the backups maintain replicas of the PSI from the virtualization layer and the protocols above. Thus, the VN can work even when individual PNs fail or leave the region, as long as there remains at least one PN inside.

The PSI managed at the virtualization layer (which is the cornerstone of VN emulation) consists of two tables that can be read from the upper layers:

– The *region activeness* table keeps track of the regions from which messages can be heard by the VN. Each entry maintains a region id, the MAC address of the current leader of the region and counters (of nodes and different types of messages) to measure the activeness of the region. An exponentially-weighted moving average of the number of PNs is computed, too, that provides a basis for QoS estimations.

- The *neighbor list* maintains the list of PNs from which messages have been heard recently. Each entry maintains a node id, region id and a lifetime. The maintenance of neighbor/region state is done by exchanging "Hello" messages and overhearing messages generated by leader nodes.

The VaNetLayer's interface to the protocols above exposes the notion of regions, the role (leader or backup) played by a PN at each moment, and functions to send/receive messages and to get/set/check the PSI. Since the PSI may be crucial for the protocols to run properly, the VaNetLayer implements one mechanism to try to preserve it, even if a region becomes depleted of PNs (see [7]).

2.2   The Virtualized Routing Protocol: VNIBR

The layout of the VNs provided by the VaNetLayer provides convenient grounds to develop a combination of topological and geographical routing, with road-based paths connecting successive intersections that lead from sources to destinations [22]. The routing protocol of our approach, called VNIBR (*Intersection-Based Routing on Virtual Nodes*), differentiates three types of routing entities:

- Level 1 entities (L1VNs) are the VNs placed at the intersections. This is where the routing decisions are made, using a procedure adapted from AODV logic. Routing tables are kept as PSI, with entries indicating which is the next road segment (identified by the L1VN at the other end) that the packets must traverse in order to reach the corresponding destination.
- Level 2 entities (L2VNs) are the VNs neighboring an intersection. These VNs start forwarding packets along a road segment as mandated by the neighboring L1VN, irrespective of whichever PN actually does the transmission. Furthermore, L2VNs act as backing entities that may try to relay packets onto other road segments during downtimes of the neighboring L1VNs.
- Finally, the VNs in intermediate positions of road segments are level 3 entities (L3VNs) that simply relay packets from one side to the other, again irrespective of specific PNs.

Monitoring QoS Along the Road Segments. L1VNs which are one road segment away from one another steadily exchange *HELLO* packets to keep track of the connectivity conditions they provide. The estimation of QoS is based on the following elements as indicated in Eq. (1) where $VN(S)$ is the set of VNs that make up the road segment (L1VNs included):

- AV_PNs_i: The average numbers of PNs supporting each VN, computed at the virtualization layer and inserted by the L1VNs, the L2VNs and the L3VNs in successive fields of the *HELLO* packets.

- *D*: An exponentially-weighted moving average of the L1VN-L1VN transmission delay, measured by the L1VNs themselves using the timestamps included in the *HELLO* packets. This value correlates with the length of the road segment, but it can also provide early signs of congestion due to packets waiting in the VN outbound queues.
- *AV_LH*: An exponentially-weighted moving average of lost *HELLO* packets.
- *AR*: The number of active communication routes established through the road segment, captured in the routing tables kept by the L1VNs. The point here is to prevent congestion of the primary routes.

$$QoS(\mathcal{S}) = \frac{\prod_{i \in VN(\mathcal{S})} AV\_PNs_i}{[D \cdot (AV\_LH + 1)] + AR} \tag{1}$$

The numbers provided by Eq. 1 vary largely depending on various factors (e.g. the density of road traffic, the level of network congestion and the signal propagation conditions). However, as proved in [8], we do not need an absolute scale for the routing decisions, and relative comparisons work.

Route Creation. Communication routes in VNIBR are created when a source PN needs to send a packet but it does not know a route to the intended destination. In that case, the source PN buffers the packet and starts a flooding process by sending a *Route Request* packet (*RREQ*) to the L1VNs that delimit its road segment. The L1VNs then propagate the *RREQ* over the connected segments in decreasing order of QoS values, with a 10 ms delay between transmits. If the QoS value for one road segment is lower than a certain fraction of the previous one, that segment and the remaining ones are skipped.

The L2VNs and L3VNs forward the *RREQ* packets without any other processing than setting a *delivery bit* in the header to 1 if the destination PN is in the current region. The L1VNs reached put their ID as the first element of a list in the *RREQ* and continue the flooding process unless a route has been established, which happens in the following cases:

1. When the *RREQ* packet reaches an L1VN that knows a valid route to the destination PN.
2. When an L1VN receives the *RREQ* packet with the delivery bit set to 1, meaning that the destination PN is in the road segment just traversed.
3. When an L1VN receives the *RREQ* packet with the delivery bit set to 0 but the destination PN is in the current intersection.

In these cases, a *Route Reply* packet (*RREP*) is created that travels along the backpath, allowing the L1VNs on the way to set up a route to the destination PN in their routing tables—just like the L1VN list in the *RREQ* packet header allowed the traversed L1VNs to set up route entries to the source PN.

Route Maintenance. Once a route between source and destination PNs has been established, as explained in Sect. 2.1, the data packets are sent VN by VN through unicast transmissions between leader nodes. The VaNetLayer raises the link layer notifications to the network layer whenever it is not possible to resolve the MAC address of the next hop node, when the RTS/CTS mechanism of IEEE 802.11 cannot reserve the shared channel, or when no acknowledgement for a data packet can be received and retransmission attempts also failed. When the transmitting PN detects a failure, it reports the error to the preceding L1VN by sending a *Route Error* packet (*RERR*), and then the L1VN can take one of two possible actions:

- The L1VN can try a *local repair* by broadcasting an *RREQ* packet and waiting for an *RREP* to restore the route. Data packets that were being relayed for the route are buffered as long as possible.
- The L1VN can report the error further upstream by forwarding the *RERR* packet along the backpath. In this case, the data packets are discarded, so they will not make it to their destinations.

Route repairs are attempted in two cases: (i) when some of the road segments connected to the L1VN have QoS values, at least, double of the one measure on the segment from where the *RERR* packet was received, or (ii) when the route is longer than 3 road segments and the L1VN happens to be among the last $\frac{1}{3}$ of the steps. These conditions are checked by all the L1VNs that receive *RERR*, meaning that VNIBR attempts to repair long routes when breakages occur nearing the end and explores broader areas progressively.

3 Mechanisms for Cloud-Based Mobile Augmentation in ViVeFog

Leaning on the services provided by the VaNetLayer and VNIBR, we have developed ViVeFog as a hybrid approach that can seek resources to augment the capabilities of any of the devices in a VANET (the AppN) by using resources provided by both servers in distant clouds or CNs in proximate clouds. The distant servers can be reached either by 3G/4G connections available to the AppN itself or to any of the CNs, or via roadside Internet access points (hereafter denoted by APs). In turn, the communications between AppN and CNs happen via 802.11p links, using single-hop or multi-hop routes.[1,2]

---

[1] Without loss of generality, in the rest of the paper we will assume that AppNs do not have 3G/4G connections of their own, but only the capability of communicating V2V and V2I via 802.11p. In the same line, for simplicity, we will assume that Internet APs are always placed in intersections.

[2] Multi-hop routes to CNs or APs can go through any vehicles, not only those who offer (part of) their resources as CNs. We assume that all vehicles participate in the operation of the VaNetLayer and VNIBR—a study of how the performance of the former degrades when not all the nodes collaborate can be found in [7].

As depicted in Fig. 2, the proximate clouds are confined to the street segments between intersections, involving the aggregate of the resources offered by the CNs that happen to be in the regions of the corresponding L2VNs and L3VNs (Sect. 2.2) at any given moment. In this regard, the clouds can be considered *proximate immobile clouds* as per the terminology of [9], but only because the virtual nodes are stationary. The proximate resources used by any AppN are provided by individual CNs, and both are allowed to move freely once they collaboration has started. This way, it will typically be the case that an AppN starts using some resources provided by a given CN in a moment that they are right next to each other, within one hop of 802.11p communication, but then start to move apart; VNIBR deals with the extension to a multi-hop route in a completely transparent manner, so in this sense our approach incorporates the notion of *proximate mobile clouds* too.[3]

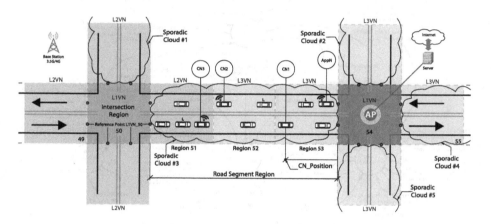

Fig. 2. Sporadic clouds in ViVeFog.

The operation of ViVeFog relies on the exchange of information about the resources offered by the CNs, which is aggregated and kept as PSI in the L1VNs. This involves two processes:

– On the one hand, every CN sends *M_ResourceInfoFromCN* messages to the L1VNs that delimit its current street segment, whenever it leaves an intersection or there is any change in the resources it offers. The messages contain information about the resources offered (e.g. bandwidth in 3G/4G connections, sensing capabilities, pieces of information to share, etc.) in a non-prescribed format, so it is up to the applications to encode and interpret the information.

---

[3] In Fig. 2, we use the term *sporadic cloud* to emphasize the point that the encounters among collaborating vehicles can be merely coincidental. The important fact, however, is that the underlying protocols simplify access to the shared resources and, at the same time, increase the stability of the communications to support proper completion of the tasks allocated to the CNs.

- On the other hand, there is a steady exchange of *M_SporadicCloudResources* messages between all pairs of L1VNs that are one road segment away from one another, in order to keep fresh PSI about the resources available in the L2VNs and L3VNs in between.

The operation of ViVeFog is driven by messages, timers and flags that take AppNs and CNs through different states, yielding the state machine of Fig. 3.

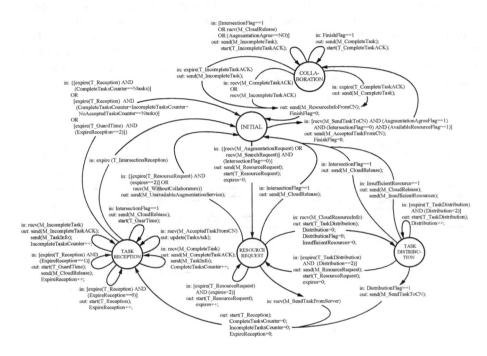

Fig. 3. The state machine of ViVeFog.

Discovery of CNs. When an AppN is in a street segment (which is denoted in Fig. 3 by *IntersectionFlag = 0*) and the application requests to use external resources (by means of an *M_AugmentationRequest* message), ViVeFog sends an *M_ResourceRequest* message to the corresponding L1VNs, in order to discover CNs that could serve those needs. The AppN changes from INITIAL to RESOURCE REQUEST state and waits for responses from those L1VNs during the time set in the *T_ResourceRequest* timer. Looking at the PSI they store, the L1VNs prepare their replies considering not only the resources available in the AppN's street segment, but also the adjacent ones –this way, for example, the AppN in region 53 of Fig. 2 could do not only with resources from *Sporadic Cloud #3* (which covers its current segment) but also from any of the 6 neighboring sporadic clouds (3 touching the L1VN of region 50, the other 3 touching region 54).

If any of the L1VNs find that the request can be fulfilled, it sends to the AppN an *M_CloudResourceInfo* message, which makes it transition to TASK DISTRIBUTION state and start the *T_TaskDistribution* timer. On the contrary, if the L1VN finds that the request cannot be fulfilled according to the PSI it stores, it sends an *M_WithoutCollaborators* message; upon receiving two of those, the AppN changes to INITIAL state and the application layer is notified via an *M_UnavailableAugmentationService* message. The AppN also goes back to INITIAL state if the *T_ResourceRequest* times expires 3 times.

The fact that each L1VN handles different PSI (summarizing the resources available on the adjacent street segments) implies that their replies to the AppN are based on local views. Therefore, in the example of Fig. 2, it might be possible to fulfill a request from the AppN in region 53 with resources from all the surrounding sporadic cloud, but none of the L1VNs would know that and, as a result, the AppN would get two *M_WithoutCollaborators* messages. This behavior suggests that the applications on top of ViVeFog should be written in such a way that they make fine-grained request rather than aggregated ones.

Task Allocation. When an AppN knows about CNs that could fulfill its augmentation requests, the application running on top of ViVeFog can decide which CNs should be allocated the tasks in question (there may be several candidates, and the application may decide one way or another owing to any information included in the *M_ResourceInfoFromCN* and *M_ResourceRequest* messages). Once the allocation has been decided (indicated by *DistributionFlag = 1* in Fig. 3), the AppN sends the allocated tasks to the CNs via *M_SendTaskToCN* messages and changes to TASK RECEPTION state. At this point, the (possibly multi-hop) communication routes between the AppN and the CNs are established, which VNIBR will attempt to maintain (extending or shortening, if necessary) in a seamless way.

There are three other possible transitions out of TASK ALLOCATION state:

- If the *T_TaskDistribution* timer expires three times before concluding the allocation of tasks (e.g. because the application takes too long to decide), the AppN returns to RESOURCE REQUEST state and sends again the *M_ResourceRequest* messages to the corresponding L1VNs. This happens because the availability of augmentation resources changes as the CNs move or change their resource offerings.
- If the AppN leaves the current street segment (i.e. enters an intersection, as indicated by *IntersectionFlag = 1*) before concluding the allocation of tasks, the augmentation request is discarded and triggered again in the sporadic cloud corresponding to the new segment it enters. To this aim, the AppN broadcasts an *M_CloudRelease* message to inform the L1VNs and CNs, and then returns to INITIAL state.

- If, for whichever reason, the application decides not to do with the discovered CNs, the AppN broadcasts an *M_CloudRelease* message and changes from TASK DISTRIBUTION to INITIAL state.

Task Resolution. The tasks assigned to CNs can be completed, abandoned at some point or even rejected. As the AppN receives notifications from the CNs, it sends the corresponding information to the application layer via *M_TaskInfo* messages (one per task). When all the tasks are done, the AppN changes from TASK RECEPTION to INITIAL state. If any of them cannot be completed before the *T_Reception* timer expires twice, a *T_GuardTime* is set to wait before sending the *M_CloudRelease* message. When this timer expires, the AppN returns to INITIAL state and the augmentation process ends.

The Collaborators' Side. A CN changes from INITIAL to COLLABORA-TION state after the reception of the *M_SendTaskToCN* message. The CN can confirm acceptance of the task by sending an *M_AcceptedTaskFromCN* message to the AppN. Successful completion is notified to the AppN through an *M_CompleteTask* message.

If the CN receives an *M_CloudRelease* message, it can send to the AppN any partial results by means of an *M_IncompleteTask* message. The same happens when it decides to stop sharing resources. Both complete and partial results are retransmitted while the AppN does not acknowledge their reception. In the end, the CN returns to INITIAL state.

4   Experimental Evaluation

For the assessment of the ViVeFog approach, we have made simulations of an application of collaborative mapping and navigation, in which a set of CNs in a city share storage, computing and communication resources so that a few lightweight AppNs (with no capacity to store map chunks or to run route seeking algorithms) can get indications to reach their destinations, containing only the map information along the proposed routes. The experiments were twofold:

- On the one hand, we measured the benefits brought by the collaboration features in comparison with having the AppNs get indications exclusively from remote servers (i.e. without seeking assistance from CNs). Hereafter, we will use the moniker ViVeFogless to refer to the configuration in which the application is built directly on VNIBR (e.g. removing the collaboration layer from Fig. 1, but keeping the underlying virtualization constructs).
- On the other hand, we compared ViVeFog and ViVeFogless with another fog computing approach inspired by MobTorrent, a framework presented in [23] to optimize mobile Internet access from vehicles. MobTorrent put forward an original solution in which mobile clients, rather than always waiting for being within reach of any of the APs deployed in a city, use their 3G/4G connection to send a request to a central server that, in turn, instructs selected APs to

prefetch content. The prefetched data are then replicated on *mobile helpers* (other vehicles) in the vicinity of those APs, that propagate the information in a store-carry-forward fashion by direct (one-hop only) communications. The central server runs mobility prediction and scheduling algorithms to select the best APs to prefetch content, processing mobility traces from each one of the vehicles that offer themselves as mobile helpers. In our adaptation of MobTorrent (which we shall refer to as MobFog), the mobile helpers map directly to CNs in the terminology of the preceding sections.

In order to fairly compare the three configurations (ViVeFog, ViVeFogless and MobFog) supporting the same application, we set the following conditions in our simulation scenarios:

- All the vehicles were equipped with 4G (LTE) and 802.11p connections. The latter would be used as the preferred means to communicate with remote servers, either in one hop to reach an AP (in the three configurations) or through multi-hop routes (only in ViVeFog and ViVeFogless).
- In ViVeFog and MobFog, the CNs offered 15% of their LTE bandwidth to other vehicles. Their storage resources were considered unlimited, and they started with no map chunks in their memories.
- In ViVeFog and MobFog, the requests issued by the AppNs could be allocated to either remote servers or CNs (whichever replied first). The requests would be specifically targeted to the servers only after two consecutive attempts to use CN resources for a certain task failed to complete the work.
- The round trip times from the APs or the LTE antennae to the servers (for ViVeFogless too) were always 300 ms.
- The execution of all the algorithms (mobility prediction, scheduling and route seeking, where applicable) was assumed to take a constant time of 10 ms in the remote servers, whereas route seeking in the CNs took 200 ms.
- The number of AppNs was fixed to 10, and their sequences of destinations were fixed, too.[4]
- 8 APs were placed in major intersections, their coverage areas adding up to 15% of the city area.
- Finally, to make up for the fact that MobFog allows CNs to support one another by exchanging previously-downloaded map chunks, we allowed the CNs in ViVeFog to request the chunks they needed from other CNs, using the same mechanisms described for AppNs in Sect. 3.

We used ns-3 as network simulator and SUMO (*Simulation of Urban MObility*) to get realistic mobility traces for the vehicles. We looked at the following metrics in scenarios of sparse, medium or heavy traffic, with different percentages of vehicles offering themselves as CNs (25%, 50% or 75%).

---

[4] We defined sequences of destinations to ensure the AppNs would be asking for routes throughout the entire duration of the simulations, not only at the beginning.

Overall Amount of Traffic Entering + Leaving the Remote Servers.
Table 1—with the figures normalized with regard to the performance of
ViVeFog—shows that the collaboration features brought by the latter cause substantial savings in comparison with ViVeFogless, owing to the fact that the CNs
keep copies of the map chunks. While this is true also for MobFog, the savings are
lower because of the location information uploaded to the server as required by
the mobility prediction and scheduling algorithms. Only in scenarios of heavy
traffic and abundance of CNs does MobFog reduce the burden on the servers
more than ViVeFog does, because the location updates are less frequent and the
dissemination of chunks by the store-carry-forward mechanisms serves to make
them available throughout the whole set of CNs quickly enough.

Table 1. Relative amounts of traffic handled by the remote servers.

	25% of CNs			50% of CNs			75% of CNs		
	ViVeFogless	ViVeFog	MobFog	ViVeFogless	ViVeFog	MobFog	ViVeFogless	ViVeFog	MobFog
Light traffic	5.42	**1.00**	3.84	6.53	**1.00**	3.11	8.09	**1.00**	2.26
Medium traffic	4.99	**1.00**	3.17	6.41	**1.00**	2.51	8.03	**1.00**	1.41
Heavy traffic	4.60	**1.00**	2.15	6.38	**1.00**	1.66	7.98	**1.00**	0.94

Overall Amount of Traffic Going Through the LTE Network. The normalized figures of Table 2 show that the configurations relying on the virtualization layer (ViVeFogless and ViVeFog) managed to deliver much more information
through the VANET than MobFog, particularly due to VNIBR's ability to create and maintain multi-hop routes to the APs. The fact that ViVeFogless did
not allow the AppNs to get map data from other vehicles implied extra LTE
communications, especially with low traffic densities (when it is harder to establish or maintain the multi-hop routes). Part of the overhead with MobFog was
due to the updates of location information, which had to be uploaded via LTE
whenever the CNs were not within the areas covered by the APs.

Table 2. Relative amounts of traffic going through the LTE network.

	25% of CNs			50% of CNs			75% of CNs		
	ViVeFogless	ViVeFog	MobFog	ViVeFogless	ViVeFog	MobFog	ViVeFogless	ViVeFog	MobFog
Light traffic	1.14	**1.00**	2.91	1.18	**1.00**	3.04	1.25	**1.00**	3.65
Medium traffic	1.09	**1.00**	3.11	1.15	**1.00**	3.08	1.23	**1.00**	3.77
Heavy traffic	1.04	**1.00**	3.18	1.12	**1.00**	3.22	1.22	**1.00**	4.06

Average Latency for an AppN to Get a Route. The time needed to get routes in the case of ViVeFogless was constant: 310 ms (300 ms round-trip time to the remote servers + 10 ms in computing). In contrast, the latencies varied largely with ViVeFog and MobFog, since it was possible to have the route-seeking task fulfilled by CN just one (802.11p) hop away, but also to end up asking the remote servers after failing to get a route from any CN nearby. The normalized figures of Table 3 show that ViVeFog and MobFog yielded significantly greater latencies that ViVeFogless in scenarios of light traffic or only 25% of vehicles offering their resources, since the attempts to communicate with the CNs were more likely to fail. In contrast, in scenarios of heavy traffic and abundant CNs, ViVeFog and MobFog did attain improvements in the service to the AppNs. Noticeably, MobFog caused slightly lower latencies than ViVeFog because it would never try multi-hop routes.

Table 3. Relative average latencies for AppNs to get routes upon request.

	25% of CNs			50% of CNs			75% of CNs		
	ViVeFogless	ViVeFog	MobFog	ViVeFogless	ViVeFog	MobFog	ViVeFogless	ViVeFog	MobFog
Light traffic	0.38	**1.00**	0.88	0.41	**1.00**	0.92	0.53	**1.00**	0.94
Medium traffic	0.81	**1.00**	0.91	0.82	**1.00**	0.93	0.98	**1.00**	0.95
Heavy traffic	0.83	**1.00**	0.93	0.97	**1.00**	0.95	1.04	**1.00**	0.93

5   Conclusions

The results gathered in Tables 1, 2 and 3 show that ViVeFog achieves good performance as a framework for mobile augmentation in urban VANET scenarios. On the one hand, the comparison with ViVeFogless justifies the idea of augmenting the capabilities of lightweight devices by resorting to resources from nearby collaborators, which contributes to reducing the burden on remote servers without putting at risk the responsiveness of services with no hard real-time constraints, and at the same time saves 10%–20% usage of the 3G/4G connections, which are still an expensive resource. On the other hand, the comparison with MobFog demonstrates the benefits of the processes running at the virtualization and routing layers under ViVeFog (Fig. 1), which enable transparent exploitation of multi-hop routes within the VANET and, thereby, greater possibilities to reach (and maintain lasting communications with) Internet access points and a greater number of collaborator nodes. This is where the key contribution of this work lies, with a hybrid fog computing approach that offers *proximate immobile clouds* while not restricting the relative movements of AppNs and CNs. The downside is that the virtualization processes depend on having sufficient traffic densities, so the proposal cannot work properly during periods of very light traffic or in non-urban scenarios. In such settings, it is more convenient to resort to mechanisms like the ones presented in [24].

Acknowledgment. This work has been supported by the European Regional Development Fund (ERDF) and the Galician Regional Government under agreement for funding the AtlantTIC Research Center for Information and Communication Technologies, and through its Program for the Consolidation and Structuring of Competitive Research Groups as well as the Ministerio de Educación y Ciencia (Gobierno de España) research project TIN2017-87604-R.

References

1. Bar-Magen Numhauser, J.: Fog computing: introduction to a new cloud evolution. University of Alcalá (2012)
2. Bonomi, F., Milito, R., Natarajan, P., Zhu, J.: Fog computing: a platform for internet of things and analytics. In: Bessis, N., Dobre, C. (eds.) Big Data and Internet of Things: A Roadmap for Smart Environments. SCI, vol. 546, pp. 169–186. Springer, Cham (2014). https://doi.org/10.1007/978-3-319-05029-4_7
3. Khekare, G.S.: Design of emergency system for intelligent traffic system using VANET. In: International Conference on Information Communication and Embedded Systems (ICICES), pp. 1–7, February 2014
4. Liu, B., Jia, D., Wang, J., Lu, K., Wu, L.: Cloud-assisted safety message dissemination in VANET-cellular heterogeneous wireless network. IEEE Syst. J. **11**(1), 128–139 (2017)
5. Gerla, M., Wu, C., Pau, G., Zhu, X.: Content distribution in VANETs. Veh. Commun. **1**(1), 3–12 (2014)
6. Jia, S., Liu, Z., Zhu, K., Zhang, L., Fadlullah, Z., Kato, N.: Bus-Ads: bus-based priced advertising in VANETs using coalition formation game. In: IEEE International Conference on Communications (ICC), June 2015
7. Bravo-Torres, J.F., López-Nores, M., Blanco-Fernández, Y., Pazos-Arias, J.J., Ramos-Cabrer, M., Gil-Solla, A.: Optimizing reactive routing over virtual nodes in VANETs. IEEE Trans. Veh. Technol. **65**(4), 2274–2294 (2016)
8. Saiáns-Vázquez, J.V., López-Nores, M., Blanco-Fernández, Y., Ordóñez-Morales, E.F., Bravo-Torres, J.F., Pazos-Arias, J.J.: Efficient and viable intersection-based routing in VANETs on top of a virtualization layer. Ann. Telecommun. **73**(5–6), 317–328 (2018)
9. Abolfazli, S., Sanaei, Z., Ahmed, E., Gani, A., Buyya, R.: Cloud-based augmentation for mobile devices: motivation, taxonomies, and open challenges. IEEE Commun. Surv. Tutor. **16**(1), 337–368 (2014)
10. Karim, R., et al.: VANET: superior system for content distribution in vehicular network applications. Technical report, Rutgers University, Department of Computer Science, pp. 364–370 (2008)
11. Hussain, S., Hamid, Z., Khattak, N.S.: Mobility management challenges and issues in 4G heterogeneous networks. In: International Conference on Integrated Internet Ad Hoc and Sensor Networks, p. 14. ACM (2006)
12. Wang, C., Li, Y., Jin, D., Chen, S.: On the serviceability of mobile vehicular cloudlets in a large-scale urban environment. IEEE Trans. Intell. Transp. Syst. **17**(10), 2960–2970 (2016)

13. Olariu, S., Khalil, I., Abuelela, M.: Taking VANET to the clouds. Int. J. Pervasive Comput. Commun. **7**(1), 7–21 (2011)
14. Lee, E., Lee, E.-K., Gerla, M., Oh, S.Y.: Vehicular cloud networking: architecture and design principles. IEEE Commun. Mag. **52**(2), 148–155 (2014)
15. Abolfazli, S., Sanaei, Z., Shiraz, M., Gani, A.: MOMCC: market-oriented architecture for mobile cloud computing based on service oriented architecture. In: IEEE International Conference on Communications in China (ICCC), Beijing, China, pp. 8–13, August 2012
16. Xu, K., Wang, K.-C., Amin, R., Martin, J., Izard, R.: A fast cloud-based network selection scheme using coalition formation games in vehicular networks. IEEE Trans. Veh. Technol. **64**(11), 5327–5339 (2015)
17. Firooz, M.H., Roy, S.: Collaborative downloading in VANET using network coding. In: IEEE International Conference on Communications (ICC), Ottawa, Canada, pp. 4584–4588, June 2012
18. Kumar, N., Rodrigues, J.J., Chilamkurti, N.: Bayesian coalition game as-a-service for content distribution in internet of vehicles. IEEE Internet Things J. **1**(6), 544–555 (2014)
19. Arkian, H., Atani, R., Diyanat, A., Pourkhalili, A.: A cluster-based vehicular cloud architecture with learning-based resource management. J. Supercomput. **71**(4), 1401–1426 (2015)
20. Gerla, M.: Vehicular cloud computing. In: 11th Annual Mediterranean Ad Hoc Networking Workshop (Med-Hoc-Net), pp. 152–155, Ayia Napa, Cyprus, June 2012
21. Yu, R., Zhang, Y., Gjessing, S., Xia, W., Yang, K.: Toward cloud-based vehicular networks with efficient resource management. IEEE Netw. **27**(5), 48–55 (2013)
22. Jerbi, M., Senouci, S., Rasheed, T., Ghamri-Doudane, Y.: Towards efficient geographic routing in urban vehicular networks. IEEE Trans. Veh. Technol. **58**(9), 5048–5059 (2009)
23. Chen, B.B., Chan, M.C.: MobTorrent: a framework for mobile internet access from vehicles. In: INFOCOM, pp. 1404–1412, Rio de Janeiro, Brazil, April 2009
24. Liu, J., Ge, Y., Bi, J., Guo, L.: Cooperative downloading strategy on highway scenario. In: International Conference on Computer and Information Technology (CIT), Chengdu, China, pp. 828–832, October 2012

Credit Based Incentive Approach for V2V Cooperation in Vehicular Cloud Computing

Lylia Alouache[1,2], Nga Nguyen[2(✉)], Makhlouf Aliouat[1], and Rachid Chelouah[2]

[1] Ferhat Abbas Setif1 University, Setif, Algeria
maliouat@univ-setif.dz
[2] Paris Seine University, EISTI, Cergy, France
{lae,nn,rc}@eisti.eu

Abstract. The Vehicular Cloud Computing (VCC) represents an important factor of smart cities through which Internet access can be offered to vehicular networks to store and download content via mobile gateways. The deployment of this service is focused on the exchange and the share of information between network entities. However, selfish nodes are an obstacle in a totally distributed network. As a solution, a compensation could be provided to the vehicles that are willing to participate in VCC or to become an Internet gateway, while preserving their anonymity. Different credit-based incentive schemes are discussed in this paper. A scenario based on the Blockchain technology which implements a virtual payment service for the VCC members, for the resource consumption and for the gateway service in V2V routing mode, is proposed.

Keywords: IoV · Vehicular Cloud Computing · Communication
V2V · Routing · Mobile gateways · Incentive scheme
Cryptocurrency · Blockchain

1 Introduction

Today, vehicles as well as all connected objects within the smart cities evolve from a passive consumer of simple data to active and intelligent agents which enable collaborations with content creating and sharing. The vehicular cloud can be the basis that makes this evolution possible. In fact, the large amount of underused storage space and computing power coupled with embedded sensors provide a unique opportunity to use vehicles as a mobile cloud with high-speed connectivity such as 4G and Long Term Evolution (LTE). Vehicular Cloud Computing (VCC) [15] is presented to effectively exploit vehicular network resources and thus provide users secure and robust information services as well as richer experiences.

The VCC is opportunistic. It gathers the vehicles by geographical proximity, by specific criteria, or coincidentally. Although the VCC solves a lot of problems

© Springer Nature Switzerland AG 2018
A. M. J. Skulimowski et al. (Eds.): IOV 2018, LNCS 11253, pp. 92–105, 2018.
https://doi.org/10.1007/978-3-030-05081-8_7

locally by improving some Quality of Service (QoS) metrics like resources consumption, overhead delay and latency, it is still dependent on the classic Internet cloud, where the durable and the global useful information is deported to. In the literature, there are some works about extending the Internet to VCC. To do this, the VCC members have two means: fixed gateways and mobile gateways [16,18]. In the approaches with fixed gateways, fixed Road Side Units (RSUs) installed along the roads are used as an Internet access point. Each vehicle can communicate directly with the RSU or via multi-hop communications while in the approach with the use of mobile gateways, private vehicles are equipped with several interfaces and serve as gateways to other vehicles in the network. We note that in both mobile and fixed gateways, multi-hop scenario is used, hence the importance of V2V communication. The gateway discovery method can be proactive or reactive depending on whether it is initiated by the gateway or by the client vehicle. The two methods can be launched in both fixed and mobile gateways approaches.

In this paper, we focus on the different approaches in the literature to offer Internet on board vehicles, using Vehicle-to-Vehicle (V2V) communication mode and mobile gateways. Some existing approaches of incentive schemes for V2V collaboration are highlighted. We also propose a scenario of credit-based incentive scheme for VCC formation and V2V collaboration based on the Blockchain of cryptocurrency. The Blockchain represents a distributed register, hosted on a peer-to-peer network of participating nodes where the cooperation is authorized and moderated by a consensus protocol which defines the rules of the network. The unique cryptographic fingerprint used by each block and the consensus protocol provide a very high level of security. The fingerprint (hash) takes a lot of computing time and resource to generate it initially. The miner who adds one block to the Blockchain performs the computational work to earn a bitcoin reward (the proof-of-work protocol). Altering the block would require generating a new hash. Since hashes also serve as links in the blockchain (each block contains the unique hash of the previous block), if an at-tacker wants to modify the contents of the block retroactively, he must first compute a new hash not only for the current block, but also calculate it for each block below. Second, there is the time con-straint. The attacker must modify the contents of a block and recalculate the hash of the chain quickly in order to avoid another node adding a new block to the blockchain, which would distort the new calculated hash. This attack is only possible if the attacker owns a computer more powerful than the rest of the com-bined nodes (and even in this case, the success is not guaranteed). In the opposite case, any added block, the blockchain's signature thus modified will be in conflict with the blockchain signatures avail-able on the other existing nodes in the network and they will automatically reject its modifications.

The rest of paper is organized as follows. Section 2 describes several important routing and gateways selection protocols for Internet access in vehicular networks. Some existing credit-based incentive mechanism are also enumerated in this section. We propose in Sect. 3 a case study of virtual payment for collaborative formation of VCC as well as gateways selection, based on the Blockchain and cryptocurrency that will be implemented in our HSDN-GRA routing protocol [2]. Finally, Sect. 4 summarizes the article with some perspectives concerning the improvement of our work.

2   Related Work

2.1   Gateways to Internet Access

In this section, we present some contributions of how to access to Internet services from vehicles using fixed of mobile gateways. As example of fixed gateways approach, Bechler et al. [6] propose the DiscoveRy of Internet gateways from VEhicles (DRIVE) protocol, which combines a discovering available gateways mechanism with a best gateway selecting procedure according to some fixed parameters. The fixed RSU along the roads broadcast periodically messages to signal their presence. The vehicles which are in their transmission area receive these messages then store the contained information in a local database. Given the periodicity of the messages and the local database, a vehicle can at any time know if there is a gateway within its transmission area or not by consulting the database. If multiple gateways are available in the database, the best one is chosen according to the traffic density, the Euclidean distance between the vehicle and the gateway, the number of vehicles connected to the gateway and the bandwidth. DRIVE reduces the gateway discovery time because the gateways discovery mechanism is limited to consulting the local database. However, the solution is proactive, the routes are established even if the vehicles do not have packets to transmit. Besides, the position and the speed of vehicles are not considered when the gateway is chosen. This may result in a short connection time which will cause a frequent link failure.

The protocols based on static gateways can provide connectivity only in areas where they are deployed. As the distribution and requirement of static gateways represents big drawbacks of this approach, we are more interested in the mobile gateways. Mobile gateways reflect of the Internet of Vehicles (IoV) problem, in which an ubiquitous and performing connectivity must be guaranteed even in the absence of any fixed infrastructure.

Namboodiri et al. [16] propose Prediction Based Routing Protocol for Vehicular Ad Hoc Networks (PBR) as a multi-hop routing protocol developed specifically for mobile gateways. In PBR, the route discovery phase is reactive and is initiated by a Route Request (RREQ) packet broadcasting. When multiple gateways respond, the source vehicle selects the closest gateway in terms of distance, and if there is equality the nearest gateway in terms of hops is chosen or vice versa. However, PBR differs from conventional reactive protocols as the routes are repaired proactively. The route life is estimated thanks to the geo-location information, then a new route is created before the current one became obsolete. The advantage of PBR is that the roads are repaired even before they become obsolete avoiding the repair time of these roads. Consequently it reduces the delay of packets transmission. This protocol also considers the mobility of vehicles in the gateway selection. However, this proactive technique of road repair and the RREQ broadcasting for the gateways discovery step results in a large number of control packets, which leads to high bandwidth usage just for the control packets. As a result, the global performance of the network can be degraded.

Taleb et al. [20] propose a Clustering-based Multi-metric adaptive mobile Gateway Management mechanism (CMGM) where vehicles access to the Internet via the base stations which are the RSUs, either directly or by multi-hop scenario. A zone named 3G active region is delimited around each RSU. CMGM combines a dynamic clustering technique for vehicles according to their direction criterion incoming or outgoing from the 3G zone, with an adaptive management of mobile gateways. Two groups are then formed. The first one contains the vehicles going to the 3G active region and the second one groups the vehicles leaving the 3G active region. Then, a subgroup is formed by the mobile gateways that are in the perception area and whose signal to the RSU is greater than a defined threshold. This subgroup represents the potential gateways of a cluster. In each cluster, the closest vehicle to the group center is designated as a cluster head who manages communications and controls signaling messages between candidate gateways. The gateways discovery procedure can be done proactively with a periodic warning from the gateways or re-actively by solicitation messages from source vehicles. A gateway is chosen from all the candidates when the strength of its relative signal strength to the RSU as well as the stability of its link with respect to the source vehicle are higher than the thresholds fixed in each cluster. Only the gateway with the optimum values will be selected from all the gateways satisfying the signal and stability conditions. By limiting the number of vehicles communicating directly with the RSUs, CMGM allows avoiding their saturation. In addition, organizing vehicles in clusters helps to a better management of V2V communications as well as reducing the redundancy of control messages. However, the cluster head election process independently of the speed is inadequate to the vehicular networks. In addition, CMGM does not implement a load control mechanism that can be very useful to avoid the gateway overloading.

A simplified gateway selection (SGS) scheme for the multi-hop relay in a VANET-UMTS, where UMTS is Universal Mobile Telecommunication System, integration network is proposed by Alawi et al. [1]. The proposed solution allows vehicles to continue to be connected even in not well-covered zones by soliciting the vehicles located inside the UMTS coverage zone to assist other vehicles that move outside the UMTS coverage zone in order to communicate to the UMTS infrastructure network. All vehicles in the UMTS coverage zone use its 3G universal terrestrial radio access network interface to connect to UMTS. When a vehicle is moving between two cells areas or entering a dead spot zone the Received Signal Strength (RSS) degrades below the predefined threshold. So, when any vehicle wants to connect to the UMTS network, it broadcasts the relay request (RReq). At the reception of RReq, all the intermediate vehicles compute their RSS from UMTS and compare it to the RReq packet. The vehicle with the greater RSS represents one of the gateways and transmits the relay respond

(RRep) packet to the source vehicle. This last one chooses as gateway the RRep best one with respect to three metrics namely received signal strength, route lifetime, and available route capacity. When the current gateway degrades these metrics, the same approach is relaunched to select another one and continues to help the source vehicles to forward their data. The SGS can increase the network coverage area by the integration of vehicles to the UMTS network. Nevertheless, it will suffer from high delays if the zone area of the VANET network is large [5].

Ansari et al. proposed in [4] a system where the public buses, taxis, and lorries called High Tier Nodes (HTN) equipped with Dedicated Short Range Communications (DSRC) and LTE interfaces act as gateways. The selection of an HTN is launched by the rest of private vehicles called Low Tier Nodes (LTNs) periodically as it is activated by the reception of periodic beacons from the HTN. Each HTN has records of the LTNs currently attached to them, which are constantly reported and updated with the traffic control center via the LTE network. At the reception of beacons from HTN, LTN places this later in the candidate registration set, then calculates the connection delivery delay for every HTN in this candidate registration set. Based on beacons information, the HTNs with the negative values of the calculated delays are dropped, while the one with the highest delay is selected as gateway. Once LTN has registered with the HTN, it stays connected with it until the distance between LTN and HTN remains below the predefined transmission range. Having authority owned gateways makes the network more secure, so it has been a promising candidate for vehicular networks. However with the current growth in cellular users, vehicular networks would require much more capacity with respect to cellular network.

Another protocol that supports trust in the gateways selection process is proposed by Baraa et al. in [5] called routing protocol for Robust and Trust Mobile Gateway Selection (RTMGwS). It is based on vehicle movements and variant routing parameters namely: Route Lifetime, Available Load Capacity, Number of Hops and Trust parameter, in order to select an optimal mobile gateway with highly robust and trust connection to the infrastructure network. This selection of gateways is done in a locally reactive manner and global proactive way. The selection of relay is based on the routing parameters in the relay selection step, then the route establishment process is launched. RTMGwS also stores multiple paths in mobile vehicles tables received by relays for mobile gateway selection, which improves its performances. They also propose in [5] an improvement of CMGM mechanism and SGS by adding a trust parameter for selecting their mobile gateway.

Finally, Alouache et al. [2] a multi-criteria routing protocol based on a hybrid SDN architecture is proposed for selecting step by step the mobile gateway until Internet access is reached. The Hybrid SDN-based and Geographic Routing Protocol (HSDN-GRA) tries to increase the communication reliability and availability while minimizing link breaks, reducing resolution costs and keeping a good end-to-end delay. The controllers that make decisions about where data is sent combine three different criteria for HSDN-GRA. The contact duration and the free load metric are embedded on each vehicle while communication error logs are handled by an elected node within clusters. Knowledge of inter-vehicle contact time is an important and useful parameter as it permits a proactive avoidance and anticipation of premature link failures. Secondly, a load balancing parameter called free load is added in order not to saturate the intermediate nodes. Finally, a dedicated log of error communications is hosted on a cluster head containing all error occurrences of the cluster members. Before choosing a relay, the error log is solicited to verify if the vehicle does not have a high frequency of communication problems. This avoids premature communication disruptions, packet loss, and security issues, and reduces the resolution costs and the redundancy of some system messages.

The related work presented shows that offering Internet access for vehicular networks as well as the VCC is totally based on a collaborative system and V2V communications, but V2V is only useful if many vehicles around are equipped and collaborative [11]. For this reason, we are looking for an incentive approach which proposes a profit in return for the vehicles accepting to rent their resources and which act as vehicular cloud resource providers.

2.2 Incentive Mechanism Approach for Selfish Nodes

The need of comfort and Intelligent Transportation Systems (ITS) can be satisfied by the formation of an opportunistic mobile cloud as well as the sharing and the transfer of data by cooperation V2V. However, in a public environment with a total absence of a third party, it is very difficult to guarantee the cooperation of all vehicles and suppose the total absence of selfish vehicles which do not wish to share their resources and satisfy the users and the target institutions requests, especially without any reward in return to their participation. There are existing works about the incentive schemes which seem to be an attractive approach where any participant is satisfied. Figure 1 shows a non exhaustive list of credit-based incentive mechanisms inspired from [10].

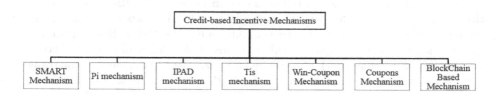

Fig. 1. Non-exhaustive list of credit-based incentive mechanisms

Referring to incentive approaches in vehicular networks, it is possible to propose a credit-based payment system using only virtual money [22]. There are also reputation-based and trust-based incentive processes for nodes, such that network nodes can evaluate neighbor node activity and collectively revoke uncooperative nodes [13]. Existing incentive systems rely entirely on a central trusted third party. However, in vehicular networks where the V2V communication mode is the most widespread, it is interesting to propose a credit-based incentive system in the total absence of a third party, in an exclusively cooperative way.

In [9], Jun et al. propose to address the problem of selfish nodes behavior while guaranteeing security requirements and preserving the location and identity privacy. To do so, the proposed privacy-preserving distance-based incentive scheme uses a secure multiparty computation and homomorphic encryption. Furthermore, this incentive scheme can suppress nodes with harmful behaviors fairly and reasonably while stimulating the active helpers. For the payment scheme, a cost and a distance are associated with the transmission of a packet at each hop. When a relay successfully transmits a message, it obtains a ticket which is passed to a local trusted authority for verification. The destination also forwards the total cost of the message to the same local authority. This local authority compares the two estimated costs to be able to verify the good reception of the message and thus pays each relay participant according to the fixed unit price. This approach is based on a third party, which is not always achievable in vehicular network environment.

In order to inhibit nodes from being selfish, Xu et al. [21] propose an incentive scheme for delivering packets in Mobile Social Network. Nodes obtain and use virtual currency for relaying packets from node to another, while the nodes which refuse collaboration will not get paid. Therefore, they will lose a chance to earn currency to afford the relay service from other nodes in the future. According to the defined status related to limited resources, a sender chooses the relay. Specifically, if the status of the sender is loose, it will select one of its neighbors to be a relay with a low agreement price. In contrast, if the status of the sender is tense, it will select any node it encounters even a non-friend-node with a high agreement price. Finally, they employ negotiation game to model the transaction pricing between the sender and the relay node.

Park et al. [19] propose an architecture for store-carry-forward communication service with a Bitcoin-based incentive scheme for the service. Bitcoin is the first cryptocurrency representing a decentralized electronic cash system, based on peer-to-peer network and distributed consensus protocol without any trusted third party. Each user has one or multiple private and public key pairs, and unique address associated with user's account namely called wallet and the private key for transactions signature about coins. The validity of the transactions is verified by Bitcoin network nodes called miners. After a time period, the transactions are collected by the miners into a single unit as a block. The new block accepted by the majority of miners according to a consensus protocol is then be added to the Bitcoin public ledger called Blockchain. In this proposition, they try to transfer messages from RSU acting as a local server to another RSU. Transactions are launched between the vehicle and the concerned RSUs. The actor entities have their Bitcoin accounts to give and receive Bitcoins. When an RSU solicits a vehicle to transfer packets to another one, it entrusts the packets together with a Bitcoin transaction to give coins to the vehicle. The source RSU's Bitcoin transaction is locked under the condition that the coins can be spent to the vehicle which forwards the packets to the destination RSU. The Bitcoin transaction for the relay is registered to the Bitcoin network by the destination RSU only if this vehicle faithfully transfers the packets. In this system, vehicles identity is preserved as well as the authenticity of the transactions without any third party.

In [12], Li et al. propose the CreditCoin network representing a privacy-preserving incentive announcement network based on Blockchain via an efficient anonymous vehicular announcement aggregation protocol. The proposed CreditCoin network is performed in a non-fully trusted environment as it allows users to generate and to send announcements anonymously while motivates them to share traffic information in incentives. In addition, transactions and account information in CreditCoin are tamper-resistant. Besides, malicious users identities in anonymous announcements with related transactions are identified by the CreditCoin Trace Manager.

3   Blockchain Based Credit Payment Scenario in VCC

In smart cities area and distributed vehicular networks, some intelligent transportation services can be achievable in a reliable manner, as well as a vehicular cloud computing can be formed without any third party in a fully distributed way, using only V2V communication mode. But it is still difficult to use the V2V communication mode without revealing users identities. Besides, vehicles usually lack the motivation to be gateways or relays for other vehicles. This communication mode also suffers from the intermittent connectivity and the instability of the network, especially in isolated areas without fixed access points as well as in dense areas with a lot of obstacles (buildings, ...).

In this paper, we propose a combination of the Blockchain paradigm with the routing protocol proposed in our previous work [2], in order to form and exploit the VCC as well as find mobile gateways to Internet access.

3.1   Blockchain

Blockchain is a combination of different innovations such as public key cryptography, distributed consensus, and peer-to-peer (P2P) networking. The chain of blocks forms a ledger of every successfully performed transaction between nodes. This ledger is shared between all nodes participating in the network, which do not fully trust each other. The transactions contained in each block represent an ordered list of events. Each block references the cryptographic hash of the previous block. Consequently a chain of blocks is formed. The first block, called the genesis block does not reference any block. The transactions are mutually agreed upon by the nodes in the network as a distributed consensus algorithm ensures the nodes agreement on the block's content through a process called Mining [17].

Thanks to the Blockchain mechanism, data sharing, ride sharing, payment (toll, energy, insurance, etc.), communication, transactions, security, and smart transport system are achievable in totally distributed vehicular networks. One of the application of Blockchain is the Bitcoin [14] invented in 2008. It is a cryptographic currency representing an e-money on a P2P or decentralized network where each client, called a node, is also a server. In order to secure this currency, the transaction system is based on the concept of Blockchain, based in part on cryptography processes.

The goal of this work is to propose a scenario for creating VCC as well as publishing, discovering, and exchanging data and services against cryptocurrencies such as Bitcoin where only permitted the vehicles that can participate in the network activities including forming vehicular cloud, connecting, mining, and sending or receiving transactions.

3.2   Incentive Scheme for Gateway Selection Based on HSDN-GRA Routing Protocol

Even if a good routing protocol is designed, it is still depending on whether the vehicles will follow the protocol or not. This problem of QoS in V2V communication is splitted into two observed cases. First of all, a private vehicle belonging to an individual person can be selfish and thus refuses to transmit the messages of others for nothing, because carrying messages will overload its own resources. Secondly, for the specific vehicles like taxis and buses, the situation is worse, because they will rapidly be overloaded and their resources are consumed by the relaying services for others, even though they are willing to forward messages initially [7]. As a result, they try to save their own resource and ignore the routing protocol instructions.

To solve this problem of QoS in V2V communication, we propose to combine an incentive scheme with a routing protocol. It is highly important to give vehicles incentives and stimulating them to cooperate in forwarding messages while considering the contact duration, the free load as well as the log of communication errors inspired by the routing algorithm described in [2]. The vehicles which are moving in the same direction, having a relative speed that tends to 0, and presenting an error frequency less than the fixed threshold are grouped to form a VCC which collects data dedicated to ITS services, so each vehicle needs to access to the Internet, and communicate with the conventional cloud. To do so, a vehicle is chosen as a mobile gateway according to the HSDN-GRA algorithm [2] for link stability and load balancing. Besides, the problem of selfish vehicles is resolved by rewards. Each vehicle entering in the network has it own account for virtual coins. A Blockchain ledger, representing a distributed data structure as blocks which are linked together and forming a chain, where all the transactions as well as their related information are saved. The account of a vehicle is credited with virtual coins, when it performs a successful operation between the VCC member and the conventional cloud, or when it acts as a gateway for Internet access.

The Bitcoin Blockchain can be used to reward cooperative vehicles while revoking selfish ones. In our system, each vehicle represents a node of the Bitcoin network, and has a Bitcoin account and wallet for storing, sending and receiving

Bitcoins, as well as tracking transactions. The transactions represent the transfer of crypto currency between the vehicles for the data relay service, but also for the formation of a vehicular cloud dedicated to IoV services and which collaborates with a traditional cloud.

A Bitcoin wallet allows to generate and store the public key/private key pair. These keys will help to carry out transactions and to ensure their integrity. The public key represents the Bitcoin address of a vehicle that can receive Bitcoins, while the private key allows it to make a signature because spending Bitcoins means signing an outbound transaction with the private key. Transactions are done through asymmetric cryptography. These transactions are recorded in a block, then broadcasted to the one hop neighbors that will take care of the mining operation to validate the transaction. Once validated, it will be added to the longest chain of transaction blocks and the transfer of crypto currency will be definitively realized without possibility of reversing or alteration. We choose to limit the validation of transactions to one-hop neighbors because it is difficult to keep a global view of a non-hierarchical network. In our protocol, a relay node is chosen among the visible neighborhood in a totally distributed network in order to guarantee the robustness, since network segmentation and intermittent connection are rather frequent.

We opt for light (simple) nodes, i.e. when transactions are made and confirmed for several generations of successive blocks, they can be removed from the nodes for memory space constraints. The light nodes will have a block header string, they store only the last blocks validated in complete, with a fingerprint or a hash of the transactions and the oldest blocks. This footprint is calculated using the Merkle trees, which makes it possible to verify the authenticity of the Blockchain without having all the data distributed on each of the nodes of the network. Light nodes will not be able to verify transactions, but given the fact that the others have accepted them previously, it is considered that the block is valid. The number of cryptocurrency to pay against a service is calculated according to the quantity n of data, the utility U of the data [8] and a fixed unit price PU. The utility of data is calculated from its size S and after a period of time T, the value of data utility is computed by Formula 1. The variable λ represents the commission rate [8].

$$U = S \times e^{-\lambda T} \tag{1}$$

The price of a given service is estimated by Formula 2.

$$Price = \sum_{i=1}^{n} U_i \times PU \tag{2}$$

To sum up, this proposition transforms the routing protocol into a credit network model between relays in the vehicular network through a directed and weighted graph, where the value of each edge shows the amount of credit that a vehicle is willing to extend to another in exchange for a data transfer service [3].

There is a large amount of applications and services using V2V communication such as local signaling obstacles, emergency services, accident or weather

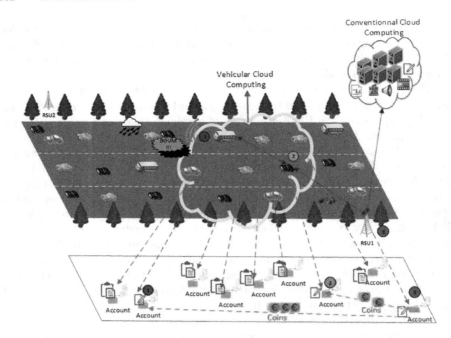

Fig. 2. An incentive scheme scenario in Vehicular Cloud Computing

problems share information, video transfer, etc. This is especially useful when the information has a position and a delay constraints. Figure 2 describes a scenario to cooperatively form a VCC, and relaying information from a vehicle to conventional cloud against virtual money. The vehicles inside the white cloud form a cooperative VCC. Conventionally, every one of them has already installed the application of e-payment and created an account. These vehicles form a weighted graph. The weight of each exploited edge is calculated by using Formulas 1 and 2. In Fig. 2, a Bus (the vehicle with the red circle number (1) detects a collision, so the information needs to be sent to the remote cloud computing via V2V communication mode. A Car (the vehicle with the blue circle number (2) is selected as a best relay according to three criteria: the contact duration, the load balancing and the communication errors frequency [2]. In this use case, the Car is able to access to Internet via the RSU (the infrastructure with the orange circle number (3). The purple arrows represent the transactions generated for this service as well as the payment of the relays. The transaction between the Bus and the Car is created and signed by the Bus, then the Bus will publish the transaction within neighboring in order to be validated. The transaction will contain the public key of the Bus, the public key of the Car, the amount of the transaction according to the utility of the data as well as a reference to the previous transactions of the Bus. When the neighboring validates this transaction, it will be added to the Blockchain of our e-payment network, and the cryptocurrencies will be transferred to the account of the Car. This account is not registered anywhere, however, it can be estimated from the Blockchain ledger. To ensure that the Bus does not commit double spending, i.e. to send the same amount to two different vehicles without having this sum on his account, we assume that the distributed system is synchronous and we opt for the dating of the transactions. The goal of this proposition is to improve our previous work on the HSDN-GRA routing protocol by inciting and rewarding selfish vehicles on which the routing protocol is based.

4 Conclusion

In this paper, the vehicular cloud computing has been described, as well as the different strategies guaranteeing Internet access in vehicular networks. The problem of selfish vehicles has been studied, especially in the totally distributed V2V communication mode. The communication QoS is deteriorated even if a good routing protocol is designed, because, on the one hand, it is still a crucial question whether nodes will follow the protocol or not, and in the other hand, the incentive mechanisms have as principal challenge the disconnections and link failures between vehicles.

We propose in this paper a scenario of execution, where an incentive scheme based on virtual coins payment using the Blockchain is combined to a mobile gateway selection algorithm using as input three criteria namely: contact duration, free load and communication error log. As a result, this approach could ensure the load balancing, the stability of links in the gateway selection while proposing rewards to selfish gateways, in a completely anonymous manner.

The choice of the Blockchain technology will ensure the integrity of the rewards, the anonymity, the security of the transactions and the immunization against group cheating group. One limit of our approach could be the creation of a common framework that needs to be followed by all the vehicles. However, our financial incentives could be implemented in parallel with the routing protocol, if the car manufacturers let the drivers the choice of being a relay node in the V2V communication or not.

In this paper, the feasibility of a new incentive paradigm to IoV geographical protocols has been explored, and up to our knowledge, there is no other research work that proposes the same scheme in order to make a direct comparison. As future work, this incentive scheme will be integrated in the HSDN-GRA framework implementation [2] and tested under realistic scenarios. Comparisons with incentive schemes of selfish vehicles will be presented.

References

1. Alawi, M., Saeed, R., Hassan, A., Alsaqour, R.: Simplified gateway selection scheme for multihop relay in vehicular Ad hoc network. Int. J. Commun. Syst. **27**(12), 3855–3873 (2013)
2. Alouache, L., Nguyen, N., Aliouat, M., Chelouah, R.: Toward a hybrid SDN architecture for V2V communication in IoV environment. In: Fifth International Conference on Software Defined Systems (SDS), Barcelona, Spain, pp. 93–99, April 2018
3. Aniket, K.: Introduction to credit networks: security, privacy, and applications. In: ACM SIGSAC Conference on Computer and Communications Security, New York, USA, pp. 1859–1860 (2016)
4. Ansari, S., Boutaleb, T., Sinanovic, S., Gamio, C., Krikidis, I.: Vehicular multitier gateway selection algorithm for heterogeneous VANET architectures. In: Advances in Wireless and Optical Communications (RTUWO), pp. 180–185. IEEE, November 2017
5. Baraa, T., Alsaqour, R., Alawi, M., Abdelhaq, M., Sundararajan, E.: Robust and trust dynamic mobile gateway selection in heterogeneous VANET-UMTS network. Veh. Commun. **12**, 75–87 (2018)
6. Bechler, M., Wolf, L., Storz, O., Franz, W.J.: Efficient discovery of Internet gateways in future vehicular communication systems. In: The 57th IEEE Semiannual Vehicular Technology Conference, Jeju, South Korea, vol. 2, pp. 965–969. IEEE, April 2003
7. Chen, T., Wu, L., Wu, F., Zhong, S.: Stimulating cooperation in vehicular ad hoc networks: a coalitional game theoretic approach. IEEE Trans. Veh. Technol. **60**(2), 566–579 (2011)
8. Chou, C.M., Lan, K.C., Yang, C.F.: Using virtual credits to provide incentives for vehicle communication. In: 12th International Conference on ITS Telecommunications, pp. 579–583, November 2012
9. Jun, S., ChunJiao, H., Fan, Y., HuanGuo, Z.: A privacy-preserving distance-based incentive scheme in opportunistic VANETs. Secur. Commun. Netw. **9**(15), 2789–2801 (2015)
10. Kadam, R., Bangare, M.: A survey on credit-based incentive schemes in delay tolerant network. Int. J. Sci. Res. **5**(6), 782–786 (2016)
11. Kuchinskas, S.: Telematics and new V2V/V2X business models, January 2012. http://analysis.tu-auto.com/safety-adas-autonomous/telematics-and-new-v2vv2x-business-models
12. Li, L., et al.: Creditcoin: a privacy-preserving blockchain-based incentive announcement network for communications of smart vehicles. IEEE Trans. Intell. Transp. Syst. **19**(7), 2204–2220 (2018)
13. Li, Q., Malip, A., Martin, K.M., Ng, S.L., Zhang, J.: A reputation-based announcement scheme for VANETs. IEEE Trans. Veh. Technol. **61**(9), 4095–4108 (2012)
14. Martins, S., Yang, Y.: Introduction to bitcoins: a pseudo-anonymous electronic currency system. In: Conference of the Center for Advanced Studies on Collaborative Research, Riverton, NJ, USA, pp. 349–350 (2011)
15. Mekki, T., Jabri, I., Rachedi, A., Ben Jemaa, M.: Vehicular cloud networks: challenges, architectures, and future directions. Veh. Commun. **9**, 268–280 (2017)
16. Namboodiri, V., Gao, L.: Prediction-based routing for vehicular ad hoc networks. IEEE Trans. Veh. Technol. **56**(4), 2332–2345 (2007)

17. Odiete, O., Lomotey, R.K., Deters, R.: Using blockchain to support data and service management in IoV/IoT. In: Peng, S.-L., Wang, S.-J., Balas, V.E., Zhao, M. (eds.) SICBS 2017. AISC, vol. 733, pp. 344–362. Springer, Cham (2018). https://doi.org/10.1007/978-3-319-76451-1_33
18. Pan, H.Y., Jan, R.H., An-Kai, A., Jeng, C., Chen, C., Tseng, H.R.: Mobile-gateway routing for vehicular networks. In: Eighth IEEE VTS Asia Pacific Conference on Wearable Computing Systems (APWCS 2011), pp. 1–5. IEEE Computer Society, July 2011
19. Park, Y., Sur, C., Kim, H., Rhee, K.H.: A reliable incentive scheme using bitcoin on cooperative vehicular Ad-Hoc networks. IT CoNvergence PRActice (INPRA) 5(4), 34–41 (2017)
20. Taleb, T., Benslimane, A.: Design guidelines for a network architecture integrating VANET with 3G beyond networks. In: 2010 IEEE Global Telecommunications Conference GLOBECOM 2010, pp. 1–5. IEEE, Miami, December 2010
21. Xu, Q., Su, Z., Guo, S.: A game theoretical incentive scheme for relay selection services in mobile social networks. IEEE Trans. Veh. Technol. 65(8), 6692–6702 (2016)
22. Zhu, H., Lin, X., Lu, R., Fan, Y., Shen, X.: Smart: a secure multilayer credit-based incentive scheme for delay-tolerant networks. IEEE Trans. Veh. Technol. 58(8), 4628–4639 (2009)

Vehicular Grouping and Network Formation: Virtualization of Network Self-healing

Duaa Zuhair Al-Hamid[✉] and Adnan Al-Anbuky

Electrical and Electronic Engineering, Auckland University of Technology,
Auckland, New Zealand
{duaa.alhamid,adnan.anbuky}@aut.ac.nz

Abstract. The enhancement of vehicular network management and connectivity can significantly improve road safety and pave the way towards unmanned vehicular operation. Variable speeds and densities associated with constant movement of vehicles, changeable routes adopted by vehicles under diverse traffic conditions, would inevitably result in different dynamic vehicular network cluster formation/re-organization possibilities. Such dynamic re-organization for vehicular networks necessitates aspects of self-formation, self-joining and self-healing. Member nodes located in close vicinity to each other may formulate a group within the network. New members may join a group in case they arrive within close proximity of the group while existing members may depart in the event of change of route or if the group become distance away. The departure of a vehicle (an active network node) may create rupture in the data communication network operation. The paper presents the organization of vehicular network considering the dynamic self-healing in the event of departure of a key network-connectivity component. The Contiki-Cooja simulation tool is used for implementation wherein various network scenarios are created to test and analyze the process. The results indicate the efficiency of election process at minimal network downtime. It also reflects how the network down time can be minimized or even totally removed using appropriate vehicular sensed parameters. The study also offers preliminary analysis to the impact of connectivity dynamics on the network re-organization process.

Keywords: Vehicular network · Vehicular grouping · Self-healing

1   Introduction

Vehicular Network (VN) domain covers numerous applications such as traffic management in the direction of emergency, traffic alert messages and route planning. In addition, it enhances the driving system by creating a self-organized and protected solution.

The need for VN encourages manageable, scalable and intelligent operation. This can establish communication with the internal and external environments via the wireless connection. For example communication like vehicle to on-board sensors (V2S), vehicle to vehicle (V2V), vehicle to infrastructure (V2I) to meet the requirements of efficient data communication and acceptable quality of service (QoS) [1, 2]. The various types of data relevant to driving style like real-time traffic information, or

© Springer Nature Switzerland AG 2018
A. M. J. Skulimowski et al. (Eds.): IOV 2018, LNCS 11253, pp. 106–121, 2018.
https://doi.org/10.1007/978-3-030-05081-8_8

information related to the location and condition of vehicles in an emergency can be exchanged through vehicular communication.

Owing to the mobility of vehicles, the highly dynamic topology of VN requires a physically adjacent group management for the moving vehicles in the road. This would provide efficient and stable routes for data dissemination. Hence, the vehicular grouping or clustering could be one of the proposed solutions that plays imperative role in facilitating the connectivity of network of vehicles that are within each other's line of sight and are reachable through single or multiple hops connectivity. Vehicular grouping approach tends to involve frequent events of constituent vehicular nodes leaving or joining any group.

That approach could be correlated with the data traffic considering a highway scenario as it is a continuous flow of vehicles. The long stretch of a highway with vehicles moving for around 100 km/h could reflect the combination of vehicles that can formulate a group. Looking at the distance between two cars within the same lane (as governed by the 2-second rules), the number of hops and connectivity radio signal strength RSSI for a given group can define the stretch of the group along the road. This stretch may reflect the ideal modeling density or vehicular capacity of a vehicular group. It may also offer indication on the maximum number of groups presented at a given sector of the highway. An example of the above traffic scenario is shown by Fig. 1. The shaded areas reflect potential for groups to formulate on that direction of the motorway.

Fig. 1. Traffic grouping scenario on a typical highway [3]

Considering the sudden departure of a vehicular node (that has acted as a router node) from its group would most likely result in abrupt disruption of the sensed data flow and communication within the group. Certain dependent nodes on the departing nodes get disconnected from the group and thus be rendered unmonitored. Such events are highly transitory in nature necessitating adaptive, real-time and autonomous self-organizational mechanism. Enhancing such aspects of vehicular network related to the configuration process, virtualization offers a testing ground for running and analyzing soft-trials of dynamic network scenarios.

The objective of this paper is to look at the organization of vehicular network with emphasis on self-healing in the event of departure of a vehicle acting as a router node causing partial disruption to the network. For this purpose, an operational dialogue and fitness model for election process have been implemented using the Contiki-Cooja simulation tool wherein the best-fit replacement vehicular node gets elected and positioned to replace the departing node with minimal or no disruption to the network.

2 Literature Review

The main issues in formulating a scalable, more robust and delay tolerant network are the high mobility and the frequent changes of vehicular network topology. Hence, clustering technique is proposed to be used as an approach to explore these issues. In spite of the comprehensive research on dealing with group of vehicles based on clustering [4–9], the challenges of managing the network connectivity and flow of data in highly dynamic processes have not been fully investigated.

Clustering algorithms could be based on vehicles moving in the same direction that can be clustered in one group [10]. Rawashdeh et al. [8] have proposed a clustering algorithm for vehicular network on highways where the speed difference among neighboring vehicles travelling in the same direction is the main parameter to achieve a stable clustering structure. The authors have clustered the vehicles with high speed in one group and the vehicles with slow speed in another group. However, any vehicle could be left out of any cluster when its speed deviates too much from the speed of other vehicles in the cluster. Hence, multiple clusters could affect the network stability. Wu et al. [11] have proposed a group routing protocol based on temporary mobile social relationship between vehicles. The approach is based on the similar movement behavior of the nodes at an intersection to be considered as one group. However, the social interaction among the vehicles may not necessarily achieve the optimal data route. Also, there is no indication about the size of the vehicular group.

In the context of achieving the stability, Maslekar et al. [12] have proposed a stable clustering algorithm for one hop communication where they have assumed that each vehicle knows its own location, destination and the route in advance using GPS and digital maps. The formation of the cluster is initiated before the road intersections and is based on the travel path of the vehicle. However, the algorithm has been tested for one hop only.

Some researchers have pointed out the importance of the involved parameters in the cluster head election approach. According to Hadded et al. [9], the moving vehicles in one direction could not be moving on the same end-to-end route, which could lead to the departure for some vehicles after a short period of notification time. Thus, the authors have emphasized the importance of the road ID (RID) where only neighboring vehicles that move on the same road and in the same direction are considered to provide a stable cluster. In their approach, the method of electing a cluster head based on mobility features and a weight function is the key for achieving more stable cluster. Each vehicle (v) calculates its current weight W (v, t) using the following equation:

$$W (v, t) = w1 * \delta (v, t) + w2 * |v (v, t) - \rho (v, t)| - w3 * n (v, t) \qquad (1)$$

The weight equation model involves the parameters of average distance, average speed, and number of neighboring vehicles. The vehicle that meets the requirements of the proposed model is elected as a cluster head. Then, all vehicles that are within transmission range of the cluster head become members and are not allowed to participate in another cluster head election procedure. Although the method has been presented by the weight function, it was fully depending on the map and road ID which may not be the ideal/ achievable approach for formulating the cluster.

Touil et al. [7] have proposed an algorithm based on four metrics: unique ID, connectivity, distance and mobility of mobile ad hoc network to find the best one that suits the vehicular network for formulating the cluster. However, the authors have not considered multi-hop neighboring nodes in formulating the cluster and have not considered the road side unit (RSU) for supporting the cluster head in the support for involved computation or involved communication through the Internet.

To enhance the network connectivity, the delivery of warning or emergency messages in case of accidents or assistance in improving the network performance [13], RSU is utilized as a gateway to the cloud through the Internet. This node is considered as one of the crucial elements of vehicular communication network owing to its deployment over the road infrastructure wherein the related data (speed, position, vehicle counting, etc.) can be collected and transmitted to the required destination [14]. The bidirectional flow of information which is either from RSU to vehicles or from vehicles to RSU emphasizes the importance of the infrastructure that could be represented by stationary or mobile RSU [15]. Nevertheless, the cost of deploying number of stationary RSUs along the road particularly on a large scale needs to be considered as well as the area of deployment so that a maximum number of vehicles can be covered [16].

According to Cavalcante et al. [17], the use of minimal number of RSUs with the maximum possible coverage of the region (and consequently, vehicles) should be considered to assist in disseminating the information and operating the network smoothly. Mehar et al. [18] have emphasized the placement of RSUs for delay-sensitive vehicular network applications wherein the duration of communication messages and the discontinuous connectivity should be considered. However, some applications may require additional deployment of RSUs for more coverage.

Clustering can assist in load balancing, disseminating the information in the network and aggregating it on the cloud [5]. Arkian et al. [5] have formulated vehicular cloud architectural framework based on network clustering to overcome the mobility of the network and improve its performance. Herein, the clustering scheme targets cooperative provisioning of resources among the member nodes within a group. The authors have emphasized the cluster head selection which is responsible for formulating and maintaining the vehicular cloud. However, issues related to the possible dynamic changes in network members association such as departing of cluster head and the possible replacement by a cluster member have not been addressed in their work.

The focus of this paper will be on the dynamic healing area of the self-organized network by offering the ability for a group to be re-grouped and for members to join and leave dynamically. The GPS rout, RSSI (Received Signal Strength Indicator) and vehicular speed will be used in this research as key parameters in the operation. Furthermore, the look-ahead approach through the use of route information would also be considered as part of the overall vision in sustaining the dynamic structure of the mobile vehicular group. This will further be supported by the inclusion of hand-off among the roadside units.

3   Approach for Vehicular Grouping

The vehicular network topology is structured based on the nature of the road wherein the vehicles are distributed over multiple organized lanes and along the length of each lane. Connectivity in tree network formation is seen as authentic approach that could align with the road structure. The number of hops within the topology can be identified based on the natural grouping on the road. This in effect reflect the stretch of the road that can be covered within one group. The flow of data could also be enhanced through the consideration of the load balance among the routing nodes.

The main concept involves the aspects of network self-formation, members joining & leaving and network self-healing in the event of the departing routing node. Here, new vehicles may join if they get close to the group and others may depart in the event of moving away from the group. This could be associated with several reasons such as divergent routes to be traversed by the various nodes, switching from one group to another, and vehicles moving with dissimilar and varying speeds.

The network structure of connectivity is illustrated by Fig. 2 wherein a one direction of the road has been considered for the communication to avoid the inter-ference between the two directions. The tree approach could be configured based on the number of connectivity to RSU, the connectivity to each routing level of the network and the number of allowable hops. The process of generating sub-trees can be initiated by the RSU wherein it will be connected to the set maximum number of router nodes. Then each router node sets the connection to the leaf or lower level router nodes according to identified parameters such as RSSI to have a complete organized structure.

Therefore, establishing a grouping or clustering structure to partition the network into small groups of moving vehicles to make the dynamic network more manageable and stable, simplify the routing in the network and achieve load balance.

Besides, offering the solution of grouping vehicles to adequately control and manage information on the roads, offering drivers and passengers new services focused on safety and collaborative driving.

The self-healing aspect has been considered for the departing of the router node (cluster head) from its initial position and leaving its cluster. The departing node leaves its dependent children or leaf nodes unconnected. Hence, a new router node should be elected to replace the departed one and be able to accommodate the unconnected nodes. Network re-organization to recover from this situation could involve the cloud looking

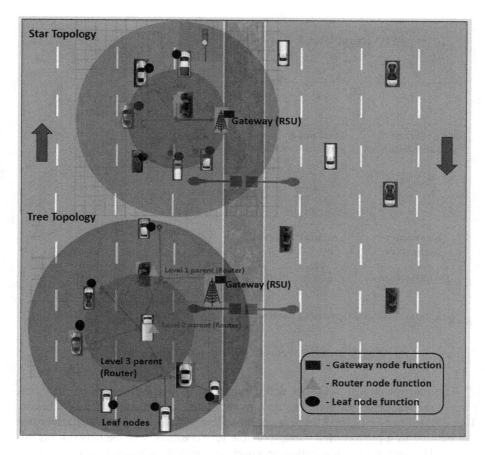

Fig. 2. Structure of vehicular network topology

at the virtual structure and elect a potential replacement (i.e. the fittest possible vehicular node). This will then take over the missing routing role. The latency in executing the healing process is highly important as it leaves some of the network nodes unable to pass their data. Preplanning using available vehicular routing data is therefore highly important for avoiding this blind region.

4   Vehicular Network Virtualization Architecture

The proposed system architecture for the vehicular network is illustrated by Fig. 3. It reflects the overall organization of the system wherein the physical vehicular network is connected over the Internet via the roadside unit or gateway to the cloud. The resources that are available in the cloud such as data storage, network virtualization and other capabilities for processing and intelligence that can offer intelligent interaction with the physical network of vehicles.

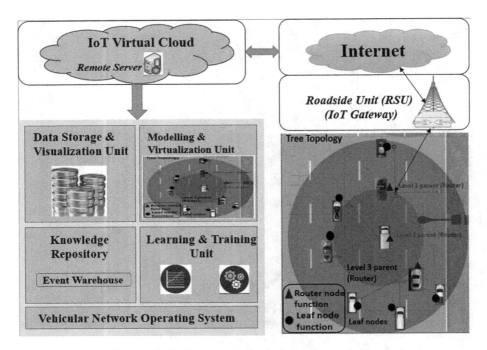

Fig. 3. Vehicular network physical-virtual organization

The functionality of vehicular nodes can be supported by three core functions, namely the leaf or sensor node function, router node function, and gateway function. This concept can be utilized for network modelling which offer the virtualization that can be used as a platform for testing possible re-orchestration of the network organization. The proposed virtualization approach involves the dissociation of the three functions to be loaded as software functional components within the remote cloud.

It is anticipated that the virtualization approach could allow for the reformulation and integration of the network and related virtual functions to be deployed onto virtual motes. This could support dynamic re-orchestration. For example, the functional role of a node through software reformulations at the virtual level could be switched via implementation of any of the three functions such as reconfiguring a leaf node to act as a router node and vice versa. Hence, the operational behavior of the vehicular network can be modified to meet the service requirements.

5   Router Fitness Model

The objectives of a router fitness model is to facilitate the election of a replacement router to the departing router. The process involves measurements relevant to the possible candidate nodes for this election. These are related to the load balance as well as ability to cover connectivity of the departing router's Childs by any of the existing same level routers. It also relates to the reachable Childs (that can be reached by one level up router in reference to the departing router) of the departing node. A router fitness model facilitates the competition among such eligible candidate nodes is discussed in this section. The role of fitness model is to achieve effective selection in term of efficient connectivity and load balance at no or minimal network downtime.

5.1   Description of Election Parameters

The approach used utilizes several measured parameters that helps in preplanning, allowing for routers load balance and insuring reliable connectivity. The parameters used are discussed in the followings:

Pre-Election Parameters

GPS Data (or GIS Route Plan): GPS is assumed to be used for route planning and end-to-end journey guidance. It could offer an estimation as to when the departing node is going to leave the network. Such information help plan-ahead of node departure time and allow for the option of delay tolerance in re-orchestrating the network before the rupture in the network takes place.

Vehicular Speed: This data in conjunction with GPS data could be used to calculate the time available before departure. Alternatively, this information can be used to calculate at what distance should the information pertaining to initiating the process of re-orchestration be broadcasted.

A Record of the Associated Nodes Addresses: The departing router possesses an updated record of the associated nodes (i.e. an updated list of vulnerable child leaf nodes). Such nodes, if reachable by the RSU or the router at one level above the departing router are duly notified by the RSU to participate in the election process. Herein, they are to compete with same level routers to replace the departing router. If unsuccessful, they need to be associated with an alternative router.

Election-Specific/Decision Making Parameters

Distance of the Potential Router from the Related RSU: Herein, sensed RSSI values are used directly as a mean of connectivity signal strength and hence covering for the need for calculating the distance. All routing enabled nodes present their RSSI to the RSU or related router. This, in effect, presents a more realistic means for connectivity.

Distance of the Potential Router from the Departed Router's Leaf Nodes: The eligible router nodes in the election process, including affected leaf nodes within the reach of upper layer router or RSU, as well as router nodes of other clusters attempt to check their RSSI values with respect to the affected leaf nodes beyond the reach of the RSU. Such RSSI-based checking of connectivity enables identification of the unreachable leaf nodes which could be accommodated by a certain router node and thus, could get re-connected to the network.

Ability of a Router to Cover Maximum Number of Affected Nodes: The potential departing router replacement node should be capable of encompassing as many affected leaf nodes as possible. Herein, the number of affected leaf nodes that could be connected to the candidate nodes can be determined. The affected leaf nodes would set the priority of connection to the potential node through the distance. Affected leaf nodes with RSSI signal below a threshold value, with respect to a particular candidate node, will not be able to connect.

Battery Level of the Potential Router Node: The battery level of the potential nodes has also been considered as a parameter in the election process even though the energy aspect may not be of much concern in vehicular network. It may be of more significance in other mobile objects like bikes or other subject carrying wireless smart device.

5.2   Formulation of Router Fitness Model

The model for the election process attempts to identify a replacement router node among the leaf nodes when the current router departs the network. The focus will be on those nodes that can communicate with the upper level to the departing router or RSU wherein they have been identified as reachable nodes. The competition here will be among the reachable leaf nodes (the nodes in the communication range of the router). The following model is suggested for the replacement router election:

$$W_v = \{N_w[RSSI_{RL-RSU} + RSSI_{RL-L} + C_{CL-RL} + B_{RL}]\} \tag{2}$$

Where, $N_w = W \times f$, f represents fiddle factor pertaining to the respective variable, $RSSI_{RL-RSU}$ represents the received signal strength indication for reachable leaf node with respect to RSU. $RSSI_{RL-L}$ represents the received signal strength indication for reachable leaf node with respect to other leaf nodes. C_{CL-RL} represents the number of leaf nodes that are reached by the reachable leaf. B_{RL} represents the battery level of RL.

In the above model, the fiddle factors corresponding to each of the parameters have been formulated independently so as to attain uniformity of weightage (normalized values) assigned to each of the variables under consideration (and their final summation).

5.3   Communication Dialog During the Routing Recovery Process

The departing router node in the vehicular network is the main trigger for the sequence of messages among the participated nodes in the replacement election process. Each node disseminates its message according to chosen parameters so that the RSU can start running the fitness model based on the selected criteria to elect one of the eligible nodes. Description of each action undertaken by the various nodes to disseminate their messages are provided as below:

(1) The departing router node identifies that its vehicle will depart the cluster after predefined distance as declared by the GIS measurements. The departing node then collects the vehicle speed and calculates the time remaining prior to departure. It then disseminates the necessary information pertaining to its departure, viz., remaining distance, time, current speed and associated leaf nodes' (children) addresses. Departing router message, M_{DR} (message 1) is as depicted in Fig. 4.

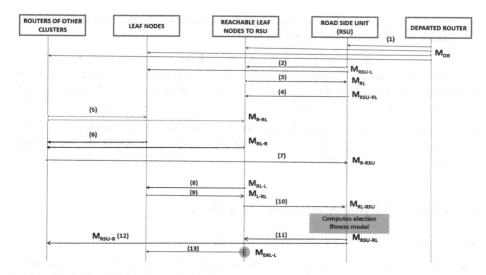

Fig. 4. UML diagram for the sequence of messages among the participated nodes in the election process

(2) Upon receiving the above information from the departing router, the RSU vies to check for, and subsequently establish connection with the departed router's leaf nodes (children). For this, it broadcasts message 2 M_{RSU-L} (see Fig. 4). This message, intended to measure the individual nodes' RSSI with respect to the upper level router. It will helps in identifying the reachable leaf nodes via encouraging a response from each such node. Message M_{RL} is acknowledgement transmitted back by the reachable leaf nodes (along with their respective RSSI values). In response, the RSU or upper level router transmits an acknowledgement message, M_{RSU-RL} notifying the reachable leaf nodes of their participation in the election process (see Fig. 4).

(3) Routers other than the departing router test their reachability with respect to the departing router's leaf nodes. They then notify the RSU on the number of reachable leaf nodes and their addresses, the number of existing leaf nodes that they are currently taking care of as well as the average signal strength with departing routers leaf nodes. The messages M_{R-RL}, M_{RL-R} and M_{R-RSU} are the related messages 5, 6 and 7 respectively (see Fig. 4).

(4) Leaf nodes that could become routers disseminate signals to all departing router's leaf nodes in an attempt to identify those with whom they could establish connection. Again, the RSSI signal values are considered for the identification of the connectable nodes. This information will then be passed to the RSU. The Messages M_{RL-L}, M_{L-RL}, and M_{RL-RSU} respectively perform these actions as depicted by the three messages 8, 9 and 10 in Fig. 4.

(5) As per the information collected from the reachable nodes and other routers, RSU will work out the fitness values for each of the participant nodes and elect the one with the highest fitness value. Subsequently, all participant nodes will be notified about the outcome of the election by broadcasting the node ID of the elected

router to them. This message will also contain information about the leaf nodes for which the elected router bears responsibility.

The process attempts to elect a reachable node that connects to the maximum number of leaf nodes. Messages M_{RSU-RL} and M_{RSU-R} notify the elected reachable node to take responsibility of the leaf nodes within its range, including the router(s) that could cover the remaining leaf nodes. Messages 11 and 12 cater for these respectively.

(6) Owing to the assignment of the leaf nodes to a new router(s), the relevant routers notify the related leaf nodes and resume their connectivity within the network in accordance with the new arrangement.

6   Network Virtual Model and Test Results

6.1   Network Modelling Using Contiki-Cooja

The vehicular network-based clustering scenario has been modelled using Contiki-Cooja simulator. The vehicular network scenario model is formulated based on the main functional nodes: RSU, router and leaf nodes. The election process can be initiated based on the parameters and the sequence of messages discussed in Sect. 5. Using the proposed fitness model, one of the reachable leaf nodes will be elected as a replacement node for the departing router. The functional role of the elected node can be switched to a router node via flexible software-invoked formulation of router virtual function.

The following Fig. 5 depicts the implementation and modelling of the vehicular nodes-based clustering scenario. The network is represented by the nodes of departing router, RSU, reachable leaf node and unreachable leaf node. The node number could be scaled by including more reachable leaf nodes. In terms of extracting the results to test the approach, two reachable leaf node (4 and 6) have been considered.

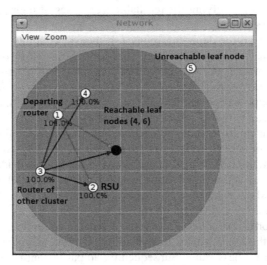

Fig. 5. Network model implemented within the Cooja simulator

6.2   Results and Discussion

The following Table 1 depicts the simulation parameters that are utilized in cooja scenarios.

Table 1. Simulation Parameters

Parameter	Value
Speed	0–100 km/h
Transmission power	20dBm
Receiver sensitivity (SNR)	−100dBm
Packet data rate	256 Kbps
Battery	95%

The following performance measures are being conducted for analyzing the self-healing process and the performance of the network.

- **The Consistency of the Election Process**

A cooja scenario is designed for the VN with both stationary and mobile nodes. The Fig. 6 below shows a comparison between the static and dynamic scenarios wherein the election process is being repeated multiple times (for 10 trials). During this process, the number of election rounds that is related to the successful transmission of the packets has been achieved for 10 times by the candidate node for the static scenarios. However, one have to take into consideration cases where one or more of the candidate are within the low RSSI range in communication or are occasionally have transmission been blocked by neighboring vehicles. In this case, successful arrival of all the important data may not take place in all operational cycles. For example six out of ten result in completing the election scenario for the dynamic operation of Fig. 6. This type of uncertainty may result in significant delay and hence need to be catered for.

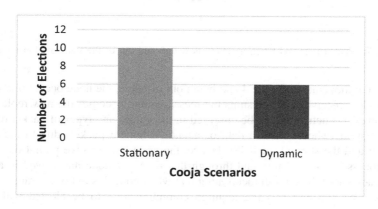

Fig. 6. The consistency of the election process

From the results, the stationary node that meets the election requirements will be elected successfully to replace the departed router. However, introducing the mobility factor to the network wherein the candidate node has a weak RSSI cause irregularity in the election or variability with respect to the election outcome.

- **Possible communication irregularities**

The message received in the network is affected by the distance of the nodes (RSSI). As the distance increases (the signal gets weaker), there will be more message drops. RSSI parameter has an impact on the rate of message drops wherein the efficiency of communication is influenced by this parameter. Various scenarios have been tested in cooja wherein one or some of the nodes can be out of the transmission range, close to the boundary or blind by neighboring nodes. Hence, the node(s) may not receive or/and transmit some of the related messages based on the proposed UML.

The Fig. 7 below depicts the result of a scenario wherein the reachable leaf node 4 moves in and out of the transmission range. As can be clearly seen from Fig. 7, the packet received by node 4 is 100% represented by the red bar at trial 2 while it is 80% for node 6. This indicates that both nodes are within the transmission range, node 4 is receiving and transmitting all the messages based on the proposed UML while node 6 is missing 20% of the messages as it is not elected as a replacement node.

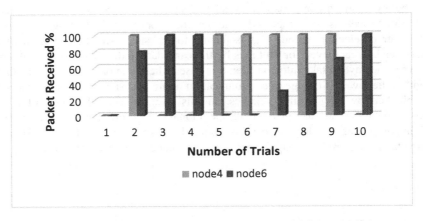

Fig. 7. Packet received when node (4) is within and out of the transmission range

Upon the movement of node 4 and being out of range, the node occurs packet loss. Hence, node 6 receives and transmits the messages and becomes the new replacement node. However, fluctuation can be observed in the values and types of packet received in this scenario (whether it is a data or acknowledgment packet) due to the node's movement and the strength of RSSI. Hence, the node may receive partial data as the whole process is taking 2 min and through that time, the node has moved in and out causing packet loss. It is worth mentioning that when node 4 is out of the range, node 6 works as a backup and sets the required communication to be elected within less latency.

The other scenario is considered where there is an obstacle represented by node 6 on the way of node 4. Hence, the connectivity becomes blind until the node gets reconnected again. The following Fig. 8 shows that node 4 occurs packet loss due to the isolation of the node while node 6 receives and transmits all the packets for about 1 min from the simulation time. The blinding condition of the node could be considered as part of the election criteria. However, node 4 is able to reconnect and receive all the packets once it gets a strong signal and its line of sight becomes clear. It is clear that node 6 receives only 20% of the packets in the last minute of the simulation as it losses some of the data and acknowledgment messages based on the node situation. Hence, node 4 is recovering and being elected at the last three trials as shown by Fig. 8.

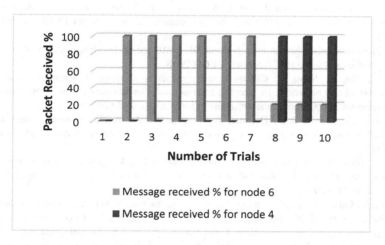

Fig. 8. Packet received when node (6) is the obstacle on the way of node (4)

7   Conclusion

The paper explored the organization of vehicular network with emphasis on resolving the vehicular clusters self-healing in the event of a routing node's departure. The concept has been implemented using Contiki-Cooja simulation tool taking into consideration the communication among the nodes and the fitness model for electing the eligible node to replace the departed one. The model has been tested based on status of the competing nodes. The percentage of data received reflects the node being at the boundary or within the range and that also is offering a backup for election. Furthermore, some nodes could be disadvantaged by either being blinded or being outside the line of sight boundary occasionally. Hence, in future we will be considering the communication reliability impact factor as part of the router election criteria.

The work for the next stage will take into consideration the capacity of the system in absorbing messages when implementing specific protocol like Lora. This includes looking into the relation between the size of the vehicular group and the stretch of the road that could accommodate the group. This factor may allow customization of the generic solution to a given application and physical environment such as urban or highway roads. It may also investigate type of mobility groups like vehicles, motor bikes or bicycles. Furthermore, the use of history and planning information like the recent reliability of connectivity, or GPS routing plan for each individual node (or vehicle) as influential factors in the router selection criteria.

References

1. Lu, N., Cheng, N., Zhang, N., Shen, X., Mark, J.W.: Connected vehicles: solutions and challenges. IEEE Internet Things **1**(4), 289–299 (2014)
2. Sanguesa, J.A., Barrachina, J., Fogue, M., Garrido, P., Martinez, F.J., et al.: Sensing traffic density combining V2 V and V2I wireless communications. Sensors **15**(12), 31794–31810 (2015)
3. The Press-Enterprise. https://www.pe.com/2017/09/09/temecula-calling-for-regional-summit-to-tackle-traffic-on-15-freeway. Accessed 14 Oct 2018
4. Jin, D., Shi, F., Song, J.: Cluster based emergency message dissemination scheme for vehicular ad hoc networks. In: The 9th International Conference on Ubiquitous Information Management and Communication, Bali, Indonesia, pp. 1–8 (2015)
5. Arkian, H.R., Atani, R.E., Diyanat, A., Pourkhalili, A.: A cluster-based vehicular cloud architecture with learning-based resource management. J. Supercomput. **71**(4), 1401–1426 (2015)
6. Joe, I., Shin, M.: An energy-efficient mobile cluster-based approach for vehicular wireless sensor networks. In: The 6th International Conference on Networked Computing (INC), pp. 1–5. IEEE (2010)
7. Touil, A., Ghadi, F.: Implementation of clustering metrics in vehicular ad-hoc networks. In: Rocha, A., Serrhini, M., Felgueiras, C. (eds.) Europe and MENA Cooperation Advances in Information and Communication Technologies 2017, LNCS, vol. 520, pp. 441–449. Springer, AG (2017). https://doi.org/10.1007/978-3-319-46568-5_45
8. Rawashdeh, Z.Y., Mahmud, S.M.: A novel algorithm to form stable clusters in vehicular ad hoc networks on highways. EURASIP J. Wirel. Commun. Netw. **2012**, 15 (2012)
9. Hadded, M., Muhlethaler, P., Zagrouba, R., Laouiti, A., Saidane, L.A.: Using road ids to enhance clustering in vehicular ad hoc networks. In: The 2015 International Wireless Communications and Mobile Computing Conference (IWCMC), pp. 285–290. IEEE (2015)
10. Gupta, N., Prakash, A., Tripathi, R.: Adaptive beaconing in mobility aware clustering based MAC protocol for safety message dissemination in VANET. Wirel. Commun. Mob. Comput. **2017**, 1–15 (2017)
11. Wu, H., Tang, H., Dong, L.: A novel routing protocol based on mobile social networks and internet of vehicles. In: Hsu, C.-H., Wang, S. (eds.) IOV 2014. LNCS, vol. 8662, pp. 1–10. Springer, Cham (2014). https://doi.org/10.1007/978-3-319-11167-4_1
12. Maslekar, N., Boussedjra, M., Mouzna, J., Labiod, H.: A stable clustering algorithm for efficiency applications in VANETs. In: The 7th International Conference on Wireless Communications and Mobile Computing (IWCMC), pp. 1188–1193. IEEE (2011)
13. Charalampopoulos, G., Dagiuklas, T., Chrysikos, T.: V2I applications in highways: How RSU dimensioning can improve service delivery. In: The 23rd International Conference on Telecommunications (ICT), pp. 1–6. IEEE (2016)
14. Parrado, N., Donoso, Y.: Congestion based mechanism for route discovery in a V2I-V2 V system applying smart devices and IoT. Sensors **15**(4), 7768–7806 (2015)

15. Aslam, B., Amjad, F., Zou, C.C.: Optimal roadside units placement in urban areas for vehicular networks. In: IEEE Symposium on Computers and Communications (ISCC), pp. 000423–000429. IEEE (2012)
16. Kuo, W.H., Tung, Y.S., Fang, S.H.: A node management scheme for R2 V connections in RSU-supported vehicular adhoc networks. In: International Conference on Computing, Networking and Communications (ICNC), pp. 768–772. IEEE (2013)
17. Cavalcante, E.S., Aquino, L.L., Pappa, G.L., Loureiro, A.A.: Roadside unit deployment for information dissemination in a VANET: an evolutionary approach. In: The 14th Annual Conference Companion on Genetic and Evolutionary Computation, PA, USA, pp. 27–34 (2012)
18. Mehar, S., Senouci, S.M., Kies, A., Zoulikha, M.M.: An optimized roadside units (RSU) placement for delay-sensitive applications in vehicular networks. In: 12th Annual IEEE Consumer Communications and Networking Conference (CCNC), pp. 121–127. IEEE (2015)

Evaluate Good Bus Driving Behavior with LSTM

Qingwen Han[1], Xiaochang Hu[1], Shibiao He[2], Lingqiu Zeng[1(✉)], Lei Ye[1], and Xiaohan Yuan[1]

[1] Chongqing University, Chongqing 400044, China
{hqw,xch,zenglq,Yelei}@cqu.edu.cn, ciel07yxh@gmail.com
[2] Chongqing College of Humanities, Science and Technology, Chongqing 401524, China
hdoctor@vip.sina.com

Abstract. Drivers' behaviors and their decision can affect the probability of the traffic accident, pollutant emissions and the energy efficiency level, good driving behavior can not only reduce fuel consumption, but also improves ride comfort and safety. In this paper, a new concept, evaluation zone, is defined to distinguish special driving areas which has much influence on energy consumption and ride comfort. Then, based on reducing fuel consumption and improving ride comfort, evaluation zone based driving behavior model is proposed to obtain good driving behavior dataset for the long short-term memory (LSTM) to apply the driving behavior evaluation and driving suggestion providing tasks. By using 687# bus line's driving data of Chongqing City, China, test results demonstrate that the developed model performs well and the LSTM could provide reliable driving evaluations and suggestions for drivers.

Keywords: Driving behavior · Long short-term memory
Electric bus · Driving suggestion

1 Introduction

With development of autonomous vehicles, evolving vehicles are expected to revolutionize transportation supporting safer, faster, and more entertaining smart objects, rather than being just a mobility unit. Industry people think that autonomous driving technologies should be firstly applied in some special vehicles, such as agriculture vehicles, mining vehicles, logistics vehicle, and public transportation vehicles, whose decision control strategies are relatively simple than that of general vehicles. It is noticeable that public transportation vehicles closely relate with daily life of people. Due to the features of energy saving and manpower saving, autonomous driving related application could greatly decrease running cost, and show great attraction to public transit companies [1,2]. Researchers believe that the commercialization progress of public transportation autonomous vehicles greatly depended on the rationality of customized driving strategy.

© Springer Nature Switzerland AG 2018
A. M. J. Skulimowski et al. (Eds.): IOV 2018, LNCS 11253, pp. 122–132, 2018.
https://doi.org/10.1007/978-3-030-05081-8_9

The running lines of public bus relatively fix. Generally, the drivers of same bus line shall face the same driving environment. Both of energy consumption and quality of passengers travel experience are largely depended on the driver's driving behavior [3]. Past studies have shown that different driving behaviors have a great influence on automobile energy consumption, and the driver's good driving behavior can reduce energy consumption by about 15% [4]. On the other hand, aggressive driving behavior, such as rapid acceleration and rapid deceleration, anxious to keep the vehicle at high speed, etc., should bring both bad travel experience and high-energy consumption [5]. In past few years, researchers devote to improve the performance of public transportation system and believe that an appropriate model should be helpful in autonomous control. In recent years, neural networks and deep learning methods are introduced to realize driving behavior modeling, and show powerful advantage in function and technique. In [6], Liu et al. propose a deep learning based feature extraction method to extract essential features from redundant driving behavior data. Literature [7] present a driving behavior modeling method, which employs hidden Markov models (HMMs) and deep learning algorithm, to explore bad driving behavior from large amounts of driving data, and provide risky alarming function. In actual, the performance of deep learning based approach is influenced by two key techniques; training data labeled method and network architecture. In [8], predefined abnormal patterns and manually labeled training data are used to identify similar patterns, which are marked as anomalies. Literature [9] proposed a rule-based method, in which two kind of typical driving manner, car-following behavior and evasive behavior, are selected to model.

It is well known that driving behavior can be influenced by several factors, such as personal characteristics (personality, ability and skills, attitudes, perceptions, socio-economic characteristics–age, gender, experience, etc.), vehicle related (type, model, characteristics, etc.), mobility patterns (trip distance, traffic conditions; road geometry, etc.) and environmental indicators (weather conditions, etc.) [10]. The more factors are considered, the more complex the model should be. According to the relationship among driving factors and fuel consumption [11], the fuel consumption related factors, such as accelerator [12], velocity [13] and gear position [14], are used in driving behavior model construction [4]. Autonomous control mechanism should be designed according to good driving behavior. Hence, in this paper, we focus on good driving behavior discovery, and try to give reasonable driving suggestion for corresponding road section.

In our previous work [15], three factors, which are accelerated rate, velocity, and gear position respectively, are selected as model inputs. A fuel based labeling criterion is defined, while a bus stop area oriented modeling rule is presented. According to this line of thought, in this paper, evaluation zone is defined to divide bus line into several sections. A deep learning model is used to find good driving behavior. Two-year data of 687# bus, Chongqing City, is employed to realize good driving behavior discover, while 1-month data is used as validation data set. A three steps procedure, which includes data preprocessing, data segmentation, and cluster analysis respectively, is used to obtain good driving behavior.

This paper is organized as follows. The experiment and the methodology used in this work is given in Sect. 2. Section 3 is experiment results, in which experiment results of driving behavior evaluation and driving suggestion providing are introduced. Finally, the conclusion and future work are given in Sect. 4.

2   Methodology

The experiment and the methodology used in this work is shown in Fig. 1, which illustrates the general system architecture. The raw dataset is firstly collected from 687# bus line in Chongqing. Then, we proposed an evaluation zone based driving behavior model to get good driving behavior dataset. Finally, the LSTM model is applied to the evaluation and driving advice providing tasks.

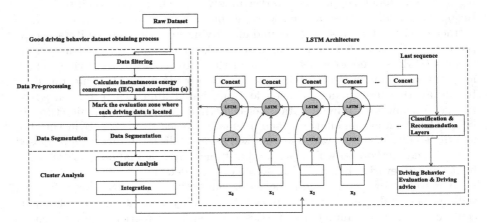

Fig. 1. Overall system architecture.

2.1   Raw Dataset

Hengtong intelligent public transport management cloud platform, which is used by Chongqing Bus Company, is a bus dispatching and management system. The platform manages all 3000 buses in Chongqing city. Corresponding bus-driving records are collected and stored on back-end data server. The record of one object bus includes GPS information and running state. The collection interval is set as 1 s. Examples of some of the explanatory variables contained within each category include:

- Mechanical properties: engine state, battery state, motor speed, gas pressure
- Running state: velocity, gear, brake, and accelerator
- Position information: GPS position

In this paper, 2 years driving records of 26 buses of line 687 is used to construct evaluation zone based driving behavior model, while the detailed digital map is shown in Fig. 2.

2.2   Data Segment and Pre-processing

As aforementioned, proposed driving behavior evaluation model is an evaluation zone oriented one. That is said, all raw dataset are firstly mapped to critical driving area for the drivers.

Definition 1. *Evaluation zones of bus driving denote the specific road section, such as bus stop, steep slope, sharp turn, etc., whose energy consumption and ride comfort greatly influenced by driving behaviors.*

In this paper, the evaluation zone is defined as a circle area whose radius is 50 m.

$$Zone = \{Z(x,y) | d\overline{Z \cdot A_i} \le 50\} \tag{1}$$

where $Z(x,y)$ is the dataset of bus line, and Ai is the position of evaluation zone i.

$$d\overline{Z \cdot A_i} = \sqrt{(X_z - X_{A_i})^2 + (Y_z - Y_{A_i})^2} \tag{2}$$

As shown in Fig. 2, there are 120 evaluation zones along 687# bus line, which are denoted by red circles. According to evaluation zone division output, the raw dataset is divided into 120 segments. After that, a pre-processing procedure is used to filter invalid data, such as redundant data, erroneous data and long term parking data.

8 indicators, which are bus ID, speed (V), longitude (Lo), latitude (La), time (Tim), instantaneous energy consumption (IEC), acceleration (a) and Evaluation Zone label (EVL) respectively, are selected to construct efficient original data set D. EVL is defined in data segment process. 5 of the 8 indicators are provided by raw dataset, while the other 2 indicators, which are energy consumption and acceleration parameter respectively, should be calculated. All buses running on 687# bus line are pure electric vehicles. Then the instantaneous energy consumption (IEC) can be calculated as follows,

$$IEC_i = Voltage_i \times Current_i \tag{3}$$

where IEC_i, $Voltage_i$ and $Current_i$ represent the i_{th} record of the raw dataset, and $Voltage_i$ and $Current_i$ can be obtained from the raw dataset.

Moreover, acceleration (a) parameter should be obtained according to the classical formula,

$$a = \frac{\Delta V}{\Delta Tim} \tag{4}$$

where ΔV is speed difference in a certain period ΔTim. Then the original data set D could be denotes as,

$$D = data[h][8] = \left\{ \begin{array}{c} (Id_1, V_1, Lo_1, La_1, Tim_1, IEC_1, a_1, EVL_1) \\ \cdots\cdots \\ (Id_i, V_i, Lo_i, La_i, Tim_i, IEC_i, a_i, EVL_i) \\ \cdots\cdots \\ (Id_h, V_h, Lo_h, La_h, Tim_h, IEC_h, a_h, EVL_h) \end{array} \right\}, i = 1, 2, \ldots, h \tag{5}$$

where h is the number of rows that are in the data set D. Examples of data set D is listed in Table 1.

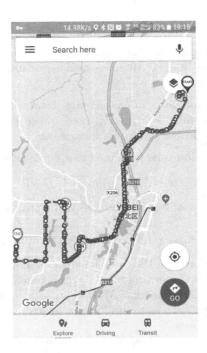

Fig. 2. 687#bus line & evaluation zones.

Table 1. Efficient original data structure.

Id	Time	Longitude	Latitude	Speed (km/h)	Instantaneous energy consumption (kW)	Acceleration (m/s^2)	Evaluation zone label
90	2016/1/28 18:14:12	106.6435	29.7508	19.53	101.521	1.58	0
13	2016/1/28 18:14:12	106.6252	29.71886	15.33	98.461	−2.6	3

2.3 Dataset Clustering

In this paper, a K-means clustering algorithm is used for good driving behavior discovery, and the parameter used in the K-means experiment is K, which illustrates the number of clusters.

Here a 3 steps procedure is used.

Step 1: Cluster Analysis

Cluster analysis is based on segmented dataset, as shown in Fig. 3, 3 clusters, which represent high energy consumption (red), medium energy consumption (blue) and low energy consumption (green) respectively, are generated by clustering process. Here note that normalized data are used in this process.

Step 2: Outlier data removal

In this step, the black points shown in Fig. 3, which are considered as outliers and correspond to bad driving behaviors, should be removed.

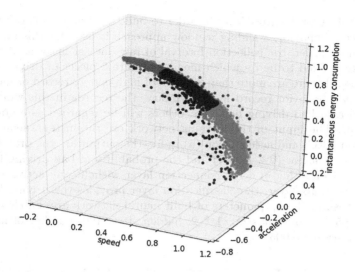

Fig. 3. Cluster results of data piece in evaluation zone 1. (Color figure online)

Step 3: Labeling

In this step, the dataset D is labeled according to energy consumption and acceleration parameter. Here three energy consumption levels, high, medium and low, which are denoted as "2", "1", "0" respectively, are labeled to each data piece. On the other hand, the data piece, whose acceleration parameter is higher than $3m/s^2$ or less than $3m/s^2$ in 3 s, is labeled as "0", which illustrates the data piece is a bad bad-driving behavior record. Then the extended dataset D is obtained. Examples of data set D' is listed in Table 2.

Table 2. Data structure of zone1 dataset.

Time	Longitude	Latitude	Speed (km/h)	Instantaneous energy consumption (kW)	Acceleration (m/s^2)	Energy label	Driving behavior label
2017/2/16 17:25	106.6435	29.7508	28.5	105.90364	−0.2	0	1
2017/2/16 18:18	106.6252	29.71886	31.9	168.6215	2.4	0	1

2.4   Training Methodology

In this paper, two learning network is used. The one is employed to evaluate driving behavior, while the other is used to generate driving suggestion.

Driving Behavior Evaluation: In order to build a learning network for evaluating driving behavior, a sliding window approach is used for this evaluation. As mentioned earlier, the collection interval of raw dataset is set as 1 s and the window size is fixed to be 5 s which mean there are 5 pieces of driving data in each window. If there are more than 2 pieces of high-energy record or more than 1 piece of bad behavior record in one window, the records in this window will be assessed as a bad driving behavior, others will be regarded as a good driving behavior. The input of the learning network are the instantaneous energy consumption (IEC) and acceleration (a) in 5 s, the output are the probability of good driving behavior (0%−100%) and the probability of bad driving behavior (0%−100%). Consisting of a full connection layer without any activation function and a Softmax layer, the classification layer provides the driving behavior evaluation results. The parameters of built neural network are: batch size = 32, input size = 5 * 2, output size = 1 * 2, hidden size = 100, number of layers = 2 and learning rate = 0.005.

Driving Suggestion Data Generation: The work is based on a sliding window approach for a short term future prediction. The window size is fixed to be 6 s with an overlap of 5 s' information and prediction is made for 1 s in future. The window will be skipped if there are more than 2 pieces of high-energy record or more than 1 piece of bad behavior record in the 6 s. The inputs of the learning network are the speed (V) and acceleration (a) in 5 s, the output is the one recommended driving behavior of speed (V) and acceleration (a) for the 5 s record. Recommendation layer gives the driving suggestion and the parameters of this built neural network are as same as Driving Behavior Evaluation's network.

3   Experiment Results

Here a validation process is used to validate effectiveness of the proposed method. One-month bus data (1/5/2018, 31/5/2018) is selected as test dataset to realize conformance test. As mentioned earlier, in this paper, two learning networks are used to realize driving behavior evaluation and driving suggestion data generation. Hence, in this part, two corresponding experiments are done. Moreover, to fulfill above two functions for all 120-evaluation zones, 240 trained networks are needed.

3.1   Experiment Results of Driving Behavior Evaluation

Training results of 5 evaluation zones are listed in Table 3, in which positive samples and negative samples correspond to good driving behaviors or bad driving behaviors. The accuracy of driving behavior evaluation is shown in Fig. 4. As shown in Fig. 4, accuracy of evaluation is up to 90%.

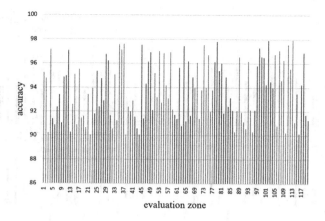

Fig. 4. Accuracy of Driving Behavior Evaluation.

Table 3. Some evaluation zone's results of driving behavior evaluation

Evaluation zone id	Training dataset			Test dataset			Correct forecasts	Prediction accuracy
	Training samples	Positive samples	Negative samples	Test samples	Positive samples	Negative samples		
1	24164	7461	16703	2859	1381	1478	2723	95.24%
22	49459	30644	18815	3802	1513	2289	3423	90.03%
34	51374	26842	24532	3453	1934	1519	3151	91.25%
56	55723	29203	26520	2986	1573	1413	2812	94.17%
115	59171	34218	24953	4951	2334	1617	4630	93.51%

3.2 Experiment Results of Driving Suggestion Providing

Here two scenarios are considered. In scenario 1, 40 good driving behavior samples are used to realize suggestion providing process, while in scenario 2, 33 good driving behavior samples and 7 bad driving behavior samples are considered.

Corresponding experiment results are discussed as follows.

Scenario 1: All good driving behavior

As shown in Fig. 5, the predicted speed is coincident with real driving speed, while the predicted acceleration presents a slight deviation with real value. Besides, the mean square error of speed and acceleration are 0.054729 and 0.156187 after normalization.

Scenario 2: Partial bad driving behavior

In Fig. 6, sample 21st to 27th are bad driving behaviors samples, whose real driving parameters differ greatly from the suggestion parameter in both speed and acceleration.

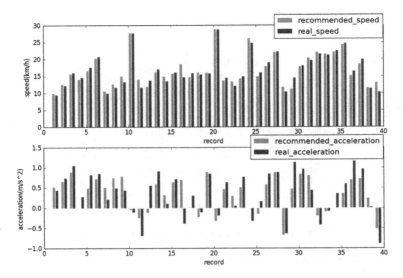

Fig. 5. Driving advice providing in evaluation zone 1 with all good driving behavior.

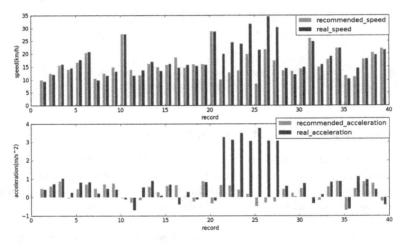

Fig. 6. Driving advice providing in evaluation zone 1 with partial bad driving behavior.

From the experiment results of this part, if the driver performs good driving behavior, then the recommended driving behaviors has small differences with his own driving behaviors. On the contrary, if the driver performs bad driving behavior, the recommended driving behavior and his own driving behavior will be very different. The fact indicates this network can provide reliable driving suggestions for drivers.

4 Conclusion

Driving behavior modeling is a key point in autonomous driving decision-making research. In general, energy consumption and acceleration factors are reflections of driving performance. In this paper, an energy consumption and acceleration oriented model is put forward to fulfill good driving behavior discovery, while LSTM network is used to evaluate driving behavior and provide driving suggestion.

Two-year driving data of 687# bus, Chongqing city, are used to discover good driving behavior and train neural network. Another 1-month data are used as our test dataset. Simulation results show that proposed method perform good in driving behavior evaluation and driving suggestion providing.

In future works, the complexity of training network should be considered. Then the network reuse method should be take into account.

Acknowledgement. The authors would like to thank Chongqing Hengtong Bus Co., Ltd. for providing the raw bus driving data. This research is supported by National Nature Science Foundation of China, Project No. 61601066. Thanks for the graduate research and innovation foundation of Chongqing, China, Grant No.CYS17033. Thanks for Fundamental Research Funds for the Central Universities No.2018CDXYTX0009.

References

1. Lárusdóttir, E.B., Ulfarsson, G.F.: Effect of driving behavior and vehicle characteristics on energy consumption of road vehicles running on alternative energy sources. Int. J. Sustain. Transp. **9**, 592–601 (2015)
2. Sabiron, G., Thibault, L., Degeilh, P., Corde, G.: Pollutant emissions estimation framework for real-driving emissions at microscopic scale and environmental footprint calculation. In: IEEE Intelligent Vehicles Symposium (IV), pp. 381–388 (2018)
3. Wilhelem, T., Okuda, H., Levedahl, B., Suzuki, T.: Energy consumption evaluation based on a personalized driver-vehicle model. IEEE Trans. Intell. Transp. Syst. **18**, 1468–1477 (2017)
4. Ericsson, E.: Independent driving pattern factors and their influence on fuel-use and exhaust emission factors. Transp. Res. Part D **6**, 325–345 (2001)
5. Thew, R.: United evidence and research strategy: driving standards agency. CIECA, version (1.2) (2007)
6. Liu, H., Taniguchi, T., Tanaka, Y., Takenaka, K.: Essential feature extraction of driving behavior using a deep learning method. In: Intelligent Vehicles Symposium (IV), pp. 1054–1060 (2015)
7. Miyajima, C., Takeda, K.: Driver-behavior modeling using on-road driving data: a new application for behavior signal processing. IEEE Signal Process. Mag. **33**, 14–21 (2016)
8. Zhang, M., Chen, C., Wo, T., Xie, T., Bhuiyan, M.Z.A., Lin, X.: SafeDrive: online driving anomaly detection from large-scale vehicle data. IEEE Trans. Ind. Inform. **13**, 2087–2096 (2017)
9. Chong, L., Abbas, M.M., Flintsch, A.M., Higgs, B.: A rule-based neural network approach to model driver naturalistic behavior in traffic. Transportation Res. Part C Emerg. Technol. **32**, 207–223 (2013)

10. Goldenbeld, C., Levelt, P.B.M., Heidstra, J.: Psychological perspectives on changing driver attitude and behaviour. Recherche - Transports - Sécurité **67**, 65–81 (2000). Accessed 01 Apr 2000
11. Tang, T.Q., Huang, H.J., Shang, H.Y.: Influences of the driver's bounded rationality on micro driving behavior, fuel consumption and emissions. Transp. Res. Part D Transp. Environ. **41**, 423–432 (2015)
12. Liu, X., Xie, H., Ma, H., Chen, S.: The effects of bus driver's behavior on fuel consumption and its evaluation indicator. Automot. Eng. **36**, 1321–1326 (2014)
13. Meng, X., Zeng, C., Yang, D., Cai, F., Xia, H.: Analysis of the vehicle fuel consumption for different driving operation behavior. Energy Conserv. Environ. Prot. Transp. **8**, 14–20 (2012)
14. Beckx, C., Panis, L.I., Vlieger, I.D., Wets, G.: Influence of gear-changing behaviour on fuel use and vehicular exhaust emissions. In: Morrison, G.M., Rauch, S. (eds.) Highway Urban Environment. Alliance For Global Sustainability Bookseries, vol. 12, pp. 45–51. Springer, Dordrecht (2007). https://doi.org/10.1007/978-1-4020-6010-6_5
15. Han, Q., Zeng, L., Hu, Y., Ye, L., Tang, Y., Lei, J., et al.: Driving behavior modeling and evaluation for bus enter and leave stop process. J. Ambient. Intell. Humaniz. Comput. **9**, 1–12 (2018)

Social Knowledge to Improve Situation Awareness of Assistance Systems in City Driving

Alberto Fernández-Isabel[1] and Rubén Fuentes-Fernández[2]([✉])

[1] Universidad Rey Juan Carlos, Móstoles, Spain
alberto.fernandez.isabel@urjc.es

[2] Research Group on Agent-based, Social & Interdisciplinary Applications
(GRASIA), Universidad Complutense de Madrid, Madrid, Spain
ruben@fdi.ucm.es
http://grasia.fdi.ucm.es

Abstract. City traffic is getting more multi-modal, with a variety of actors and mobility options in mixed spaces. This makes decisions on traffic behaviour and control more complex. Beyond traditionally considered aspects (e.g. traffic state or used vehicle), human aspects (e.g. physical state, displacement goal, or companion), gain increasing relevance. They can greatly modify how people move and interact with others. Introducing social knowledge about human behaviour and context can help to better understand and anticipate the environment and its actions. This paper proposes the development of Social-Aware Driver Assistance Systems (SADASs) for that purpose. A SADAS uses *traffic social properties* that formalize social knowledge using a template organized around diagrams. The diagrams are compliant with a specific modelling language, which is intended to describe social aspects in a given context. They facilitate the integration of this knowledge with system specifications, and its semi-automated verification both in design and run time. A case study on a distributed obstacle detection system for vehicles extended with social knowledge to anticipate people' behaviour illustrates the approach.

Keywords: Multi-modal traffic · Mixed space · People' behaviour
Social knowledge · Traffic social property
Social-Aware Driver Assistance System

1 Introduction

City traffic is quickly changing worldwide over the last years due to several converging trends. First, growing concerns on pollution and recovering spaces for non-transport uses are leading changes in policies intended to reduce the presence of conventional fuel vehicles [22]. Banning these vehicles from city centers, reducing their lanes, or charging them for parking in streets are some examples of

A. M. J. Skulimowski et al. (Eds.): IOV 2018, LNCS 11253, pp. 133–145, 2018.
https://doi.org/10.1007/978-3-030-05081-8_10

these measures. Second, other means of transport (e.g. bicycles, scooters, or electric cars) are gaining momentum as alternatives. They offer a more individually tailored mobility, meet better users' requirements regarding the environment, health, and costs, and circumvent constraining policies [22].

These trends are creating mixed spaces [16]. There, the traditional segregation of traffic according to the type of vehicle used is blurred, and combined traffic flows appear. Interactions among participants become more complex [18,19], as there is a great variety of perceptions on traffic and the environment, capabilities of vehicles, and people' features and situations.

This context makes necessary that assistance systems enrich the aspects they consider to provide their services. Some information is widely used even in commercial systems, such as traffic signals, lanes, and obstacles [4]. Other aspects only appear in research systems. Among this later group, *social aspects* are information on features of people (e.g. gender and age), their companion (e.g. travelling with different types of passenger), and the resources they use (e.g. different vehicles or mobile phones while driving), that affect people' behaviours in traffic activities. Literature already acknowledges the influence of these aspects (e.g. [20] for pedestrians in groups, [23] for bicycles, or [3] for passengers). However, there is little work on how to incorporate them to assistance aids, and when existing, it usually adopts an ad-hoc approach [4].

The current work develops a framework for Social-Aware Driver Assistance Systems (SADASs) in Vehicle Ad-hoc NETworks (VANETs) that incorporates those social aspects. This information allows to anticipate better how different actors can behave, and thus to improve decision making. The approach has two elements: components that work with social aspects and interact with the rest of the system; means to represent and manage that information.

The SADAS approach introduces those elements by extending a general framework to model Intelligent Transport Systems (ITSs) [9] and its Modelling Language (i.e. the ITSML). It adds to its component model the required *social components*: *converters* transform low-level data from sensors into social information, while *notifiers* use this to send recommendations and actions to the rest of the system; *reasoners* derive new social information from available one. It also adds to the ITSML information model the primitives to represent *social information* and its transformations, and reliability levels to indicate different degrees of certainty of the information. The resulting extension is the SADAS-ML.

The use of social information relies on *traffic social properties* and a pattern matching algorithm among specifications of social information. Properties formalize *social knowledge* on traffic and its transformation with the SADAS-ML. This knowledge is information about social aspects applicable in a wide range of situations, extracted from literature in Social Sciences or observations in specific environments. For instance, that children are prone to make unexpected quick movements. The processing of social information relies on a pattern matching between observed or derived information and descriptions of properties. This is used to check information or produce new one.

A case study about an intelligent warning system for traffic illustrates the approach. It extends the work in [13] on the distributed detection of pedestrians from cars. In it, images allow discovering people around cars and some of their features, and track them [25], e.g. groups, children playing, and bikers. Here, social components use this information to derive new one on people' potential behaviours given their activities. This in turn allows providing more tailored warnings to drivers.

The rest of the paper is organized as follows. Section 2 introduces the background regarding the ITS framework [9]. Then, Sect. 3 describes the components of the SADAS architecture and its traffic social properties. The case study of a distributed obstacle detection system with social knowledge illustrates the approach in Sect. 4. Section 5 compares those results with related work. Finally, Sect. 6 discusses some conclusions on the approach and future work.

2   Background

SADASs appear in the technological context of VANETs. Their components and information models are described using extensions of the general modelling framework for ITSs and their environments in [9].

Its ITSML considers *persons* (some of them in *vehicles*), and an external *environment* (that comprehends *things*) that interact. These elements are sub-classes of the general *place* class. A place is a position for multiple *spots*. A *spot* is both an element that can be observed and where *containers* can be located. Containers are computational nodes for *sensors*, *actuators*, *utilities*, and their controller *managers*. Sensors and actuators interact with the environment, while utilities are pure software components that only work inside an ITS. Communication *channels* link these containers. An ITS comprehends multiple containers and channels.

All the previous elements are specified as *components*. These are characterized by their internal state and a method-based interface. They can also have other components as parts. The state, and the parameters and results of methods, are defined as pieces of *information* with a name, a type, and maybe values for their attributes. Types can be primitive ones or a reference to an already defined type of information. Flows of control and information among components use those methods.

Sensors perceive events from the environment, and use their methods to generate notifications to other components. Managers use available information to check their goals and decide what tasks to attempt. The execution of these tasks invokes methods, that can generate new notifications. Some of these notifications trigger the execution of actuator methods, which act on the environment.

The ITSML specifies this conceptual framework using a metamodel. Metamodels are used to define the abstract syntax of graph-based MLs, i.e. their available primitives and the constraints applicable to them [12]. Working with metamodels facilitates reusing parts of other MLs. Usual primitives available in ML for metamodels include *nodes*, *relationships*, and *roles* (i.e. the ends of the relationships). *Properties* are attributes or adornments of the previous elements. For instance, the numbers in roles that are cardinality indications.

At the level of ITSML diagrams, the language also provides mechanisms for the instantiation of classes. For each type of element in the ML of name *name*, there is another class of name *Iname* that represents its instances at the model level. In this way, only algorithms need to be specified with code.

In next diagrams and in the vein of the Unified Modelling Language (UML) [21], relationships with triangles represent inheritance, and those with diamonds represent aggregation, with filled diamonds for composition and hollow diamonds for mere aggregation. Elements can be located in packages, and their fully qualified name includes that package name. For instance, "ITS" for the ITSML.

3   SADASs

The SADAS approach pursues that driver assistants get a better understanding of the situation around their vehicles by incorporating social knowledge. A SADAS interprets the actual observations from sensors using that knowledge to derive additional information. This extra information can include people' features, how they are moving, and the kind of activity they are performing and with whom. With it, the system can infer what interactions are expected with surrounding people in the near future.

Next sections describe the main aspects of a SADAS. Section 3.1 shows the use of social information to reason on traffic. Section 3.2 discusses its architecture based on the ITS framework (see Sect. 2).

3.1   Social Information for Traffic

SADASs need elements to represent social information and its processing rules. They are described with the SADAS-ML, which is an extension of the ITSML.

The focus is currently on two groups of social aspects that affect speed and risk perception when moving [17]. First, the individual features of age, gender, and vehicle used if any; second, movement in groups. Figure 1 shows the specific concepts in the SADAS-ML to manage this information. They are sub-types of the ITSML *information*, as they represent information on elements of an ITS.

The class *object* represents an element with a unique *id* in a given *position* in the space. The *near* relationship allows indicating proximity among positions.

Additionally, *mobile objects* have associated a *movement*. It includes a *speed* to indicate its direction and module, a *maneuverability* to indicate its ability to change direction, and a *fastness* to describe its potential fastest speed. As sub-types of the mobile object appear the *person* and *vehicle* (e.g. *car*, *bicycle*, and *scooter*). People can travel in vehicles as drivers or passengers. They can also move together in *groups*.

Traffic information is specified using these types (e.g. *person* or *gender*) and values for their attributes when there are constraints on them. For instance, a type of *person* without a value for *gender* corresponds to instances of any gender,

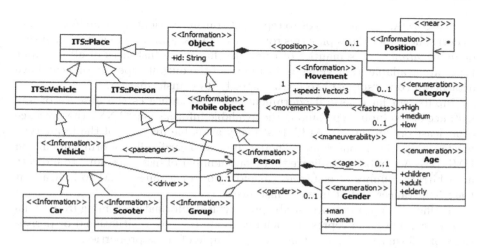

Fig. 1. Partial SADAS-ML specification with its elements to specify information. Elements from package "ITS" belong to the ITSML [9].

but with a value, only to instances of that specific gender. As a convention, specific values are written with their literal, and variable names start with an underscore. For instance, a variable _GENDER can be used to specify that two types of *person* have different *gender* values.

Observations from vehicle sensors provide evidences to categorize surrounding objects under the previous classes, and assign to them the related attribute values. For instance, a person walking alone with a speed below the average (i.e. *fastness low*) may suggest an elderly person (i.e. *age elderly*) or somebody with mobility impairments [17].

All the previous information types also include two more types of attributes. Tags to characterize them, and reliability attributes to describe the level of confidence in their information.

Objects can have attached an arbitrary number of string *tags*. For instance, they allow describing an object as a traffic signal or a hospital.

Information has also assigned three attributes that help to evaluate its reliability, and this can prioritize decisions based on them. *Certainty* considers how sure is regarded the information. It can be *high, medium,* or *low. Source* is intended to distinguish between *observed* and *derived* information. For instance, the distance to an obstacle offered by a sensor is *observed*, while the identification of an object as a scooter rider from its speed is *derived. Scheduling* distinguishes between *current, foreseen,* and *stale* information. Current information is applicable at the current moment, foreseen is expected to be in the future, and stale was applicable or foreseen in the past but no longer. For instance, an observed group of people moving regularly following paths are current information, the expectation that they continue moving that way is foreseen, and when they disappear from images, the information on their expected position will become stale after some time.

The SADAS-ML also needs to represent transformations of social information to derive new one. *Rules* play this role. A rule takes as input and generates pieces of *information*. The semantics of rules are that when instances of all its input types are available, they generate instances of the output types. A rule can have attached a code "snippet" to further specify its transformation.

Inputs can have several adornments. "NOT" indicates the absence of any instance of the input type among the available information; "ANY" the presence of at least one instance; "ALL" that every available instance of the input type meets the specified constraints. There can be also cardinality adornments like in UML [21]. A number to indicate that exact number of instances, an * to indicate an arbitrary number of instances (including 0), or a range N..M to indicate at least N instances and at most M instances.

Traffic social properties describe prototypical information coming from social knowledge. They can represent social contexts (i.e. given situations) or derivations of information. Figure 2 shows an example of these properties.

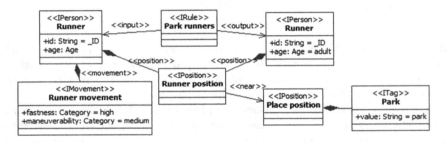

Fig. 2. Rule to derive person information from observations in a park environment.

The property considers driving near a park. There, one *person Runner* is observed moving *fast* (over the average speed). That person must be probably a children or a runner. The first one is expected to have a high *maneuverability* (thus making unexpected changes in speed and address), while the second one has a medium one (thus changes in address are slower). Since in this case the movement seems regular, the rule derives that the *person* is probably a *runner* of *age adult*.

The previous diagram shows instances that can correspond to different actual pieces of information. For instance, when the property is triggered is because the sensors detected an actual object (the current instance) that was identified as an example of the type *person* with certain movement. Following the conventions of the ITSML, the SADAS-ML diagrams use for every type *name* the stereotype *Iname* to represent its instances.

The variable *_ID* in the *runner id* attribute allows indicating that the rule modifies an instance. As the *id* value is unique among all known instances, the input and output instances of *person* are the same.

3.2 Architecture

The integration of social information in assistance systems requires components to interact with the rest of the system and manipulate that information. Figure 3 shows these and related components. Following the ITSML, the new components are *utilities* (i.e. software components that do not interact with the external environment), as there are already sensors and actuators that play that role.

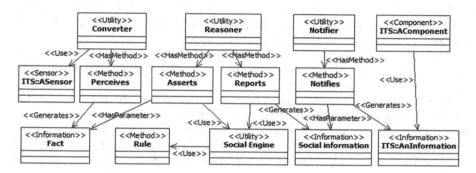

Fig. 3. Specific components in the SADAS architecture. Components from package "ITS" correspond to the ITS framework [9].

Converters manage the interaction with sensors, and transform their observations into SADAS-ML facts. They have *perceives* methods (from the ITSML) that implement that transformation. These facts are representations of instances conform to the SADAS-ML.

Those facts are sent to the *reasoner* using its *asserts* methods, which add them into the base of the *social engine*. The engine is a resource *utility* that implements a rule-based engine and facts base. It carries out the derivation of new information with rules. Then, the interpreter uses its *reports* methods to read that base and extract the *information* for the *notifiers*.

Notifiers use their *notifies* methods to transform SADAS-ML facts into suitable formats for the rest of the assistance system. They have also *consult* methods to support information requests to the *reasoner*.

This design aims at facilitating the flexible management of information. The rule-based approach in the core components of the reasoners allows changing the used social knowledge by merely modifying the included traffic social properties. Changing the information received from or sent to the rest of the system requires modifying converters and notifiers. Their transformations to and from the SADAS-ML are coded. Nevertheless, as they are tailored to specific transformations (e.g. certain types of sensors), they can be reused among systems.

4 Case Study: Distributed Obstacle Detection

The case study develops a SADAS that extends the distributed system for pedestrian detection from cars described in [13]. The proposed system uses social information to anticipate potential actions of surrounding people, and thus proposing specific warning measures for them, either for the driver or the external person.

The original system [13] considers cars equipped with several sensors. Using techniques of image processing and information fusion, each car is able to detect pedestrians. A pedestrian is characterised as a *track* that includes the time, position, and speed. Cars are able to communicate this information to other nearby cars in order to reduce accidents caused by pedestrian occlusion.

The SADAS uses social knowledge to consider obstacles beyond pedestrians, e.g. bicycles and scooters. It also pursues anticipating their potential next positions according to their features and activities.

The architecture of this SADAS is very close to the generic one (see Sect. 3.2). There are two groups of components: those from the original system; and the new ones added for the SADAS.

The original components are represented by the *utility tracker* and the *communication manager*. In the general SADAS architecture (see Fig. 3), they respectively correspond to the *ASensor* element that provides input to the SADAS, and the *AComponent* element that provides the output of the SADAS to the rest of the system. The tracker integrates the information from multiples sensors and manages the actual observed previous detections. It uses and generates *track information*. The manager takes SADAS derived *track information* on expected future positions, and notifies this information to other vehicles using ITS *channels*. It also receives this kind of information from other managers. This allows the detection system to track obstacles over time around the VANET of cars.

Following the architecture for SADAS, there are also new components: a *converter*, a *reasoner* with its *social engine*, and a *notifier*. The converter takes the observed *track* information from the tracker and provides to the social engine as an *observed* fact (which corresponds to the *fact* in Fig. 3). The notifier takes the new derived track information labelled as *foreseen* and provides it to the *communication manager*.

Note that from the point of view of the original components, the only modification regarding information is the difference between observed and derived tracks. The first ones reproduce the original observations, and the second ones are derived from social knowledge.

In order to get more information from tracks, the rule base of the social engine includes traffic social properties. In this case, it uses the property about runners in parks seen previously (see Sect. 3.1) and two other about groups (see Fig. 4) and means of transport (see Fig. 5).

The first property (see Fig. 4) considers a group of people moving together. This information comes from the original system as multiple track observations. The SADAS considers that a group appears when tracks of several individuals have a close position (e.g. less than one meter) and move within that range for at least some time (e.g. three minutes).

After identifying a group, properties allow distinguishing different potential types of group. The rule considers the description of a *tourist group*. Such groups

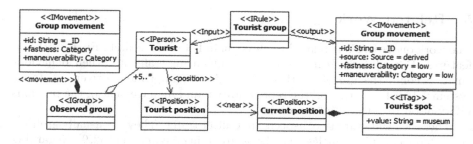

Fig. 4. Rule to derive group information from observations in a tourist spot.

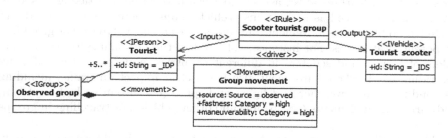

Fig. 5. Rule to derive information on used vehicles from observations.

move *near* cultural facilities (e.g. museums and palaces) and are large (over 5 persons). They are expected (i.e. *source derived*) to move regularly (i.e. *maneuverability low*) and with low speeds (i.e. *fastness low*).

The second property (see Fig. 5) considers that, if observations show that a group of tourist is moving fast, they can be using electric scooters to take a walk. This could be represented associating them instances of that type of vehicle.

The previous information allows making more precise expectations on movements around the cars in the original system. Instead of just considering the actual information, the expected *maneuverability* and *fastness* of an obstacle can determine a safety area around it. For instance, the runner will have a rectangular safety area, larger in front of her/him; on the contrary, children will have circular areas around them, though with a radius shorter than the distance in front of the runner as their highest speed is lower. In the case of scooters assigned to groups, safety areas will be round and with a higher radius.

In this case, the information exchanged among the SADASs of cars is reduced to the tracks extended with the safety areas. Nevertheless, as people move closer to different cars belonging to the VANET, their related social information could also migrate to other car SADASs. This would allow using already observed or derived information in other cars.

5   Related Work

The work on SADASs is related to three main fields of research. First, works on features of people and their environment influencing traffic and their behaviour on it. Second, the use of all this information to implement driver assistance systems. Third, research on the representation and management of the previous information to get new information.

There is a wide variety of aspects that affect traffic. They are usually grouped as related to people, vehicles, and the surrounding environment [2,9]. Regarding people is common considering age and gender [17] or socio-economic [15] characteristics. These features affect aspects like risk perception and taking, response time, or moving speed as pedestrians. Vehicles largely determine the speed and maneuverability of the movement, but also affect people' behaviour or give hints on potential attitudes. For instance, [24] studied the personality traits of usual riders of bicycle and scooters in different countries, and [23] factors affecting the riding itself. The environment also has a clear impact on traffic, including its conditions (e.g. weather and light) and space (e.g. urban or highway) [14], and surrounding elements (e.g. people and other vehicles, or travelling in groups [3,20]).

Though all those aspects can be relevant for traffic, assistance systems only consider some of them [4]. These systems mainly use information on the driving area (e.g. type of road), environmental conditions (e.g. rain and light), and surrounding obstacles (i.e. position, speed and size). There are works on abstraction and fusion of information to allow more complex systems [7]. However, when considered at the level of driving, they focus on low-level sensor processing (e.g. multiple vision techniques to track obstacles). Other architectures relying on notify-observe patterns [8] are not widely used in the area. The distributed system for pedestrian detection in [13] is an example of such efforts, though the actual mechanism to report information between cars is not discussed. Social aspects only appear when considering problems affecting to traffic in wider areas, like incident detection or traffic forecasting and demand estimation [7].

As pointed out before, the use of this information is assistance systems happens usually at a low-level of abstraction. It is highly dependant on the specific algorithms that use them. For instance, systems based on artificial vision use raw images. Abstraction is limited, frequently to bounding boxes and speeds as in [13]. Some works have considered the use of more abstract representations of information. For instance, [5] use rules to adjust image processing, or [6] to control traffic signals. More general representations (e.g. key-value tuples [1]) have been proposed also for context-aware systems. They offer higher flexibility, but have the disadvantage of lacking specific methods for knowledge management, so these must be developed according to the problem needs. Nevertheless, these works do not apply these mechanisms like in SADASs to vehicle driving and reasoning on social aspects.

Regarding the representation of this information using MLs, there is little work on the area. The ITSML [9] has been used to study infrastructures like smart roads [11] using simulations, and also in the context of model-driven development for integration with other systems [10]. These uses have not dealt with social information like in the SADAS approach.

6   Conclusions

This paper has presented an approach called SADAS to develop driver assistance systems that consider social aspects. This information is used to get a better understanding of the context around traffic (e.g. activities in progress and limitations of surrounding people and vehicles) from observations. All this available information is used in turn to deduce actual movement constraints and anticipate potential next events.

SADASs rely on two main elements. A set of social components allows extending common driver assistance systems to integrate social aspects. A SADAS-ML allows specifying social information and its transformation rules. The ML is an extension of the ITSML for the specification and simulation of ITSs.

The SADAS-ML is focused on social information related to individual features, travel companion, vehicles and positions. Its rules allow defining transformations from input to output instances of that information.

The actual use of SADAS-ML information relies on a pattern matching algorithm. It identifies in the available information instances of the searched information. For this, it compares the types of information, and the classes and values of their attributes.

A case study on the extension of a distributed pedestrian detection system [13] illustrated the use of SADASs. Social information allowed deriving information on potential activities and the vehicles used by surrounding people, which in turn was used to determine better the potential area of their movements.

The SADAS approach has still several open issues. First, sensors can provide additional observations to integrate as social information, e.g. regarding weather or lighting. Moreover, smart cities are deploying a variety of sensors that could be also integrated in these systems, like cameras or presence sensors in traffic lights. Second, additional sources of information can help to better identify some social contexts. For instance, authorities publish local events (e.g. accidents, traffic congestions, or concerts). Third, the SADAS-ML has to be enriched in order to consider additional information (e.g. impairments or use of devices) and facilitate the specification of rules, reducing the need to resort to code snippets. This would allow addressing the description of other social settings. Fourth, the approach needs to be tested in additional case studies, in particular extending systems beyond vehicles.

Acknowledgment. This work has been done in the context of the projects "RISE Women with disabilities In Social Engagement (RISEWISE)" (grant 690874) supported by the European Commission in the Horizon 2020 programme, "Collaborative Ambient Assisted Living Design (ColoSAAL)" (grant TIN2014-57028-R) and "Research Thematic Network on Smart Cities" (grant TIN2016-81766-REDT) supported by the Spanish Ministry for Economy, Industry, and Competitiveness, MOSI-AGIL-CM (grant S2013/ICE-3019) supported by the Autonomous Region of Madrid and co-funded by

EU Structural Funds FSE and FEDER, and the "Programa de Creación y Consolidación de Grupos de Investigación" (UCM-BSCH GR35/10-A).

References

1. Alfonso-Cendón, J., Fernández-de Alba, J.M., Fuentes-Fernández, R., Pavón, J.: Implementation of context-aware workflows with multi-agent systems. Neurocomputing **176**, 91–97 (2016)
2. Amditis, A., Pagle, K., Joshi, S., Bekiaris, E.: Driver-vehicle-environment monitoring for on-board driver support systems: lessons learned from design and implementation. Appl. Ergon. **41**(2), 225–235 (2010)
3. Baxter, J.S., Manstead, A.S., Stradling, S.G., Campbell, K.A., Reason, J.T., Parker, D.: Social facilitation and driver behaviour. Br. J. Psychol. **81**(3), 351–360 (1990)
4. Bengler, K., Dietmayer, K., Farber, B., Maurer, M., Stiller, C., Winner, H.: Three decades of driver assistance systems: review and future perspectives. IEEE Intell. Transp. Syst. Mag. **6**(4), 6–22 (2014)
5. Cucchiara, R., Piccardi, M., Mello, P.: Image analysis and rule-based reasoning for a traffic monitoring system. In: Proceedings of 1999 IEEE/IEEJ/JSAI International Conference on Intelligent Transportation Systems, pp. 758–763. IEEE (1999)
6. Dion, F., Hellinga, B.: A rule-based real-time traffic responsive signal control system with transit priority: application to an isolated intersection. Transp. Res. Part B: Methodol. **36**(4), 325–343 (2002)
7. El Faouzi, N.E., Leung, H., Kurian, A.: Data fusion in intelligent transportation systems: progress and challenges-a survey. Inf. Fusion **12**(1), 4–10 (2011)
8. Fernández-De-Alba, J.M., Fuentes-Fernández, R., Pavón, J.: Architecture for management and fusion of context information. Inf. Fusion **21**, 100–113 (2015)
9. Fernández-Isabel, A., Fuentes-Fernández, R.: Analysis of intelligent transportation systems using model-driven simulations. Sensors **15**(6), 14116–14141 (2015)
10. Fernández-Isabel, A., Fuentes-Fernández, R.: An integrative modelling language for agent-based simulation of traffic. IEICE Trans. Inf. Syst. **E99–D**(2), 406–414 (2016)
11. Fernández-Isabel, A., Fuentes-Fernández, R.: Extending a generic traffic model to specific agent platform requirements. Comput. Sci. Inf. Syst. **14**(1), 219–237 (2017)
12. France, R., Rumpe, B.: Model-driven development of complex software: a research roadmap. In: 2007 Future of Software Engineering, pp. 37–54. IEEE Computer Society (2007)
13. García, F., Jiménez, F., Anaya, J.J., Armingol, J.M., Naranjo, J.E., de la Escalera, A.: Distributed pedestrian detection alerts based on data fusion with accurate localization. Sensors **13**(9), 11687–11708 (2013)
14. Golob, T.F., Recker, W.W.: Relationships among urban freeway accidents, traffic flow, weather, and lighting conditions. J. Transp. Eng. **129**(4), 342–353 (2003)
15. Goodman, A.: Walking, cycling and driving to work in the english and welsh 2011 census: trends, socio-economic patterning and relevance to travel behaviour in general. PloS one **8**(8), e71790 (2013)
16. Hamilton-Baillie, B.: Shared space: reconciling people, places and traffic. Built Environ. **34**(2), 161–181 (2008)

17. Holland, C., Hill, R.: The effect of age, gender and driver status on pedestrians intentions to cross the road in risky situations. Accid. Anal. Prev. **39**(2), 224–237 (2007)
18. van der Horst, A.R.A., de Goede, M., de Hair-Buijssen, S., Methorst, R.: Traffic conflicts on bicycle paths: a systematic observation of behaviour from video. Accid. Anal. Prev. **62**, 358–368 (2014)
19. Kaparias, I., Bell, M.G., Miri, A., Chan, C., Mount, B.: Analysing the perceptions of pedestrians and drivers to shared space. Transp. Res. Part F: Traffic Psychol. Behav. **15**(3), 297–310 (2012)
20. Moussaïd, M., Perozo, N., Garnier, S., Helbing, D., Theraulaz, G.: The walking behaviour of pedestrian social groups and its impact on crowd dynamics. PloS one **5**(4), e10047 (2010)
21. OMG: OMG Unified Modeling Language (OMG UML), Version 2.5.1, December 2017. http://www.omg.org/. Accessed 1 July 2018
22. Rode, P., et al.: Accessibility in cities: transport and urban form. In: Meyer, G., Shaheen, S. (eds.) Disrupting Mobility. LNM, pp. 239–273. Springer, Cham (2017). https://doi.org/10.1007/978-3-319-51602-8_15
23. Terzano, K.: Bicycling safety and distracted behavior in the Hague, the Netherlands. Accid. Anal. Prev. **57**, 87–90 (2013)
24. Yao, L., Wu, C.: Traffic safety for electric bike riders in China: attitudes, risk perception, and aberrant riding behaviors. Transp. Res. Rec. **2314**(1), 49–56 (2012)
25. Yazdi, M., Bouwmans, T.: New trends on moving object detection in video images captured by a moving camera: a survey. Comput. Sci. Rev. **28**, 157–177 (2018)

Development of a Mobile Functional Near-Infrared Spectroscopy Prototype

Nils Volkening[1](✉), Anirudh Unni[2], Jochem W. Rieger[2],
Sebastian Fudickar[3], and Andreas Hein[1]

[1] OFFIS Institute for Information Technology, 26121 Oldenburg, Germany
{nils.volkening,andreas.hein}@offis.de
[2] Applied Neurocognitive Psychology Lab, University of Oldenburg,
26111 Oldenburg, Germany
{anirudh.unni,jochem.rieger}@uni-oldenburg.de
[3] Division of Assistance Systems and Medical Device Technology,
University of Oldenburg, 26111 Oldenburg, Germany
sebastian.fudickar@uni-oldenburg.de

Abstract. Driving is a complex and cognitively demanding task. It is important to assess the cognitive state of the driver in order to develop cognitive technical systems that can adapt to different cognitive states of the driver. For this purpose, we have developed a mobile functional near-infrared spectroscopy (mofNIRS) prototype. This paper describes the improvements of this mobile prototype with freely placeable optodes on a subject's head and the results of an evaluation study. We conducted a motor cortex experiment with four subjects, whereby the mobile prototype was mounted on the right hemisphere and a commercial, stationary fNIRS on the left hemisphere above the motor cortex area. One data set had to be discarded due to incorrect synchronization between both systems. The results of the remaining three subjects are presented and discussed in this paper. Here, we report the results from the time-series and Statistical Parametric Mapping (SPM) analyses, which shows t-values with high differentiability of the Results. Furthermore, both analysis methods show comparable results between the commercial system and the mobile prototype.

Keywords: Mobile fNIRS prototype · Motor cortical activity
Validation study · Driver cognitive states

1 Introduction

The degree of automation in vehicles is continuously increasing [6]. Many assistive systems have been introduced in the last decade that provide specific information to the driver and reduce their cognitive workload. For example, navigation systems provide important information to the driver, anti-lock braking systems stabilize the car in the event of a safety-critical situation and cruise control supports speed regulation [14]. However, the information channel between the driver and the assistive system is unidirectional, as most of these systems receive little or no information regarding the driver's internal state or goals.

© Springer Nature Switzerland AG 2018
A. M. J. Skulimowski et al. (Eds.): IOV 2018, LNCS 11253, pp. 146–161, 2018.
https://doi.org/10.1007/978-3-030-05081-8_11

1.1 Critical Systems Engineering for Socio-Technical Systems

The aim of our project 'Critical Systems Engineering for Socio–Technical Systems' (CSE) is to integrate humans in the control loop of socio-technical systems. The subproject 'The Car that Cares' (CTC) is responsible for the automotive domain. The overall objective of CTC is to develop processes, techniques and software tools to enable the development of socio-technical car systems, that offer situation-aware cooperative interaction with the driver of the car. This means that in CTC, the driver should become a part of the control loop so that assistive systems will receive feedback of different driver states e.g. cognitive states. Therefore, a mobile fNIRS prototype was developed and tested as part of the CTC project.

The results of the first evaluation study looked promising [30], but there were still many problems and improvements to be tested. In this paper, we present the extended hardware of the mofNIRS prototype and the results of a successive evaluation study. First, we will briefly introduce the physiological and physical properties as well as the biological processes that functional near-infrared spectroscopy makes possible in the first place. Subsequently, we will examine the current state of the art in the field of fNIRS. Section 4 describes the hardware used and the test setup in more detail. Afterwards we will present the results and discuss them in detail in Sect. 6. At the end of the paper, there is a summary and an outlook on the next steps.

2 Fundamentals

The fNIRS is a non-invasive method for the imaging of brain activity [28], by measuring the relative concentration changes in oxyhemoglobin (HbO) and deoxyhemoglobin (HbR) in the blood. For a validation of the mofNIRS prototype, the motor cortex along with the primary motor cortex and pre-motor cortex are particularly suitable. On the one hand, this region is very close to the scalp tissue, making it easily accessible for optical measurements [13, 19] and produces clearly distinguishable and strong signals. On the other hand, this area of the head is normally covered with a lot of hair and placement of the optodes could be challenging.

2.1 Physiological Context

When neural activity is elicited, it results in stronger blood circulation in the corresponding cortex area. This is referred to as neurovascular coupling or hemodynamic response and can be measured by a corresponding increase in HbO with a simultaneous decrease in HbR concentration [31]. However, there is a latency of several seconds between neuronal activity and the hemodynamic response, which is also reflected in the fNIRS imaging [23]. Few seconds after the end of the neuronal activity, the blood flow decreases slowly and the HbO and HbR concentration changes return to the base level.

2.2 Physical Context

With oxygen binding the color of the hemoglobin changes, for example, HbO has a lighter shade of red than HbR [17] due to the conformational change of the iron ion, which means that both variants also have a different absorption maximum (HbO at approximately 760 nm, HbR at approximately 850 nm) which is used in the fNIRS [34]. To convert the change in absorption to relative concentration changes of HbO and HbR respectively, the modified Beer-Lambert law is used [24, 29].

3 State of the Art

NIRS is a non-invasive, safe technique [12] for the optical recording of brain activity [9, 21]. FNIRS provides finer temporal information and a better image of cortical hemodynamic activity compared to functional magnetic resonance imaging (fMRI) [10]. FNIRS is also less susceptible to motion artifacts and represents a comparatively insignificant physical limitation for the subjects [5, 8], or allows for greater mobility [2] compared to fMRI. However, Tachtsidis et al. and Cohen et al. showed that the individual blood circulation of the headache and changes in blood pressure and heart rate can lead to false positive fNIRS signals [7, 26]. In addition, fNIRS has a lower signal-to-noise ratio (SNR) than fMRI [8], and there is also a risk of motion artifacts in optodes, due to the weight of the fiber optic cables [22]. Most experimental setups still offer a spatially limited frame [11, 18]. Therefore, fNIRS development is moving in the direction of miniature probes as well as wireless devices [32]. Recently, there has been a tendency to increase the number of channels to allow higher resolution tomographic imaging [11, 16] and to allow for greater coverage of one or more areas of the head [20]. But one of the main reasons to increase the number of channels is to achieve short channel separation which allow us to measure extra-cortical activity (e.g. muscle activity) [15, 25, 33] and possibly reduce the influence of extra-cortical signals from cortical brain activation measurements.

4 Methods

4.1 Subjects

In this study, fNIRS brain activation was measured from four healthy volunteers (1 female/3 male) aged 22 to 27 years, while carrying out grip movements with the hands using hand-held strength trainers. The subjects were informed about the procedure prior to the measurement. None of the subjects took medication or had a history of cardiovascular, neurological or psychiatric diseases. The motor functions of both upper extremities were not restricted at the time of the examination. The experimental set-up was approved by the Ethics committee of the Carl von Ossietzky University of Oldenburg (Drs 14/2016) and complied with the Helsinki Declaration. We obtained written consent for the storage and publication of data from all subjects.

4.2 Motor Cortex Study-Design

The subjects were measured with both the commercial fNIRS (cofNIRS) and mofNIRS devices simultaneously, with the cofNIRS having coverage of the left motor area and the mofNIRS having coverage over the right motor area. The data were processed with the nirsLAB 2017.6 toolbox [33]. The subjects were sitting in front of a computer screen, whose brightness was adapted to the darkened environment. The distance from the screen was about 70 cm. First, the baseline brain activity was recorded for 2 min during which the subjects relaxed with their eyes closed. After notification by an employee, the actual measurement began. The instructions (right hand, rest, left hand, rest) were displayed on the screen via a MATLAB script using Psychtoolbox [4]. The subjects had to complete a total of 30 sets. Each set was structured as follows: hand strength exercises with the right hand for 15 s and a 15 s level out phase. This was followed by a rest period for 30 s and then 15 s hand strength exercises with the left followed by another 15 s level out and 30 s resting phase (2 min in total). At the end of the measurement, there was a 2-min rest period. The total duration of the measurements was 64 min. During the experiment, the subjects were measured with both fNIRS devices simultaneously to ensure that the conditions for data collection by both systems were as equal as possible and to register potential changes, delays or errors by the subjects in carrying out the experiment with both devices. The sources and detectors were placed in a standard 10–20 layout (Fig. 1) by means of a standard fNIRS cap. To ensure that the cap was placed in a reliable way across all participants, we checked if the position of the optode holder on the fNIRS cap for the anatomical location Cz on the midline sagittal plane of the skull is equidistant to the nasion and the inion and equidistant to the ears. Before the optodes were plugged into the cap at their respective locations (cf. Fig. 1), transparent gel was applied locally on the corresponding scalp location to reduce the refractive index between scalp and the optode's glass fiber. This also made it easier to push the hair towards the sides, so that the optode comes in direct contact with the scalp. The mofNIRS was placed over the right motor area and mainly recorded the influence of motor activation of the left hand. The cofNIRS was placed on the left motor area and mainly recorded the influence of motor activation of the right hand. In the following sections, the main cortical activities considered for both systems are referred to as contralateral activity, i.e. in case of the mobile prototype, cortical activity of the right motor area or the left hand and for the cofNIRS, cortical activity of the left motor area or the right hand. The experiment was carried out in a darkened, acoustically shielded room. The raw data were recorded at a sampling frequency of 7.81 Hz with the cofNIRS, and approximately 5.34 Hz with the mofNIRS. Both devices were synchronized by 3 trigger signals (right hand/left hand/rest phase) which were output by the MATLAB script via a parallel port. To process the data uniformly, the data from the mobile prototype was converted by means of a Python script into the file format of the cofNIRS and then processed further with the analysis package of the program nirsLAB 2017.6, so that the following analysis steps are the same for the mofNIRS and the cofNIRS.

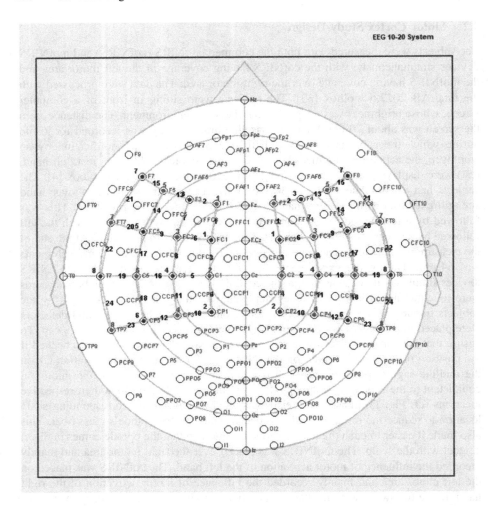

Fig. 1. Schematic picture of the placement of the optodes on a head (Red: Sources, Blue: Detectors) and the channel numbers (numbers on the green lines). (Color figure online)

4.3   Mobile FNIRS Prototype

The mofNIRS prototype is made of four main components: digital detectors, sources, daughterboard and mainboard, a detailed description of the hardware could be found in [30]. In this paper, we provide a rough overview over all components and a detailed description of the improvement, compared to the first version.

Digital Detectors: The detectors are self-developed digital detectors, i.e., each detector carries out its own A/D conversion and the motherboard can read the digital value directly. A Si photodiode is used as a receiver and its output is amplified transimpedance amplifier with a gain of 120 dB. The generated voltage is then converted by a 16bit A/D converter. During the first evaluation [30], we had some stability problems, in terms of movement or loosening of the optodes over time. Therefore, we add a little skirt (indicated by black arrow in Fig. 2B) around the original housing of the detectors, which delivered new fixation points for a second cap. This cap was made of elastic rubber cords and an adjustable plastic holder on each side (see Fig. 2) and placed over the standard fNIRS cap.

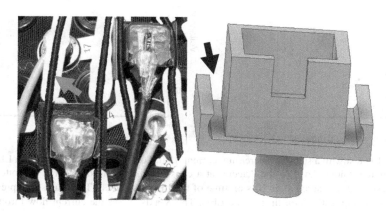

Fig. 2. A: Detail view of the cap with mounted detectors and sources and the additional cap of rubber bands (red arrow) to fixate the detectors; B: Schematic drawing of the new detector housing with the small skirt (black arrow) to hold the rubber bands for a better stability (Color figure online)

Sources: Dual-wavelength light emitting diodes (LEDs) (760 nm/850 nm) are used as sources. Each LED has a continuous current limit of 60 mA and a maximum pulse current rating of 100 mA regarding the datasheet. During the first evaluation we had a very low signal strength and to the fact that we could not easily increase our amplification and the commercial LED emitted twice as bright as our LED, we try to increase the brightness of the LEDs. Therefore, a test was performed how much current our LEDs could handle without causing damage and how the brightness evolved respectively. Therefore, an experiment was performed, where the maximum current flow through the LED was raised stepwise by 10 mA increments. One detector recorded the increasing brightness. The source and detector were attached to a reference tube, which is approximately 5 cm long and has an opaque inner core to absorb and scatter the light and an aluminum shell to reduce the influence of ambient light. As shown in Fig. 3, for the 760 nm LED and the 850 nm LED, both LEDs have a linear increase of brightness up to 140 mA. As the current increases, a flattening of the curve can be seen, which indicates that the LED chip heats up too much and thus loses efficiency and may be damaged. In a pulse mode (max 200 ms duty cycle), an approximate increase in linear brightness up to 190 mA (760 nm) or, 200 mA (850 nm) could be measured. Since only two LED drivers are installed on the daughterboard, an increase to maximum of 120 mA per LED can be achieved without hardware modifications and by parallel operation of the two LED drivers.

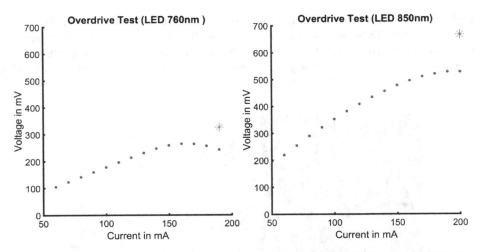

Fig. 3. LED test with a stepwise increasing current. Left: 760 nm LED, Right: 850 nm LED. On the Y-axis the voltage level of the detector at a constant distance to the source is plotted. The voltage level was measured after 10 s on time of the LED (red dots). The blue star represents a measurement after 200 ms on time of the LED. The X-axis shows the current flow through the LEDs. (Color figure online)

Daughter Board: In order to control the detectors and sources, a daughter board has been developed, which provides connections for up to 16 detectors and 8 sources. Two LED drivers are used to control the brightness of the LEDs. The current can be adjusted in 255 steps from 0 mA to 60 mA. During the first evaluation, we found that the signal strength was too low for reliable results. To increase the output power of the LEDs, we constructed Y-Cable, so that one LED could be plugged to one output of each LED driver. Therefore, we achieved a maximum output current of 120 mA per source. The LEDs can be plugged into the daughter board with simple Y-Cable with two 3-pin Molex connectors.

Main Board: The daughter board is connected to a Beagle-Board Black, which is the main board. External communication takes place via LAN, WLAN or serial data transmission. It also has a micro-SD card slot which is used as local memory for the measurement data. The operating system used is an Internet of Things (IoT) version of Linux Debian 9 without the graphical user interface (GUI). The housings of the optodes for the mofNIRS are designed to fit into the same holders as the commercial optodes. This makes it possible to attach both systems side by side to the same cortex regions.

4.4   Block Averaging of the Time-Series Data

The unfiltered raw times-series data were transformed with the modified Beer-Lambert's law from voltage (V) to relative concentration change in mmol/l of HbR and HbO [24]. The HbO and HbR time-series data were exported to MATLAB via the data export function of nirsLAB 2017.6. The time-series data was z-scored and split into separate blocks (right hand activity, left hand activity and rest phase), according to the timestamps of the trigger device. We also performed a baseline correction for each block, in such a way that we subtracted the first value of each block from the following values in this block. Therefore, each block starts from zero. We then performed a block-averaging of the time-series data.

4.5 SPM Analysis

The statistical parametric mapping (SPM) analysis was performed in nirsLAB 2017.6 software. For the SPM analysis, we also used the unfiltered HbO and HbR data. To reduce effects of movement artifacts and systemic physiology, we used an autoregressive model (AR(n); n_{max} = 30). It is based on autoregressive iteratively reweighted least squares developed by Barker et al. [3] and is implemented in the nirsLAB 2017.6 Toolbox [1, 27]. With the resulting autoregressive coefficients, a pre-whitening filter was generated that was applied to reduce the influence of large outliers caused by movement artifacts and serially correlated noise from the physiological artifacts and the temporal correlation of the time-series data. Pre-whitening can handle such noise correlated time series data where an autoregressive model considers the correlation between the current time sample and its neighboring samples and models the temporal correlations. To characterize the pattern of brain areas involved during left and right-hand activity, we performed univariate regression analyses on a single-subject level separately for each fNIRS channel using the generalized linear model (GLM) analysis of the nirsLAB Toolbox. Our design matrix consisted of three regressors that corresponded to the entire blocks of right-hand, left-hand and rest period. The autoregressive model AR(n) from [3] that generated the pre-whitening filter and was applied to the fNIRS time-series data was also applied to the design matrix, with a weighting of 1 (right hand) −1 (rest) for the computation of the t-values for the right-hand activity and with −1 (rest) 1 (left hand) for the left-hand activity. The results are presented as unthresholded t-value maps (difference: Activity-Rest) from the channel-wise linear regression of HbR and HbO data, which were computed by using nirsLAB,

4.6 Commercial FNIRS

We used the NIRScout Extended system from NIRx Medical Technologies, LLC as a commercial functional near-infrared spectroscope. For this study we used 8 detectors and 8 sources. The LED sources were dual-wavelength LEDs with the two wavelengths 760 nm and 850 nm. The detectors consisted of an extended glass fiber, transmitting the returning light to the detector card without any additional attenuation. In order to increase the SNR, both wavelengths were modulated at two different frequencies (1/1.5 kHz) and the channel separation was achieved by time-division multiplexing.

5 Results

During measurement of the first subject, the trigger device failed and therefore the synchronization between the mofNIRS and the cofNIRS was lost. Therefore, we excluded all measurements of the first subject. For the results from block averaging of time-series data, we present only an exemplary result of a channel with a high t-value for the cofNIRS as well as the mofNIRS for subject 2. Also, in the remaining two subjects, one can find corresponding channels with the same characteristics. For the SPM analysis we present all results for the three subjects.

5.1   Block-Average of the Time-Series Data

In the first step, the time series for the mobile and commercial fNIRS were plotted by using a MATLAB script (as described in Sect. 4.4). Each time series plot shows the relative concentration changes of HbO (red) and HbR (blue) as a mean value over all 30 sets for the activity phase (continuous line) and the following rest phase (dotted line). The standard error is plotted as an error-bar. The block average of subject 2 (see Figs. 4 and 5) for the mofNIRS shows an increase in the HbO concentration during the first 6 to 7 s of activity. Subsequently, a plateau formation up to 17 s can be seen, followed by a slow decrease of the concentration back to the starting level. The concentration of HbR is approximately inverse to the HbO curve. This can be seen both in contralateral activity and somewhat reduced in ipsilateral activity. The concentration of HbO in the ipsilateral activity (Fig. 5) after 30 s still shows a slightly increased level, compared to the start concentration and the concentration of HbR is slightly below the start level. The plot of the following rest-phase doesn't seem to show much concentration changes over the block average.

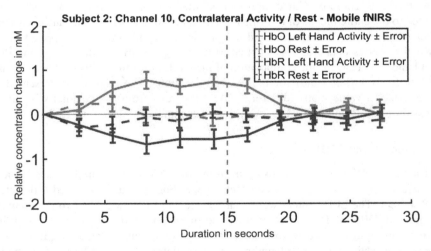

Fig. 4. Block average of the time-series data of the contralateral activity and clear down phase (continuous line) and the following rest phase (dotted line) for the relative concentration change for HbO (red) and HbR (blue). The dotted vertical line shows the end of the activity phase. (Color figure online)

The plots of the block averages of the time-series data for the contralateral and ipsilateral activity of the cofNIRS and the mofNIRS are comparable. There is an increase of the concentration of HbO over the first 6 to7 s after the activity starts and then a plateau formation for the next 10 to 11 s, following by a decrease over the next 4

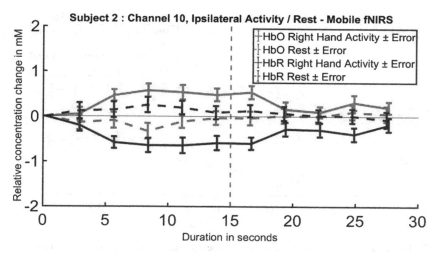

Fig. 5. Block average of the time-series data of the ipsilateral activity and clear down phase (continuous line) and the following rest phase (dotted line) for the relative concentration change for HbO (red) and HbR (blue). The dotted vertical line shows the end of the activity phase. (Color figure online)

to 5 s. But the final concentration level after 30 s is still slightly higher compared to the start concentration. The curve of HbR concentration is nearly inverse to the HbO, as we have seen before from the plot of the mofNIRS. The time series of the following contralateral rest phase is more stable, compared to the first seconds of the of the time series of the mofNIRS, and shows a steady concentration level over the whole 30 s. The time series of the following ipsilateral rest phase shows a relative increase of the HbR and a decrease of the HbO concentration changes over the first 12 s. Afterwards it also reached a plateau for the rest of the 30 s (Figs. 6 and 7).

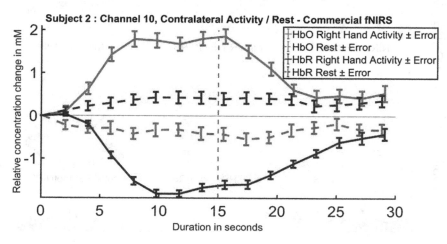

Fig. 6. Block average of the time-series of the contralateral activity and clear down phase (continuous line) and the following rest phase (dotted line) for the relative concentration change for HbO (red) and HbR (blue). The dotted vertical line shows the end of the activity phase. (Color figure online)

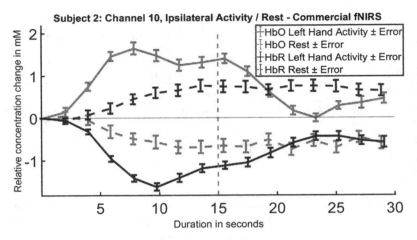

Fig. 7. Block average of the time-series of the ipsilateral activity and clear down phase (continuous line) and the following rest phase (dotted line) for the relative concentration change for HbO (red) and HbR (blue). The dotted vertical line shows the end of the activity phase. (Color figure online)

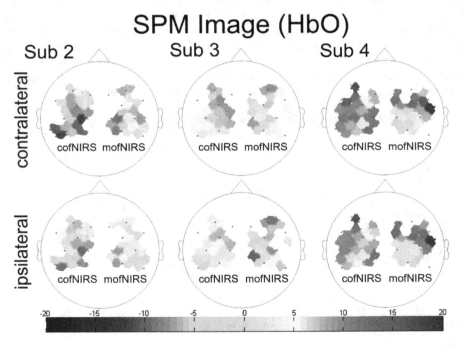

Fig. 8. Results of the SPM analysis from both systems for the HbO data for all subjects. The upper row shows the contralateral activation and the lower row shows the ipsilateral activation. Each colored voxel represents the t-value of a channel. (Color figure online)

5.2 SPM Analysis

In a second step, we performed a SPM analysis as described in Sect. 4.5 to check if any channel shows high differentiability brain activation during the activation phase compared to the rest phase. As mentioned in Sect. 4.2, the cofNIRS was mounted on the left hemisphere and the mofNIRS was mounted on the right hemisphere. The results of both systems for the contralateral and ipsilateral activation for the HbO time series are combined in Fig. 8 and the HbR time series in Fig. 9. Over all subjects and conditions, the cofNIRS has more and higher differentiability brain activation channels as compared to the mofNIRS. Both systems show a comparable local distribution of the t-value within subjects. The distribution of the highest t-values varies between each condition and subject of the HbO results. Thus, the HbO measurements (Fig. 8) of the cofNIRS for subject 2 show the higher values, both for the contralateral activity and for the ipsilateral activity. In the measurement of subject 3, the cofNIRS also has a slightly higher max. t-value for contralateral activity. However, the measurements of the mofNIRS from the ipsilateral activity of subject 3 show higher t-values, as well as for both measurements from the subject 4. Overall, there are a larger number of highly differentiated channels in contralateral activity than in ipsilateral activity.

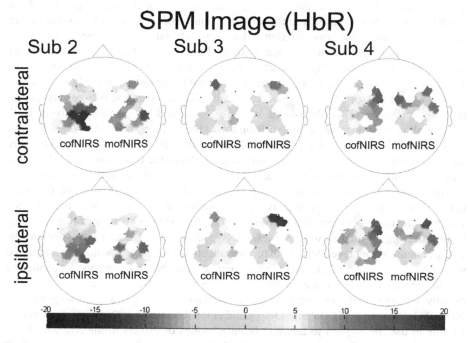

Fig. 9. Results of the SPM analysis from both systems for the HbR data for all subjects. The upper row shows the contralateral activation and the lower row shows the ipsilateral activation. Each colored voxel represents the t-value of a channel. (Color figure online)

For the HbR results, the picture is slightly different, here the cofNIRS shows a higher number of channels with higher discriminability and therefore higher t-values for all measurements, but the local distribution of the t-value within subjects is still comparable.

6   Discussion and Conclusion

The results from the block averaging of the time series as well as the SPM analysis show comparable results between the mobile prototype and the commercial fNIRS. The block averaging shows a few seconds after the start of the activity phase, the concentration of HbO in the region increases and HbR is simultaneously washed out. This effect lasts a few seconds longer than the end of the motor activity and then the concentration of HbO and HbR slowly returns to the baseline. The initial changes in concentration during the rest phase of the mofNIRS can be explained by the fact that the hemodynamic response to the stimulus was so strong that the 15 s of level out phase after the end of the activity was not enough to return to the basic rest concentration and a kind of overshoot occurred. This is also very well visible in the results of the ipsilateral activity at cofNIRS. Here the signal needs about 10 s before it reaches the pre-activity level again. Furthermore, you can see that the signal quality of the mofNIRS is not as good as that of the cofNIRS. The error bars are higher and the space between HbO and HbR concentration is lower, which indicates that the measurement results are less stable, and the dynamic is lower. Nevertheless, the curves of the activity and rest phase are sufficiently far apart. The error margin of both curves overlaps in the 15 s of activity only in the first 5 s, which is normal to the facts that the hemodynamic response has a lack of a few seconds. Afterwards a clear separation between the curves is to be recognized. This observation was also confirmed by the SPM analysis. Both systems show a comparable spatial distribution of the t-values over the covered area for each subject. The results of the SPM analysis for the HbO time-series data has more highly differentiated channels, compared to the results of the HbR time-series data. The reason for this is not yet quite clear and must be clarified in further experiments. Overall, the results look very promising and significantly better than in the first validation study. There is a significantly higher number of usable channels and the raw values of the detectors have also become even higher. This indicates that our measures to improve signal quality were successful. We also did not detect any spontaneous changes in the signal level during the measurements, which indicates that the additional rubber band cap and the added skirts to the optodes, prevents movements or decoupling of the optodes during the measurements. In the first study, this occurred more frequently through slight movements of the subject or through a loosening optode. Nevertheless, there is still potential for optimization, but we hope that soon we will also be able to use this system to measure brain activities of drivers in the real world and confirm the results of our ongoing research [1, 31] in real traffic situations. To confirm the reliability and the correctness of the results of the mofNIRS a larger study has to be carried out.

Acknowledgments. This work was supported by the funding initiative Niedersächsisches Vorab of the Volkswagen Foundation and the Ministry of Science and Culture of Lower Saxony as a part of the Interdisciplinary Research Centre on Critical Systems Engineering for Socio–Technical Systems.

References

1. Anirudh, U., et al.: Brain activity measured with fNIRS for the prediction of cognitive workload. In: 6th IEEE Conference on Cognitive Infocommunications (2015)
2. Atsumori, H., et al.: Development of a multi-channel, portable optical topography system. In: Conference Proceedings: Annual International Conference of the IEEE Engineering in Medicine and Biology Society. IEEE Engineering in Medicine and Biology Society, pp. 3362–3364 (2007)
3. Barker, J.W., Aarabi, A., Huppert, T.J.: Autoregressive model based algorithm for correcting motion and serially correlated errors in fNIRS. Biomed. Opt. Express **4**(8), 1366–1379 (2013)
4. Brainard, D.H.: The psychophysics toolbox. Spat. Vis. **10**(4), 433–436 (1997)
5. Brigadoi, S., Cutini, S., Scarpa, F., Scatturin, P., Dell'Acqua, R.: Exploring the role of primary and supplementary motor areas in simple motor tasks with fNIRS. Cogn. Process. **13**(Suppl 1), S97–S101 (2012)
6. Brookhuis, K.A., De Waard, D., Janssen, W.H.: Behavioural Impacts of Advanced Driver Assistance Systems-an overview (2001)
7. Cohen, I.R., Lajtha, A.: Oxygen Transport to Tissue XXX. Advances in Experimental Medicine and Biology, vol. 645. Springer, Dordrecht (2009). https://doi.org/10.1007/978-0-387-85998-9
8. Cui, X., Bray, S., Bryant, D.M., Glover, G.H., Reiss, A.L.: A quantitative comparison of NIRS and fMRI across multiple cognitive tasks. NeuroImage **54**(4), 2808–2821 (2011)
9. Custo, A., Wells, W.M., Barnett, A.H., Hillman, E.M.C., Boas, D.A.: Effective scattering coefficient of the cerebral spinal fluid in adult head models for diffuse optical imaging. Appl. Opt. **45**(19), 4747–4755 (2006)
10. Cutini, S., Moro, S., Bisconti, S.: Review: functional near infrared optical imaging in cognitive neuroscience: an introductory review. J. Near Infrared Spectrosc. **20**(1), 75–92 (2012)
11. Eggebrecht, A.T., et al.: A quantitative spatial comparison of high-density diffuse optical tomography and fMRI cortical mapping. NeuroImage **61**(4), 1120–1128 (2012)
12. Ferrari, M., Quaresima, V.: A brief review on the history of human functional near-infrared spectroscopy (fNIRS) development and fields of application. NeuroImage **63**(2), 921–935 (2012)
13. Franceschini, M.A., Toronov, V., Filiaci, M., Gratton, E., Fantini, S.: On-line optical imaging of the human brain with 160-ms temporal resolution. Opt. Express **6**(3), 49–57 (2000)
14. Freyman, R.: Möglichkeit und Grenzen von Fahrerassistenz- und Aktiven Sicherheitssystemen. Aktive Sicherheit durch Fahrerassistenz (2004)
15. Goodwin, J.R., Gaudet, C.R., Berger, A.J.: Short-channel functional near-infrared spectroscopy regressions improve when source-detector separation is reduced. Neurophotonics **1**(1), 15002 (2014)

16. Habermehl, C., et al.: Somatosensory activation of two fingers can be discriminated with ultrahigh-density diffuse optical tomography. NeuroImage **59**(4), 3201–3211 (2012)
17. Huppelsberg, J., Walter, K.: Kurzlehrbuch Physiologie. Thieme electronic book library. Thieme, Stuttgart [u.a.] (2009)
18. Krüger, A., et al.: Imaging of motor activity in freely moving subjects using a wearable NIRS imaging system. In: Digital Holography and Three-Dimensional Imaging. Part of Biomedical Optics and 3-D imaging, 28 April–2 May 2012, Miami, Florida, United States. OSA annual topical meeting. OSA technical digest (online). OSA The Optical Society, Washington, DC, BM4A.3 (2012). https://doi.org/10.1364/biomed.2012.bm4a.3
19. Leff, D.R., et al.: Assessment of the cerebral cortex during motor task behaviours in adults. A systematic review of functional near infrared spectroscopy (fNIRS) studies. NeuroImage **54**(4), 2922–2936 (2011)
20. Mehnert, J., et al.: Developmental changes in brain activation and functional connectivity during response inhibition in the early childhood brain. Brain Dev. **35**(10), 894–904 (2013)
21. Okada, E., Delpy, D.T.: Near-infrared light propagation in an adult head model II Effect of superficial tissue thickness on the sensitivity of the near-infrared spectroscopy signal. Appl. Opt. **42**(16), 2915 (2003)
22. Piper, S.K., et al.: A wearable multi-channel fNIRS system for brain imaging in freely moving subjects. Celebrating 20 Years Funct. Near Infrared Spectrosc. (fNIRS) **85**(Pt 1), 64–71 (2014)
23. Roy, C.S., Sherrington, C.S.: On the regulation of the blood-supply of the brain. J. Physiol. **11**(1–2), 85–158 (1890)
24. Sassaroli, A., Fantini, S.: Comment on the modified Beer-Lambert law for scattering media. Phys. Med. Biol. **49**(14), N255–N257 (2004)
25. Schecklmann, M., Mann, A., Langguth, B., Ehlis, A.-C., Fallgatter, A.J., Haeussinger, F.B.: The temporal muscle of the head can cause artifacts in optical imaging studies with functional near-infrared spectroscopy. Front. Hum. Neurosci. **11**, 456 (2017)
26. Tachtsidis, I., Leung, T.S., Devoto, L., Delpy, D.T., Elwell, C.E.: Measurement of frontal lobe functional activation and related systemic effects. A near-infrared spectroscopy investigation. Adv. Exp. Med. Biol. **614**, 397–403 (2008)
27. Tachtsidis, I., Scholkmann, F.: Erratum: publisher's note: false positives and false negatives in functional near-infrared spectroscopy: issues, challenges, and the way forward. Neurophotonics **3**(3), 39–801 (2016)
28. Tak, S., Ye, J.C.: Statistical analysis of fNIRS data. A comprehensive review. NeuroImage **85**(Pt 1), 72–91 (2014)
29. Villringer, A., Planck, J., Hock, C., Schleinkofer, L., Dirnagl, U.: Near infrared spectroscopy (NIRS) A new tool to study hemodynamic changes during activation of brain function in human adults. Neurosci. Lett. **154**(1–2), 101–104 (1993)
30. Volkening, N., Unni, A., Becker, S., Rieger, J.W., Fudickar, S., Hein, A.: Development of a mobile functional near-infrared spectroscopy prototype and its initial evaluation. In: Proceedings of the 11th PErvasive Technologies Related to Assistive Environments Conference on - PETRA 2018, pp. 214–221. ACM Press, New York (2018). https://doi.org/10.1145/3197768.3201534
31. Volkening, N., Unni, A., Löffler, B.S., Fudickar, S., Rieger, J.W., Hein, A.: Characterizing the Influence of Muscle Activity in fNIRS Brain Activation Measurements. IFAC-PapersOnLine **49**(11), 84–88 (2016)
32. Wyser, D., Lambercy, O., Scholkmann, F., Wolf, M., Gassert, R.: Wearable and modular functional near-infrared spectroscopy instrument with multidistance measurements at four wavelengths. Neurophotonics **4**(4), 41413 (2017)

33. Xu, Y., Graber, H.L., Barbour, R.L.: nirsLAB. A computing environment for fNIRS neuroimaging data analysis. In Biomedical Optics, 26–30 April 2014, Miami, Florida, United States. OSA technical digest (online). OSA The Optical Society, Washington, DC, BM3A.1 (2014). https://doi.org/10.1364/biomed.2014.bm3a.1
34. Zijlstra, W.G., Buursma, A., van Assendelft, O.W.: Visible and near infrared absoption spectra of human and animal haemoglobin. Determination and application. VSP, Utrecht (2000)

Vehicular Modelling and Simulation

AMoDSim: An Efficient and Modular Simulation Framework for Autonomous Mobility on Demand

Andrea Di Maria[1], Andrea Araldo[2(✉)] (ID), Giovanni Morana[1],
and Antonella Di Stefano[3]

[1] Aucta Cognitio R&D Labs, 95123 Catania, Italy
{adimaria,gmorana}@auctacognitio.net
[2] Réseaux et Services de Télécommunications, Télécom SudParis, Evry 91011, France
andrea.araldo@telecom-sudparis.eu
[3] Universitá di Catania, 95125 Catania, Italy
ad@dieei.unict.it

Abstract. Urban transportation of next decade is expected to be disrupted by Autonomous Mobility on Demand (AMoD): AMoD providers will collect ride requests from users and will dispatch a fleet of autonomous vehicles to satisfy requests in the most efficient way. Differently from current ride sharing systems, in which driver behavior has a clear impact on the system, AMoD systems will be exclusively determined by the dispatching logic. As a consequence, a recent interest in the Operations Research and Computer Science communities has focused on this control logic. The new propositions and methodologies are generally evaluated via simulation. Unfortunately, there is no simulation platform that has emerged as reference, with the consequence that each author uses her own custom-made simulator, applicable only in her specific study, with no aim of generalization and without public release. This slows down the progress in the area as researchers cannot build on each other's work and cannot share, reproduce and verify the results. The goal of this paper is to present AMoDSim, an open-source simulation platform aimed to fill this gap and accelerate research in future ride sharing systems.

Keywords: Smart mobility · Smart city
Shared mobility · Autonomous vehicles · Simulation

1 Introduction

Transportation is traversing a period of big transformations driven by Information and Communication Technology (ICT). For instance, the ubiquitous connectivity guaranteed by 3G and 4G has triggered the emergence of *ride sharing* services, e.g., Uber and Lyft, in which users reserve a ride through a smartphone app and service providers match them to a fleet of vehicles. Goldman Sachs

A. M. J. Skulimowski et al. (Eds.): IOV 2018, LNCS 11253, pp. 165–178, 2018.
https://doi.org/10.1007/978-3-030-05081-8_12

quantifies the importance of these services by predicting a market of 285 billion dollars in 2030 [11]. In more and more cities, ride sharing services are also determining a transformation of every-day life [12]. This revolution will become even deeper when these services will be provided by Autonomous Vehicles (AVs). Autonomous Mobility on Demand (AMoD) services [8] will be very cheap for the users, since providers will not have to sustain the cost of labor of the drivers.

One reason for the efficiency of these systems is that vehicles can be shared among many users. To do so, efficient and scalable algorithms are needed. While the Vehicle Routing Problem [4] has been studied from the 1950s, the success of ride sharing systems has lead to a renovated interest in this decade, where the problem has been specialized to the case of matching ride requests from passengers to available vehicles, while respecting some constraints on users' waiting and riding time. A particular focus has regarded the computation of condensed vehicle trips to properly aggregate many rides in order to minimize provider's costs while keeping the user quality of level acceptable. The request-vehicle matching problem has been shown to be NP hard [7]. Therefore, a vast literature has developed to propose "good" heuristics with a reasonable computation time to be used in practice and has resorted to simulation to evaluate them. Unfortunately, up to now no reference simulation tool has emerged for this, which is shown by the fact that most of the authors have been forced to build from scratch their own case-specific simulator. The negative consequences are:

- Waste of time and effort, to create every time a simulator.
- Impossibility to build on the effort of past research.
- Difficulty for the community to reproduce and verify results.

On the other side, there are few exceptions of complex transportation simulation tools extended with models of ride sharing systems. However, they are not suitable for the researchers interested in the development of algorithms for ride-sharing, whom we target in this work. The reasons are:

- They require to specify scenarios with high level of realism, like economic indicators of the population and of the area, which are not usually available.
- Even if available, it takes a long time and effort to figure out how to set them up into the simulators, which would instead be preferable to spend in the inner workings of the algorithms.
- They lack flexibility: when developing an algorithm, it is necessary to test it in a vast range of scenarios, instead of just super-realistic one, to generalize the findings.
- The level of detail transportation represents an overhead: part of the computation time is spent in representing the detailed movement of vehicles at millisecond scale, which has no big impact on the ride sharing logic.

For these reasons, transportation simulation tools are to be used a-posteriori when, for instance, a transportation authority or company wants to check what is the impact of a ride sharing strategy, already developed and thoroughly studied, on the particular scenario of interest.

In this paper we present AMoDSim, a simulation framework open to researchers in future-generation ride-sharing systems whose design goals are:

- Launching massive simulation campaigns to simultaneously test the performance of the algorithms under study, under different settings, is easy and scalable.
- By means of modularity, it is easy to implement new algorithms, with minimum modification of the other components.
- Results on the performance for both the provider and the user perspective are produced automatically and are simple to analyze.

The code is available[1] under the *CC BY-NC-SA 4.0* license. The rest of the paper is organized as follows: In Sect. 2 we review the work in simulation of ride sharing systems. In Sect. 3 we present the model of AMoD used in AMoDSim. In Sect. 4 we describe its architecture and in Sect. 5 we showcase it in a case study in which we compare several provider and user-related metrics of two different matching algorithms.

2   Related Work

In this section we describe the state of the art of the research on autonomous mobility on demand and future generation ride sharing systems, focusing on the simulation tools used. We divide this research in works that use case-specific simulators and complex transportation simulators. The limitations of both has been discussed in the previous section.

2.1   Work Based on Case-Specific Simulators

We emphasize that no code has been made public with any of the studies listed in this subsection, nor the simulators have been described enough to be reproducible. This reinforces the utility of our effort. Santi, Frazzoli et al. published a series of papers [7,22,24] where they proposed mathematical formulations of ride sharing problems and heuristics to solve them. Case studies are shown in New York. Similarly, Ma et al. [19] study ride-sharing algorithms using GPS taxi trajectories collected in Bejing. Agatz et al. [5] built a simulator for a case study in Atlanta. Within their simulator, an agent can subscribe to a provider either as a rider or a driver. The study better represents systems like BlaBla Car [1], in which a traveler can publish her future trip in a web portal and other users can hop-in. These systems are now called "carpooling" and are different from ride sharing systems like Uber and Lyft and the future AMoD, in which (i) drivers are continuously operating for hours just to serve other individuals' trips and (ii) requests for rides arrive continuously in real time and are not announced in advance. Other case-specific simulators were developed for case studies in Seul and Boston in [16] and [17], respectively.

---

[1] https://github.com/admaria/AMoDSim.

2.2 Work Based on Complex Transportation Simulators

Some case studies have been performed extending commercial transportation simulators, like Aimsun [18,20]. However, commercial tools are usually not available to researchers and their code is closed, impeding the verification and the reproduction of results. To the best of our knowledge, three simulation tools developed by academic institutions have been extended and employed in studies related to AMoD, namely SimMobility [8] and MATSim [9,10] and SUMO [6]. The main issue with the first two is the level of complexity that the researcher is required to handle and the performance. They are agent-based, i.e., they simulate the behavior of each single traveler through transportation-specific economic models. In order to do so, the researcher must construct first a synthetic population and describe the economic indicators of the urban network. As discussed in Sect. 1, this is overkill for research focused on algorithms, which is what we target here. The unsuitability of these tools is testified by the fact that: (i) they are generally used, at least as far as published research visible to us is concerned, only by the very same group that developed them and (ii) researchers have preferred to craft their own case-specific simulators instead of using them. SUMO is a microscopic simulator that has been employed in a recent case study on AMoD in the city of Milan [6]. However, that study does not fill the gap we aim to fill. First, SUMO is a purely microscopic simulator, i.e., it computes the detailed movement of each vehicle,[2] which is an overhead that we want instead to avoid, since it has limited interest when studying the dispatching logic in an AMoD system. Second, SUMO does support natively Mobility on Demand services and the authors of [6] had to write from scratch this functionality, which, however, they do not make publicly available. Third, SUMO needs detailed input, that the authors needed to obtain by cross-correlating several data-sources (Google APIs, mobile phone traces, etc.), while the choice we made in AMoD is to streamline the input definition, sacrificing some realism. Finally, is it not possible in [6] to specify user-specified quality of service requirements.

2.3 Other Work

Loosely related to our work is an entire stream of research devoted to the simulation of swarms of autonomous robots that, by combining individual decision capabilities and exchange of information between each other, can successfully achieve a goal. A part of this research [23] is devoted to the resiliency of such formations to individual faults or communication disturbances. A fleet of autonomous vehicles can be seen as a swarm of intelligent robots whose goal is to satisfy the set of user requests. However, the aim of AMoDSim is mainly allowing the researcher to study dispatching algorithms, abstracting the details of where and how the intelligence is distributed and of the information exchange between vehicles.

---

[2] A particular version of SUMO, called SUMO MESO [2], is intended to reduce the details in vehicle movement simulation. However, we are not aware of any published study on AMoD systems based on SUMO MESO.

3   Model of Autonomous Mobility on Demand

We now present the model of AMoD service implemented into the simulator. The model includes a fleet of *vehicles*, a *coordinator* managing it and *users*. Users send trip requests to the coordinator, which runs matching algorithms or simply orchestrates the distributed computation running in the vehicles, in order to decide how to match them to the available vehicles. A trip request consists of two *stop*-points, one for the pick-up and one for the drop-off. Each stop point is a tuple $sp = \{q, t, \Delta t\}$, where q is the pick-up or drop-off point, t is the *preferred time* at which the user wishes to be picked up or dropped off, Δt is the *maximum extra-time* the user tolerates to be picked up or dropped off, with respect to the preferred time.

At any given time, each vehicle v has a set of planned *stop*-points organized in a certain sequence $S_v = [sp_1, sp_2, \dots]$, that we call *schedule*. Each schedule is associated with a *cost* $c(S_v)$, which can be defined in different ways to take into account provider or user-related metrics. For example, this cost could be the kilometers traveled to accomplish that schedule, or some indication of the travel or waiting time of the users served by that schedule. The goal of the provider is to create and continuously update the schedule S_v of each vehicle of its fleet, in order to optimize the costs $c(S_v)$, subject to respecting the time constraints of all the users. Observe that this model is general enough to represent different types of optimization: (i) both provider cost or user level of service can be optimized, as this boils down to the way the cost $c(S_v)$ is defined; (ii) one can simply study the overall cost optimization, or min-max optimization, etc.; (iii) the optimization can be both centralized, in case a single coordinator decides all the schedules S_v, or distributed, in case, for instance, each vehicle v optimizes its own schedule. While the model is general, we have currently only implemented the strategies described in Sect. 3.2.

3.1   Time Constraints

We define a schedule $S_v = [sp_0, \dots, sp_n]$ of a vehicle v *feasible*, if the time constraints of all its stop-points is satisfied. Let us suppose $sp_i = (q_i, t_i, \Delta t_i)$ and that b_i is the time needed to complete sp_i, i.e., the time for the passenger to board (alight), in case of pick-up (drop-off), that the current time is t_{now} and the current vehicle location is q_v. Let us denote with $\tau(q, q')$ the estimated time to go from a location q to q'. Then the estimated time at which the stop-point sp_i will be served is:

$$\hat{t}_i = t_{\text{now}} + \tau(q_v, q_0) + \sum_{j=1}^{i} [b_{j-1} + \tau(q_{j-1}, q_j)] + b_i$$

The *estimated delay* of each stop-point $d_i = \hat{t}_i - t_i \le \Delta t_i$, for $i = 0, \dots, n$. The provider must only compute feasible schedules S_v for each vehicle v in the fleet. AMoDSim is able to simulate on-line optimization algorithms, in which the schedules are continuously modified. To avoid violating some user constraints, the feasibility should be checked at any modification. For example, suppose we modify S_v by inserting a new stop-point $sp = (q, t, \Delta t)$ at position k, obtaining a new schedule $S_v^{(k)} = [sp_0, \ldots, sp_{k-1}, sp, sp_k, \ldots, sp_n]$. The detour the vehicle does to serve sp determines an additional delay on all the stop-points after the k-th. If we denote with $\hat{t}_i^{(k)}$ the estimated stop-point time of sp_i after the insertion, the additional delay is $\Delta d_i^{(k)} \equiv \hat{t}_i^{(k)} - \hat{t}_i$ and it is easy to show that:

$$\Delta d_i^{(k)} = \begin{cases} 0, & \text{if } i < k \\ \tau(q_{k-1}, q) + b + \tau(q, q_k) - \tau(q_{k-1}, q_k), & \text{if } i \geq k \end{cases}$$

where b is the time for alighting or boarding related to sp. To check whether the modified schedule is feasible, not only must we check that the time constraints of the new sp are satisfied, but also that the time constrains are satisfied for all the stop-points already present in the schedules, i.e., $d_i + \Delta d_i^{(k)} \leq \Delta t_i$ for $i = 0, \ldots, n$.

3.2 Examples of Optimization Strategies

To give a more concrete idea of the model we discussed in the previous section, we now describe two heuristics we implemented in AMoDSim and some possible assumptions about the request constraints expressed by users. We adopt such heuristics and assumptions in the case study of Sect. 5. However, we emphasize that the simulator is more general and can be used in different ways.

Recall a request sent by a user is composed by a stop-point $sp = (q, t, \Delta t)$ for the pick-up and another $sp' = (q', t', \Delta t')$ for the drop-off. We assume that the user would like to be picked-up immediately, i.e., $t = t_{\text{now}}$ and to be dropped-off as in the ideal case in which a vehicle is immediately at her disposal and can bring her to the destination in the shortest path, without detours, i.e., $t' = t_{\text{now}} + \tau(q, q')$.

We implement two optimization strategies, namely Radio-Taxi and Insertion Heuristic. With the former each vehicle can serve one passenger at a time, while the latter allows ride sharing, i.e., the same vehicle can serve multiple passengers at a time.

We first describe the *Insertion Heuristic*, loosely inspired by [15]. The cost function $c(S_v)$ is chosen in order to represent the user experience. More precisely, the cost of a schedule $S_v = [sp_0, \ldots, sp_n]$ is the sum of the estimated delays d_i, as defined in Sect. 3.1, of all its stop-points, i.e., $c(S_v) = \sum_{i=0}^{n} d_i$. The Insertion Heuristic attempts to minimize the marginal cost when serving an additional request. Suppose a new request is sent, consisting of the stop-points sp, sp' for the pick-up and drop-off, respectively. Assigning the new request to any vehicle, will increase the cost of its schedule, i.e., the sum of the delays suffered by its stop-points. Let us take any vehicle v and denote with $S_v^{(k,k')}$ the schedule obtained from S_v by inserting the pick-up sp in the k-th position and the drop-off sp' in the k'-th position, with $k' > k$. If the modified schedule is infeasible, we set $c(S_v^{(k,k')}) = \infty$). We compute the best placement of drop-off and pick-up, which minimizes this increase in cost, i.e.,

$$(k^v, k'^v) = \arg \min_{(k,k'),k'>k} \left(c(S_v^{(k,k')}) - c(S_v) \right)$$

We repeat the same computation for all the vehicles and we choose the one whose marginal cost is minimum, i.e.:

$$v^* = \arg \min_v \left(c(S_v^{(k^v,k'^v)}) - c(S_v) \right)$$

Finally, we assign the request to vehicle v^* and place the pick-up and drop-off in the k^{v*}-th and k'^{v*}-th positions, respectively.

The *Radio-Taxi* strategy is a constrained version of Insertion Heuristic, in that we impose that each pick-up be followed in any schedule by the correspondent drop-off, which ensures that at most one passenger is in the vehicle at any moment.

3.3 Vehicle Movement

All vehicles travel through the links of the network, i.e., roads, at a predefined *cruising speed*. Each link has a length, which determines the time needed to traverse it. Obviously, when a vehicle alternates between a stop-point and another, its speed does not go from 0 to the cruising speed and back to 0 instantaneously. Therefore, we introduce a parameter t_a (t_d), which represents the time lost for accelerating (decelerating). When a vehicle reaches a stop-point sp_i, we keep it in that node for an additional time $b_i + t_a + t_d$, before sending it again to the link toward the next stop-point.

4   Software Architecture

AMoDSim is a simulation platform developed on top of Omnetpp [3]. It is designed to be configurable, modular, event-based, algorithm-oriented and extensible with custom optimization strategies and network topologies.

The simulator models the road network as a set of nodes, i.e., geographical locations that could be origins and destinations of the service requests, connected through links, i.e., road connections between different locations. A *vehicle* is represented as a *packet* traveling through the links (Fig. 1). A node is a compound-module composed of three sub-modules: queue, routing and application. A node has one queue module per each outgoing or incoming link. Each *Queue* module forwards (receives) packets to one of the outgoing links (from one of the incoming links). The *Routing* module (i) decides to which of the outgoing links a packet should be forwarded and (ii) checks, every time a vehicle passes, whether the node is one of its stop-points, in which case the vehicle is passed to the Application module. The *Application* module implements multiple functions:

- It generates user requests, as pairs of stop-points (one for the pick-up and one for the drop-offs). The generation obeys to a pre-determined stochastic process. So far, Poisson arrivals are implemented.
- It receives all the vehicles for which the node in question is a stop-point, checks the next stop-point, accessing a data-structure storing all the schedules and sends the vehicle to it. At the same time, it also notifies the coordinator, so that it can update the schedule in question.
- It keeps the vehicles that are idling at the node with an empty schedule. In this case, it also receives a signal from the coordinator if a new schedule is assigned to the idling vehicles and sends them to their new stop-point.

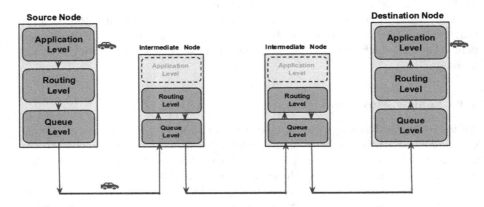

Fig. 1. A *trip* example

The *Coordinator* manages the incoming trip requests, implements the trip allocation strategies and assigns each request to a vehicle, according to the implemented optimization strategy. It has been designed to be easily extensible with custom allocation strategies. We implemented a modular Coordinator within a hierarchical structure where the superclass implements the standard functions. One can extend such superclass and implement the logic of her matching algorithm.

4.1   AMoD Performance Metrics

AMoDSim collects data during its execution and produces a set of results that enable statistical analysis related to both the point of view of the provider and of users.

Regarding the provider viewpoint, AMoDSim provides the following information per-vehicle: (i) distance traveled, (ii) number of passengers on board, (iii) requests picked-up but not yet dropped-off, (iv) number of pick-ups already in the schedule but not yet completed, (v) total requests assigned, (vi) the time the vehicle has spent idle or with p passengers, where p ranges from 1 to the number of per-vehicle seats.

Moreover, for each of the collected metric, AMoDSim computes aggregated fleet statistics, as sum, minimum, maximum, mean, standard deviation, median and 95th percentile.

At each time frame, the following information about the users' requests received up to that time are collected: (i) length of the submitted requests, (ii) number of requests that the system has received and assigned to the vehicles, (iii) number of requests that the system has rejected because it could not serve them within the time constraints, (iv) number of requests that the system is processing at the snapshot time.

The level of quality for the users is described by the following per-user quantities: (i) time that users spent in the pick-up location waiting for the vehicle, (ii) actual time that the user spent in the vehicle, (iii) *Stretch*, i.e., the ratio between the actual trip time and the preferred one, which is the time between the preferred pick-up and drop-off times.

5 Case Study

We showcase the capabilities of AMoD in a simple case study, in which we launched a campaign of 1800 simulations. We compare the performance of the Insertion Heuristic to the Radio-Taxi. We show how AMoDSim allows to find interesting insights on the AMoD systems and answer questions like: what is the fleet size needed to sustain a certain request rate? Which kind of vehicles should be employed (of how many seats)? What is the sharing level, i.e., how effectively are we able to condensate different user rides in few vehicle schedules? By how much sharing rides allows to reduce the fleet size needed? How efficient is vehicle usage, e.g., how much time vehicles are idle? We underline that the findings we get are not necessarily general properties of every AMoD systems, but depend on the particular optimization strategy we adopt and the particular scenario. Therefore, our goal is to show how other researchers can obtain similar findings with AMoDSim about their strategies and their scenarios. Finally, we show the computational performance of AMoDSim. We are aware that the quality of AMoDSim cannot be validated only by the case study we present here. Part of our future work is to apply AMoDSim to different scenarios and to validate by comparing it with other simulators. This latter point requires careful thinking, since other simulators are not directly comparable, for the reasons discussed in Sect. 1. We also believe that the best way to make AMoDSim reach full maturity is its adoption by other researchers for their studies, which would help in understanding and improving its limits.

5.1 Scenario

We use Manhattan Grid that covers an area of $60\,km^2$, equivalent to Manhattan, with static link travel times as in [14]. We consider different configurations of the fleet of vehicles to study the performance of multiple ride-sharing degrees and fleet size. We perform simulations starting from single-seater up to 10-seater minibus and a fleet of 500 up to 9000 vehicles. We assume a cruising speed of 35 kmph and a constant acceleration and deceleration of 1.676 mpss, resulting in a $t_a + t_d = 11.5$ (see Sect. 3.3) as in [21]. Thus, the vehicles have a constant acceleration (deceleration) of 1.676 mpss (-1.676 mpss). Users submit requests with Poissonian arrivals as in [16] with rate ranging from 20 up to 640 requests per hour per km^2 compatible with the scenarios employed in the literature [7,15]. As for the b_i of a pick-up (drop-off) stop point sp_i, i.e. the time need for boarding (alighting), we assume 5 s (10 s) as in [13]. All results are collected running 4 h simulations.

5.2   Results

In this section, we first give an example of analysis possible in AMoDSim and then discuss its computational performance.

Sharing Opportunities for an AMoD Provider. We investigate the factors determining the *sharing degree* and its impact on the provider and the users. The sharing degree is the capacity of an AMoD provider to exploit the fact that a single resource (vehicle) can be used to serve multiple requests. This concept, at the core of the sharing economy, cannot be quantified in a single value, but emerges from a set of different indicators that we discuss here. Figure 2 shows the performance of Radio-Taxi. It is clear that the system is saturated: only 35K requests are served over 65K and the number of idle vehicles goes down to zero in few minutes. Figure 3 shows that under the same conditions, Insertion Heurisitc with a fleet of 4-seater 2K vehicles allows to meet all the requests. Observe also that the total number of kilometers traveled, a proxy for the provider cost, decreases considerably by increasing the number of seats, since the sharing opportunities increase.

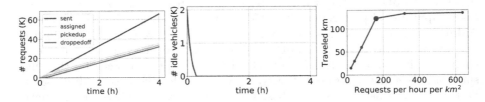

Fig. 2. RadioTaxi: maximum extra-time $\Delta t = 15$ min, 2K vehicles. In the left and middle figure, the rate is 320 req/h/Km^2

The sharing degree is well summarized by Fig. 4, which shows the fraction of time vehicle spend, on average, with 0 (idle), 1, 2, ... passengers. Intuitively, if we allow users to express a tight extra-time constraint Δt, the sharing opportunities

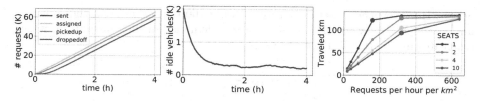

Fig. 3. Insertion Heuristic: $\Delta t = 15$ min. In the left and middle plots, 320 req/h/Km^2 and 2K 4-seater vehicles are used.

shrink and we can just afford few passengers at a time, in order to meet the constraints of all of them.

Note that, even with a long Δt, more than 6 seats are rarely utilized. This suggests that, if we want to implement a minibus-like service, strategies different from Insertion Heuristic must be used (which is an interesting subject to investigate). Observe also that high capacity vehicles would be fully utilized only if Δt is too tight. In other words the type of vehicles to be used depends on the type of service that the provider wishes to offer and the level of service users expect.

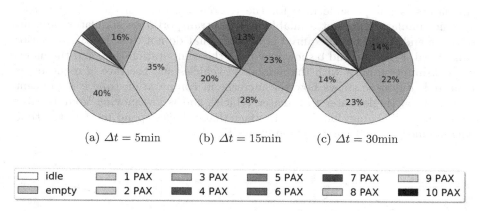

(a) $\Delta t = 5$min   (b) $\Delta t = 15$min   (c) $\Delta t = 30$min

| idle | 1 PAX | 3 PAX | 5 PAX | 7 PAX | 9 PAX |
| empty | 2 PAX | 4 PAX | 6 PAX | 8 PAX | 10 PAX |

Fig. 4. Vehicle occupancy with 1K 10-seater vehicles and a rate of requests 320 per hour per km^2

Mean Waiting Time. In a RadioTaxi-based AMoD system, the only way to serve a higher service demand is to increase the fleet size. Moreover, a large fleet reduces the Waiting Time (WT), which is shown in Fig. 5a. With the Insertion Heuristic another parameter impacts the user experience, namely the vehicle seats. In Fig. 5b we use large points to indicate the first value of request rate in which we observed the system is in saturation, i.e., it is not able to serve all the requests, e.g., Fig. 2. Observe that when the system is not saturated, the best WT are measured with 1 seater vehicles, since each is dedicated entirely to a single user each time and the user does not make detours due to sharing with others. However, the system saturates at only 160 req/h/km². On the contrary, larger vehicles allow to serve a more intense demand without saturation, which translates in a better WT for the users.

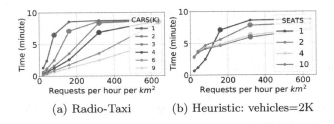

(a) Radio-Taxi   (b) Heuristic: vehicles=2K

Fig. 5. Mean waiting time with a maximum delay $\Delta t = 10$ min.

Computation Time and Memory Consumption. In this section we discuss the single-run computation time and the peak memory consumption of AMoD-Sim, which we observed in our case study. Note that comparison with other simulators is not possible here for the reasons discussed in Sect. 2: the case-specific simulators are not available and the transportation simulators are out of scope and would have required input data that do not exist for the scenarios considered. Figure 6a and b show how both the computation time and the memory consumption grow with the number of vehicles and the rate of requests, as expected. Figure 6c shows how the increase in computation time is significant moving from single-seater to 2-seater vehicles and is low moving from 4-seater to 10-seater. This may be due to the fact that vehicles spend most of the time with no more than 4 passengers anyway (Fig. 4).

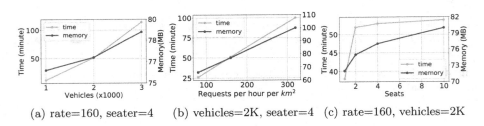

(a) rate=160, seater=4   (b) vehicles=2K, seater=4   (c) rate=160, vehicles=2K

Fig. 6. Computation time and Memory consumption: $\Delta t = 15$ min

6   Conclusion

This paper proposed the open-source simulation framework AMoDSim to study future-generation ride-sharing systems. Its modularity and flexibility simplify the evaluation of new scheduling algorithms via extensive simulation campaigns in a vast range of scenarios. AMoDSim cannot be directly compared with other simulators. Indeed, case-specific simulators are of restricted usefulness and, usually, not even released, while the code of commercial tools is closed. This prevents verification and reproduction of the results. On the other hand, transportation-engineering open-source tools are simply not suitable for designing new algorithms, since they are intended for a later stage, when a planning or transportation authority wants to predict the impact of a specific AMoD service within their own geographical area.

In contrast, this work proposes an open-source platform with the aim to enable researchers to assess their solutions, verify and reproduce their results, comparing them on a common base, and contribute to its evolution with proper code extensions as new requirements arise.

The case study presented here showed how easy it is to test different settings and to study the impact of the relevant parameters of the scheduling algorithm under study. Finally, some measures and insights were given on the performance of the simulator itself and its capability to scale.

Acknowledgement. This work is supported by the CLARA - CLoud plAtform and smart underground imaging for natural Risk Assessment - project, funded by the Italian Ministry of Education, Universities and Research, within the Smart Cities and Communities and Social Innovation initiative.

References

1. BlaBla Car. https://www.blablacar.com/
2. MESO: Mesoscopic version of SUMO. http://sumo.dlr.de/wiki/MESO
3. OMNeT++. https://www.omnetpp.org/
4. Toth, P., Vigo, D.: Vehicle Routing. SIAM-MOS, 2nd edn. (2014)
5. Agatz, N.A.H., Erera, A.L., et al.: Dynamic ride-sharing: a simulation study in metro Atlanta. Transp. Res. B-Method **45**(9), 1450–1464 (2011)
6. Alazzawi, S., Hummel, M., Kordt, P., Sickenberger, T., Wieseotte, C., Wohak, O.: Simulating the impact of shared, autonomous vehicles on urban mobility - a case study of Milan. In: SUMO User Conference (2018)
7. Alonso-Mora, J., Samaranayake, S., et al.: On-demand high-capacity ride-sharing via dynamic trip-vehicle assignment. PNAS **114**(3), 462–467 (2017)
8. Basu, R., et al.: Automated mobility-on-demand vs. mass transit: a multi-modal activity-driven agent-based simulation approach. Transp. Res. Rec. https://doi.org/10.1177/0361198118758630
9. Bischoff, J., Maciejewski, M.: Simulation of city-wide replacement of private cars with autonomous taxis in Berlin. In: ANT. Elsevier Masson SAS (2016)
10. Boesch, P.M., Ciari, F., et al.: Autonomous vehicle fleet sizes required to serve different levels of demand. Transp. Res. Rec. **2542**, 111–119 (2016)
11. Burgstaller, S., Flowers, D., et al.: Rethinking mobility: The 'pay as you go' car: ride hailing just the start. Technical report (2017)
12. Clewlow, R.R., Mishra, G.S.: Disruptive transportation: the adoption, utilization, and impacts of ride-hailing in the United States. Technical report, UC Davis (2017)
13. Elpern-Waxman, J.: Transportation Terms: Dwell Time (2017)

14. Hyland, M., Mahmassani, H.: Dynamic autonomous vehicle fleet operations: optimization-based strategies to assign AVs to immediate traveler demand requests. Transp. Res. C-Emer. **92**, 278–297 (2018)
15. Jaeyoung, J., Jayakrishnan, R., et al.: Design and modeling of real-time shared-taxi dispatch algorithms. In: TRB 92nd Annual Meeting (2013)
16. Jung, J., Jayakrishnan, R., et al.: Design and modeling of real-time shared-taxi dispatch algorithms. In: TRB Annual Meeting, vol. 8 (2013)
17. Lam, A.Y.S., Leung, Y., et al.: Autonomous-vehicle public transportation system: scheduling and admission control. IEEE Trans. Intell. Transp. Syst. **17**(5), 1210–1226 (2016)
18. Linares, M.P., Montero, L., et al.: A simulation framework for real-time assessment of dynamic ride sharing demand responsive transportation models. In: WSC (2016)
19. Ma, S., Zheng, Y., et al.: T-share : a large-scale dynamic taxi ridesharing. In: ICDE (2013)
20. Martinez, L.M., Correia, G.H.A., et al.: An agent-based simulation model to assess the impacts of introducing a shared-taxi system: an application to Lisbon. JAT **49**, 475–495 (2015)
21. Robinson, S.: Measuring bus stop dwell time and time lost serving stop with London ibus automatic vehicle location data. Transp. Res. Rec. **2352**(1), 68–75 (2013)
22. Santi, P., Resta, G., et al.: Quantifying the benefits of vehicle pooling with shareability networks. Proc. Natl. Acad. Sci. **111**(37), 13290–13294 (2014)
23. Skulimowski, A.M.J., Ćwik, A.: Communication quality in anticipatory vehicle swarms: a simulation-based model. In: Peng, S.-L., Lee, G.-L., Klette, R., Hsu, C.-H. (eds.) IOV 2017. LNCS, vol. 10689, pp. 119–134. Springer, Cham (2017). https://doi.org/10.1007/978-3-319-72329-7_11
24. Vazifeh, M.M., Santi, P., et al.: Addressing the minimum fleet problem in on-demand urban mobility. Nature **557**, 534 (2018)

Aggregated Multi-deep Deterministic Policy Gradient for Self-driving Policy

Junta Wu[1,2] and Huiyun Li[1,2(✉)]

[1] Shenzhen Institutes of Advanced Technology, Chinese Academy of Sciences,
Shenzhen 518071, China
hy.li@siat.ac.cn

[2] Shenzhen College of Advanced Technology, University of Chinese Academy
of Sciences, Shenzhen 518071, China

Abstract. Self-driving is a significant application of deep reinforcement learning. We present a deep reinforcement learning algorithm for control policies of self-driving vehicles. This method aggregates multiple sub-policies based on the deep deterministic policy gradient algorithm and centralized experience replays. The aggregated policy converges to the optimal policy by aggregating those sub-policies. It helps reduce the training time largely since each sub-policy is trained with less time. Experimental results on the open racing car simulator platform demonstrates that the proposed algorithm is able to successfully learn control policies, with a good generalization performance. This method outperforms the deep deterministic policy gradient algorithm with 56.7% less training time.

Keywords: Self-driving · Deep reinforcement learning · Deep deterministic policy gradient

1 Introduction

Self-driving vehicles capable of sensing environment and navigating intelligently attract enormous interest in both research and industry area [1]. The two main foundation stones behind the self-driving vehicles are perception and decision. The former enables the vehicles to percept the world, whilst the latter yields the control policies. Generally, control policies giving intelligent action commands (such as steering, acceleration and brake command) are essential for self-driving vehicles after they get the environment information from various sensors. However, how to learn optimal control policies is a challenge for self-driving vehicles.

Recently, with the accessibility of large amount of training data and computation resources, interest of applying machine learning techniques to self-driving vehicles has grown explosively. Particularly, the success of deep neural network (DNN) technique [2, 3], raises a new upsurge of study on self-driving vehicles. The DNN has been applied onto an end-to-end learning system for self-driving vehicles, which maps raw pixels from camera directly to steering commands [4].

Reinforcement learning [5] whose essence is learning through interaction [6] is an active branch of machine learning and had some success for solving challenging

A. M. J. Skulimowski et al. (Eds.): IOV 2018, LNCS 11253, pp. 179–192, 2018.
https://doi.org/10.1007/978-3-030-05081-8_13

problems in control theory. As DNN was developed, reinforcement learning with DNN, i.e., deep reinforcement learning algorithms was proposed in [7]. The so-called deep Q-network (DQN) [7] is the first deep reinforcement learning algorithm to successfully learn an optimal control policy for an autonomous braking system [8]. There are also other deep reinforcement learning algorithms inspired by DQN are used in the field of self-driving vehicles. For example, deep Q-learning with filtered experiences (DQFE) algorithm [9], which extended experience replay technique, successfully learned a steering policy on the open racing car simulator (TORCS) [10, 11].

However, DQN is only applicable for the tasks with discrete and low-dimensional action spaces. One has to discretize action spaces to apply DQN onto self-driving vehicles, where action space is continuous. But this may result in the unstable control of vehicles. In order to solve this problem, researchers proposed deep deterministic policy gradient (DDPG) algorithm to directly learn continuous control policy [12]. Unfortunately, DDPG usually demands long training time to find an optimal policy.

Aggregation method has been proved to be successful in reinforcement learning [13–15]. In this paper, we propose a deep reinforcement learning algorithm with aggregation method to reduce the training time, which is able to learn multiple sub-policies at the same time by utilizing centralized experience replay technique and output the final control policy by aggregating all the sub-policies.

The remainder of this paper is organized as follows. Section 2 provides background knowledge. Section 3 describes details of the proposed method. Experimental results of the proposed method are presented in Sect. 4 and analysis of aggregation is provided in Sect. 5. Finally, the paper is concluded in Sect. 6.

2 Background

2.1 Reinforcement Learning

In a standard reinforcement learning setup, an agent interacts with environment ε at discrete time steps. In each time step t, the agent observes the state s_t and takes the action a_t according to its policy π which maps a state to a deterministic action or a probability distribution over the actions. Then it receives an immediate reward $r(s_t, a_t)$. The accumulated reward the agent can get from a specific time step t is defined as:

$$R_t = \sum_{i=t}^{T} \gamma^{i-t} r(s_i, a_i), \tag{1}$$

where $\gamma \in [0, 1]$ is a discount factor. The goal in a reinforcement learning task is to learn an optimal policy π^* by maximizing the expected accumulated reward from the start state, which is $E[R_t]$.

2.2   Q-Learning and DQN

Q-Learning. Q-Learning [5] is an important branch of reinforcement learning. Q refers to the action-value function [5] $Q^\pi(s_t, a_t) = E_\pi[R_t|s_t, a_t]$, which describes the expected accumulated reward after taking action a_t in state s_t by following the policy π. Generally, the action value function can be expressed as recursive form known as Bellman equation [7]:

$$Q^\pi(s_t, a_t) = E_{s_{t+1}-\varepsilon, a_{t+1}-\pi}[r(s_t, a_t) + \gamma E_\pi[Q^\pi(s_{t+1}, a_{t+1})]]. \tag{2}$$

Q-Learning makes use of temporal-difference learning method and greedy policy to iteratively update Q function [5]:

$$Q(s_t, a_t) = Q(s_t, a_t) + \alpha[r(s_t, a_t) + \gamma \max_{a_t} Q(s_{t+1}, a_{t+1}) - Q(s_t, a_t)]. \tag{3}$$

DQN. DQN [7] combines deep neural network technique with Q-learning. The Q function is approximated with a deep neural network and converges to the optimal Q function Q^* by minimizing the following loss function:

$$L(\theta) = E_{s_t, a_t - \rho(\bullet)}\left[(Q^*(s_t, a_t|\omega) - y_t)^2\right], \tag{4}$$

where $\rho(\bullet)$ is the behavior distribution, $y_t = r(s_t, a_t) + \gamma \max_{a_{t+1}} Q(s_{t+1}, a_{t+1}|\omega')$ is the target and the parameter ω' is duplicated from the previous iteration.

Besides deep neural network technique, another key to the success of DQN is experience replay technique, which breaks the strong correlations of consecutive samples and therefore reduces the variance of updates [7].

2.3   Policy Gradient Algorithms and Deterministic Policy Gradient Algorithm

Policy Gradient Algorithms. Policy gradient algorithms derived from the policy gradient theorem [5] are used for learning stochastic policies $\pi_\theta : S \mapsto P(A)$, where S, A represent state space and action space respectively and $P(A)$ is the set of probability measures on A. They are strongly suited for reinforcement learning tasks with continuous action spaces. The basic idea behind the policy gradient algorithms is to maximize the performance $J(\theta) = E_{s \sim \rho^\pi, a \sim \pi_\theta}[R]$, by updating the parameter along the policy gradient, i.e. the gradient of the policy's performance:

$$\nabla_\theta J(\theta) = E_{s \sim \rho^\pi, a \sim \pi_\theta}[\nabla_\theta \log \pi_\theta(a|s) Q^\pi(s, a)], \tag{5}$$

where ρ^π is the state distribution and Q^π is the true action value function. Different policy gradient algorithms differ in how they estimate Q^π. Alternatively, approximating Q^π with the temporal-difference learning method [5] leads to the actor-critic (AC) algorithm [5].

Deterministic Policy Gradient Algorithm. Derived from deterministic policy gradient theorem [16], the deterministic policy gradient algorithm is used to learn deterministic policies [16] $\mu_\theta : S \mapsto A$ instead of stochastic policies. The deterministic policy gradient algorithm maximizes the performance function in the direction of deterministic policy gradient [16], which is:

$$\nabla_\theta J(\theta) = \mathrm{E}_{s \sim \rho^\mu, a \sim \mu_\theta}\left[\nabla_\theta \mu_\theta(s)\nabla_a Q^\mu(s, a)\big|_{a=\mu_\theta(s)}\right]. \tag{6}$$

Deterministic policy gradient algorithm also utilizes actor-critic (AC) framework where action value function Q^μ is used as a critic and the deterministic policy μ_θ is considered as an actor.

2.4   DDPG Algorithm

DDPG is a variant of deterministic policy gradient algorithm [12], which adopts deep neural network to approximate deterministic policy μ and action value function Q^μ. The gradient of the objective can be formulated as:

$$\nabla_\theta J(\theta) = \mathrm{E}_{s \sim \rho^\mu, a \sim \mu}\left[\nabla_\theta \mu(s|\theta)\nabla_a Q^\mu(s, a|\omega)\big|_{a=\mu_\theta(s)}\right], \tag{7}$$

where θ is parameter of actor network corresponding to the policy and ω is the parameter of critic network corresponding the action value function. The diagram of DDPG is shown in Fig. 1:

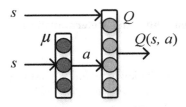

Fig. 1. Diagram of deep deterministic policy gradient

The actor network updated according to the chain rule and back-propagation of neural network eventually converges to the optimal policy which maximizes the overall performance. DDPG is an off-policy algorithm, utilizing the experience replay technique introduced in DQN to break the correlation of the samples and to keep samples independent identically distributed. In addition, the learning method of Q function is similar to that in DQN as well.

2.5 TORCS

TORCS is the competition software for the simulated car racing championship, which takes the client-server structure [11]. Figure 2 presents the client-server structure of TORCS. In TORCS, a controller of a car perceives the racing environment through a number of sensors to get the current state. Then it can perform the typical driving actions, such as accelerating, braking and steering the wheel, by following a specific control policy. The controller connects to the race server through UDP connection. In every time step, the server sends the current sensor information to the controller and waits for 10 ms to receive an action from the controller. If no action is received, the last performed action is taken.

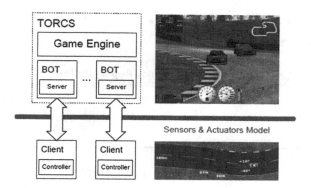

Fig. 2. Server-client structure of TORCS

Since TORCS simulates real driving environment well and its sensor information of the simulated car can be easily accessed, it is a suitable platform for the research of self-driving vehicles. Additionally, the interactive mechanism between the server (driving environment) and client (controller of a car) makes TORCS an excellent benchmark for deep reinforcement learning algorithm.

3 Proposed Method

3.1 Structure of Multi-DDPG

We have explained earlier that DDPG is more suitable for continuous control tasks than DQN. However, it takes long time to learn the optimal policy. In order to reduce the training time, we proposed an aggregated method with multi-DDPG structure. More specifically, we use multi-DDPG structure to learn several sub-policies simultaneously, which takes less training time. The structure of multi-DDPG is shown in Fig. 3. Then we achieve the aggregated policy by averaging the outputs of all the sub-policies, as shown in Fig. 4.

During training time, each sub-policy is learned with DDPG which utilizes AC framework. In each time step, the agent receives the environment state and acts according to one sub-policy. Then the performance of the action is evaluated by the corresponding Q network. By following the updating rule of DDPG, each sub-policy is improved gradually. Experiences encountered by all sub-policies are to be stored in the centralized experience replay buffer. We will go into details of centralized experience replay buffer in Sect. 3.2.

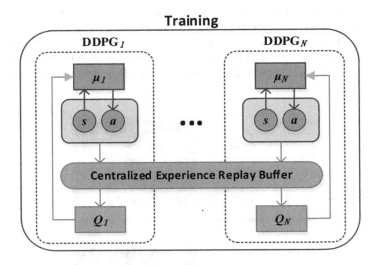

Fig. 3. Structure of multi-DDPG

We illustrate the aggregation of sub-policies in Fig. 4 where $\mu_1, \cdots, \mu_N$ are sub-polices, $a_1, \cdots, a_N$ are the corresponding outputs of the sub-policies and a is the output of the aggregated policy. After training, we get several different sub-policies. Since the sub-policies take less time to train than the optimal policy, each sub-policy performs worse than the optimal policy. However, we are able to improve the performance by aggregating these sub-policies to achieve the optimal policy. Considering that sub-policies are of equal importance and their outputs are real valued, the aggregation method we used in this paper is to average the outputs of the sub-policies. We name the above method as aggregated multi-DDPG (AMDDPG) since it bases on the aggregation of several sub-policies learned from multi-DDPG structure.

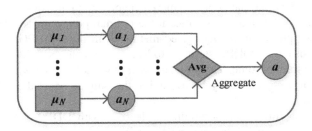

Fig. 4. Aggregation of sub-policies

3.2 Centralized Experience Replay Buffer

As introduced in Sect. 2.4, DDPG is an off-policy algorithm, which means it is capable of learning one policy through the experiences from other policies. Additionally, DDPG utilizes the experience replay technique to break the correlation of the samples and to keep samples independent identically distributed. Under such condition, it seems a natural idea to use a centralized experience replay buffer for AMDDPG. Specifically, during training time, each DDPG keeps the same experience replay buffer.

In a specific time step, the agent interacts with the environment, receiving environment state, acting according to one sub-policy and getting an immediate reward. We then store all state, action and reward information in the centralized experience replay buffer as the experiences the agent experienced. Basically, the experiences in centralized experience replay buffer are from all the sub-policies.

One intuitive insight to the centralized experience replay buffer is that the agent is able to utilize the experiences from multiple policies, which makes the agent broaden its view and have more knowledge of the environment. In this way, the agent can learn multiple sub-policies more efficiently.

3.3 Training Scheme and Algorithm

Multiple sub-policies are learned simultaneously with AMDDPG, but in a specific time step, the environment allows the agent use only one sub-policy to interact with it. Therefore, the training scheme we proposed in this paper is to alternately train multiple sub-policies. More specifically, we train one sub-policy in each episode. The full algorithm of AMDDPG is presented in Table 1.

Table 1. Aggregated multi-DDPG algorithm

Algorithm 1 Aggregated Multi-DDPG

Randomly initialize N critic networks $Q_i(s,a\,|\,\theta_i^Q)$ and actor networks $\mu_i(s\,|\,\theta_i^\mu)$
Initialize centralized experience replay buffer R
for episode = 1, M **do**
    Receive initial environment state s_1
    for t = 1, T **do**
        Select $Q_j(s,a\,|\,\theta_j^Q)$ and $\mu_j(s\,|\,\theta_j^\mu)$ according to the training scheme
        Execute action $a_t = \mu_j\left(s_t\,|\,\theta_j^\mu\right)$ and observe reward r_t and new state s_{t+1}
        Store experience $\left(s_t, a_t, r_t, s_{t+1}\right)$ in R
        Update θ_j^Q and θ_j^μ according to DDPG algorithm based on experiences
    end for
end for
---

4 Experimental Results

4.1 Setup

Reward Function. One key to learn a good policy for reinforcement learning task is to design an appropriate reward function. In this section, we discuss how to design the reward function in TORCS for AMDDPG.

In TORCS, one agent, i.e., a simulated car, can percept the environment through various sensors. Some of the sensor information are perfect for designing the reward function to guide the agent. We use the sensor information in Table 2 to construct the reward function.

Table 2. Sensor information for constructing the reward function

Name	Range (unit)	Description
φ	$[-\pi, +\pi]\ (rad)$	Angle between the car direction and the direction of the track axis
v	$[-\infty, +\infty]\ (km/h)$	Speed of the car along the longitudinal axis of the car
d_1	$[0, 200]\ (m)$	Distance between the car and the track edge in front of the car
d_2	$[-\infty, +\infty]$	Distance between the car and the track axis. $d_2 = 0$ when the car is on the axis, $|d_2| = 1$ when the car is on the track edge, $|d_2| > 1$ when the car is outside of the track

The reward function is presented in Eq. (8). In short, the performances we expect should be reflected through the terms in the reward function.

In each interaction between the car and TORCS environment, we expect the reward, r, to be as large as possible.

$$r = \left(v \times \left(\frac{1 - |v - \beta|}{\alpha} \right)^{\mathrm{I}[d_1 \leq 10]} \right) \times \cos \varphi \times (1 - |\sin \varphi|) \times (1 - |d_2|)$$
$$\times \left(\frac{|d_1|}{50} \right)^{\mathrm{I}[d_1 \leq 50]}. \tag{8}$$

The term v indicates that, in order to maximize the reward, the car has to run along the track fast. In Eq. (8), the $\cos \varphi$ and $(1 - |\sin \varphi|)$ terms expects φ to be zero, which means the car runs along the track. The $(1 - |d_2|)$ term keeps the car in the center of the track. $\mathrm{I}[\bullet]$ is an indicator function, which outputs 1 when the condition is satisfied, otherwise, 0. Therefore, the first term and last term of Eq. (8) can be reformulated as Eqs. (9) and (10).

$$v \times \left(\frac{1 - |v - \beta|}{\alpha} \right)^{\mathrm{I}[d_1 \leq 10]} = \begin{cases} v \times \left(\frac{1 - |v - \beta|}{\alpha} \right), & d_1 \leq 10 \\ v, & d_1 > 10 \end{cases}. \tag{9}$$

$$\left(\frac{|d_1|}{50}\right)^{\mathbf{I}[d_1 \le 50]} = \begin{cases} \frac{|d_1|}{50}, & d_1 \le 50 \\ 1, & d_1 > 50 \end{cases}. \tag{10}$$

The first term in Eq. (8) lets the car slow down when a turn is encountered and makes the car run as fast as possible at the straight. Besides, it is important to note that α and β are hyper parameters. They need to be fine-tuned to ensure the speed at turns is appropriate. The last term of Eq. (8) indicates that the car should observe the turn in advance and control steering angles.

Training. We trained a simulated car in TORCS to learn several self-driving policies with AMDDPG and get the optimal policy by aggregating those policies. During training process, the car received the sensor information as the environment state and executed the action given by one sub-policy. The action consists of the steering, accelerating and braking commands, whose detailed information is presented in Table 3. We have argued in Sect. 3 that AMDDPG demands less training than DDPG. Figure 6 illustrates the training time comparison between AMDDPG and DDPG.

Table 3. Commands description within one action

Commands	Range	Description
Steering	$[-1, +1]$	-1 and $+1$ mean respectively full right and full left
Acceleration	$[0, 1]$	Virtual gas pedal (0 means no gas, 1 means full gas)
Brake	$[0, 1]$	Virtual brake pedal (0 means no brake, 1 means full brake)

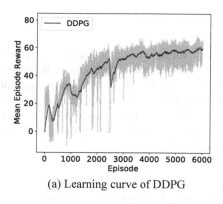

(a) Learning curve of DDPG

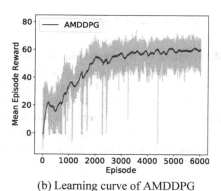

(b) Learning curve of AMDDPG

Fig. 5. Learning curve of DDPG and AMDDPG

We have trained the car 6000 episodes on Aalborg track of TORCS. The learning curve of DDPG is demonstrated in Fig. 5(a) and that of AMDDPG is presented in Fig. 5(b). As Fig. 5 shows, after 6000 episodes, the policy of DDPG and the policy of AMDDPG both converge to and oscillate around the optimal one. Figure 6 demonstrates that AMDDPG takes less time to train since each sub-policy is trained with less iterations. The training time of AMDDPG for 6000 episodes is 22.84 h while that of DDPG is 52.77 h, showing that the AMDDPG is able to reduce the training time by 56.7%. However, the difference during the first 1500 episodes is not notable enough. It is because the car paid more attention on exploring the environment at the beginning and exploration episodes do not last long. The AMDDPG and DDPG take nearly equal episodes and time to explore the new environment. Alternatively, the first 1500 episodes can be considered as the initialization.

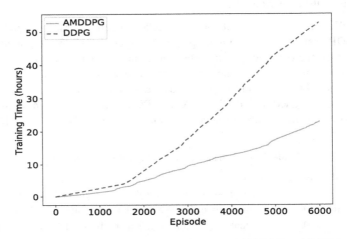

Fig. 6. Comparison of training time between AMDDPG and DDPG

4.2   Performance Test

Effectiveness of Aggregation. We show in this subsection the comparison of performance between the aggregated policy and sub-policies so as to illustrate the effectiveness of aggregation. For the sake of simplicity, we only show the performance of three sub-policies. We let the car run one lap on Aalborg track to test the policies. As Table 4 shows, the cars with sub-policies are not able to finish any lap of Aalborg track while the car with the aggregated policy can pass the track. This fully testify that aggregation does improve the performance of sub-policies.

Table 4. Comparison of performance between sub-policies and aggregated policy

Policy	Steps	Total reward (points)	Finish one lap or not
Sub-policy0	246	16690.60	No
Sub-policy1	246	15413.12	No
Sub-policy2	102	−1252.46	No
Aggregated policy	457	31603.37	Yes

Figure 7 presents the comparison of reward between the aggregated policy and sub-policies. Since the cars with sub-policies run out from the track before finish one lap, the last half of their reward curves is flat.

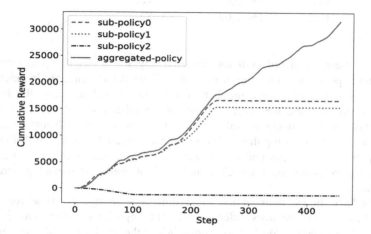

Fig. 7. Comparison of performance between the aggregated policy and sub-policies

Generalization Performance. We have learned self-driving policies on Aalborg track with AMDDPG successfully and the car performed well on the training track. However, in machine learning, one model might overfit the training dataset and perform worse on test dataset. Therefore, we test the aggregated policy learned by AMDDPG not only on the training track, Aalborg, but also on the test tracks, CG1 and CG2. Figure 8 illustrates the maps of the tracks for training and test.

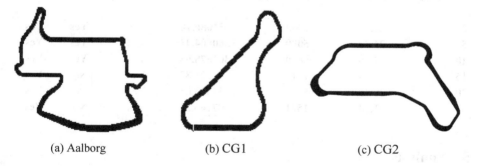

(a) Aalborg   (b) CG1   (c) CG2

Fig. 8. Maps of tracks for training and test

As Table 5 shows. The car passed the training track and the test tracks, which demonstrates the aggregated policy learned by AMDDPG does not overfit the training track and have a good generalization performance on the test tracks.

Table 5. Generalization performance of aggregated policy

Track name	Total reward (points)	Finish one lap or not
Aalborg	30007.61	Yes
CG1	23755.62	Yes
CG2	35602.09	Yes

Effect from Number of Sub-policies. Theoretically, the aggregated policy converges to the optimal policy when the number of sub-policies is large enough. In practice, it is inefficient to aggregate a large number of sub-policies. Additionally, the larger the number of sub-policies, the more the memory overhead would be. Therefore, we choose some small numbers for sub-policies and compare the performance to decide the suitable number of sub-policies. We test the aggregated policies on Aalborg track and compare the total steps and total reward in one episode. In addition, we test the aggregated policies on the track CG1 and CG2 as well to compare generalization performance.

As Table 6 shows, there is not large difference in training time for different numbers but the performances differ largely. The aggregated policy with 3–10 sub-policies performs better. With 3–10 sub-policies, the total steps in one episode of Aalborg can reach the maximum steps and the car is able to gain much more reward than the car with more than 10 sub-policies. Besides, the car with 3–10 sub-policies can pass not only Aalborg track but also CG1 and CG2 track, which means the aggregated policy with 3–10 sub-policies has better generalization performance.

Table 6. Comparison of performance of aggregated policies with different numbers of sub-policies

Number of sub-policies	Training time (hours)	Total steps in Aalborg	Total reward in Aalborg	Pass Aalborg	Pass CG1	Pass CG2
3	22.84	**5000**	**331086.10**	Yes	**Yes**	Yes
5	24.40	**5000**	**360804.43**	Yes	**Yes**	Yes
10	24.16	**5000**	**303678.65**	Yes	**Yes**	Yes
15	22.09	771	47121.87	Yes	No	Yes
20	20.49	567	34343.05	Yes	No	Yes
30	21.74	1541	97146.37	Yes	No	Yes

5   Analysis

In this section, we aim to explain why the aggregated policy performs better than sub-policies. Assume the environment state is s in a specific time step. $\mu(s)$ is the action given by the policy μ. Suppose N sub-policies are trained in AMDDPG, and each sub-policy is denoted as $\mu_i(i = 1, 2, \cdots N)$. In Addition, the optimal policy to which the aggregated policy converges is denoted as μ^*. For simplicity, the policy output at state s is represented as μ in the following formulas instead of $\mu(s)$. The aggregated policy $\bar{\mu}$ can be formulated as:

$$\bar{\mu} = \mathbf{Avg}[\mu_i] = \frac{1}{N} \sum_{i=1}^{N} \mu_i, \tag{11}$$

where $\mathbf{Avg}[\mu_i]$ is the average of sub-policies. Suppose the average bias between the sub-policies and the optimal policy is $\mathbf{Avg}[(\mu_i - \mu^*)^2]$, and the bias between the aggregated policy and the optimal policy is $(\bar{\mu} - \mu^*)^2$. We establish the relation between $\mathbf{Avg}[(\mu_i - \mu^*)^2]$ and $(\bar{\mu} - \mu^*)^2$ in Eq. (12):

$$
\begin{aligned}
\mathbf{Avg}\left[(\mu_i - \mu^*)^2\right] &= \mathbf{Avg}\left[\mu_i^2 - 2\mu_i\mu^* + (\mu^*)^2\right] \\
&= \mathbf{Avg}[\mu_i^2] - 2\mu^*\mathbf{Avg}[\mu_i] + (\mu^*)^2 \\
&= \mathbf{Avg}[\mu_i^2] - 2\mu^*\bar{\mu} + (\mu^*)^2 \\
&= \mathbf{Avg}[\mu_i^2] - 2\bar{\mu}^2 + \bar{\mu}^2 + \left(\bar{\mu}^2 - 2\mu^*\bar{\mu} + (\mu^*)^2\right), \\
&= \mathbf{Avg}[\mu_i^2 - 2\mu_i\bar{\mu} + \bar{\mu}^2] + (\bar{\mu} - \mu^*)^2 \\
&= \mathbf{Avg}\left[(\mu_i - \bar{\mu})^2\right] + (\bar{\mu} - \mu^*)^2 \\
&= \mathbf{Var}(\mu_i) + (\bar{\mu} - \mu^*)^2 \\
&\geq (\bar{\mu} - \mu^*)^2
\end{aligned} \tag{12}
$$

where $\mathbf{Var}(\mu_i)$ represents the variance of sub-policies. Equation (12) demonstrates the bias between the aggregated policy and the optimal policy is smaller than the average bias between the sub-policies and the optimal policy. Therefore the aggregated policy is closer to the optimal policy than sub-policies and performs better. As Eq. (12) shows, the variance of sub-policies is reduced when using the aggregated policy as the final policy and the aggregated policy is closer to the optimal policy.

6 Conclusion

This paper presented a new deep reinforcement learning algorithm, aggregated multi-deep deterministic policy gradient (AMDDPG), to find the optimal control policies for self-driving vehicles. We demonstrated AMDDPG improved the performance of sub-policies by aggregating them. The method reduced the training time by 56.7%. We also illustrated the aggregated policy generalizing well on other test tracks of TORCS. Finally, we investigated the effect from number of sub-policies.

However, a few limitations remain to our approach. One is unstable learning due to the high variance of DDPG algorithm. This leads the final policy to oscillate around the optimal policy. We leave this investigation to the future work.

Acknowledgment. This work was supported by Shenzhen Engineering laboratory on Autonomous Vehicles, NSFC 61672512, and the Shenzhen S&T Funding with Grant No. JCYJ201605 10154531467.

References

1. Urmson, C.: Self-driving cars and the urban challenge. IEEE Intell. Syst. **23**(2), 66–68 (2008)
2. Krizhevsky, A., Sutskever, I., Hinton, G.: ImageNet classification with deep convolutional neural networks. In: NIPS 2012 Proceedings of the 25th International Conference on Neural Information Processing Systems, pp. 1097–1105. Curran Associates Inc., New York (2012)
3. LeCun, Y., Bengio, Y., Hinton, G.: Deep learning. Nature **521**, 436–444 (2015)
4. Bojarski, M., Del Testa, D., Dworakowski, D., et al.: End to end learning for self-driving cars. arXiv preprint arXiv:1604.07316 (2016)
5. Sutton, R.S., Barto, A.G.: Reinforcement Learning: An Introduction. MIT Press, Cambridge (1998)
6. Arulkumaran, K., Deisenroth, M.P., Brundage, M., et al.: Deep reinforcement learning: a brief survey. IEEE Signal Process. Mag. **34**(6), 26–38 (2017)
7. Mnih, V., Kavukcuoglu, K., Silver, D., et al.: Human-level control through deep reinforcement learning. Nature **518**, 529–533 (2015)
8. Chae, H., Kang, C.M., Kim, B.D., et al.: Autonomous braking system via deep reinforcement learning. arXiv preprint arXiv:1702.02302 (2017)
9. Xia, W., Li, H.Y.: Training method of automatic driving strategy based on deep reinforcement learning. J. Integr. Technol. **6**(3), 29–40 (2017)
10. Wymann, B., Espié, E., Guionneau, C., et al.: TORCS: the open racing car simulator (2015)
11. Loiacono, D., Cardamone, L., Lanzi, P.L.: Simulated car racing championship: competition software manual. Politecnico di Milano, Dipartimento di Elettronica, Informazione e Bioingegneria, Italy (2013)
12. Lillicrap, T.P., Hunt, J.J., Pritzel, A., et al.: Continuous control with deep reinforcement learning. In: ICLR (2016)
13. Jiang, J.: A framework for aggregation of multiple reinforcement learning algorithms. Dissertation, University of Waterloo, Waterloo, Ontario, Canada (2007)
14. Jiang, J., Kamel, M.S.: Aggregation of reinforcement learning algorithms. In: The 2006 IEEE International Joint Conference on Neural Networks, pp. 68–72. IEEE, Vancouver (2006)
15. Lowe, R., Wu, Y., Tamar, A., et al.: Multi-agent actor-critic for mixed cooperative-competitive environments. In: Advances in Neural Information Processing Systems (2017)
16. Silver, D., Lever, G., Heess, N., et al.: Deterministic policy gradient algorithms. In: ICML 2014 Proceedings of the 31st International Conference on International Conference on Machine Learning, pp. I-387–I-395. ICML, Beijing (2014)

HESAVE: An Approach for Online Heuristic GPS Trajectory Sampling

Zexin Yan, Zhihan Liu[✉], and Quan Yuan

Beijing University of Posts and Telecommunications, No. 10, Xitucheng Road, Haidian District, Beijing 100876, People's Republic of China
{axlent, zhihan, yuanquan}@bupt.edu.cn

Abstract. In location based service system, online trajectory compression can help to relieve the whole system's pressure by reducing communication, storage and computation cost during network transmission, storage and business computing. Segment simplified sampling method is a kind of trajectory compression methods which is widely used in online trajectory compression, but current methods have the problems such as temporal information loss and difficulty of parameter selection. In this paper, we propose an online heuristic trajectory sampling algorithm base on segment simplification, HESAVE (HEuristic SAmpling based on VEctor feature). HESAVE introduces Iterator Vector to describe motion semantics of trajectory points. Furthermore, Iterator Vector Information is proposed to quantify the information of trajectory points based on Iterator. Moreover, HESAVE adopts a data-driven window called Sliding Mode Window to split multi-mode trajectory into isolated process units and a priority queue for each unit to select trajectory points. Extensive experiments on Geo-Life 1.3 dataset show that HESAVE can gain more reservation of trajectory's temporal and positioning information after sampling under the same sampling ratio compared to SQUISH. In addition, HESAVE's computation resource consumption is quite acceptable.

Keywords: Trajectory compression · Heuristic sampling
Trajectory vector feature · Data-driven window

1 Introduction

In recent year, with the development of mobile communication technology and the proliferation of intelligent devices, Location Based Services (LBS) [1] are becoming popular. Service providers collect users' location information via various devices such as smart phones and GPS terminals by various location-acquisition techniques [2, 3]. These continuous location points collected from a certain user constitute the user's travel trajectory. Massive trajectory data impel the evolution of LBS and can be excavated and analyzed with other multi-source and heterogeneous big data to obtain more valuable results [4–6].

Processing and management of user-generated GPS trajectory data are important parts of LBS and other relative applications [7]. An online compression approach in data collecting and preprocessing phase can reduce the data capacity, which can relieve

A. M. J. Skulimowski et al. (Eds.): IOV 2018, LNCS 11253, pp. 193–207, 2018.
https://doi.org/10.1007/978-3-030-05081-8_14

the whole system's pressure by reducing communication, storage and computation cost during network transmission, storage and business computing [8].

Generally, the core method of trajectory compression is reducing the amount of data represented by sampling or recoding trajectory data within certain limitation of information loss. Segment simplified sampling method [9] is a kind of trajectory compression method by discarding several trajectory points when information loss caused by removing them from original trajectory, which called *error* in many algorithms, is under certain threshold.

Deformation of trajectory after sampling is a common error criterion and many segment simplified sampling methods treat trajectory as a polyline in a two-dimensional plane, and use certain standard such as Vertical Euclidean Distance (VED) or Synchronized Euclidean Distance (SED) to quantify the deformation [10, 12]. VED is the vertical distance from the original trajectory point to the compressed trajectory, and SED is the distance from the original point to the point on compressed trajectory which is selected according to time scale.

These methods have several shortcomings:

1. **Loss of temporal information of trajectories.** We divide information of certain trajectory point into two parts: temporal information and positioning information. Positioning information is the result of motion. Shape of trajectory is one expression of positioning information, both VED and SED are suitable metrics for deformation. Temporal information can reflect the process and pattern of motion combined with positioning information. Speed and acceleration information are expressions of temporal information, which is worthy in the high-level data processing and analyzing. Indeed, VED and SED ignore the better part of temporal information.
2. **Difficulty of threshold selection.** The effect of trajectory sampling is greatly affected by the thresholds. However, thresholds are closely related to trajectory characteristics such as motion patterns, and it needs some domain knowledge to select a proper threshold.

To overcome these shortcomings, we propose a trajectory sampling approach HESAVE (HEuristic SAmpling based on VEctor feature) which can be applied in trajectory data acquisition and preprocessing phase. HESAVE is a heuristic online segment simplified sampling approach, it uses priority queue and Sliding Mode Window (SMW) to support multiple motion pattern trajectory sampling with low latency. In HESAVE, we propose Iteration Vector (IV) to describe motion semantics of trajectory points and Iteration Vector Information (IVI) as a measurement of information contained in certain trajectory point. IVI preserves both temporal and positioning information of the trajectory point to ensure feature similarity after sampling.

The remainder of this paper is organized as follows: Sect. 2 introduces the situation of other trajectory compression algorithms, and we introduce HESAVE in detail in Sect. 3. Next, we design and perform a serial of experiments and the results are analyzed in Sect. 4. Finally, we carry out summary of present work and future work.

2   Related Work

HESAVE is an online trajectory sampling algorithm based on segment simplification. This section discusses several similar algorithms.

Keogh et al. [10] propose sliding window algorithm and open windows algorithm. These two methods use window to split online trajectory point stream into process units, and use certain metrics related to Vertical European Distance (VED) or SED as the error criterion to select points to be sampled by comparing to certain threshold.

Potamias et al. [11] propose threshold-guided sampling algorithm which uses the latest point's speed vector to predict a position range as security areas to determine whether the newcomer should be retained. This algorithm can compress trajectories with low computation cost but may meet cumulative error problem in some particular situations. They propose ST-Trace algorithm in [11] to handle this problem.

ST-Trace uses previous speed of two points p_{i-1} and p_{i-2} to calculate two security areas z_{i-1} and z_{i-2}, and adopts the intersection of two security areas as the final security zone. If a coming point is in the final zone, this point's motion is consistent with the previous two movements. ST-Trace algorithm's computation resource consumption is quite low and the process speed is fast, but compression ratio is strongly correlated with trajectory and it is hard to control.

The above algorithms all need to specify a set of fixed thresholds to judge whether to retain the trajectory point in sampling result. To solve this problem, heuristic sampling algorithm has become the focus of research in recent years. Heuristic sampling algorithm does not need to explicitly specify threshold to complete trajectory sampling. Muckell et al. [12] propose SQUISH algorithm which adopts priority queue to maintain candidate trajectory points for sampled trajectory and retains most valuable points by ranking. SQUISH algorithm is effective with acceptable time and space complexity. As an enhancement, Muckell et al. [13] propose SQUISH-E which allows to specify a threshold to control the upper bound of error.

3   Heuristic Sampling Based on Vector Feature

A heuristic trajectory compression algorithm HESAVE is described in detail in this section. After analyzing the characteristics of trajectory data, we propose IV and IVI as the metrics of trajectory point's information, and the data-driven SMW for splitting process unit during online sampling. First, we give some basic definitions.

Definition 1: GPS Trajectory Point. The GPS trajectory point is a triple $p(lat, lng, t)$ which records the position and timestamp, where t is the timestamp, recording data acquisition time, and lat is the latitude of this point, and lng is the longitude of this point.

Definition 2: GPS Trajectory. GPS trajectory $Traj = \{p_1, p_2, ..., p_n\}$ is time series of trajectory points, and an upper bound of time interval for every two successive trajectory points is specified.

In the following parts, we will introduce the framework of HESAVE and the calculating process of IVI in detail.

3.1   Calculation of Trajectory Point's Iteration Vector

To gain the minimum information loss after sampling, we need a standard to measure how much information each trajectory point contains. The essence of the trajectory is a sample of certain motion process at several points in time. Velocity is the standard for measuring motion process, so if a trajectory point contain more velocity information, it has more capacity for reflecting the motion process. We can retain more velocity information after trajectory sampling by preserving more velocity variations, which can be described using an acceleration vector.

For two successive trajectory points $p_{i-1}(lat_{i-1}, lng_{i-1}, t_{i-1})$ and $p_i(lat_i, lng_i, t_i)$, the spherical coordinate system can be converted to the plane rectangular coordinate system. In our works, we assume that the origin is p_0, the x-axis positive direction is east direction, and the y-axis positive direction is north direction, the unit is meter.

After coordinate system conversion, speed vector $\overrightarrow{v}_i$ and acceleration vector $\overrightarrow{a}_i$ of a trajectory point can be calculated using formula 1, 2 and 3.

$$\Delta t = t_i - t_{i-1} \tag{1}$$

$$\overrightarrow{v}_i = (\frac{x_i - x_{i-1}}{\Delta t}, \frac{y_i - y_{i-1}}{\Delta t}) \tag{2}$$

$$\overrightarrow{a}_i = \frac{(\overrightarrow{v}_i - \overrightarrow{v}_{i-1})}{\Delta t} \tag{3}$$

$\overrightarrow{a}_i$ is used to describe the degree of change in velocity during this time period. Acceleration vector can reflect the motion semantics of trajectories to a certain extent. Acceleration vector of certain trajectory point can reflect the tendency of movement at that point, and acceleration vectors of multiple continuous trajectory points can further reflect high level semantics of trajectory, such as turning or being stuck in jam.

However, the sampling frequency of a trajectory is relatively high, the acceleration vector in a small time period is difficult to reflect the deformation of the trajectory and reflect enough semantics in a larger time window. For example, considering a uniform speed U-shaped trajectory with equal time interval (the reality may be the vehicle on the roundabout, or the vehicle turn around, etc.), angles between accelerate vector and velocity vector and modules of accelerate vector for each points both are same. However, after several such trajectory points, the direction of the trajectory has completely changed.

The solution proposed by other algorithms such as ST-Trace [11] to this issue is to consider vector characteristics of this point and the previous trajectory points' synthetically. Similarly, we calculate the weighted sum of the acceleration vector to retain the previous acceleration characteristics synthetically.

$$d_i = \cos <\overrightarrow{v}_i, \overrightarrow{v}_{i-1}> = \frac{\overrightarrow{v}_i \cdot \overrightarrow{v}_{i-1}}{|\overrightarrow{v}_i| \times |\overrightarrow{v}_{i-1}|} \tag{4}$$

$$it_i = t_i + f(d_i) \cdot it_{i-1} \tag{5}$$

$$\overrightarrow{ia}_i = \frac{\overrightarrow{a}_i \cdot t_i + \overrightarrow{ia}_{i-1} \cdot f(d_i) \cdot it_{i-1}}{it_i} \qquad (6)$$

The purpose of introducing formula 6 is recording the acceleration information in a larger time range when the velocity direction of the trajectory is changed, but it will blur the single point short time acceleration information as the time range expanded. Actually, we only need to record a larger time range of acceleration information when the direction of velocity changes. And the greater the speed direction changes, the more previous information needed to record. Therefore, we use $f(d)$ in formula 5 as a weight factor, d calculated in formula 4 is the cosine of the angle between velocity vector and accelerate vector to measure the variability of speed direction, whose range is $[-1, 1]$. With the decrease of d, $f(d)$ increases, whose range is $[0, 1]$. We have pointed several key points and their empirical values showed in Table 1.

Table 1. Empirical values of $f(d)$ on key points.

d	Empirical value of $f(d)$
1.00	0.00
0.86	0.50
0.50	0.80
0.00	0.90
-1.00	1.00

Fitted with a two-item exponential function, the expression of $f(d)$ is determined. The expression is shown as Formula 7 and $f(d)$ is plotted in Fig. 1.

$$f(d) = -0.0008988e^{6.776d} + 0.8893e^{-0.1203d} \qquad (7)$$

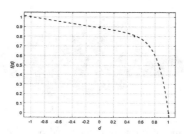

Fig. 1. Graph of $f(d)$

3.2 Measurement of Trajectory Point's Information

IV describes the motion semantics of trajectory points. In order to quantify the value of different semantics, we propose IVI to measure the amount of information contained in

IV for next step. First, transform the vector $\vec{ia}_i$ in plane rectangular coordinate system to polar coordinate system. In the physical sense, $\vec{ia}_i$ will be decomposed into the size and direction of two parts. Assume $\vec{ia}_i$ is expressed as (ax_i, ay_i) in plane rectangular coordinate system and as (ρ_i, θ_i) in polar coordinate system, and direction of polar axis is same as velocity vector. (ρ_i, θ_i) is determined using formula 8 and 9.

$$\rho_i = \sqrt{ax_i^2 + ay_i^2} \tag{8}$$

$$c_i = \cos(\theta_i) = \cos <\vec{v}_i, \vec{ia}_i> = \frac{\vec{v}_i \cdot \vec{ia}_i}{|\vec{v}_i| \times |\vec{ia}_i|} \tag{9}$$

In essence, θ_i is the angle between the direction of IV and the direction of velocity, which reflects the degree of displacement of acceleration direction and moving direction of certain trajectory point. In order to facilitate the calculation, without losing physical significance, we use cosine value of θ_i in the following process, which is labeled as c_i.

For certain trajectory, it can be treat as a continuous information source. To simplify the problem, we assume the probability of (ρ_i, c_i) and (ρ_{i-1}, c_{i-1}) are independent. In order to calculate the amount of information, the probability density function is needed. We calculated 2,354,838 trajectory points of the 1584 trajectories on the Geolife 1.3 dataset [14–16], and the density distributions on different dimensions are shown in Figs. 2 and 3-(a) and (c).

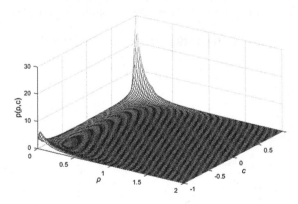

Fig. 2. Graph of ρ-c two-dimensional probability density

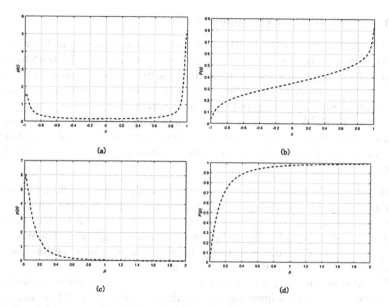

Fig. 3. (a) and (b) are graphs of c' probability density and probability distribution, (c) and (d) are graphs of ρ' probability density and probability distribution

From the probability density figure, the distribution of ρ and c are independent of each other. So, for any (ρ_i, c_i), the probability $p(\rho_i, c_i)$ is multiply of ρ's and c's probability.

$$p(\rho_i, c_i) = p_\rho(\rho_i) \times p_c(c_i) \tag{10}$$

In order to calculate probabilities $p_\rho(\rho_i)$ and $p_c(c_i)$, we use the probability distribution function to compute the probability. The probability distribution graphs of ρ and c are shown in Fig. 3-(b) and (d). Fitted with a two-item exponential function, the expressions of probability distribution functions are determined as formula 11 and 12.

$$P(\rho) = 0.8752e^{0.06431\rho} - 0.8173e^{-4.808\rho} \tag{11}$$

$$P(c) = \begin{cases} 0.3471e^{0.5056c} + 1.746 \times 10^{-10}e^{21.16c} & c \geq 0 \\ 0.3547e^{0.5639c} - 3.681 \times 10^{-5}e^{-8.373c} & c < 0 \end{cases} \tag{12}$$

Finally, we can get the amount of information using formula 13.

$$I_i = -\log_2 p(\rho_i, c_i) = -\log_2 p_\rho(\rho_i) - \log_2 p_c(c_i) \tag{13}$$

3.3   Framework of HESAVE Approach

In previous parts, we proposed IVI as the information measurement for trajectory points. Trajectory sampling is essentially to choose a subset of the trajectory points which obtain the larger amount of information as the sampling results. How to pick points is the key to trajectory sampling. HESAVE adopts a priority queue to maintain the subset of trajectory points with largest information.

In HESAVE, SMW is used to divide a trajectory into isolate processing units. SMW is a sliding window with a fixed size w, trajectory points within same SMW will be operated in same priority queue. The introduction of the SMW is trying to solve two problems:

1. SMW can limit the range of trajectory operated in algorithm to reduce the latency of the trajectory point processing. Using the window rather than the whole trajectory as the processing unit of trajectory compression, the result of trajectory sampling can be submitted periodically. Although the result of trajectory sampling result is not global optimal, it can effectively improve the real-time performance. It is necessary in some applications that have real-time requirements.
2. SMW can split trajectory points which are under different motion modes into isolated process units, thus improves the reliability of HESAVE. Many users upload trajectories collected under different transportation, or with changing of speed, acceleration and other characteristics. We call the trajectory containing a variety of motion patterns as **multi-mode trajectory**. The statistical characteristics of IVI are different among motion modes, because the distributions of speed and accelerate which are correlated with IVI are different. It is not reasonable to process trajectory points under different motion modes in the same unit.

HESAVE maintains separate priority queue for each SMW to isolate different process units. When the trajectory motion pattern changes or the number of trajectory points reaches SMW's limitation, according to the specified compression ratio, select some trajectory points with the largest IVI from the priority queue to join the sampled subset, discarding the trajectory points remained in priority queue. Finally, set up a new SMW from the new trajectory point and maintain a new priority queue. Process of HESAVE is shown by pseudo code Algorithm 1.

Algorithm 1 : *HESAVE (r, w, pstream)*

Input: **r** – target sampling ratio
    w – size of sliding mode window
    pstream – trajectory points input stream

Output: **T** – Sampled trajectory

```
//trajheap sort by point's ivi in descending order.
Create a priority queue trajheap
//counter records the number of points in window.
counter = 0
While(pstream.hasMorePoints() == true)
  counter++
  pi = pstream.getAPoint()
  Calculate IVI ivii of pi
  Add pi to trajheap
  //if counter reach the window size or motion mode
  //changed, we need to open a new window to deal with
  //new points and sample points in current window.
  if(counter >= w OR motion mode changed)
    //nreserve is the number of points to be reserved
    nreserve = trajheap.size * r
    for(i = 0; i < nreserve; i++)
      preserve = trajheap.poll()
      Add preserve to T
    end for
    //reset window and counter
    trajheap.clear()
    counter = 0;
  end if
end while
return T
```

3.4 Strategy of Window Sliding for SMW

It is necessary to identify the change of motion modes in a trajectory timely. Obviously, if we can identify the motion mode of trajectory fragments, it is easy to figure out the point where motion mode changes. The detection of trajectory motion mode is a multiple classification problem, and there are many mature methods to handle it. Feng et al. [17] propose that SVM can achieve an accuracy rate more than 90% using speed and acceleration characteristics.

In this paper, we use a fixed size sliding window to divide calculation units, then calculate the average and extreme values of the trajectory point's velocity in window as features. The motion patterns of trajectory points are divided into four categories using decision tree, including walk, bike, car and subway.

4   Evaluation

In this section, we conduct a series of experiments on the Geolife 1.3 dataset to verify the effectiveness of HESAVE and evaluate the performance. SQUISH algorithm is compared primarily.

4.1   Dataset and Experimental Environment

This study uses the Microsoft GeoLife 1.3 dataset [14–16] as a test dataset. It was collected by 172 users over a period of three years and there are various motion modes in the dataset. The sampling rate of most trajectory is 2–5 s and most of the data are collected around Beijing, China.

Experiments performed on a PC, which has an Intel Core i5-3470 CPU and 12 GB memory. The operation system is Window 10 professional edition. All algorithms are implemented in Java 1.8.0_11. All configures for JVM are the default values.

4.2   Effectivity Verification

First, we examine the sampling results under HESAVE to show its effectiveness. We select a trajectory from dataset randomly as an example, compress it with 20% target sampling ratio. Original trajectory and sampled trajectory are plotted in the plane rectangular coordinate system, as Fig. 4-(a) shows.

There are a large number of trajectory points gathered in two locations in the higher left corner of Fig. 4-(a), which are called stay points. Objects moves slowly around stay points, and it may have some high-level semantics. After sampling, only one point of a stay point is retained. To hold more information within stay points, we can isolate these points using a separate SMW by adjusting sliding strategy. This "negative example" clearly demonstrates the necessity of the mode window, although it is not a mistake to discard the stay point during trajectory compression. (Generally, we detect stay points before trajectory compression.)

Though HESAVE does not use the trajectory's geometrical characteristics directly, it can guarantee the shape similarity before and after sampling. In order to quantify the deformation after compression, we adopt **Mean Distance** (MD) as metrics of deformation, which counted the average VED of each dropped original trajectory point to the compressed trajectory. SQUISH is slightly superior to HESAVE on ME, especially at lower sampling rate. But there is little difference between them the trend of change is similar (Fig. 5).

For temporal information, a distribution map for trajectory points transient acceleration vector before and after sampling is showed in Fig. 4-(b). Assume all vectors' initial points are origin, and original trajectory point vectors' terminal points are plotted as a cross label and sampled trajectory point vectors' are plotted as a circle label. We calculated the ratio of retained trajectory points in different acceleration ranges, and the result is showed in Fig. 4-(c). From the acceleration vector distribution diagram and retain ratio, better part of the trajectory points with larger acceleration vector are retained, and the direction distribution of acceleration before and after compression is quite consistent. The sampled trajectory can hold the main speed characteristics of the original trajectory.

In summary, HESAVE is effective, and IVI as the measurement of information is reliable.

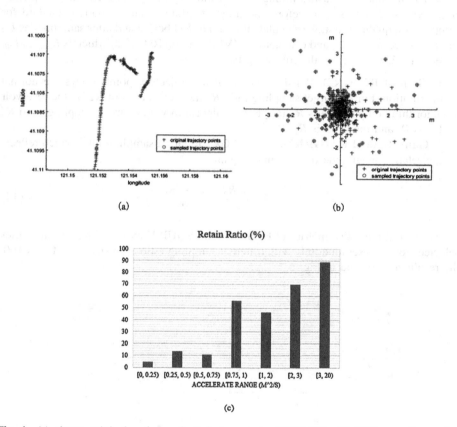

Fig. 4. (a) shows original and sample trajectory under HESAVE with 20% sampling ratio, (b) shows acceleration vector distribution before and after sampling and (c) shows trajectory points retain ratio in different accelerate ranges

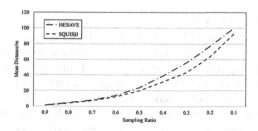

Fig. 5. MD under different sampling ratio for SQUISH and HESAVE

4.3   Comparison of Information Loss

Including SQUISH, ST-Trace, the error metrics of many trajectory sampling algorithms adopt SED as a standard [10, 12]. SED can describe the change of trajectory shape after sampling but it may not reflect temporal information loss sufficiently.

IVI is reliable to measure timing and positioning information for each trajectory point, we use IVI loss ratio before and after sampling as an evaluation standard for compression quality. First, we calculate the sum of IVI before and after sampling, as I_{all} and $I_{sampled}$ respectively, and calculate the IVI Retention Rate (R2) which is $I_{sampled}/I_{all}$. Based on R2, we propose the following two metrics:

1. Gain of R2 (GR2). IVI distribution of the trajectory points obeys the normal distribution. For the target sampling ratio R_t, the expectation of R2 by the reservoir algorithm compression is R_t, too. For an algorithm with a target sampling ratio R_t, R2 is R_s and the GR2 is R_s- R_t.

2. Gain Ratio of R2 (GRR2). Ratio of GR2 to target sampling ratio which reflects the relative magnitude of information gain.

$$GRR2 = \frac{GR2}{R_t} = \frac{R_s - R_t}{R_t} \tag{14}$$

We record these two metrics of HESAVE and SQUISH by sampling 20 trajectories selected from dataset randomly with different sampling ratio. The size of SMW is 100. the results are showed in Fig. 6.

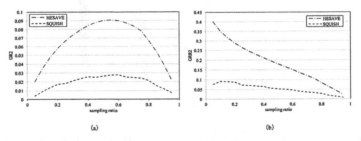

Fig. 6. (a) and (b) showed the average GR2 and GRR2 under different sampling ratio for SQUISH and HESAVE

From Fig. 6, HESAVE is much better than SQUISH. It is worth noting that from the Fig. 6-(a), the GR2 curves of HESAVE and SQUISH appear to be convex arcs. The reason is that the number of points that algorithms can eliminate or retain is not much under extreme sampling ratio, and the gaps of IVI among the trajectory points are small. The GR2 curve of SQUISH has smaller curvature than that of HESAVE, because SQUISH does not use windows as a processing unit and operate trajectory points in a larger range, so it can be less affected by a high or low target sampling ratio. It is suggested to enlarge the size of HESAVE processing window when the target sampling ratio is extreme.

4.4 Comparison of Computational and Space Complexity

Time efficiency of algorithm has great influence on the usability of algorithm, which reflects the demand of computing resources. We measure the process time of HESAVE and SQUISH by sampling 100 trajectories with different length. The target sampling ratio is 0.3 and the size of SMW is 100. The results are shown in Fig. 7.

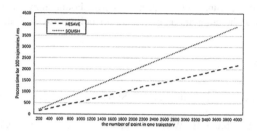

Fig. 7. Process time of HESAVE and SQUISH for trajectories with different length

The process time of HESAVE is quite smaller than SQUISH, and the difference between the two algorithms increases with the increase of trajectory length. In fact, both time and space complexity of HESAVE are better than SQUISH.

Priority queue is used to maintain trajectory points to be operated in these algorithms, and it is the main factors affecting the computational and space complexity. HESAVE uses SMW to reduce the size of processing unit, it can limit the time and space complexity of the algorithm and improve the real-time performance of the algorithm effectively (Table 2).

Table 2. Computational and space complexity comparison

Algorithm	Computational complexity	Space complexity
SQUISH	$O(n \log(n))$	$O(\log(n))$
HESAVE	$O(n \log(w))$	$O(\log(w))$

5 Conclusion

As a heuristic sampling method, HESAVE adopts priority queue to improve the generality, abandons thresholds which are relative with trajectory semantics. Using SMW, HESAVE can sample multi-mode trajectory effectively with acceptable latency by dividing trajectory into different processing units according to the trajectory semantics.

For information measurement, the time range for calculating IV can adjust dynamically to take into account the vector characteristics of trajectory at different scales for more obvious motion semantics. What's more, as the measurement for information of trajectory points, the representation of IVI owns scalability, it is flexible to add other influence factors according to the demand into the computation process of IVI.

The following work mainly includes further research on sliding window strategy of SMW by analyzing trajectory points semantics based on IVI. Current sliding window strategy has no association with IVI.

Acknowledgements. This work is supported by the Natural Science Foundation of Beijing under Grant No. 4181002, and the Natural Science Foundation of China under Grant No. 61876023. We thank the anonymous reviewers for helpful suggestions.

References

1. Schiller, J., Voisard, A.: Location-Based Services, 1st edn. Morgan Kaufmann, San Francisco (2004)
2. Potdar, V., Sharif, A., Chang, E.: Wireless sensor networks: a survey. Comput. Netw. **38**(4), 393–422 (2002)
3. Baniukevic, A., Jensen, C.S., Lu, H.: Hybrid indoor positioning with Wi-Fi and bluetooth: architecture and performance. In: IEEE 14th International Conference on Mobile Data Management, pp. 207–216. IEEE, Milan (2013)
4. Wang, Y., Zheng, Y., Xue, Y.: Travel time estimation of a path using sparse trajectories. In: KDD, pp. 25–34, ACM, New York (2014)
5. Yuan, J., Zheng, Y., Xie, X., et al.: Driving with knowledge from the physical world. In: KDD, pp. 316–324, ACM, San Diego (2011)
6. Yuan, J., Zheng, Y., Xie, X.: Discovering regions of different functions in a city using human mobility and POIs. In: KDD, pp. 186–194, ACM, Beijing (2012)
7. Zheng, Y.: Trajectory data mining: an overview. ACM Trans. Intell. Syst. Technol. **6**(3), 1–41 (2015)
8. Trajcevski, G.: Compression of spatio-temporal data. In: IEEE International Conference on Mobile Data Management, pp. 4–7. IEEE, Proto (2016)
9. Douglas, D.H., Peucker, T.K.: Algorithms for the reduction of the number of points required to represent a digitized line or its caricature. Int. J. Geogr. Inf. Geovis. **10**(2), 112–122 (1973)
10. Keogh, E., Chu, S., Hart, D., et al.: An online algorithm for segmenting time series. In: IEEE International Conference on Data Mining, pp. 289–296. IEEE, San Jose (2001)
11. Potamias, M., Patroumpas, K., Sellis, T.: Sampling trajectory streams with spatiotemporal criteria. In: IEEE International Conference on Scientific and Statistical Database Management, pp. 275–284. IEEE, Vienna (2006)
12. Muckell, J., Hwang, J.H., Patil, V., et al.: SQUISH: an online approach for GPS trajectory compression. In: International Conference on Computing for Geospatial Research and Applications, pp. 1–8. ACM, Washington DC (2011)
13. Muckell, J., Olsen, P.W., Hwang, J.H., et al.: Compression of trajectory data: a comprehensive evaluation and new approach. Geoinformatica **18**(3), 435–460 (2014)
14. Zheng, Y., Zhang, L., Xie, X., Ma, W.: Mining interesting locations and travel sequences from GPS trajectories. In: International Conference on World Wild Web, pp. 791–800, ACM Press, Madrid (2009)

15. Zheng, Y., Li, Q., Chen, Y., Xie, X., Ma, W.: Understanding mobility based on GPS data. In: ACM Conference on Ubiquitous Computing, pp. 312–321. ACM Press, Seoul (2008)
16. Zheng, Y., Xie, X., Ma, W.: GeoLife: a collaborative social networking service among user, location and trajectory. IEEE Data Eng. Bull. 33(2), 32–40 (2010)
17. Feng, T., Timmermans, H.J.P.: Transportation mode recognition using GPS and accelerometer data. Transp. Res. Part C Emerg. Technol. 37(3), 118–130 (2013)

Mobility as a Service Enabled by the Autonomous Driving

Christian Rakow[✉] and Manzoor Ahmed Khan

DAI Labor, Technische Universität Berlin, Ernst-Reuter-Platz 7,
10587 Berlin, Germany
{christian.rakow,manzoor-ahmed.khan}@dai-labor.de

Abstract. The future of transport network fueled by vision of Autonomous driving is expected to revolutionize the classical ways of mobility. In this paper, we focus on enabling the autonomous mobility of specially enabled students within the Technical University Berlin Campus. In this connection, we digitize segments of the roads by deploying various sensors and communication infrastructure for V2X and sensors-to-central cloud communication. We present our vehicle disposition system for the so called "Uni-Shuttle", which integrates the various sensors information and optimizes the vehicles' schedules by means of local search operations and meta-heuristics. Our evaluation in a simulated environment shows that our approach is more efficient than a traditional bus with a fixed time-schedule and line network.

Keywords: Autonomous vehicle · Street digitization · V2X
Dial-a-ride

1 Introduction

Rapidly increasing population and mobility demand in urban areas becomes a serious concern of our time that significantly affects the everyday lives of citizens. Traffic congestion, air pollution and limited parking places are among the prominent problems of our cities as a result of urbanization. Rather than making constructional extensions on the city infrastructures, which is time-consuming, expensive and unsafe, optimized use of the existing roads with innovative approaches is believed to be a more feasible solution. Based on this common understanding, more flexible, on-demand and integrated mobility options gain interest rather than using traditional ways of transportation. The technological advancements in ICT sector, newly emerging shared mobility concepts and enhancements in the autonomous driving are the major driving forces behind this behavior change. In this context, we address the recently emerging paradigm of "Mobility as a Service" (MaaS), having a great potential of leading more efficient and sustainable transport. Fueled by the rapidly realizing autonomous driving concepts, MaaS is expected to exist in different modes in future e.g., MaaS for general public, MaaS for university campus, MaaS for hospital patients, etc.

A. M. J. Skulimowski et al. (Eds.): IOV 2018, LNCS 11253, pp. 208–219, 2018.
https://doi.org/10.1007/978-3-030-05081-8_15

Being the part of a flagship project of Germany focusing on driving test-road, we study the impact of autonomous driving on different modes of MaaS. However, in this paper, the focus is confined to an approach for a so called "dial-a-ride" service, with a fixed graph of stations where users can request transport to their desired destination. We do not only optimize for shortest routes and travel times, but also focus on a holistic view of real-life challenges. In practice, unforeseen circumstances such as road congestion, crashes or severe weather can happen and the system has to react accordingly.

Our approach consist of a continuous rolling horizon planner, which optimizes current trips by local search and various configurable metaheuristics, such as late acceptance or tabu search. Any changes in the environment or deviations from a plan, e.g., a delayed vehicle, are submitted to the planner, which adjusts plans in real-time.

2   Related Work

Most recent "Vehicle Routing Problems" (VRP) variants differ widely from the original problem formulation given by [6]. Hence, there is a huge variation of available methods. [7] developed a taxonomy based on over 1000 journal articles and classified the most impactful papers. [11] extend the idea and define the so called Rich Vehicle Problems (RVRPs), which focuses on recent methods that solve inherently more complex challenges.

For basic problem variants exact methods have been developed, that minimize the total round-trip time [14]. As the VRP is a np-hard problem, these scale not well and are generally not suited for practical problems with more than a thousand customers. For this reason approximate methods based on heuristic and metaheuristics are often used in practical applications as shown in a survey by [1]. An extensive review of the history of VRPs and classical methods can be found in [14].

Authors in [8] propose a multi-agent simulation approach to demonstrate the feasibility of on-demand mobility operated by shared, autonomous and electric cars. In the presented work, the dynamic interactions between customers, a dispatching center and a shared, autonomous, electric vehicle fleet are studied. The main entities of the simulation model are given as "control center", "taxi" and "fleet management", each of which is represented as a software agent on a Java based platform. Authors consider three different simulation scenarios within the city of Munich, covered by shared autonomous vehicle (SAV) fleet. As a result of performed simulation runs on different scales, it is indicated that SAV fleets provide around 15% increase in mileage compared to a situation with privately owned vehicles. In addition, the average customer waiting time is found to be below 3 min in all scenarios.

An online mechanism is presented by the authors of [2] to enable fair allocation in payment for passengers of autonomous taxis. In the envisaged scenario, shared autonomous taxis are modeled on a grid city network with clients occasionally requesting a ride. Authors make use of a finite state machine to demonstrate the sharing scheme and explain the algorithm. It is highlighted that the proposed algorithm provided fair payment allocation for the passengers with the guarantee of envy freeness and maximum utilities.

Authors of [12] propose a public transportation system based on autonomous vehicles by addressing two major problems: "scheduling" and "admission control". The scheduling refers to assigning designated vehicles to the admissible transportation requests, determining routes of vehicles and the times by which they should reach their destinations. On the other hand, the admission process finds out the set of requests suitable for scheduling to produce maximum profit. While the scheduling is formulated as a mixed-integer linear problem, the admission control is handled by a genetic-algorithm based solution. Authors validate the proposed architecture by performing simulations on a real taxi dataset recorded in Boston.

Authors in [3] simulate the city-wide replacement of private cars with autonomous taxi (AT) fleets by considering a typical weekday in Berlin. The proposed simulation model optimizes a real-time AT dispatching algorithm to handle high number of requests at a low computation time. Based on the simulation results, authors indicate that one AT can replace the demand served by ten conventionally driven vehicles.

In this paper we consider changes in the environment and multiple constraints such as maximum allowed customer waiting times. Most taxonomies would classify the problem at hand as (i) a rich VRP and (ii) a dynamic dial-a-ride problem. [13] carried out a survey specially for these problem variants, where knowledge is not complete, but revealed during runtime. Up until now most research focuses on special VRP variants with a few specific characteristics, as pointed out by multiple authors [5, 11, 13]. Our approach advances current research on dynamic and real-life routing problems and tackles challenges that arise with the advent of next generation transportation infrastructure. It is the first step of our effort to carry out research of future mobility concepts in a real-life test-bed with the integration of upcoming and novel technologies.

3   Mobility as a Service - the DigiNet-PS Perspective

To elaborate on our perspective of MaaS, we will first introduce a flagship project of Germany, DigiNet-PS[1] that is led by an author of the paper.

3.1   Overview of DigiNet-PS

DigiNet-PS is an ambitious project that aims to develop a smart city infrastructure at the center of Berlin, Germany, as an urban test field for automated and networked driving functions. For this purpose, the project offers a highly digitized infrastructure along a road stretch of over 3.4 km that spans the TU Berlin campus and the historical Brandenburg Gate, together with the surrounding streets. DigiNet-PS project aims at creating a live test road that: (i) Enables

---

[1] www.diginet-ps.de.

the stakeholders (automobile makers, communication providers, etc.) to create and test their solutions for autonomous driving in the real urban environment. (ii) Enable the study of evolving ecosystems for autonomous driving and digitized cities. (iii) Enable smaller entrants/entrepreneurs to be the part of future autonomous driving industry. (iv) Solutions for migration towards Level 4/5 autonomous driving.

To achieve these objectives, DigiNet-PS follows a philosophy different to many autonomous driving initiatives around the world i.e., we believe that "Intelligent vehicle is good, but Intelligent environment is better". This is to say that with the limited visibility (enabled by on-vehicle sensors) of vehicle, the goals of L-4/L-5 may not be achieved. This provisions that both the visibility and environmental perception of the autonomous vehicles need to be improved. For instance, it is still unclear as to how capable the autonomous vehicles will be to cope with different situations and environments? Obviously, accurate identification of objects and street furniture lead to predicting the behavior e.g., a car in front will behave differently than a pedestrian or a tree. The question is, will the autonomous vehicles cope with unprecedented and complex situations e.g., roads with unregulated traffic, temporary/dynamic obstacles such as vehicle looking for parking or road construction, making way for fire-brigade, etc. This reinforces the fact that not all the variables for every decision-making instance or not all the situations for decision-making are known in advance. Hence, the vehicle needs additional/external sources of information, improved techniques for creating its environment, equipped with human like instinct, etc. These requirements lead us in DigiNet-PS to carry out research in three levels:

- **Vehicle research:** to improve the perception of the vehicle by introducing new functions and approaches. Within DigiNet-PS, we aim at introducing new layers of information and improved approaches (including ML) to improve the decision-making of autonomous vehicles. The idea is to also make the autonomous vehicle capable of predicting the environment.
- **Street digitization/Edge Computing:** In order to increase the visibility of autonomous vehicles and provide them with additional external information, different types of sensors (parking, traffic analysis, environmental, road-condition, etc.) and communication infrastructure (components for short-range and cellular communications) are deployed. The research focus at this level remains on creating the perception of the environment by edge computing, sensory data fusion, and AI approaches. The idea is to create an "Edge Dynamic Map (EDM)" very similar to the "Local Dynamic Map (LDM)" of the vehicle and feed the LDM with the information from EDM in real-time for better/more informed decision-making.
- **Cloud:** It has the global view, as it can communicate both with edge computing entities and the vehicles. This level implements the most computation intensive tasks. The data-analytics approaches, high level patterns for different scenarios, data-fusion, sensors selection, Machine learning for situational awareness, etc. are the research topics at this level. So the distributed AI

based decision-making, 5G and CV2X are the research areas at all the three levels.

3.2 MaaS in DigiNet-PS

Within the scope of DigiNet-PS we also plan to deploy an autonomous vehicle equipped with up-to six passenger seats that will be available for the transportation needs of specially enabled students. The so called "Uni-Shuttle" integrates the solutions developed in all three research areas to provide (i) a demonstrator and show-case for state-of-the art research and (ii) better mobility for students on the campus. The Uni-Shuttle is the ideal testbed as it not only relies on autonomous driving functions in the vehicle itself, but also sensory data of the traffic situation to adjust current routes. Furthermore, the cloud backend enables the service to schedule routes in advance based on future demand and forecasted traffic congestion. The concept can be extended to other areas with large campuses and is for instance very valuable for hospitals where many passengers with special needs are relying on the provided mobility services.

4 Realization of DigiNet-PS MaaS

We now discuss the technical and conceptual constituent components of MaaS that include: environment digitization, communication infrastructure, and vehicle disposition planner. In what follows next, we provide the details of these constituent components.

4.1 Infrastructure Digitization

By the digitization, it is meant that the street furniture is equipped with different types of sensors including: parking sensors, traffic analysis sensors, road-condition sensors, environmental sensors, etc. These sensors are deployed with the goal to collect autonomous vehicles' environment information for further processing in edge or cloud and making it available to other vehicles for more informed decision-making.

4.2 Communication Infrastructure

The communication infrastructure enables vehicle to vehicle (over the roadside unit), vehicle to sensors, vehicle to datacenter, and sensors to datacenter communication. Figure 1 presents an overview of the communication infrastructure. As evident from the figure the roadside units (RSU) on the downstream allow vehicles and sensors to communicate over short range communication technologies with vehicles and nearby sensors. In further work it is planned to pursue cooperative approaches for resource-allocation [10] and load-balancing [15] in order to maintain network efficiency with an increasing number of participants. On the upstream the RSU communicates with the DigiNet-PS backend/cloud via backhaul network. For the backhaul network, we rely on two communication links: microwave based and 5 G.

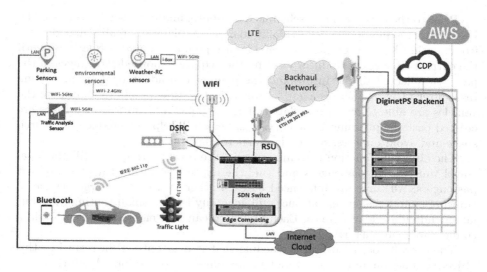

Fig. 1. DigiNet-PS communication infrastructure

4.3 Vehicle Disposition Planner

Figure 2 shows our disposition system architecture, which realizes the well known MAPE-K loop [9] for self-adaptive systems.

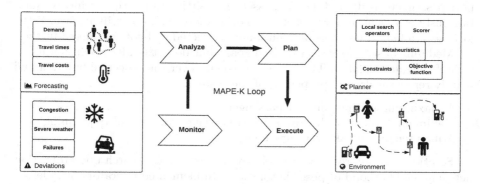

Fig. 2. The execution cycle of the vehicle dispatching system.

The planner component generates and optimizes plans for the vehicle fleet, by means of metaheuristics and local search operators. These plans are executed in the environment and feedback is used to adapt to changes and re-optimize continuously in the background. The demand is not known beforehand and passenger requests have to be scheduled as soon as they arrive. However, forecast data is available not only for the demand, but also for the stochastic travel time and costs.

Prior to the execution of a schedule only approximate knowledge is available. Due to unforeseen events such as traffic congestion, plans and reality may deviate from one another. To compensate for this each plan is updated regularly up until the current time t_{now}. By incorporating the acquired knowledge, changes in the past are reflected to the future and the planner can adapt to it by modifying tasks after t_{future}. There is a gap between the two time points to make sure the vehicles are able to execute updated plans without interruptions. No tasks are created past the planning horizon $t_{horizon}$, which is helpful to reduce the search space and avoid unnecessary re-plannings too far in the future.

The objective function is to minimize (i) the total routing cost, (ii) the total travel time for all passengers and (iii) the expected waiting time for forecast passengers. All three are influenced by each other, e.g. using a large vehicle to transport many passengers at once will generally lead to small routing cost, but larger individual travel times. Each objective can be weighted differently via a configurable parameter.

The overall goal is to find a schedule that is near optimal in regard to this objective function and does not violate any physical constraints. A solution constitutes the schedules of all vehicles, where each schedule is represented by an ordered list of stops that define the path the vehicle will follow. Additionally, each stop also includes departure times that allows the vehicle to stay at a specific location and the set of passengers that are picked-up or dropped-off at this stop.

A solution that fulfills all hard constraints is called "feasible". In practice those are all schedules, which are realizable by the given vehicle fleet and transport passengers as desired, i.e. no passenger is sitting in multiple vehicles simultaneously or a vehicle does not have to drive more than one trip at once. If the local search finds a non-feasible solution it is rejected and not considered further.

Medium constraints reflect desired goals, but do not render a solution infeasible if they are violated. They have precedence over the objective function and mainly represent desired properties of the system:

– A maximum waiting time for passengers
– Maximum detour for already boarded passengers in case of re-planning
– A maintenance break every few hours.

Solutions are improved iteratively by means of local search operators, that define a neighborhood of possible solutions. Implemented operators include:

– Inserting or removing stops into a schedule, which is randomly selected from all available stops or assigned more greedily with stops where passengers are currently waiting.
– Driving to a nearby parking space or depot.
– Pickup and drop-off of a passenger.
– Swapping two vehicles. (Although in the case of Uni-Shuttle there is only one)

Solutions are generated for the time-span between t_{future} and $t_{horizon}$. Each operation constitutes a new solution that will be scored according to the objective function. We implemented incremental score calculation in order to reduce the computational effort by only accounting for facts that changed between two solutions. Each step a fixed number of solutions will be generated and a meta-heuristic selects one, which will become the new solution. Late-acceptance [4] is used in the default configuration, though other options are also available. The whole vehicle disposition planner, including the domain model, score calculation and search operators is implemented in Java with support by the OptaPlanner[2] framework.

5 Evaluation

To evaluate the performance of our disposition algorithm we created a simulation to compare it with a traditional bus that operates on a fixed route. Figure 3 shows the area that is digitized by DigiNet-PS and also the operational area of the bus shuttle.

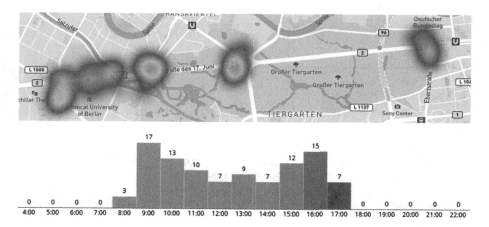

Fig. 3. Spatial and temporal distribution of passenger request in the evaluation.

In total the section is around 3.4 km long and a vehicle needs roughly 20 min for one round-trip. There are seven bus stations along the road, which are near to train stations, university buildings or attractions like the "Siegessäule" or "Brandenburger Tor".

Especially stops near train stations exhibit a larger amount of requests at which students usually arrive first. Furthermore, there are two peaks in the morning and afternoon at times when most of the lectures start or end. In total, we generated 100 requests during the operational time between 8:00 and 18:00. The demand that is also shown in Fig. 3 is based on data we gathered from the course catalog. Based on the lectures' time slots and room sizes we generated requests drawn from a normal distribution centered at the peak hours. In future

---

[2] www.optaplanner.org.

work we would like to replace our estimations with actual data collected by e.g. a people counting sensor.

To model the planned deployment as close as possible, there was only one vehicle simulated with six passenger seats. The system was configured with $t_{future} = 2$ min and $t_{horizon} = 3$ h. The fixed bus that is used for comparison drives the whole route in circles without further delay after each round-trip. All configurations were simulated 5 times and averaged at the end.

One of the most important criteria for evaluating the service quality is the time a passenger needs to wait for the bus to arrive. Passengers send their desired pickup location and destination via an app to the backend and receive a preliminary schedule which includes the estimated time to wait. Figure 4 shows the waiting time percentiles for a fixed bus service and our disposition planner.

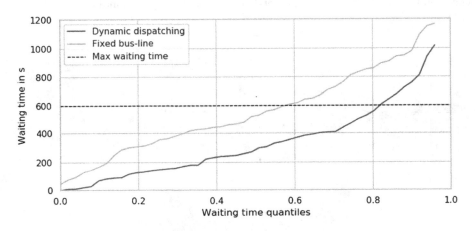

Fig. 4. Comparison of waiting times for dynamic disposition and fixed bus route.

The maximum desired waiting time, a medium constraint to ensure a certain level of service quality, was set to ten minutes. The figure shows that with our on-demand disposition 80% of passenger request could be met. In contrast, the fixed bus line could only transport around 60% of the passengers within the given constraints. Furthermore, the median waiting time for the fixed bus was up to three minutes higher.

Figure 5 shows the maximum amount of boarded passengers in 5-min intervals. One can see that the dynamic dispatching is able to transport slightly more passengers by utilizing nearly all passenger seats during the peak times.

One important aspect of the journey is not only the waiting time but also the travel time itself. A short wait period might be meaningless if passengers have to accept huge detours because of the ride sharing. Table 1 shows the waiting time and detour compared with a direct connection.

Detour is defined as the time a trip takes compared to a direct trip from the origin to the destination. Because of the service area, which is only one

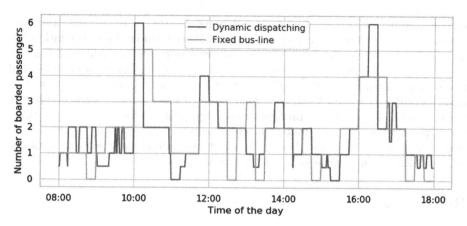

Fig. 5. The maximum occupancy over 5 min intervals.

Table 1. Comparison of dynamic dispatching and a fixed bus-line.

Metric		Dynamic dispatching	Fixed bus-line
Waiting time	$Q_{0.25}$	**144.50 s**	349.50 s
	$Q_{0.5}$	**281.0 s**	523.01 s
	$Q_{0.75}$	**477.25 s**	819.25 s
Detour	$Q_{0.25}$	**20.0 s**	30.0 s
	$Q_{0.5}$	**30.0 s**	40.0 s
	$Q_{0.75}$	**77.0 s**	286.75 s

long road segment there are only small detours in both operations modes. These
are mainly caused by the time the bus needs to stop in order to board other
passengers. But it is also apparent that the detour can be significantly higher
in our scenario when using a fixed bus. For instance the bus might be going in
the wrong direction so a passenger needs to wait until the bus completed its
round-trip and changes the direction.

Overall the evaluation shows that the dynamic dispatching is much more
effective than a fixed bus-route in the case of DigiNet-PS. However, the current
scenario includes only one autonomous vehicle. If the testbed is extended to a
larger area or more vehicles are added to the fleet the comparison needs to be
reevaluated.

6   Conclusion

In this paper, we discussed the evolving mobility modes specifically those enabled
by the autonomous driving. We also provided a brief overview of an initiative
of autonomous driving in Berlin, which is used as the testing facility to validate

different solutions of the autonomous driving. Furthermore, we discussed our perspective of mobility as a service and contributed model. Our simulation has shown that the dynamic disposition is more effective than a traditional bus-line in the case of DigiNet-PS. We see this only as the first step in carrying out research for future mobility services with integration into new communication and road infrastructure. With the deployment of more sensors we would like to try new machine learning approaches to combine the collected data and validate the approach not only in simulation, but also in practice as soon as the vehicle is deployed. Moreover, extending the testbed with additional road segments and more vehicles is one major point for future work.

References

1. The vehicle routing problem: state of the art classification and review. Comput. Ind. Eng. 300–313 (2016). https://doi.org/10.1016/j.cie.2015.12.007
2. Bai, W., Quan, J., Fu, L., Gan, X., Wang, X.: Online fair allocation in autonomous vehicle sharing. In: GLOBECOM 2017 - 2017 IEEE Global Communications Conference, pp. 1–6, December 2017. https://doi.org/10.1109/GLOCOM.2017.8254671
3. Bischoff, J., Maciejewski, M.: Simulation of city-wide replacement of private cars with autonomous taxis in Berlin. In: The 7th International Conference on Ambient Systems, Networks and Technologies (ANT 2016) (2016). https://doi.org/10.1016/j.procs.2016.04.121
4. Burke, E.K., Bykov, Y.: A late acceptance strategy in hill-climbing for exam timetabling problems. In: PATAT 2008 Conference, Montreal, Canada, pp. 1–7 (2008)
5. Caceres-Cruz, J., Arias, P., Guimarans, D., Riera, D., Juan, A.A.: Rich vehicle routing problem. ACM Comput. Surv. (2), 1–28 (2014). https://doi.org/10.1145/2666003
6. Dantzig, G.B., Ramser, J.H.: The truck dispatching problem. Manag. Sci. (1), 80–91 (1959). https://doi.org/10.1287/mnsc.6.1.80
7. Eksioglu, B., Vural, A.V., Reisman, A.: The vehicle routing problem: a taxonomic review. Comput. Ind. Eng. 57(4), 1472–1483 (2009). https://doi.org/10.1016/j.cie.2009.05.009
8. Jäger, B., Agua, F.M.M., Lienkamp, M.: Agent-based simulation of a shared, autonomous and electric on-demand mobility solution. In: 2017 IEEE 20th International Conference on Intelligent Transportation Systems (ITSC), pp. 250–255, October 2017. https://doi.org/10.1109/ITSC.2017.8317947
9. Kephart, J.O., Chess, D.M.: The vision of autonomic computing. Computer (1), 41–50 (2003). https://doi.org/10.1109/MC.2003.1160055
10. Khan, M.A., Toker, A.C., Sivrikaya, F., Albayrak, S.: Cooperation-based resource allocation and call admission for wireless network operators. Telecommun. Syst. 51(1), 29–41 (2012). https://doi.org/10.1007/s11235-010-9412-1
11. Lahyani, R., Khemakhem, M., Semet, F.: Rich vehicle routing problems: from a taxonomy to a definition. Eur. J. Oper. Res. 241(1), 1–14 (2015). https://doi.org/10.1016/j.ejor.2014.07.048
12. Lam, A.Y.S., Leung, Y., Chu, X.: Autonomous-vehicle public transportation system: scheduling and admission control. IEEE Trans. Intell. Transp. Syst. 17(5), 1210–1226 (2016). https://doi.org/10.1109/TITS.2015.2513071

13. Ritzinger, U., Puchinger, J., Hartl, R.F.: A survey on dynamic and stochastic vehicle routing problems. Int. J. Prod. Res. **54**(1), 215–231 (2016). https://doi.org/10.1080/00207543.2015.1043403
14. Toth, P., Vigo, D., Scheinberg, K.: Vehicle Routing: Problems, Methods, and Applications (2014). https://doi.org/10.1137/1.9781611973594.fm
15. Yildiz, M., Khan, M.A., Sivrikaya, F., Albayrak, S.: Cooperation incentives based load balancing in UCN: a probabilistic approach. In: 2012 IEEE Global Communications Conference (GLOBECOM), pp. 2746–2752, December 2012. https://doi.org/10.1109/GLOCOM.2012.6503532

Adaptive Multiple Task Assignments for UAVs Using Discrete Particle Swarm Optimization

Kun Chen[✉], Qibo Sun, Ao Zhou, and Shangguang Wang

The State Key Laboratory of Networking and Switching Technology,
Beijing University of Posts and Telecommunications, Beijing, China
ck3621863@163.com

Abstract. The forest fire is an extremely dangerous natural disaster. The traditional fire-fighting equipment have great difficulty in performing firefighting in mountain terrain. Unmanned aerial vehicles (UAVs) are coming into a popular form in forest firefighting. In view of the suddenness of forest fires, the adaptive and dynamic firefighting task assignment for UAV is of great significance, and the current firefighting task assignment cannot address this issue. This paper proposed an adaptive and dynamic multiple task assignment method for UAVs. Firstly, the adaptive and dynamic firefighting task assignment is formulated as an optimization problem. Secondly, an assignment algorithm is proposed to solve the problem by extending the particle swarm optimization (PSO) algorithm. Finally, the experiment results verify the effectiveness of the proposed algorithm.

Keywords: UAV · Forest firefighting · Task assignment
Particle swarm optimization

1 Introduction

Forests are an important part of the national economy. Forest fires cause great threaten to the lives of firefighters. UAVs do not endanger the lives of operators in putting out forest fires, and can ensure the continuity of operations [1]. Therefore, UAVs are becoming more and more widely used in forest fire fighting [2].

Traditionally, the forest fire fighting missions can be simplified to four stages: search, detection, firefighting and verification. UAVs should work cooperatively to complete their tasks. For example, in order to successfully complete the firefighting missions in minimum time, UAVs performing detection tasks should gather more information, and feedback these data to the UAVs performing firefighting tasks.

There are plenty of methods that have been proposed for solving the multiple task assignment problem. In the early study, the generic UAV cooperative multiple task assignment problem is defined in [3]. An autonomous control model of unmanned vehicle is proposed in [4]. In the methods proposed in [5, 6], the swarm intelligence algorithms are applied to solve the problem. Besides, a network flow model is proposed to solve task assignment and route planning in [1]. Phan and Liu [7] develop a decision

© Springer Nature Switzerland AG 2018
A. M. J. Skulimowski et al. (Eds.): IOV 2018, LNCS 11253, pp. 220–229, 2018.
https://doi.org/10.1007/978-3-030-05081-8_16

making algorithm to optimally solve the task assignment problem for UAVs. However, they only focus on the firefighting task, and ignore the detection task. Ghamry [8, 9] use the auction-based algorithm to solve the task assignment and route planning. Huang [10] proposes a task assignment algorithm for underwater vehicles. Jiang [11] considers the vehicle routing problems with time windows. Oh [12] proposes a novel market-based decentralized algorithm to solve task assignment of multiple UAVs. However, none of these methods can do multiple task assignment adaptively and dynamically. It means all the assigned tasks should be completed before new-coming tasks can be assigned to the UAVS. In view of the suddenness of forest fires, the adaptive and dynamic firefighting task assignment for UAV is of great significance.

In this paper, a PSO-based algorithm is proposed to address this issue. Firstly, we formulate the adaptive and dynamic firefighting task assignment as an optimization problem. Secondly, by extending the PSO algorithm, an assignment algorithm is proposed to solve the problem. Finally, the experiment results show the advantages of our algorithm.

The rest of the paper is organized as follows. Section 2 defines the problem. Section 3 describes the technical details of our algorithm. In Sect. 4, the experiment results are described. Finally, we conclude this paper in Sect. 5.

2   System Model and Problem Formulation

2.1   System Model

The forest fire fighting mission is divided into a group of targets. Four types of tasks should be performed for completing a target: search, detection, firefighting and verification. For one target, the tasks must be executed in this special order. The key to the problem is how to insert new tasks into the original assignment strategy when new incoming targets arrive dynamically. We must ensure that the insertion would not affect the original targets. We assume that there are n vehicles and m targets at the beginning, and these targets have been assigned to the vehicle. In addition, the terrain has been already searched, and k denotes the new targets that have been found. Let $T_S = \{T_{S_1}, T_{S_2}, \ldots, T_{S_m}\}$ be the set of original targets, and let $T_N = \{T_{N_1}, T_{N_2}, \ldots, T_{N_k}\}$ be the set of new targets. Let $V = \{V_1, V_2, \ldots V_n\}$ be the set of UAVs completing these targets. Let q denote the number of task, and p denote the number of task of each target. Therefore, $q = p * (m + k)$. In this paper, we assume that the terrain has been searched. Therefore, only three types of tasks should be performed for complete a target: detection, firefighting and verification. Therefore $p = 3$. The descriptions of all parameters in this paper are presented in Table 1.

Table 1. Parameter description

Parameter	Description
n	The number of vehicles
m	The number of original targets
k	The number of new targets
p	The number of tasks of each target
q	The number of tasks of all target
V	The set of vehicles
T_S	The set of original targets
T_N	The set of new targets
T_{ij}	The time to complete target j for vehicle i
t_j	The maximum accepted completion time of target j
D_{ij}	The air distance to complete target j for vehicle i
d_i	The maximum air distance of vehicle i
X_{ij}	Whether vehicle i performs the task of target j

2.2 Problem Formulation

The goal of adaptive multiple task assignment for UAVs is to achieve the best overall effectiveness, while the total air distance and the whole task completion time are two main objects that should be minimized. We assume the UAVs have the same speed, so the task completion time can be represented by minimizing the maximum air distance among UAVs.

Minimum the total distance is calculated by the following:

$$\min \sum_{i \in V, j \in T_s \cup T_n} D_{ij} * X_{ij} \tag{1}$$

Where D_{ij} represents the distance between the vehicle i and target j.
Minimum the task completion time is calculated by the following:

$$\min \max \sum_{j=1}^{m+k} D_{ij} * X_{ij}, i \in V \tag{2}$$

where X_{ij} is an binary parameter denoting whether vehicle i performs the task of target j.

There are three constraints for adaptive multiple task assignment problem: time constraints, task constraint, and air distance constraint.

Time Constraints. The time constraints require that a certain task be performed within a given time. The requirement is of great importance for time-critical targets. The constraint is denoted by the following:

$$\sum_{i=1}^{n} T_{ij} * X_{ij} < t_j, j \in T_S \cup T_N \tag{3}$$

Where T_{ij} is the time to complete target j for UAV i, and t_j is the maximum accepted completion time.

Task Constraints. Each task should be performed only once. The constraint is denoted by the following:

$$\sum_{i=1}^{n} X_{ij} = 1, j \in T_S \cup T_N \tag{4}$$

Air Distance Constraint. The total air distance requirement of the tasks for each vehicle does not exceed its maximum air distance. The constraint is denoted by the following:

$$\sum_{j}^{m+k} D_{ij} * X_{ij} < d_i, i \in V \tag{5}$$

Where D_{ij} represents the air distance from current location of vehicle i to target j, and d_i is the maximum air distance of vehicle i.

3 Proposed Adaptive Multiple Task Assignments Algorithm

We extend the basic PSO algorithm to address the adaptive multiple task assignment algorithm. Our extension includes: (1) we propose a new encoding strategy; (2) we propose a new fitness function; (3) we propose a new initialization strategy (4) we re-define the operators in PSO.

3.1 Encoding

We propose a new encoding strategy for particles. Each particle represents a task assignment strategy in search space. We use a two-dimensional encoding strategy. The first dimension represents the UAVs, while the second dimension represents the targets. So each column represents that a vehicle is allocated to perform a task for a specific target. In addition, the length of each encoded particle is q. Each target must appear 3 times. The order of the appearance denotes the execution order. Assuming there are three targets and two UAVs, an encoding example is shown as Fig. 1.

UAV	1	2	1	2	2	1	1	1	2
Target	2	3	2	1	1	2	3	1	3

$$X_i$$

Fig. 1. Encoding example

3.2 Fitness Function Definition

The performance of each particle is calculated by a predefined fitness function based on the two objective function in Sect. 2.2. According to each column of the encoded particle, we can calculate the distance between the UAV and the location of the target. Thus, we can add the distance of each column from left to right to obtain the total distance. If vehicle i perform two or three tasks for target j consecutively, we assume that vehicle i can hover above the position of the targets. The hover distance is defined as $2 * \pi * R_{min}$, where R_{min} is the minimum turn radius of vehicle i. Due to the hypothesis of the UAV speed, we can use the air distance to indicate the task completion time.

3.3 Initialization

In order to avoid falling into local optimum values, the particle swarms are randomly initialized. First, the initial particle is generated according to the assigned task. Secondly, three numbers are randomly generated, respectively indicating the insertion position, the target and the UAV. The target and the corresponding UAV are respectively inserted into the first row and the second row of the particle according to the insertion position.

3.4 Operator Definition

According to the characteristic of the adaptive multiple task assignments problem, we can adjust the update strategy in the PSO:

$$X_i(t+1) = c_2 * F_3(c_1 * F_2(w * F_1(X_i(t)), pBest_i), gBest) \tag{6}$$

Where X_i is the position of particle i during the iteration procedure, t is the iteration number. $pBest_i$ is the personal best position of particle i. $gBest$ is the global best position. w is the mutate factor. c_1 and c_2 is the cross factor. Therefore, the particle update strategy consists of three steps: one mutation operation and two cross operations.

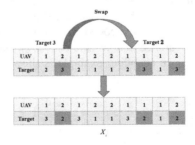

Fig. 2. Example of mutation operation

The first step is to perform particle mutation. An example is shown in Fig. 2. Firstly, the algorithm generates a random decimal w. If $w > w_0$, then the algorithm will generate two random integers between $m + 1$ and $m + k$, which represent two new targets. Then, we swap the task assignment of them.

The second step is to perform the first cross operation. An example is shown in Fig. 3. Firstly, the algorithm randomly generates a decimal c_0 between 0 and 1. If c_0 is larger than the across factor c_1, then go to the next step. Secondly, the algorithm will randomly find and record the task assignment for the new target in the local best value of particle. Finally, the algorithm will replace the task assignment in current particle with the recorded local best value.

Algorithm 1: Adaptive Multiple Task Assignments Algorithm based on PSO

Input:

　Target T, vehicle V, iteration number M, population size N and initial task assignment

Output:

　New task assignment

Procedure:

1: 　**for** each particle i

2: 　　Initialize position X_i

3: 　　Evaluate particle i and set $pBest_i = X_i$

4: 　**end for**

5: 　$gBest = \min(pBest_i)$

6: 　**for** $j : 1 \rightarrow M$

7: 　　Update the w , C_1 and C_2

8: 　　**for** $i : 1 \rightarrow N$

9: 　　　Randomly exchange two target in X_i

10: 　　　Randomly generate a target, replace its task assignment in X_i with the task assignment in $pBest_i$

11: 　　　Randomly generate a target, replace its task assignment in X_i with the task assignment in $gBest$

12: 　　　Evaluate particle i

13: 　　　**If** $fitness(X_i) > fitness(pBest_i)$

14: 　　　　$pBest_i = X_i$

15: 　　　**If** $fitness(pBest_i) > fitness(gBest)$

16: 　　　　$gBest = pBest_i$

17: 　　**end for**

18: 　**end for**

19: 　**print** $gBest$

end procedure

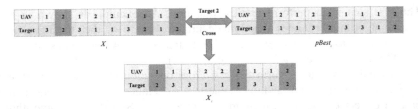

Fig. 3. Example of cross operation I

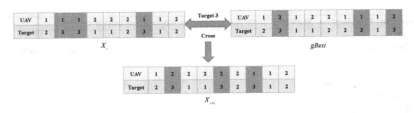

Fig. 4. Example of cross operation II

The last step is to perform the second cross operation. An example is shown in Fig. 4. Firstly, the algorithm randomly generates a decimal c_0 between 0 and 1, if c_0 is larger than the across factor c_2, go to the next step. Secondly, the algorithm will find and record the best task assignment of the new target in the global best value of the particle. Finally, the algorithm will replace the assignment method in current particle with the recorded global best value.

At the end of each iterator, each particle needs to be verified by the constraint above. Each task must be performed only once. The air distance of each UAV must be less than its maximum air distance. The completion time of each target must be earlier than its latest completion time.

3.5 Adaptive Multiple Task Assignments Algorithm Based on PSO

The adaptive multiple task assignment algorithm is shown in Algorithm 1. Firstly, the algorithm computes the fitness function of the particle. If the fitness function value of the particle is larger than its local best value, update its local best value with it. Then, the algorithm compares the fitness function of the local best value of the particle with the global best value. If the local best value is larger than the global best value, update the global best value with its local best value. Finally, when the indicated iterations are reached, the global best value is returned as the optimal solution of the adaptive multiple task assignment problem.

Table 2. Target position

Target	1	2	3	4	5	6
Coordinate X	63	46	0	64	67	51
Coordinate Y	70	53	63	4	59	65

Table 3. Vehicle position

UAV	1	2	3
Coordinate X	20	67	43
Coordinate Y	14	82	68

4 Performance Evaluation

4.1 Experiment Setup

In our simulation experiments, we assume that all targets are equally important. For each target, the tasks must be executed in the special order above. The number of original targets, the position of the new targets, and the current position of UAVs are initialized according to Tables 2, 3 and Fig. 5, respectively. The population size and max iterations number are set to 150 and 200. The number of original targets, new targets and UAVs are set to 3, 3 and 3, respectively. The weight factors w, c_1 and c_2 are set as 0.9, 0.8 and 0.3. With many contrast experiments, these parameters are optimal. In addition, the circle radius of UAVs is 3 km. The initial task assignment is shown in Table 4. We compare our adaptive multiple task assignment algorithm (AMT) with traditional PSO algorithm. It is shown in Table 4 that UAV 1 would perform three tasks, which are detection task, firefighting task and verification task for target 3. UAV 2 would perform three tasks, which are detection task for target 1, firefighting task for target 2 and verification task for target 1. UAV 3 would complete the rest tasks, including detection task for target 2, firefighting task for target 1 and verification task for target 2.

4.2 Experiment Results

The premise of adaptive task assignment is to ensure that the initial task assignment is unchanged. Figure 6 and Table 5 show the experiment results of PSO algorithm. The fitness function is defined as the maximum air distance of UAVs. It can be seen from the results that the PSO algorithm takes a long time to iterate to the global best value. Also, the order of initial task performing is changed. Figure 6 and Table 6 show the experiment results of AMT algorithm. It can be seen from the results that the AMT algorithm can quickly iterate the optimal value and tend to be more stable. Each UAV has a new task to perform with the initial task assignment is relatively changeless. In addition, Fig. 6 show the performance between the two algorithm. AMT algorithm only takes 1.2 s to iterate the optimal value, but PSO algorithm takes 8.7 s.

Table 4. Intial task assignment

UAV	Initial task assignment
1	3(D)→ 3(F)→ 3(V)
2	1(D)→ 2(F)→ 1(V)
3	2(D)→ 1(F)→ 2(V)

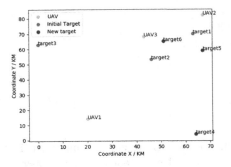

Fig. 5. Position of targets and UAVs　　　　**Fig. 6.** Air distance

Table 5. Task assignment of PSO

UAV	Task assignment
1	4(D)→ 2(D)→ 3(D)→ 2(F)→ 3(F)
2	5(D)→ 4(F)→ 5(F)→ 4(V)→ 2(V)→ 3(V)
3	1(D)→ 6(D)→ 6(F)→ 6(V)→ 5(V)→ 1(F)→ 1(V)

Table 6. Task assignment of AMT

UAV	Task assignment
1	3(D)→ 3(F)→ 3(V)
2	1(D)→ 5(F)→ 2(F)→ 4(d)→ 4(F)→ 5(V)→ 6(V)→ 1(V)
3	2(D)→ 6(D)→ 5(D)→ 6(F)→ 1(F)→ 2(V)→ 4(V)

5 Conclusion

In this paper, we formulate the adaptive firefighting task assignment as an optimization problem, and propose a PSO-based algorithm to solve the problem. Experiment results verify the effectiveness of our algorithm. We would consider the route planning problem for UAVs in the future.

Acknowledgment. This research is supported in part by NSFC (61571066, 61602054), and Beijing Natural Science Foundation under Grant No. 4174100 (BNSF, 4174100).

References

1. Kou, K.-H., Yu, J.-Y., Wang, G., Zhang, F.-X.: Task assignment and route planning method of cooperative attack for manned/unmanned aerial vehicles. In: 2017 IEEE International Conference on Unmanned Systems (ICUS), pp. 168–176. IEEE (2017)
2. Yuan, C., Zhang, Y., Liu, Z.: A survey on technologies for automatic forest fire monitoring, detection, and fighting using unmanned aerial vehicles and remote sensing techniques. Can. J. For. Res. **45**(7), 783–792 (2015)
3. Shima, T., et al.: Multiple task assignments for cooperating uninhabited aerial vehicles using genetic algorithms. Comput. Oper. Res. **33**(11), 3252–3269 (2006)
4. Skulimowski, A.M.J.: Anticipatory control of vehicle swarms with virtual supervision. In: Hsu, C.-H., Wang, S., Zhou, A., Shawkat, A. (eds.) IOV 2016. LNCS, vol. 10036, pp. 65–81. Springer, Cham (2016). https://doi.org/10.1007/978-3-319-51969-2_6
5. Zhou, S., Yin, G., Wu, Q.: UAV cooperative multiple task assignment based on discrete particle swarm optimization. In: 2015 7th International Conference on Intelligent Human-Machine Systems and Cybernetics (IHMSC), vol. 2, pp. 81–86. IEEE (2015)
6. Bello-Orgaz, G., Ramirez-Atencia, C., Fradera-Gil, J., Camacho, D.: GAMPP: genetic algorithm for UAV mission planning problems. In: Novais, P., Camacho, D., Analide, C., El Fallah Seghrouchni, A., Badica, C. (eds.) Intelligent Distributed Computing IX. SCI, vol. 616, pp. 167–176. Springer, Cham (2016). https://doi.org/10.1007/978-3-319-25017-5_16
7. Phan, C., Liu, H.H.: A cooperative UAV/UGV platform for wildfire detection and fighting. In: 7th International Conference on System Simulation and Scientific Computing (ICSC), pp. 494–498 (2008)
8. Ghamry, K.A., Kamel, M.A., Zhang, Y.: Multiple UAVs in forest fire fighting mission using particle swarm optimization. In: 2017 International Conference on Unmanned Aircraft Systems (ICUAS), pp. 1404–1409. IEEE (2017)
9. Ghamry, K.A., Zhang, Y.: Cooperative control of multiple UAVs for forest fire monitoring and detection. In: 2016 12th IEEE/ASME International Conference on Mechatronic and Embedded Systems and Applications (MESA), pp. 1–6. IEEE (2016)
10. Huang, H., Zhu, D., Ding, F.: Dynamic task assignment and path planning for multi-AUV system in variable ocean current environment. J. Intell. Robot Syst. **74**(3–4), 999–1012 (2014)
11. Jiang, X., Zhou, Q., Ye, Y.: Method of task assignment for UAV based on particle swarm optimization in logistics. In: Proceedings of the 2017 International Conference on Intelligent Systems, Metaheuristics & Swarm Intelligence, pp. 113–117. ACM (2017)
12. Oh, G., et al.: Market-based task assignment for cooperative timing missions in dynamic environments. J. Intell. Robot. Syst. **87**(1), 97–123 (2017)

Vehicular Security and Privacy

Towards the Security Measures of the Vehicular Ad-Hoc Networks

Krzysztof Stepień and Aneta Poniszewska-Marańda(✉)

Institute of Information Technology, Lodz University of Technology, Łódź, Poland
krzysztof.stepien@edu.p.lodz.pl, aneta.poniszewska-maranda@p.lodz.pl

Abstract. The vehicles currently manufactured are becoming progressively associated with the Internet, supporting a variety of new highlights that are valuable towards both drivers and automakers. Therefore, the highlights given entail the new security issues. Vehicular Ad-Hoc Networks (VANET) have recently emerged as one of the solutions that could help connecting cars to the vast network. Not only could preserve the safety, but also the efficiency of the traffic.

The paper focuses on the VANETs that are vulnerable to attacks which can directly lead to the corruption of networks and then possibly provoke a considerable loss of time, money, and even the users' lives. The analysis of the Sybil attacks is presented and the possible solutions that could solve the security leaks in vehicle networks are proposed.

Keywords: Car network · Vehicular Ad-Hoc Networks (VANETs)
Car security · Privacy · Security attacks

1 Introduction

The massive deployment of wireless technologies has emerged over the recent couple of years. Therefore, the growing number of wireless devices such as a remote keyless system and personal digital assistants could be met in the cars. Those devices achieve potential outcomes for both the drivers and the passengers. Therefore, the cars are immensely computerized and interconnected using both wired and wireless technologies.

Growing amount of modern technologies in the car systems are vulnerable to attacks. Figure 1 presents both physical and wireless systems that modern cars can be associated with. Most of those features are supported with the aid of the *Engine Control Unit (ECU)* [1].

There are plenty of circumstances in which the system architecture as a whole can be disrupted. First of all, the updates (firmware) that come to the car over the air pass through the insecure communication channels. The firmware is sent to the car using WiFi, mobile network or Bluetooth. Then, physical channels within the car (Controller Area Network, CAN) distribute all the updates through the Engine Control Unit (ECU). Unfortunately, these channels could be

A. M. J. Skulimowski et al. (Eds.): IOV 2018, LNCS 11253, pp. 233–248, 2018.
https://doi.org/10.1007/978-3-030-05081-8_17

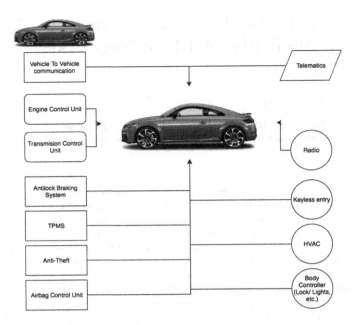

Fig. 1. Network inside the car – different shapes show how systems inside the car are usually grouped

eavesdropped by the hacker. As a consequence, the firmware can be received or modified bringing potentially devastating outcomes.

Not only the car itself may be the source of the problem. *Vehicular Ad-Hoc Networks (VANETs)* have a number of distinctive properties. Those properties are prone to attackers that could take advantage of the security leaks. Connections in a VANET base on node-to-node communication. Each node is able to act both as a host inquiring information or as a router forwarding the facts [2,3].

VANET is a technology that treats every moving vehicle as a node being a part of a mobile network. VANET turns every collaborating automobile rights into a wireless router or a node. It allows all the automobiles being in the range of the Road Side Unit to connect and create a wide network with a huge range. There are two types of nodes: (i) RoadSide Unit (RSU) – it represents fixed nodes provisioned along the route; and (ii) OnBoard Unit (OBU) – it refers to the mobile nodes (such as vehicles) equipped with an electronic interface that connects to other nodes in a wireless manner (Fig. 2).

VANET attacks may lead to catastrophic consequences: traffic accident, vast time loss (in case of tampering traffic jam by hackers), financial loss (for example in payment services). However, the publications concerning this topic are insufficient. During the research, the Sybil attack was mentioned as one of the most common and critical attack types. This attack is crucial in decentralized structures, for instance social networks. In those networks, the private data is shared brazenly and it is impossible to erase the records once they are uploaded.

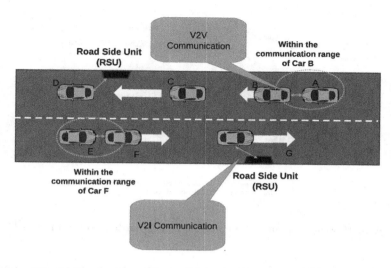

Fig. 2. The basic structure of *Vehicular Ad-Hoc Networks* [2]

This paper presents the VANETs that are vulnerable to attacks which can directly lead to the corruption of networks and then possibly provoke a considerable loss of time, money, and even the users' lives. The focus is given on the Sybil attacks to propose the methods to avoid the bottleneck that could arise during these attacks. The analysis of Sybil attacks is presented and the possible solutions that could solve the security leaks in vehicle networks are proposed.

The paper is structured as follows: Sect. 2 describes the security aspects of Vehicular Ad-Hoc Network, among others the security requirements of VANET and its threatening attacks. Section 3 deals with the Sybil attack, while Sect. 5 elaborates the outcomes of presented solution dealing with Sybil attack.

2   Security Aspects of Vehicular Ad-Hoc Network

As it was mentioned in the previous chapter, cars are getting more and more connected to one another as well as the environment surrounding them. Consequently, the security threats are believed to increase over time. Before the concept of the interconnected vehicles was introduced, the automotive industry had not paid much attention to the cyber-security. In the past, the intruders required physical access to perform an attack on the vehicle. Today the connected vehicle is surrounded by multiple connection points which use *LTE* (Long-Term Evolution) or *WiFi* to connect to the Internet.

Figure 3 shows 15 locations in the car that face the greatest possibility of being attacked according to the Intel security report [4]. Each point represents the advanced feature of the connected car. These features use different *ECUs* that are in charge of different capabilities. The ECUs are linked to the internal vehicle community referred to *CAN* (Controller Area Network).

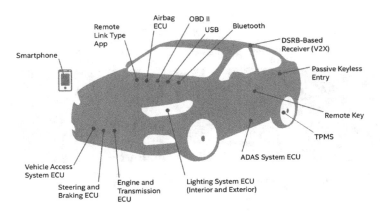

Fig. 3. 15 weakest points of a connected car according to Intel report [4]

Therefore, the main difficulties that car manufacturers needs to accomplish, were found [4]:

– *Over-the-air updates* (*OTA*) – the new cars and the computers are alike in their complexity to a great extent. The vehicles have considerably sophisticated software architecture as well as a number of applications installed inside. Every once in a while, the software given needs to be updated in order to have all the possible bugs fixed and any other discovered vulnerabilities included. It could be challenging for the car producers, because some of the updates could be crucial and potentially critical for the safety of the driver and passengers if installed on time. If the car could not be updated due to being off-line or to any other reason, it would not be clear who bears the responsibility for the accident of the car with outdated software [5, 18].
– *Low computational power* –the computational power of automobiles is low. Modern microprocessors would not be reliable enough to work in the environment with constantly changing humidity, vibration, and temperature. It could not withstand these conditions. It could be a factor that the hackers could take advantage from because they can leverage stronger computers to hack. The computers inside the car do not have enough computation power to provide the algorithms safe enough to preserve the security [5].
– *Difficult to monitor* – it is difficult to manage all the automotive electronics by a certified authority, as the car might not always be connected to the Internet.
– *No Safety without Security* – even a single infected car on the road could pose a threat to all the surrounding vehicles. Even the new security bug-fix creates the new safety issues.

Isaac et al. [6] discussed some of the major security attacks that have been reported on VANET networks since 2010. They presented some solutions that correspond to each safety issue in car network. The main safety regions include: anonymity, key management, privacy, recognition.

2.1   VANET Security Requirements

Preserving the security in VANET network is a unique challenge due to the fact that human lives are constantly at stake. Therefore, the challenges presented in VANET network shows how severe the problem is.

In conventional networks, the main safety concerns comprise confidentiality, integrity, and availability. None of them includes ordinarily safety. Nonetheless, the security in VANET also indicates the ability to determine the driver responsibility while maintaining one's privacy.

The deployment of a complete security system for VANET could be very tough in practice. A safety breach of VANET is often crucial and precarious. What is important, a vehicular community character is highly dynamic with frequent and instant arrivals and departures of cars as well as short connection intervals. Due to its dynamic nature, high mobility, and open nature of WiFi or wireless communication, VANET is liable to attacks [9].

However, some of the crucial points that are necessary to preserve *VANET* security, could be described as [10]:

Confidentiality. It refers to the "confidential communication". In a group of nodes, none of them, with the exception of a group individuals, is able to decrypt the messages which can be broadcast to each member of the group. Furthermore, none (even other participants) besides a dedicated receiver member is successful to decrypt the message committed to it [10].

Integrity. It ensures that information or messages sent among the nodes is not altered by attackers. This concept in VANETs regularly combines with the "authentication" concept to guarantee that a node is able to verify that a message is certainly dispatched and signed. Even if the authentication of the sender was evaluated properly, the receiving car performs data verification to check whether it contains corrupted information or not [10].

Availability. Even if the network is under attack, it ought to be available for nodes to connect. Moreover, it should not alter the performance of the network.

Privacy. All data concerning driver's personal information must be kept secret from unauthorized access [11]. The following cases could be considered:

- *Communications Among Cars and RSUs* – the privacy means that an eavesdropper is impossible to determine whether or not the exclusive messages derive from the same vehicle.
- *Communications between vehicles* – deciding whether two different legitimate messages coming from the car is intensely burdensome.

Traceability and Revocability. Although all the data and identity of the vehicle should be hidden from the others, there should still be a possibility to obtain the vehicles' real identities and to revoke them for the future usage.

Non-repudiation. The driver has to be diagnosed in case of an accident. A sender should have the obligatory responsibility to transmit the messages to the investigation unit. After that, the unit given will check the sequence correctness and the content of messages exchanged before the accident.

Real-Time Constraints. Cars are capable of moving in and out of the different VANET networks at any time. Therefore, the real-time constraints need to be maintained.

Low Overhead. All messages in VANETs are time critical due to the dynamic environment. Thus, the "low overhead" is essential to retain the usefulness and validity of the messages [12].

However, some of the crucial points that are necessary to preserve *VANET* security, could be described as (Fig. 4) [10, 12]: confidentiality, integrity, availability, privacy, traceability and revocability, non-repudiation, real-time constraints, low overhead. Privacy is of the greatest importance among the rest of parameters. Other requirements that are equally crucial comprise the authentication, non-repudiation and message integrity.

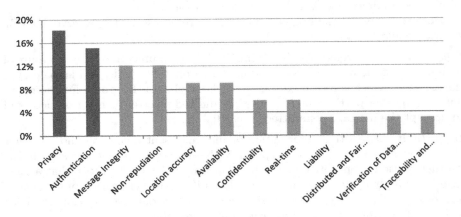

Fig. 4. The important aspects of security requirements in *VANET* [8]

2.2 Types of Attacks in VANET Network

The security environments VANET evaluated in the previous section represent the answer for the possible attacks. The attacks could be categorized as follows [6, 7]:

Insider vs. Outsider. If the attacker is a member of the network and can communicate with the other nodes (cars), it will be referred to the insider and able to perform an attack using various methods. On the other hand, outsider attack refers to the node that is not directly connected to the other members of the network. It has fewer assaults possibilities.

Malicious vs. Rational. A malicious attacker uses diverse strategies to damage the member nodes and the network without looking for its personal benefit. On the contrary, a rational attacker expects its very own benefit from the attacks. Therefore, these assaults are more foreseen and could be discovered earlier, because they follow some patterns.

Active vs. Passive. An active attacker can generate new packets to damage the network while a passive attacker most effectively eavesdrops the WiFi channel but cannot generate the new packets.

Local vs. Extended. Local attacker refers to the situation when he has a limited scope even if it possesses several entities (stations or cars). Otherwise, an extended attacker broadens his scope by controlling several entities that are scattered across the network.

In 2013, Sumra et al. [8] proposed five different classes of attacks and every class is expected to provide better perspectives for the VANET security:

- *network attack* – hackers can directly affect other vehicles and even the whole infrastructure; these attacks have the higher level of danger because these affect the whole network,
- *application attack* – the hacker is interested in changing the content of an application and abusing it for his own benefits,
- *timing attack* – a type of attacks in which the main objective for attackers is to create the empty messages in order to add some time slot; it creates the delays that cause the situation when the receiver might get his message too late,
- *social attack* – messages, which trigger the bad emotions of other drivers,
- *monitoring attack* – attacks in which monitoring and tracking activities are performed.

The greater interest is given to the safety of end users, the more important is that these programs should be very secure. Automakers wanted to create certain reliable service for customers and provide adequate safety of human life.

There are plenty of possible attacks that can occur in VANET. They are broadly categorized into three main groups, connected with: availability, authenticity, driver confidentiality and miscellaneous. Therefore it is unwanted that attacker can affect the new potentially lifesaving vehicular network. These bothersome hackers behave in very unpredictable ways and may launch diverse styles of attacks. One of such attacks is a Sybil attack.

3   Sybil Attack

The Sybil attack bases on creating a false neighbouring presence in the *VANET* network. To perform this form of attack, a vehicle proclaims to be several cars either at the same time or in succession. This attack could trigger an emergency situation considering a vehicle can claim to be in extraordinary positions at the identical time. Therefore it could create a chaos and large security risks in the community [11]. The Sybil attack damages the network topologies and connections as well as community bandwidth consumption (Fig. 5).

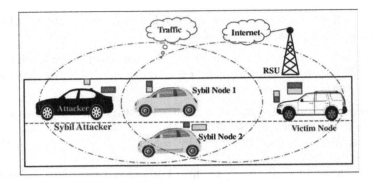

Fig. 5. Sybil attack – the attacker sends multiple messages with different identities to the other car and the innocent vehicle thinks that there is a heavy traffic [13]

The message flow (concerning information about traffic, accidents) is sent by nodes to the network. All messages could be potentially observed by hackers. They could generate false messages in the network (Fig. 5). However, when more than one vehicle reports the same issue in the road, the first innocent node sends the message to all other nodes in the network. These fake identities create the illusion of the bogus situation on the road. Increasing number of fake identities enables the attacker to gain a control of the whole network. Number of Sybil nodes depends on the computation resources and memory storage of the hacker.

There are three types of defences against Sybil attacks that can be applied in the Ad-Hoc networks: registration, position verification, and radio resource testing. First one does not enough prevent against Sybil attacks. A malicious node has a possibility to register with multiple identities by non-technical means such as stealing. Moreover, it could lead to the serious privacy troubles. In case of position verification, the system should check whether each physical node refers to the one unique identity. The last type of defence assumes that all physical entities are limited in resources [13].

Unfortunately, all these three aforementioned defence types are designed for indoor applications and they all depend on the fixed base stations under constant conditions. They cannot work appropriate without adaptation.

3.1   Sybil Attack Detection Approaches

The main crucial point in counter-mining Sybil attack is to preserve valid unique identity for a physical node. There are plenty of solutions for Sybil Attack detection and the most important are [14]:

1. *Robust Sybil Attack* Detection – it bases on the motion trajectories differences of vehicles. Each driver connected to the network drives with its individual path, chosen speed and maintains some specific distance from the following vehicle on the road. Therefore, it could detect an attack independently using *RSU (Road-Side Unit)*. Each vehicle is enabled to check the signatures of

corresponding cars and detect the Sybil nodes. Digital signatures with time-stamp are broadcasted using infrastructure. This causes high effectiveness, robust and minimum system requirements [16].

When the new node comes into the range of RSUs, the vehicle requests for the authorized messages from RSU. This authorized message proofs that this particular vehicle is present at that particular time in the range of RSU. Then one of the verified vehicle nodes computes the difference between the values of neighbouring nodes and the new node. Finally, it judges whether a new node is Sybil node or the correct one (Fig. 6) [16]. Essential information is sent and received in real time to support all road users and traffic service centres in their decision-making process [14]. The main drawback of that solution has not preserved the privacy of node [14].

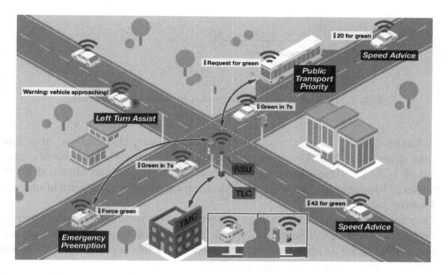

Fig. 6. Vehicles gathering RSUs' digital signatures in motion [14]

2. *Time-stamp series* – this method does not use *VPKI* (Vehicular Public Key Infrastructure) and *RSU*s with internet accessibility. Here *RSU*s are responsible only for issuing time-stamp [15]. Vehicle generates a time-stamp request which wishes to be verified using *RSU* for certificates correctness. If the certificate is valid, *RSU* will now not deliver any response. Otherwise, *RSU* extracts previous time-stamp information and combines it with the present time-stamp to generate a brand new combination of time-stamps [15].

When the car passes through the consecutive *RSU* units, it acquires licensed time-stamp that is signed through that particular *RSU*. Therefore, if any node sends a message about passing multiple *RSU*s at the same time, it will be detected as a Sybil node (Fig. 7).

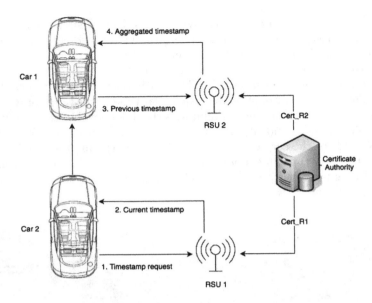

Fig. 7. Time-stamp series approach to detect Sybil attack

Unfortunately, in case of a complex urban roadway, this method may have some drawbacks. If RSUs are located near intersections, then the hacker could collect multiple time-stamps from each RSU. Then, he can obtain different values of time-stamps that could help in sending Sybil messages without being detected by the system [16].

3. *Enhanced Lightweight Sybil Attack* Detection – this technique does not require any extra hardware. The main approach includes a detection based on four parameters, such as speed, energy, frequency and latency and their threshold values which are predefined in the system [15].

   The initial network is set-up with initialized threshold values. The nodes whose parameters are less than their corresponding threshold values are recognized as legitimate nodes. When the unknown node tries to enter the network, all its parameters are checked. If all parameter's values are greater or equal to their corresponding threshold values, the new node is detected as Sybil node, otherwise as legitimate node [17].

The presented solutions to prevent Sybil attacks are compared in Table 1. All presented methods are decentralized. Besides the first one, all of them preserve the privacy. None of them use Certification Authority. Last two uses *RSS* to detect Sybil nodes. The location verification methods are used in all of them as being easy and have a fewer computational complexity than the authentication methods, which are distributed in processing.

Table 1. Comparison of Sybil Attack Detection Techniques in VANETs

Method	Ce/decentralized	Privacy	CA used	RSS based	Location based
RSA	Decentralized	No	No	No	Yes
Time-stamp	Decentralized	Yes	No	Yes	Yes
ELSA	Decentralized	Yes	No	Yes	Yes

4 Implementation of Method Against the Sybil Attract and Its Analysis

The prototype of *VANET* network was created in order to come up with a solution which could help in the Sybil attacks prevention. The project was realized in Java language. The *VANET* was designed to test the proposed security solutions.

The vehicle unique identification is preserved using *VIN* number (Vehicle Identification Number). This number is emitted once the vehicle is produced, and can never be changed, unlike the license plates. Moreover, the license plates can be used to identify the owner, which violates the privacy standpoint. To ensure that VIN number really derives from the vehicle it claims, *CA* (Certificate Authority) signature is used. It solves the problem of authentication but also messages integrity and non-repudiation of the sender. The created system mocks multiple intersections where vehicles can drive. All the ordinary vehicles are marked in green colour, on the other hand all false detected nodes are marked in red colour. (Fig. 8).

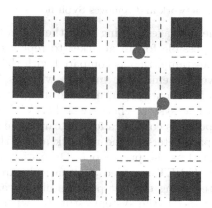

Fig. 8. Visualization of *VANET* network (green rectangles represents the valid vehicles; cars marked by the red squares represents the infected ones) (Color figure online)

Each vehicle connected to the network entails the list of features such as speed, history of positions, the time-stamp. The system is checking whether a user is not sending messages too frequently and whether the parameters of the vehicle are changed in a fluent way. Moreover the system verifies the vehicle's connection to the available *RSU*s (Fig. 9).

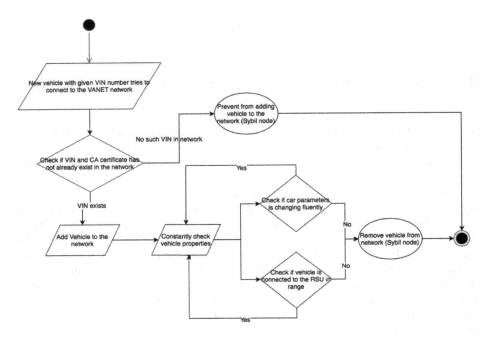

Fig. 9. Flowchart of created solution – the system constantly checks the parameters of vehicles connected to the network and removes Sybil nodes

Furthermore, all the messages coming from the car in the system presented are new, making it impossible for an attacker to replay them later on. Every message contains a time-stamp, that is compared with the current time.

At first, the new vehicle emits the message with its VIN to the network. It solves the problem of authentication, message integrity and non-repudiation of the sender vehicle. The system checks whether VIN already exists in the network and if the response is correct, adds the car to the network. The vehicle is constantly sending parameters to the network and if they are not changing rapidly, the car is treated as the proper one. Otherwise, the vehicle is treated as the Sybil node and VANET removed automatically from the network. The parameters are validated using the last position of the car and predicted with the aid of the previous speed (the system estimates where the whereabouts of the vehicle should be in the future (or at least in a valid range)). Simultaneously, the system checks if the car is in range of any RSUs connected to the VANET network.

The system intends to check whether a user is sending messages too frequently at the communication unit level (minimum delta time between messages is not high enough). It is not ignoring all the future messages (some of them might be crucial), but it drops the excess ones that will not affect road safety.

In order to analyse the created solution, several tests were performed. A particular number of public X509 keys were created for each vehicle (last tests include 100 vehicles). Multiple tests were taken for a number of cases. Figures 10 and 11 shows the borderline cases. When the time-stamp of the vehicle is not

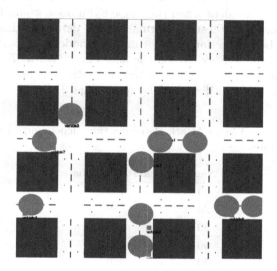

Fig. 10. Simulation of proposed solution with 10 faulty vehicles on the screen (just after initialization)

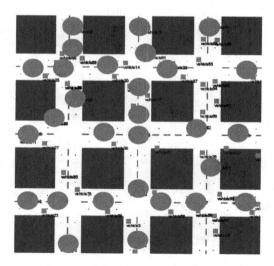

Fig. 11. Simulation of proposed solution with 100 faulty vehicles on the screen (just after initialization)

proper (sender's communication is not fresh), a vehicle drives out of the valid RSU or finally the vehicle parameters (such as speed) behaves in an unexpected way, the system detects them as Sybil nodes and removes from the system.

Table 2 depicts the time-dependent amount of the false nodes connected to the network. Greater number of the vehicles decrease the mean time of single Sybil node detection, as the system posses the higher amount of data that helps in processing all nodes linked to the particular VANET network. This could create a dangerous precedent when the single Sybil node would be detected too late. However, during the tests performance, the detection time of false node was fast enough. Low detection time for multiple nodes is caused mainly by the infrastructure (V2V – *Vehicle To Vehicle* and V2I – *Vehicle To Infrastructure*) – all positive nodes (vehicles) and infrastructure (RSUs) constantly validates all the nodes around and identifies the false ones (Fig. 12).

Table 2. Comparison of Sybil Attack Detection time depending on number of nodes connected to the system.

Number of cars	Time (ms)
10	100
20	150
30	170
40	200
50	220
60	250
70	270
80	300
90	330
100	350

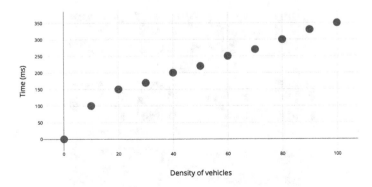

Fig. 12. The response time for Sybil node detection between different amount of cars connected to the VANET network

The presented solution could be of help in preventing the network from unauthorized access of the hacker's node or nodes that have been already connected to the network, but they are trying to hack the network themselves. The Sybil attack is one of the most aggressive types of attack, because even one false node could possibly affect the whole network and generate misleading messages that could even prevent the administrator from proper managing given VANET network.

5   Conclusions

The main purpose of VANET is not only to provide the road safety and services but also to preserve the security of all nodes in the network. Therefore, securing the VANET comes as a considerable challenge. The major issues in VANETs are privacy and authentication. Any attack could pose a serious threat to life. The Sybil attack gave the illusion of the road leading to create many serious disruptions inside the network scenario. Therefore, VANET requires the new innovative methods which include confidentiality and authenticity to provide a secure network. Most approaches are expands to detect a Sybil attack in quite a reasonable time, but the increasing number of nodes (taking a normal use case into consideration) may lead to increasing delay, which additionally expands the bottleneck in the network communication. Each method mentioned in Table 1 applies the new mechanism but - unfortunately - does not avoid minor drawbacks. Therefore, it is impossible to decide in favour of a distinctive mechanism or procedure.

Nevertheless, some essential criteria could be specified as:

- increasing number of nodes should not affect a large number of Sybil nodes detection,
- Sybil nodes should be discovered and removed infinite time,
- privacy of the user has to be preserved,
- economic should be taken into consideration in the implementation,
- number of exchanging messages in VANET should not increase.

References

1. Car network structure. https://www.globalcarsbrands.com/top-10-newest-car-technologies-that-have-revolutionized-the-auto-industry/. Accessed 14 Apr 2018
2. Al-Qutayri, M., Yeun, C., Al-Hawi, F.: Security and privacy of intelligent VANETs. In: Computational Intelligence and Modern Heuristics (2010)
3. Ad-hoc networks structure. https://www.researchgate.net/figure/VANET-Structure.fig1263545192. Accessed 14 Apr 2018
4. Vehicle weakest points. http://www.intel.com/content/www/us/en/automotive/automotive-security-best-practices-white-paper.html. Accessed 14 Apr 2018
5. Czosseck, C., Ottis, R., Ziolkowski, K.: Paradigm change of vehicle cyber security. In: Proceedings of 4th International Conference on Cyber-Conflict, pp. 380–384 (2012)

6. Isaac, J.T., Zeadally, S., Camara, J.S.: Security attacks and solutions for vehicular ad hoc networks. IET Commun. **4**, 894–903 (2010)
7. Al-kahtani, A., Abdulaziz S., Kharj, A.: Survey on security attacks in vehicular ad hoc networks (VANETs). In.: Proceedings of 6th International Conference on Signal Processing and Communication Systems (ICSPCS), pp. 1–9 (2012)
8. Sumra, I.A., Iftikhar A., Hasbullah, H., Manan, J.: Classes of attacks in VANET. In: Proceedings of Tenth International Conference on Wireless and Optical Communications Networks (WOCN), pp. 1–5 (2013)
9. Chim, T., Yiu, S.M., Hui, L.C.K., Li, V.O.K.: Security and privacy issues for inter-vehicle communications in VANETs. In: proceedings of Sensor, Mesh and Ad Hoc Communications and Networks Workshops, pp. 1–3 (2009)
10. Wing, C.T.: Secure and privacy-preserving protocols for VANETs. Ph.D. thesis, Hong Kong (2011)
11. Zhang, L.: Research on security and privacy in vehicular ad hoc networks. Ph.D. thesis, Universitat Rovira i Virgili (2010)
12. Raw, R.S., Kumar, M., Singh, N.: Security issues and solutions in vehicular ad hoc network: a review approach. In: Wyld, D.C. (ed.) ICCSEA, pp. 339–347. WimoA, SPPR, CSIA (2013)
13. Karn, C.K., Gupta, C.P.: A survey on VANETs security attacks and sybil attack detection. Int. J. Sens. Wirel. Commun. Control **6**, 45–62 (2016)
14. Chen, C., Wang, X., Han, W., Zang, B.Y.: A robust detection of the sybil attack in urban VANETs. In: Proceedings of Distributed Computing Systems Workshops, ICDCS Workshops 2009, pp. 270–276 (2009)
15. Hamdan, S., Raad, S., Al-Qassas, S., Tedmori, S.: Comparative study on sybil attack detection schemes. Int. J. Comput. Technol. **14**(7), 5869–5876 (2015)
16. Park, S., Aslam, B., Turgut, D., Zou, C.C.: Defense against Sybil attack in vehicular ad hoc network based on roadside unit support. In: proceedings of Military Communications Conference, MILCOM (2009)
17. Samara, G., Al-Salihy, W.A., Sures, R.: Security analysis of vehicular ad hoc networks (VANET). In: Proceedings of Second International Conference on Network Applications, Protocols and Services, National Advanced IPv6 Center, Universiti Sains Malaysia, pp. 55–60 (2010)
18. Dyvak, M., Stakhiv, P., Pukas, A., Voytyuk, I., Porplytsya, N., Maslyiak, Y.: Interval model of dynamics of dispersion of harmful pollution from vehicular traffic. J. Appl. Comput. Sci. **24**(3), 49–60 (2016)

Electric Vehicle Charging Queue Management with Blockchain

Subhasis Thakur(✉) and John G. Breslin

Data Science Institute, National University of Ireland Galway,
University Road, Galway H91 TK33, Ireland
{subhasis.thakur,john.breslin}@nuigalway.ie

Abstract. We will have to build adequate charging station infrastructure to support the massive proliferation of electric vehicles over the next few years. A federated structure for charging stations can serve as a solution for building a large number of charging stations. It will allow microgrids, private houses, and hotels to provide charging services. Present literature on the topic of managing electric vehicle charging queues has not addressed the problems associated with such a federated network of charging stations. In this paper, we solve the electric vehicle charging queue management problem through a federation of charging stations using blockchains. In this electric vehicle queue management solution, we show that (a) stations cannot hide information to manipulate charging queues, (b) it enhances the privacy of electric vehicles as they are not required to reveal their exact desired recharging locations, (c) it encourages electric vehicles to recharge at the prescribed charging stations, (d) it allocates better recharging stations to electric vehicles who reveal their exact desired recharging location, i.e., one pays for privacy, (e) it supports load balancing over stations, and (f) blockchain not only provides a transparent and secure solution but also provides incentives to the station owners to bear the cost of establishing a charging station.

Keywords: Electric vehicle · Charging station · Blockchain

1 Introduction

The electrification of transportation plays an important role in reducing greenhouse gas emissions as transportation accounts for 23% of greenhouse gases. Governments are starting to ban cars with internal combustion engines by as early as 2030. These policies will introduce 150 million units of Electric Vehicles (EVs) and 400 million electric two-wheelers by 2030, with 1.2 billion EVs by 2060. The availability of charging stations is a critical component for rapid EV adoption. We will need a large number of charging stations to ensure availability to a massive number of EVs.

A federation of charging stations is a potential solution to support the required growth of charging stations. It is not only large firms who can participate in establishing charging stations but small microgrids, private residential

© Springer Nature Switzerland AG 2018
A. M. J. Skulimowski et al. (Eds.): IOV 2018, LNCS 11253, pp. 249–264, 2018.
https://doi.org/10.1007/978-3-030-05081-8_18

buildings, shops, hotels, bed and breakfasts, rural firms, and others should also be encouraged to establish charging stations. Often these stations will be owned by private owners in remote locations supported by renewable energy resources. In this paper, we focus on such a federated structure of charging stations. The problems with federating charging stations are:

Trust: Stations may not trust each other to share information on their EV queues as each station will want to maximize its queue length.

Monitoring and Enforcement: We need monitoring and governance capabilities to monitor the price for recharging services and also to enforce governance rules to regulate EV queues for energy grid load balancing.

Computational Cost: Significant computational resources are needed to coordinate EV queue management for large road networks spanning over neighbouring countries such as in the European Union. Also, we need to assess the economic feasibility of developing the computational infrastructure required for the associated information processing and EV queue management.

The present literature on EV queue management does not address these problems. We have therefore made the following contributions in this paper: (**1**) We develop a platform for charging stations to interact among themselves and solve the EV charging scheduling problem in a collaborative fashion. Using blockchain, we develop a secure, traceable, distributed solution for the EV charging scheduling problem. (**2**) We develop a distributed charging scheduling algorithm which aims to minimize the waiting time for EVs to recharge and that also prevents EVs from manipulating the system. A federated charging station network is likely to be less regulated than a centralized station network. Hence in this federated environment a station will attempt to maximize its queue of EVs to increase its profit by not disclosing queue information to nearby stations. Our solution prevents stations from executing such selfish actions. (**3**) We develop a flexible charging schedule for EVs. The present solutions for EV charging schedules are restrictive in the sense that they allow limited stations for each EV to charge at. The feasibility of an EV to charge at a prescribed station depends on traffic conditions and the personal needs of the EV driver. Also an EV driver may not wish to reveal their exact destination due to privacy concerns. In this paper we assign a large number of stations in a local area to an EV. It improves the flexibility of the charging schedule and it then becomes more likely that an EV will comply with the prescribed schedule. (**4**) The proposed solution encourages EVs to remain compliant with the prescribed station schedule. (**5**) It allocates better recharging locations to EVs who have provided accurate desired recharging locations compared with other EVs who may not want to do so due to privacy concerns. (**6**)The proposed solution supports load balancing over stations. (**7**) It continuously changes the flexibility of allocation, i.e., if the stations are not congested then EVs will get more options to recharge.

The paper is organized as follows. In Sect. 2 we discuss related literature. In Sect. 3 we present a formal model for federated charging stations. In Sect. 4 we present a blockchain-based solution for the EV charging scheduling problem.

In Sect. 5 we present an experimental evaluation of the proposed solution. We conclude the paper in Sect. 6.

2 Related Literature

[7] solves the problem of charging price manipulation by cartels of charging stations by maximizing the number of owners of charging stations in each locality. [9] develops a pricing model for charging with load balancing based on frequency regulation signals from the electricity grid. [11] solves the EV queue management problem using coalitional game theory. [5] solves the EV queue management problem with load balancing among stations while minimizing the waiting time of EVs. [2] uses a genetic algorithm to solve the EV charging scheduling problem. [10] develops a pricing model considering travel patterns, EV driver behaviors, and traffic information. [6] presents a survey on economy-driven approaches such as auctions, Stackelberg games, and other potential games to solve the EV charging scheduling problem. Existing solutions for the EV scheduling problem do not address issues around the federation of stations, and they ignore the problem of developing computational infrastructure for information processing in such a federation of stations. The shortcomings of existing solutions for EV charging queue management in a set of federated charging stations are as follows: **(1)** Existing solutions do not address the requirement to evaluate trust among charging stations and EVs. **(2)** Existing solutions do not provide a secure platform for interaction. Most of these solutions assume that such a platform exists. **(3)** Existing solutions do not provide any monitoring or enforcement capabilities. **(4)** Existing solutions do not provide any incentive to EVs to remain compliant with the prescribed solution. **(5)** Existing solutions do not provide any incentive to the station owners to bear the cost of establishing charging station infrastructure and computation infrastructure. **(6)** Existing solutions are not very flexible as they only offer a small number of stations per EV for recharging. In this paper we propose a blockchain-based EV scheduling solution. We use a proof-of-work-based blockchain as developed in [4].

3 Federated Charging Station Network

Definition 1 *(Road network):* $G = (V, E)$ *be an undirected graph representing a road network with nodes V (landmarks in a city) and edges E (road segments connecting two landmarks). $D(E_i \in E)$ (positive integer) will denote the length of the road segment E_i.*

Next we define a charging station network as an undirected graph where each node represents a charging station and stations are within an average distance that a fully charged EV can travel. The intuition behind such a graph formation is that an EV can design its travel path according to such a graph as it may need multiple recharging stops.

Definition 2 *(Charging station network): $H = (N, L)$ be an undirected graph representing a charging station network where, (1) N is a set of k charging stations and L is the set of links among the charging stations. (2) $Loc(N_i) \in V$ will denote the location of the station $N_i \in N$. The location of each station is unique and one landmark $V_i \in V$ will accommodate only one charging station. (3) A link L_i among two stations N_i and N_j is a path P in the road network G such that P connects $Loc(N_i)$ and $Loc(N_j)$ and the length of the path is less than or equal to Δ (Positive integer) i.e., $\sum_{E_i \in P} D(E_i) \leq \Delta$.*

Definition 3 *(EV): We define the properties of an EV $C_i \in C$ (C is the set of all EVs) as follows: (1) $Start(C_i) \in t$ be the starting time of the EV. (2) $Source(C_i) \in V$ be the starting location of C_i and $Sink(C_i) \in V$ be the destination of C_i. (3) $Battery(C_i, t_j) \in [0, 100]$ will denote the level of battery charge of the EV C_i at time t_j. (4) $\Theta(x) \in [0, 100]$ (x is positive integer) will denote the decrement of charge if the EV has travelled a distance x since its last charge.*

Definition 4 *(Traffic): We define the traffic as follows: (1) C is a set of m EVs. (2) $t = (t_1, t_2, \dots)$ be a discrete successive time sequence. For example t_1 is 6 AM, t_2 is 7 AM and so on. (3) The traffic load at time t_i is given by the function $\theta(t_i)$ (positive integer), i.e., $\theta(t_i) \subseteq C - \cup_{x=0}^{x=i-1} \theta(t_x)$.*

Definition 5 *(Queue): $Q(N_i, t)$ will denote the queue of EVs who want to charge at location N_i in a time t. $Q(N_i, t) \in 2^C$, i.e., it is a sequence of EVs.*

We assume the following: (1) An EV chooses the shortest path (in the graph G) to travel from its source to destination. (2) An EV chooses to charge once the level of charge in its battery reaches $\rho \in [0, 100]$ and it cannot complete its journey with the remaining charge. In the experimental evaluation we assume that ρ is 40. We consider multiple owners of the stations. An owner may only own a subset of stations.

Definition 6. *There are z firms $f_1, \dots, f_z$ who provide charging services, i.e., who own charging stations. $F(f_i) \subset N$ will denote the charging stations owned by a firm f_i.*

It is assumed that the station locations for each firm are chosen uniformly at random. Now we define a partition over charging stations as groups of connected subgraphs. Each such group of stations are options given to an EV to recharge. An EV may charge at any station in such a group.

Definition 7. *A station segmentation is a partition over the charging stations into K (positive integer) groups denoted as $\Pi = (\Pi_i, \dots, \Pi_k)$ such that: (1) a station only belongs to one group $\forall \Pi_i, \Pi_j, \Pi_i \cap \Pi_j = \emptyset$ and $\bigcup_{i \in [1,k]} \Pi_i = N$, (2) the induced subgraph for each group of stations Π_i on the charging station network is a connected graph.*

Definition 8. *A station allocation function δ maps an EV to a station segmentation group, i.e., $\delta : C \mapsto \Pi$.*

Definition 9. *A station segmentation Π is stable if there is a station allocation function δ such that the following conditions hold: (1) Any two stations in a group are at most d distance apart, i.e., $\forall \Pi_i$, $\forall N_x, N_y \in \Pi_i D(N_x, N_y) \leq d$. (2) The load difference between any two groups is at most ϵ_1 (positive number), i.e.,*

$$\forall \Pi_i, \Pi_j \in \Pi, ABS(|\cup_{c_i:\delta(c_x)=\Pi_i} c_x| - |\cup_{c_i:\delta(c_x)=\Pi_j} c_x|) \leq \epsilon_1$$

where ABS gives an absolute number and $||$ is a count function. (3) The waiting time difference between any two groups is at most ϵ_2 (positive number) i.e.,

$$\forall \Pi_i, \Pi_j \in \Pi, ABS(|\sum_{N_x \in \Pi_i} Q(N_x, t_a)| - |\sum_{N_x \in \Pi_j} Q(N_x, t_a)|) \leq \epsilon_2.$$

The explanations for the above conditions are as follows: *[Condition 1:]* This ensures that stations in each group are within a fixed proximity. Note that an EV will be asked to charge at any station in such a group of stations. Hence stations in each group should be in close proximity. *[Condition 2:]* This ensures that the difference between the number of EVs who will charge in any two groups of stations is bounded by a fixed number. Note that in a federated station environment, each firm wants to maximize the number of EVs who use their charging stations. Hence this condition ensures that there is no firm that gets more EVs. *[Condition 3:]* It ensures that the difference between the waiting time for two EVs who will recharge at different groups of stations is bounded. Hence it makes sure that the benefit of EVs (in terms of how long they will wait to get recharged) is bounded. Thus there should not be any preference over groups of stations as EVs will all require an almost equal amount of time to recharge their battery.

Definition 10. *A sequence of stable station segmentations in a time duration $[t_1, t_2, \ldots, t_x]$ is a sequence of station segmentations $\Pi^1, \Pi^2, \ldots, \Pi^x$ such that Π^1 is stable at time t_1, Π^2 is stable at time t_2 and so on.*

We solve the sequence of stable station segmentations problem with blockchain.

4   EV Scheduling with Blockchain

The blockchain (BC) mechanism works as follows: **(1)** BC allows peers of a peer-to-peer network to transfer tokens among themselves using transactions. **(2)** If a peer P_1 wants to send x tokens to P_2 then it creates the transaction T_1 and announces it to its neighbours in the BC peer-to-peer network. **(3)** Once such a neighbour P_3 receives the transaction T_1, P_3 attempts to verify it. If it can verify T_1 as a valid transaction then it forwards T_1 to its neighbours. **(4)** BC stores consistent replicas of the transaction history on multiple peers. Valid transactions are grouped into a block and blocks are stored in a chain of blocks where each block has only one parent block. **(5)** A new block can be added to the

BC as the child of the most recent block. Any peer can verify transactions and add a new block to the BC provided it satisfies the conditions of the distributed consensus protocol. **(6)** The distributed consensus protocol ensures all peers have the same replica of the BC.

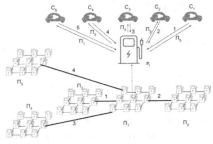

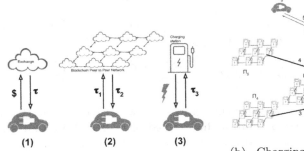

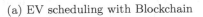

(1)   (2)   (3)

(a) EV scheduling with Blockchain

(b) Charging station allocation using blockchain transactions.

Fig. 1. (a) EV scheduling with Blockchain, (b) Charging station allocation using blockchain transactions.

As illustrated in Fig. 1, EV scheduling with blockchain works as follows: **(1)** An EV buys a set of tokens from an exchange using other types of currency. Tokens are used to find charging stations and to pay stations for recharging. **(2)** An EV sends x amount of tokens (in transaction τ_1) to a nearby charging station to find a suitable charging station. We initialize the queue management procedure by a partition over the stations and a score for each station segment that indicates the level of load on it. **(3)** Once a station receives a request from an EV to find a charging station, it evaluates if the score of its own station segment is the least when compared with surrounding station segments. It creates a transaction τ_2 whose input is τ_1 and labels it with stations from one of the surrounding station segments (including itself) which has the least score. Such a label indicates where the EV should recharge. **(4)** Once the EV receives τ_2, it chooses a station (C_x) from the list of stations mentioned in τ_2 and recharges itself by sending a new transaction τ_3 (whose input is τ_2) to it. Now we present detailed description this solution.

4.1   Blockchain Infrastructure

We assume that EVs have access to cloud-based blockchain wallets. Advances in vehicular networks, the vehicular cloud, and roadside communication facilities [1,8] justify this assumption. Every station owner is required to commit certain computational resources, i.e., they work as miners. Each station has a node in the blockchain peer-to-peer network. The identity of stations, i.e., nodes in the blockchain, is recognized with its public key, and the GPS coordinates for each station are stored in the identification information for each node.

4.2   Transactions

Blockchain uses an unspent transaction output (UTXO) data structure to express transactions. According to this, inputs to a transaction must be unspent, i.e., not used as the input to any other transaction. It ensures that funds cannot be double spent. We refer to the Bitcoin Wiki's Transaction page[1] for a detailed description of the blockchain transaction data structure. We have a few extra fields in our transaction data structure, which are (1) "Coordinates": GPS location of the creator of the transaction, (2) "Evaluated": Takes a value of True or False, and (3) "Stations": Either empty or public keys of a set of charging stations. The procedure of charging station allocation is as follows:

(1) First an EV, say C_1 gathers x amount of tokens τ. It can do so by converting any other currency into τ from a token exchange similar to Bitcoin exchanges. One token τ will represent the cost for 1 kWh. C_1 may evaluate the approximate number of tokens it needs to recharge.
(2) Once C_2 wants to find a recharging station, it first finds a nearby charging station using its own GPS location and the GPS locations of charging stations. A web service on the blockchain can be used to search for all nearby stations. Let such a station be π_i. C_1 constructs a transaction τ_x of amount x and sends it to π_i with "Coordinates" as its own GPS location, "Evaluated" as False and "Stations" as empty.
(3) The station π_i may receive many such transactions within a short interval. The interval time is fixed. It may receive transactions from C_1, C_2, C_3, C_4, C_5 in one interval. π_i will perform the station allocation operation.
(4) π_i is part of the station segment Π_1 which has neighbouring station segments, e.g., $\Pi_2, \Pi_3, \Pi_4, \Pi_5$ at a distance of 2, 1, 3, 4. The distance between two station segments is measured as the length of the shortest path that connects two stations (one in each segment) who are the most centrally located in each respective station segment. Also, each station segment is assigned a score with the following equation

$$Score(\Pi^i) = Sin(\frac{\sum_{N_x \in \Pi_i}(3.14 \times |Q_x|)/(2 \times Limit_2)}{\text{Number of stations in } \Pi_i}).$$

$Limit_2$ is the maximum allowed queue size at any station. Q_x is the queue at station N_x. The $Score$ for a station segment generates a number between 0 and 1 which reflects the average level of congestion at the stations in the station segment. Using Algorithm 1, C_i allocates stations to C_1, C_2, C_3, C_4, C_5 in such a way that it balances congestion across different station segments and it also allocates stations close to π_i to the EVs whose transaction amount is high.
(5) Algorithm 1 is as follows: Let π_i execute Algorithm 1. First it computes the amount of free spaces available in surrounding station segments. Next it allocates stations to EVs in the order of decreasing amounts of transaction

---

[1] https://en.bitcoin.it/wiki/Transaction.

value. It chooses a station for an EV in the order of increasing distance from its own station segment. Note that Algorithm 1 can be executed by several blockchain nodes in a parallel and asynchronous fashion as the station requests from EVs located long distances away need not be included as input to Algorithm 1.

(6) After π_i computes a station allocation using Algorithm 1: for each allocation, say "Allocate Π_x to C_i", it creates a transaction τ_i' whose recipient is C_i, "Evaluated" is True, "Stations" is the public keys of all stations in the segment Π_x, the input transaction is τ_i (which it has received from C_i), and the amount is $Amount(\tau_i) - TransactionFee$ where $TransactionFee$ is a small predefined value which π_i keeps to itself as a reward for processing the station allocation procedure.

(7) After C_i receives τ_i', it chooses any station, say π_x, mentioned in the "Stations" of τ_i'. C_i recharges and pays π_x with a transaction τ_i'' whose recipient is π_x, input is τ_i', "Evaluated" is False, "Stations" is empty and transaction amount is calculated according to the energy transferred from π_x to C_i.

(8) It is compulsory that C_i uses any station from the station list mentioned in τ_i' to use the token τ_i'. Hence EVs will remain compliant with having to use the prescribed charging stations.

(9) Algorithm 1 allocates the closest station segment to the EV who made the biggest transaction. Note that an EV can only use the token at prescribed stations and hence, the risk of using a high value transaction expresses an EV's desire to recharge at stations closest to π_i. By doing so the EV loses privacy but gets rewarded with a close recharging station. Hence the level of privacy is expressed using the value of the transaction.

Algorithm 1. Station allocation

Data: Station segmentation $\Pi = \Pi_1, \ldots \Pi_k$, x Transactions $\tau_1, \ldots, \tau_x$ from
$\quad\quad C' = C_1, \ldots, C_x$ to $\pi_i \in \Pi_1$ who executes the algorithm
Result: Station allocation
begin
$\quad$ $\Pi' = (\Pi_1, \ldots, \Pi_a)$ be neighbouring station segments of Π_1, $D \leftarrow$ distance
$\quad$ of Π' from Π_1, $FreeSpace \leftarrow$ vector of length a denoting available charging
$\quad$ spaces in each $\Pi_x \in \Pi'$ by using $Score$ function, $FreeSpace' \leftarrow$ vector of
$\quad$ length a denoting fraction of x EVs that each $\Pi_x \in \Pi'$ will accommodate
$\quad$ **for** $Each\ C_i \in C'$ in decreasing order of transaction amount **do**
$\quad\quad$ **for** $Each\ \Pi_x \in \Pi'$ in increasing order of distance D **do**
$\quad\quad\quad$ **if** C_i not allocated and Π_x has space **then**
$\quad\quad\quad\quad$ Allocate Π_x to C_i, $Freespace'[x] = Freespace'[x] - 1$

4.3   Distributed Consensus Protocol

The distributed consensus protocol ensures that peers of a BC peer-to-peer network reach consensus about the validity of a transaction, i.e., they all agree that the transaction is valid or invalid. Also, miners compete to add new blocks to the BC as there is a financial reward for doing so. The distributed consensus protocol determines the winner of such a race to add new blocks to the BC. It may happen that two or more miners may add a new block almost at the same time. Such an event creates a fork in the BC. The distributed consensus protocol eliminates such a fork. There are two major types of distributed consensus protocols: proof of work [4] and proof of stake [3]. In proof of work, a miner has to solve a puzzle before it can add a new block to the BC. In proof of stake, the protocol uses low complexity puzzles and peers are regularly rewarded based on their stake. Briefly the protocol is as follows:

(1) Each miner maintains a BC head which is the block whose distance (shortest path) from the first block is the maximum distance. **(2)** If a miner gets a new block (say B) it uses this procedure: (a) It checks if the new block is a valid block. If B is valid then the miner follows either of the next two steps and forwards the block to its neighbours. (b) If the parent block of the new block is the most recent block of the BC then it adds B as its child and recognizes B as the BC head. (c) If the parent block (say A) of the new block is not the most recent block in the BC then it adds B as a child of A. But it does not change the BC head. **(3)** If it creates a new block (say B) then it adds B as a child of the current BC head and recognizes B as the BC head. **(4)** If at any time, the block whose distance from the first block is the maximum distance, it is recognized as the BC head. Beside block creation and verification according to the proof of stake protocol, our miners are required to solve station segmentation adjustment problems before publishing a new block. It executes two procedures (a) "adjust station segmentation" and (b) "split or merge segments" as described in Algorithms 2 and 3.

In "adjust station segmentation", a miner swaps neighbouring stations between two station segments to reduce differences in scores among the station segments. The "split or merge segments" (the split method is shown in Algorithm 3) is performed according to historical changes in demands for charging stations. According to this, if demand is increasing at the time of creation of the block then the miner must perform a 'split' procedure as shown in Algorithm 3, otherwise it should merge station segments. The split procedure splits a station segment into two station segments in such a way that station segments induce a connected subgraph on the station graph (hence it is appropriate to allocate such segments as options for recharging an EV), and it separates/distributes stations with long queues among them (hence the resultant segments are evenly congested). We need to split a station segment to restrict EVs from choosing convenient stations (e.g. those close to the city centre) when the demand is high. It may happen that most of the EVs will choose convenient stations simultaneously, and it will not only congest certain areas but also have a negative impact on the electricity grid. The 'merge' procedure merges two neighbouring segments into one if the size of the resultant segment is within a certain range and the maximum distance between any pair of stations in the segment is less than a particular limit. A miner must execute the merge procedure if the historical demand for stations is decreasing at the time of block creation. Thus when the demand is low EVs get more options to recharge. Note that the split and merge procedures are performed at predefined times, determined by historical traffic data. This means that if the historical traffic volume increases sharply from 7 AM to 11 AM then all blocks created during this time must execute a split procedure. Similarly if the historical traffic volume decreases sharply from 11 AM to 2 PM then all blocks created during this time must execute a merge procedure.

Finally the block creation rate will be controlled using the level of complexity of the puzzle that a miner has to solve before it publishes a new block. With higher changes in the demand for stations, we create blocks more frequently to adjust station segments. Note that such modifications of the complexity of a puzzle depends on historical traffic volume information. Also, it will be a predefined in this blockchain as to whether the complexity of a puzzle will be low or high. For example, if the historical traffic volume increases sharply from 7 AM to 11 AM then the complexity of a blockchain puzzle will be low to generate blocks more frequently and to perform station segmentation adjustments and split/merge procedures more frequently. Such changes in the blockchain complexity will be predefined based on historical traffic information.

Algorithm 2. Station segmentation adjustment

Data: A station graph $H = (N, L)$, Group size limits K_1, K_2, Distance limit D
Result: Adjusted station segmentation
begin

  Station segmentation $\Pi^1, \ldots, \Pi^z$, $Score \leftarrow$ assign score to segments, Π^+ segments with score more than $AVG(Score)$, Π^- segments with score less than $AVG(Score)$

  for Each $\Pi^i \in \Pi^-$ in increasing order of score **do**

    for Each $\Pi^j \in \Pi^+$ in increasing order of score **do**

      for Each $N_x \in \Pi^i$ in increasing order of queue **do**

        $N_y \in \Pi^j$ such that, N_x has an edge with $\Pi^j - N_y$ and N_y has an edge with $\Pi^i - N_x$

        Swap N_x and N_y

        if $Score(\Pi_i) \geq AVG(Score)$ **then**

          $\lfloor$ Break;

Algorithm 3. Split a station segment

Data: A station segment $\Pi_i = (\pi_1, \pi_k)$ with queues $(Q_1, \ldots, Q_k)$
Result: Split Π_i into two segments
begin
    $Order \leftarrow$ order stations by decreasing queue length, $Group_1 \leftarrow$ station with highest queue length, $Group_2 \leftarrow$ station with second highest queue length
    while *Stations not added to $Group_1$ or $Group_2$* **do**
        $Neighbour_1 \leftarrow$ neighbouring stations of $Group_1$, $Neighbour_2 \leftarrow$ neighbouring stations of $Group_2$, $\pi^* \in Neighbour_1 \cap Neighbour_2$
        if *Distance from π^* to $Group_1$ is more than the same for $Group_2$* **then**
            Add π_i^* to $Group_1$
        else
            Add π_i^* to $Group_2$
        Add $\pi_x \in Neighbour_1 - \pi^*$ to $Group_1$ if $Score(\pi_x)$ is minimum in $Neighbour_1$, Add $\pi_x \in Neighbour_2 - \pi^*$ to $Group_2$ if $Score(\pi_x)$ is minimum in $Neighbour_2$

4.4 Observations

We note the following with blockchain-maintained EV queue management. (a) Stations cannot hide information on EV queue as all transactions are visible to all peers of the blockchain, (b) Using experimental evaluation we will show waiting time for EVs is less with blockchain maintained EV queue management, (c) an EV can choose any station in a station segment and hence it enhances its privacy, (4) as EVs can only use token to pay the prescribed stations, it will remain compliant, (5) stations segments are revised for load balancing, (6) station allocation to EVs are solved in a distributed fashion and (7) the financial incentives as transaction fees and mint coins will draw investments to build the computational infrastructure for EV queue management information processing.

5   Experimental Evaluation

We use agent-based modelling to simulate the traffic network. Stations and EVs are modelled as agents. We use asynchronous event simulation in Python to implement the activities of station and EVs. The blockchain is also modelled within the same simulation as we include block creation and associated activities within the behaviors of EVs and stations. The simulation is as follows:

(1) The simulation starts with a random partition station segmentation Π^0. We only consider the distance among stations and the maximum number of stations allowed in each station group as the factors to determine Π^0. The intuition behind generating such a partition is that we can start usage of the blockchain-based solution at 12 AM when traffic loads are negligible and such segmentation is modified over time as the traffic load changes.

(2) At every iteration of the simulation, we introduce new cars according to historical traffic information and we execute the behaviour of EVs and stations in an asynchronous fashion.

(3) We consider the following behavior of EVs: An EV proceeds towards its destination until its charge falls below a certain limit, and after that it searches for a station and moves towards the station to get recharged. After that it continues its journey towards its destination. An EV always follows the shortest paths.

(4) We consider the following behavior of stations: Each station executes three tasks as independent processes: (a) it recharges EVs, (b) it assigns stations to an EV for recharging, and (c) it creates blocks by verifying transactions and modifying station segmentations, and it either performs a 'split' or 'merge' operation according to historical demand information.

(5) We simulate the rewarding process for miners according to the proof of stake procedure. The number of blocks created in each iteration depends on the historical demand information. We create more blocks as demand increases and vice versa. The probability that a miner will receive a minted token depends on its stake, i.e., the amount of tokens it owns and when it received its last minted token.

We use the road network for Europe from Open Street Map (https://www.openstreetmap.org/) to extract major roads and highways. We process 'Shape' files for such data in R using the libraries "igraph, sp, shp2graph, rgdal". The resultant road network contains 10527 nodes and 10100 edges with a mean edge distance of 17 km. We choose 3000 nodes as charging stations uniformly at random. The station network has 26294 edges where two stations are considered as neighbours if the distance between them is at most (0.1 * mean distance amongst all pairs of stations). The mean edge length of the station graph is 77 km, i.e., on average two stations are 77 Km apart from each other. Also, the mean degree of stations is 17. The initial partition over the stations has station segments with an average segment size of 3. In any such segment, the average maximum distance between two stations is 70 km. We use four datasets (we will refer to these as datasets 1, 2, 3, 4) with 2000 EVs, and we set their source and destination locations in four local areas (i.e., four connected subgraphs of the European road network) with a diameter of 500 km, i.e., the maximum distance between any two nodes, and on average there are 150 charging stations. We set the speed of each EV as 50 km/h. Each iteration of the simulation corresponds to one hour. We set the range of EVs as 200 km. The source to destination distance for each EV is approximately 300 km. An EV searches for a charging station if (a) its battery level is less than 40%, and (b) it cannot reach its destination with the remaining charge. We compare the proposed queue management algorithm against a random allocation of stations where an EV proceeds towards the closest station for recharging. Note that existing algorithms mentioned in Sect. 2 are not immediately available for comparison because these algorithms are not designed to address issues such as (a) trust, (b) monitoring, (c) enforcement, (d) incentive and (e) cost as mentioned in Sects. 1 and 2 (Fig. 2).

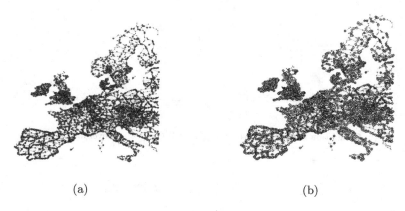

(a)   (b)

Fig. 2. The EU road network used for evaluation. The figure on the left shows station locations as 'red' nodes and the figure on the right shows station segments as stations with the same colors. (Color figure online)

Figure 3(a, b, c, d) show that the congestion level at stations for the proposed queue management solution performs much better than the random allocation (the congestion for a random station allocation is at least 12 times the congestion for the blockchain-maintained solution). We measure congestion level as the length of queues at the stations.

Next, we analyze load balancing among station segments. It is measured as a standard deviation of Score (discussed in Sect. 4.2) for the station segments. We found (Fig. 3(e, f, g, h)) that the standard deviation for our queue management solution is much lower than for random allocation. Hence the proposed solution efficiently load balances the station segments. Finally in Fig. 4, we show that the waiting time for EVs recharging with the proposed queue management solution is at most $\frac{1}{10}$ compared with a random station allocation.

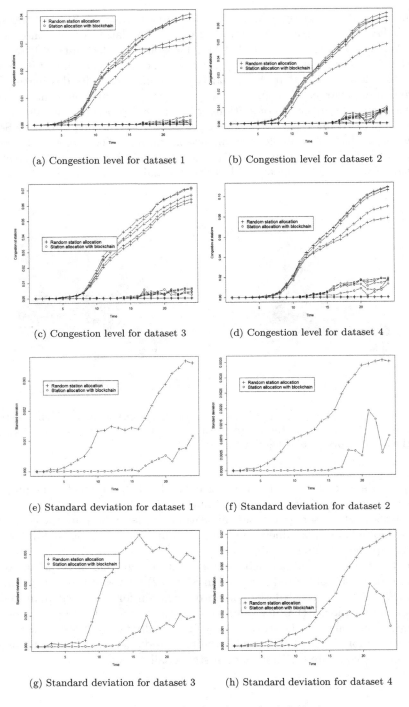

(a) Congestion level for dataset 1   (b) Congestion level for dataset 2

(c) Congestion level for dataset 3   (d) Congestion level for dataset 4

(e) Standard deviation for dataset 1   (f) Standard deviation for dataset 2

(g) Standard deviation for dataset 3   (h) Standard deviation for dataset 4

Fig. 3. Congestion level and standard deviation.

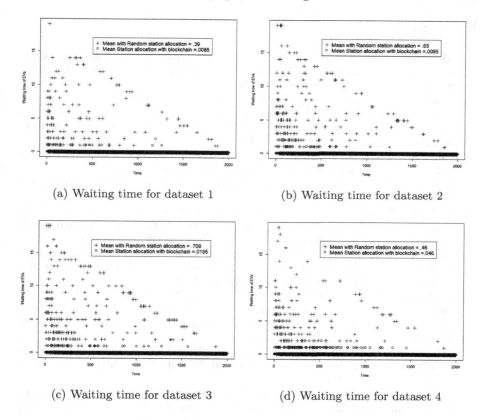

(a) Waiting time for dataset 1   (b) Waiting time for dataset 2

(c) Waiting time for dataset 3   (d) Waiting time for dataset 4

Fig. 4. Waiting time for four datasets

6   Conclusion

In this paper we proposed a blockchain-managed EV queue management procedure. It can support the federation of station networks and allow small businesses to establish charging stations by providing proper monitoring and governance tools. In the future, we will develop a dynamic station segmentation version as an improvement over this solution.

Acknowledgments. This publication has emanated from research supported in part by a research grant from Science Foundation Ireland (SFI) under Grant Numbers SFI/12/RC/2289 and SFI/16/RC/3918, co-funded by the European Regional Development Fund.

References

1. Al-Sultan, S., Al-Doori, M.M., Al-Bayatti, A.H., Zedan, H.: A comprehensive survey on vehicular ad hoc network. J. Netw. Comput. Appl. **37**, 380–392 (2014). https://doi.org/10.1016/j.jnca.2013.02.036
2. Alonso, M., Amaris, H., Germain, J.G., Galan, J.M.: Optimal charging scheduling of electric vehicles in smart grids by heuristic algorithms. Energies **7**(4), 2449–2475 (2014). https://doi.org/10.3390/en7042449. http://www.mdpi.com/1996-1073/7/4/2449
3. King, S., Nadal, S.: PPCoin: peer-to-peer crypto-currency with proof-of-stake (2012). http://www.peercoin.net/assets/paper/peercoin-paper.pdf
4. Nakamoto, S.: Bitcoin: a peer-to-peer electronic cash system (2009). http://www.bitcoin.org/bitcoin.pdf
5. Said, D., Cherkaoui, S., Khoukhi, L.: Multi-priority queuing for electric vehicles charging at public supply stations with price variation. Wirel. Commun. Mob. Comput. **15**(6), 1049–1065 (2015). https://doi.org/10.1002/wcm.2508
6. Shuai, W., Maill, P., Pelov, A.: Charging electric vehicles in the smart city: a survey of economy-driven approaches. IEEE Trans. Intell. Transp. Syst. **17**(8), 2089–2106 (2016). https://doi.org/10.1109/TITS.2016.2519499
7. Thakur, S., Gasperis, G.D.: Cartel formation in charging network for electric vehicles. In: 2016 IEEE 16th International Conference on Environment and Electrical Engineering, EEEIC, pp. 1–6, June 2016. https://doi.org/10.1109/EEEIC.2016.7555829
8. Whaiduzzaman, M., Sookhak, M., Gani, A., Buyya, R.: A survey on vehicular cloud computing. J. Netw. Comput. Appl. **40**, 325–344 (2014). https://doi.org/10.1016/j.jnca.2013.08.004
9. Wu, C., Mohsenian-Rad, H., Huang, J.: Vehicle-to-aggregator interaction game. IEEE Trans. Smart Grid **3**(1), 434–442 (2012). https://doi.org/10.1109/TSG.2011.2166414
10. Xiong, Y., Gan, J., An, B., Miao, C., Soh, Y.C.: Optimal pricing for efficient electric vehicle charging station management. In: Proceedings of the 2016 International Conference on Autonomous Agents & Multiagent Systems, AAMAS 2016, pp. 749–757. International Foundation for Autonomous Agents and Multiagent Systems, Richland (2016). http://dl.acm.org/citation.cfm?id=2937029.2937035
11. Yu, R., Ding, J., Zhong, W., Liu, Y., Xie, S.: PHEV charging and discharging cooperation in V2G networks: a coalition game approach. IEEE Internet Things J. **1**(6), 578–589 (2014). https://doi.org/10.1109/JIOT.2014.2363834

Towards a Blockchain-Based SD-IoV for Applications Authentication and Trust Management

Léo Mendiboure[1]([✉]), Mohamed Aymen Chalouf[2], and Francine Krief[3]

[1] LaBRI Lab, University of Bordeaux, Bordeaux, France
leo.mendiboure@labri.fr
[2] IRISA Lab, University of Rennes 1, Lannion, France
[3] LaBRI Lab, Bordeaux INP, Bordeaux, France

Abstract. IoV, bringing smartness into the vehicular environment, represents the future of the vehicular networks. To improve the IoV network management, resource utilization and QoS, a new architecture integrating the SDN technology have been proposed: SD-IoV. However, this architecture introduces new threats and, in particular, security is an important challenge. One of the major shortcomings with security is the lack of authentication and authorization of the applications (network, third party or user) at the distributed SD-IoV control layer. Indeed, these applications are currently able to control the SDN controllers and therefore the network behavior without any restriction. Consequently, a malicious or compromised application could easily disturb the entire network. That is why this paper proposes an innovative trust establishment system based on the blockchain technology. This system aims to control the application identity, as well as the application behavior and the network resources allocation and management. The ideas of application identity and application trust index, using the distributed nature of the SD-IoV, are introduced. Moreover, a design of this system, using smart contracts is also presented.

Keywords: Internet of Vehicles · SDN · SD-IoV · Blockchain
Security

1 Introduction

The Internet of Vehicles (IoV) is the future of the Vehicular Ad-Hoc Networks, interconnecting vehicles, and the vehicles Telematics, connecting vehicles. Combining these technologies and learning from the Internet of Things (IoT), it brings smartness into the vehicular environment, improving the vehicles' intelligence and vehicles' networking. To this end, it should integrate humans, vehicles and things in a global network interconnecting heterogeneous networks and providing services for smart transportation and, more broadly, for smart cities.

© Springer Nature Switzerland AG 2018
A. M. J. Skulimowski et al. (Eds.): IOV 2018, LNCS 11253, pp. 265–277, 2018.
https://doi.org/10.1007/978-3-030-05081-8_19

However the IoV development is facing many challenges [5, 8]. Indeed, the vehicular environment has unique features: highly dynamic topology, significant volumes of data or frequent disconnections and specific requirements: reliable communications, low latency, high Quality of Service (QoS). That is why many challenges should be addressed, including, providing a high QoS in a high-mobility environment, balancing data flows in a multi path environment and managing mobility.

To overcome that, Software-Defined Network (SDN) has rapidly been proposed as a potential solution. SDN is a new way of thinking and designing the network architecture, transforming the traditional networks into automatically programmable networks [10]. This technology decouples the network control plane, operated by one or several SDN controllers, and data plane. This separation of the network control and forwarding functions could bring many benefits: the direct network programmability, the underlying infrastructure abstraction, a central management of the network intelligence and a high level of flexibility.

Due to these benefits, a new paradigm emerged: Software Defined Internet of Vehicles (SD-IoV), the convergence of SDN and IoV. By using the SDN flexibility, centralization and programmability, the QoS, network optimization and resource utilization could be improved. To achieve that goal, [4] proposed a distributed SD-IoV architecture composed of local controllers enabling scalability and low delays. However, the integration of a distributed SDN in the vehicular environment and SDN itself give rise to a number of challenges such as mobility management, inter-networking among heterogeneous networks or security [15].

In a vehicular environment, involving autonomous vehicles or transport systems, security should be a major concern. An important point of failure in the SD-IoV architecture are the SDN controllers, the brain of the network managing the network resources utilization. In a classic case, network or third party applications, for example streaming applications, request network resources and these controllers are responsible of their allocation. However, there is no mechanism in place to secure the exchanges between the controllers and applications [13]. That is why this work focuses on the SD-IoV security and, more specifically, on building trust between the SDN controllers and the network applications.

To this end, this paper proposes an innovative SD-IoV trustworthy environment for the SDN controllers and network applications based on blockchain (BC). This solution aims to address an important issue: attackers using compromised applications consuming important network resources to disturb the proper functioning of the entire SD-IoV network. BC providing security, reliability, trust and scalability in a distributed way is currently widely studied and appears to be an interesting way of overcoming the trust issue in the distributed SD-IoV architecture. Indeed, with BC, nodes should be able to store and exchange information, transparently and securely, using a connected distributed system of registers. Therefore, this system should enable the application authentication and behavior control, as well as the network resources management.

The rest of this paper is organized as follows: Sect. 2 provides background information on the SD-IoV architecture, trust in a SD-IoV environment and BC while Sect. 3 introduces some related works on SD-IoV and trust establishment between SDN controllers and network applications. Finally, Sect. 4 proposes a BC based SD-IoV trustworthy environment and a smart contract based design of this system.

2   Background

In this section are introduced the main concepts needed to understand the context and the contribution of this paper. The background information focuses on the SD-IoV architecture, the SDN controller and the blockchain technology.

2.1   SD-IoV Overview

As shown in [8], the IoV aims to integrate different heterogeneous wireless access technologies in a global network. The IoV architecture is composed of different types of nodes: vehicles, Road Side Units (RSUs), WiFi routers designed for the vehicular networks and located along the roads, and Base Stations (BSs) providing cellular communications. With this infrastructure, different types of communication should be possible: Vehicle-to-Vehicle (V2V), Vehicle-to-Infrastructure (V2I), Vehicle-to-Network (V2N), Vehicle-to-Personal devices (V2P), etc. Using these communications, the applications are numerous: transport management (real time traffic management, parking slots booking, etc.), infotainment and advertising (multimedia applications, augmented reality, etc.) or road safety (cooperative collision warning, intersection coordinator, etc.) are a few examples.

To meet these applications needs, providing a high QoS, improving the resource utilization and optimizing the network are clearly required. SDN, transforming the network into a programmable network and simplifying the network management, could be a solution. Its main idea is to decouple the network control plane and data plane. The network traffic control is managed by the control plane, corresponding to one or several controllers, while the data forwarding is performed by the network equipments. In the vehicular environment, the SDN integration gave birth to the idea of SD-IoV and [4] proposes an interesting SD-IoV architecture. This architecture, shown in Fig. 1, is composed of four main

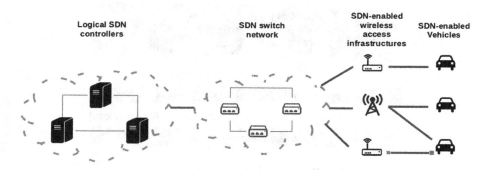

Fig. 1. Distributed SD-IoV architecture

layers: the logical SDN controllers, the SDN switch network, the SDN-enabled wireless infrastructures (RSUs, BSs) and the SDN-enabled vehicles. In order to provide a scalable architecture and to reduce delays, these controllers are placed in local areas forming a distributed network dealing with the vehicle mobility.

2.2 SD-IoV Logical Architecture

The logical architecture proposed for the SD-IoV is shown in Fig. 2. This architecture, extending the traditional SDN architecture is composed of four layers: the application layer (network services, third party and user applications), the control layer (distributed SDN controllers), the upper data plane (SDN switches and SDN-enabled wireless infrastructures) and the lower data plane (SDN-enabled vehicles).

In this architecture, the control layer, composed of a set of distributed controllers, has a prominent role. Indeed, the controllers, having a global overview of the network, dynamically and centrally manage the network resources through a modification of the SDN-enabled switches' flow tables. For example, the control layer could modify the communication paths according to the policies and requirements (QoS, security, etc.). Each controller has three main Application Programming Interfaces (APIs):

- Northbound API, the controller-applications API enabling communications between the SDN Controller and the services and applications running over the network;
- Southbound API, the controller-infrastructure API enabling communications between the SDN Controller and the SDN-enabled devices (SDN switches SDN-enabled wireless infrastructure, SDN-enabled vehicles);
- Eastbound/Westbound API, the controller-controller API enabling communications between controllers and allowing the SD-IoV distributed control plane synchronization.

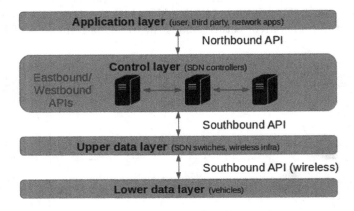

Fig. 2. Logical SD-IoV architecture

To promote the adoption of the SD-IoV, security is an important point to consider. Securing the controller APIs is a necessary part of a trustworthy environment design. As noted in [11], the trust establishment between the third party applications or network services and the SDN controller is an important point. Indeed, the Northbound API could be used to attack the SDN controller. In the current SD-IoV architecture, the applications are able to program the network (writing network policies interpreted as flow rules by the controller) and to request information (reading the network state) without any application authentication, behavior inspection and rule conflict detection. Therefore, a malicious or compromised application consuming important network resources could easily disturb the entire network. This important challenge is addressed in Sect. 4.

2.3 Blockchain

The BC [6] is currently the most popular distributed ledger technology. It can be described as a peer-to-peer (P2P) network maintaining a consistent database among all members: the BC. Through this public distributed ledger, records of all transactions are kept in the network. As the name suggests, a BC corresponds to an ordered list of chained blocks, each one containing some transactions. All the network members have the same copy of the BC and therefore modifying the BC cannot be accomplished without the agreement of most network members. The agreement of the networks members is called the consensus process and different kind of consensus have been proposed: Proof-of-Work (PoW), Proof-of-Stack (PoS), etc. Using a distributed consensus and asymmetric cryptography, the BC aims to provide a transparent, secured and scalable environment without a trusted central authority. Another interesting point with BC is the automatic and immutable smart contract. Smart contracts are softwares, BC applications, enabling two parties to negotiate the terms of an agreement, to verify fulfillment and to execute the agreed terms without a third party. Due to the possibilities offered by the BC and the smart contracts, integrating BC in the SD-IoV architecture could be an interesting solution to improve the network security.

3 Related Works

As the related works focusing on IoV are few, here, are listed some papers aiming to improve the SDN security and in particular to manage the applications trust.

First of all, some works such as [9] have already proposed methods enabling to analyze the application behavior. This paper, determining the Control-Flow Graph and the critical flows of an application, provides an overview of the activities of the applications. Therefore these works could be useful to determine whether or not an application is malicious or compromised.

Other works focus on threats containment. [14] introduced Rosemary, a micro-network operating system providing control layer resiliency. It supports the network applications failures using threat containment: the errors are isolated and the global operating system continue to function. In the same way,

[3], aiming to increase the controller availability, raises the level of abstraction between the controller and the applications. To do so, this work integrates a fault isolation layer and a network transaction layer. Thanks to that, this system should be able to protect the network. However, these two works focus on crashing applications and does not consider the application trust.

[2] studies trust, trust in application and trust in controllers. In this work is implemented an intermediary layer, called Trust-oriented Controller Proxy (ToCP), between the application layer and the infrastructure layer. To improve trust, instead of one controller, several ones (operated by different providers in different environments) are used. The network configuration requests generated by these different controllers are compared and controlled at the ToCP layer. This layer decides whether or not these requests are similar and trustable, and therefore, should be implemented at the infrastructure layer or not.

Finally some papers have already proposed global solutions aiming to establish trust between the SDN controllers and the network applications: [1,7,12]. They present different frameworks aiming to verify the network application identity and to define a trust level and permissions for each of them. [1,12] go further than [7] by introducing the idea of access control (read, write, notify and system call). Moreover, beyond the application authentication the interesting idea of controlling the applications over time is proposed in these works. Through this control the SDN controller should be able to detect the abnormal behavior of a network application and avoid the network disruption.

Nevertheless, these propositions are not suitable for the SD-IoV architecture. Indeed, they consider a centralized control layer with a single controller while the SD-IoV control layer is distributed. This paper aims to go further than these works by proposing a scalable system designed for this distributed control layer. Therefore, a distributed BC-based solution with a robust authentication mechanism is presented. This system should be able to manage the network resources allocation. Moreover, the innovative idea of trust index, enabling to manage the applications permissions, is introduced.

4   A Blockchain-Based Trust Management System

Securing the SD-IoV architecture is an important concern and in this architecture the control layer holds a central place. The northbound interface of this SD-IoV control layer is facing many issues, in particular, the trust establishment between the applications and the controllers through authentication and control.

To deal with this issue, in this section is proposed a BC-based trust management system enabling the applications authentication, control and evaluation. The theoretical approach and a smart contracts based design are presented.

4.1   System Overview

This subsection aims to introduce the proposed system. In this architecture, the SDN controllers, belonging to the SD-IoV architecture, are considered as BC

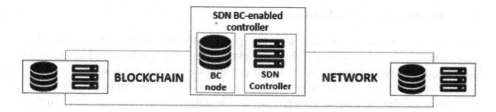

Fig. 3. SD-IoV BC-enabled architecture

nodes, forming a SD-IoV BC network. Thus, the edge equipments hosting the SDN controllers, using their computational, storage and communication capabilities should host the BC application as well. As shown in Fig. 3, all the SDN BC-enabled controllers are connected and able to communicate and interact.

This system, integrating the BC technology presents many benefits. Indeed, the SDN BC-based controllers share a distributed encrypted database that cannot be modified without the agreement of the entire network. This system aims to provide trust between the SDN BC-enabled controllers. Indeed, all the transactions and exchanges are kept in the BC and the nodes are authenticated ensuring integrity, non repudiation, authentication, availability and confidentiality.

If an outside entity, such as a Service Provider (SP), wants to modify the BC, adding information to the database, it should ask (through an API) the BC network to evaluate whether or not this request should be accepted. In our scenario, this immutable distributed ledger will be used to store the certified Applications IDentity cards (A-ID). The A-ID creation process and the A-ID use will be explained in the Subsect. 4.2. Moreover, a smart contract based implementation of the A-ID management will be presented in the Subsect. 4.5.

This A-ID should contain all the information necessary to identify an application (name, content, public key, etc.) enabling the application authentication process. In addition to this basic information, it should also contain an Application Trust Index (A-TI) used to determine whether or not the SDN BC-enabled controllers should trust this specific application. The higher is the A-TI, the higher will be the trust in the application behavior. The A-TI use and modification will be explained in the Subsects. 4.3 and 4.4.

Due to network performances consideration, the SDN controllers and the BC nodes would have to work in parallel. Indeed, the SDN controllers would only request the BC network, through APIs, according to their needs. Under this system, the SDN controllers operating speed could be maintained and the trust blockchain network operations could run in the background, providing a quick response trust management system.

In the rest of this section, on the basis of these components, are presented the main steps of the trust establishment system: applications authentication management, network resources requests management, feedback.

4.2   Applications Authentication

The applications authentication is a key point. Indeed, during a resources allocation process, the trust establishment between the applications and the control layer requires the implementation of an authentication mechanism.

The authentication process uses the A-ID briefly described in the Subsect. 4.1. Without an A-ID, an application cannot be identified. Therefore, for a SP aiming to deploy an application (network services, third party or user application) and to use the SD-IoV network, requesting an A-ID is essential.

First of all, this SP must provide the blockchain nodes with all the information enabling the application registration process (name, content, public key, author, etc.) (1). Then, the SDN BC-enabled controllers elect a BC node (2). This election is based on the Proof of Elapsed Time (PoET), a consensus algorithm with equal opportunities for all nodes to be elected. With this algorithm, a fair load balancing between the different SDN controllers could be designed.

During the A-ID creation process, the blockchain nodes act as a Certification Authority (CA) and the elected controller manages the certification process. Therefore this node controls the pieces of information provided by the SP (identity information, public key) and encrypts the A-ID with its private key certifying the application identity (3). Then, this blockchain node adds the newly created A-ID to the blockchain and provides the unique identifier corresponding to this A-ID to the SP and the application (4).

From this point on, the application will be able to establish a communication with an SDN BC-enabled controller thanks to the A-ID. The application authentication process is composed of three steps. First of all, the application provides its unique identifier to the BC network (API) (1). Then, an elected node checks if this identifier exists in the BC and if the application is certified (2). If so, using the A-ID, the controller retrieves the application public key and submits a challenge to the application (3). Once the application identity is verified, the authentication process is completed and a secured communication is established between the application and the SDN BC-enabled controller.

To conclude this part, using a distributed Certification Authority and a distributed Public Key Infrastructure (PKI) management there is not a single point of failure. This could improve the network security and robustness.

4.3   Network Resources Requests Management

Once the application is authenticated and a secured communication established, the application can request resources such as a flow table modification, implementing changes to the network, or a network state display providing an overview of the topology and the servers/end users location.

Trust is a really important point. Indeed, an authenticated application is able to disturb the network functioning through its requests. That is why its behavior should be controlled. This is where the A-TI comes in. It corresponds to the trust level of the application. The higher it is, the higher is the trust level.

The network resources requests management process, as the A-ID creation process, is managed by a node elected through the PoET. This process can be decomposed into three steps: the application's resources request (1), the request validation and the request implementation. The request validation step takes into account two parameters: the application's resources request and the A-TI.

First of all, the elected node retrieves the application A-TI and according to this value decides if the request should be accepted or not (2). If the A-TI is too low, the blockchain nodes could reject any request from this application, even network state information (a reconnaissance attack is possible). On the contrary, if the A-TI has a sufficient value, the elected node should evaluate the available network resources to determine whether or not this allocation is possible (3).

This node acts as an interface between the application and the controllers concerned by the application request. First, controllers are selected according to their location, the variety of services that they offer and the application request. Then, the supervisor checks the availability of the requested resources through an exchange with these controllers. If not available, the elected node makes a counter-proposal to the application, indicating the available resources (4). If available, or if the application accepts the counter-proposal, the request is validated.

Finally, the request is implemented (5). During the implementation process, the supervisor interprets and converts the request into a request understandable to the SDN controller and the SDN-enabled network switches (P4, Openflow, etc.). Subsequently, depending on the type of request, it is transmitted to the concerned SDN controllers. The whole process is presented in Fig. 4.

It should be noted that, if requested by either one of the parties, the concerned application or the SDN BC-enabled controller, a modification or cancellation of the resource allocation agreement could be easily managed. This modification could be initiated by the application through a new network resources request or by the controller if the allocated resources are no longer available or if the application behavior is suspicious.

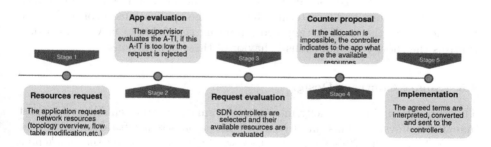

Fig. 4. Resource management flow

4.4   Feedback

The feedback is an essential part of this system allowing the application evaluation. Indeed, it aims to control the application behavior and to share the result of this analysis, providing useful information about this application.

As noted in the Sect. 3, different works have proposed methods enabling to analyze the application behavior and to determine whether or not this application is malicious or compromised. Different types of abnormal behavior can be detected and checked using these methods (service unregistration, removed dependencies, etc.). However, the behavior analysis is not beyond the scope of this paper. It will be assumed here that three types of behavior can be identified: normal, abnormal but non-dangerous, abnormal and compromised or malicious.

Once the agreed terms are implemented, if the analysis demonstrates the dangerous behavior of the application, a SDN controller could decide to cancel the resource allocation agreement. All the controllers involved in the agreement are informed and the resources can be reallocated. Nevertheless, the main purpose of the feedback is to avoid future attacks and abnormal requests. Therefore, the SDN controller will inform the whole network of this event.

The A-TI makes the dissemination of this information possible. When an application is added to the BC, its A-TI, stored in the A-ID structure, is equal to a middle value. If a dangerous behavior is detected the controller will automatically decrement the application A-TI. On the contrary, after a random period of time, all the nodes involved in the resources allocation agreement make a report of the application behavior. According to the past application behavior (abnormal but non dangerous behavior or not) and the estimated future behavior, these nodes decide to increment or decrement the A-TI of the application. The average rating given by these controllers is added to the current A-TI.

Thanks to that, this BC node or another BC node will be able to adjust its behavior. The future requests of an application with a low A-TI will not be accepted without conditions, preventing its dangerous behavior. Moreover, if the A-TI is too low, the application certificate, and therefore the application A-ID, could be revoked. To conclude this part, on the one hand, with the feedback process, the medium and long term behavior of the applications is controlled. On the other hand, the A-TI instantiation, limiting the rights of new applications, controls the short term malicious behavior of these applications.

4.5   Smart Contract Design

This subsection aims to briefly introduce the smart contract enabling this trust management system. This smart contract corresponds to a software stored in the SD-IoV blockchain. This smart contract would be executed by the blockchain system. Therefore, the applications and SP should use an API controlled by the blockchain nodes, ensuring a high level of trust and automating the exchanges between the two sides.

In the Fig. 5 is shown a simple design of this smart contract. It presents the main structures and functions of this smart contract, without which the

```
Contract ApplicationManagement:
    struct Application {};                                    # application information (pki, content, etc)
    struct Signature{};                                       # blockchain node signer
    struct ResourcesContract{};                               # agreed terms (nodes, resources, etc)
    Application application, Signature[] signatures;          # Application, Signature instantiation
    ResourcesContract[] resourcesContracts;                   # ResourcesContract instantiation
    function applicationInit(application_infos_table){}       # smart contract instantiation (Application)
    function signApplication(signer_node_infos_table){}       # application certification (Signature)
    function revokeApplication(){}                            # low A-TI, dangerous behavior: revocation
    function resourcesContractInit(){}                        # resources allocation (ResourcesContract)
    function resourcesContractCancellation(){}                # contract modification, free resources
    function decrementApplicationTrustIndex(){}               # decrement A-TI
    function computeApplicationTrustIndex(){}                 # calculation of average A-TI
```

Fig. 5. Smart contract design

trust management system could not work. With this smart contract, all the SP application lifecycle is handled, from application A-ID creation to resources allocation. The smart contract contains the application A-ID and corresponds to the application digital identity card. The smart contract address, a unique identifier, is provided to the application. This address enables the application authentication: an unknown address means that the application is not registered.

Beyond the basic structures enabling the application management: A-ID (*Application*), certification (*Signature*) and past and current resources allocations (*Resources contracts*), this smart contract also contains different function allowing its modification. These functions correspond to the A-ID creation (*applicationInit*), the application certification (*signApp*) and application revocation (*revokeApp*). There is also the resources allocation negotiation and implementation (*resourcesContractInit*) and resources freeing (*resourcesContractCancellation*), as well as the A-TI decrementation (*decrementApplicationTrustIndex*) and A-TI weighting (*computeApplicationTrustIndex*).

After the design of this smart contract, introducing a new way of establishing trust, managing identity and the interaction between the applications and SD-IoV controllers, the next phase will be to implement this system.

5   Conclusions and Future Work

The IoV development is facing many challenges including mobility management, data flow balancing or high QoS. SDN have been introduced as a solution to overcome these difficulties. Indeed, this technology should be able to improve the network management, the resource utilization and the QoS. Therefore, a new paradigm emerged: SD-IoV, an IoV architecture integrating SDN.

However, so far, this SD-IoV architecture is not secured and ensuring security in a vehicular environment should be one of the primary goals. That is why this paper aims to secure this architecture and, in particular, to secure the communications between the SDN controllers and the network and third party applications. The proposed system should enable a blockchain-based trust establishment using the distributed nature of the SD-IoV control layer. Indeed, using this technology, the SD-IoV security, robustness, reliability and scalability could be significantly improved.

The framework presented in this paper is composed of three important parts: application authentication, network resources management and allocation and application behavior control. It introduces the innovative idea of trust index (A-TI) to manage the application trust, as well as an authentication mechanism using the blockchain (A-ID). Moreover, a smart contract enabling the implementation of this system is designed and explained.

Future work will focus on four main points. The first objective is to define the algorithm handling the A-TI instantiation and modification. Then, the smart contract introduced in the Subsect. 4.5 should be implemented. This implementation will be possible with Hyperledger Fabric, an existing blockchain framework implementation enabling smart contracts' implementation with the Go programming language. Third, the APIs between the SDN controllers and blockchain network should be designed using a REST API. Finally, it will be important to evaluate the performances of this distributed management system: scalability, robustness, reliability and responsiveness.

References

1. Aliyu, A.L., Bull, P., Abdallah, A.: A trust management framework for network applications within an SDN environment. In: 31st International Conference on Advanced Information Networking and Applications Workshops, AINA 2017 Workshops, Taipei, Taiwan, 27–29 March 2017, pp. 93–98. IEEE (2017)
2. Betgé-Brezetz, S., Kamga, G., Tazi, M.: Trust support for SDN controllers and virtualized network applications. In: Proceedings of the 1st IEEE Conference on Network Softwarization, NetSoft 2015, London, United Kingdom, 13–17 April 2015, pp. 1–5. IEEE (2015)
3. Chandrasekaran, B., Benson, T.: Tolerating SDN application failures with legoSDN. In: Proceedings of the 13th ACM Workshop on Hot Topics in Networks, HotNets-XIII, Los Angeles, CA, USA, 27–28 October 2014, pp. 22:1–22:7. ACM (2014)
4. Jiacheng, C., Haibo, Z., Ning, Z., Peng, Y., Lin, G., Sherman, S.X.: Software defined internet of vehicles: architecture, challenges and solutions. J. Commun. Inf. Netw. 1(1), 14–26 (2016)
5. Fangchun, Y., Shangguang, W., Jinglin, L., Zhihan, L., Qibo, S.: An overview of internet of vehicles. China Commun. 11(10), 1–15 (2014)
6. Iansiti, M., Lakhani, K.R.: The truth about blockchain. Harvard Bus. Rev. 95(1), 118–127 (2017)
7. Isong, B., Kgogo, T., Lugayizi, F., Kankuzi, B.: Trust establishment framework between SDN controller and applications. In: 18th IEEE/ACIS International Conference on Software Engineering, Artificial Intelligence, Networking and Parallel/Distributed Computing, SNPD 2017, Kanazawa, Japan, 26–28 June 2017, pp. 101–107. IEEE (2017)
8. Kaiwartya, O., et al.: Internet of vehicles: motivation, layered architecture, network model, challenges, and future aspects. IEEE Access 4, 5356–5373 (2016)
9. Lee, C., Shin, S.: Shield: an automated framework for static analysis of SDN applications. In: Proceedings of the 2016 ACM International Workshop on Security in Software Defined Networks & Network Function Virtualization, SDN-NFV@CODASPY 2016, New Orleans, LA, USA, 11 March 2016, pp. 29–34. ACM (2016)

10. Nunes, B.A.A., Mendonca, M., Nguyen, X.N., Obraczka, K., Turletti, T.: A survey of software-defined networking: past, present, and future of programmable networks. IEEE Commun. Surv. Tutor. **16**(3), 1617–1634 (2014)
11. ONF: Principles and practices for securing software-defined networks. Open Networking Foundation Technical Recommendation TR-511 (2015)
12. Scott-Hayward, S., Kane, C., Sezer, S.: Operationcheckpoint: SDN application control. In: 22nd IEEE International Conference on Network Protocols, ICNP 2014, Raleigh, NC, USA, 21–24 October 2014, pp. 618–623. IEEE (2014)
13. Scott-Hayward, S., Natarajan, S., Sezer, S.: A survey of security in software defined networks. IEEE Commun. Surv. Tutor. **18**(1), 623–654 (2016)
14. Shin, S., et al.: Rosemary: a robust, secure, and high-performance network operating system. In: Proceedings of the 2014 ACM SIGSAC Conference on Computer and Communications Security, Scottsdale, AZ, USA, 3–7 November 2014, pp. 78–89. ACM (2014)
15. Yaqoob, I., Ahmad, I., Ahmed, E., Gani, A., Razzak, M.I., Guizani, N.: Overcoming the key challenges to establishing vehicular communication: Is SDN the answer? IEEE Commun. Mag. **55**(7), 128–134 (2017)

A Secure Authentication Protocol for Wireless Sensor Network in Smart Vehicular System

Chun-Ta Li[1], Chi-Yao Weng[2], Chin-Ling Chen[3(✉)], and Cheng-Chi Lee[4,5(✉)]

[1] Department of Information Management, Tainan University of Technology,
No. 529, Zhongzheng Road, Tainan City 71002, Taiwan (R.O.C.)
th0040@mail.tut.edu.tw
[2] Department of Computer Science, National Pingtung University,
No. 4-18, Min-Sheng Road, Pingtung City 90003, Taiwan (R.O.C.)
cyweng@mail.nptu.edu.tw
[3] Department of Computer Science and Information Engineering,
Chaoyang University of Technology, No. 168, Jifeng East Road,
Taichung City 41349, Taiwan (R.O.C.)
clc@mail.cyut.edu.tw
[4] Department of Library and Information Science, Fu Jen Catholic University,
No. 510, Jhongjheng Road, New Taipei City 24205, Taiwan (R.O.C.)
cclee@mail.fju.edu.tw
[5] Department of Photonics and Communication Engineering, Asia University,
No. 500, Lioufeng Road, Taichung City 41354, Taiwan (R.O.C.)

Abstract. As wireless sensor networks (WSN) and Internet of things (IoT) have rapidly developed over recent years, the smart vehicular system is designed in the environment of WSN to provide vehicle related applications such as traffic safety for drivers, controlling traffic signal, broadcasting traffic information and speed monitoring etc. Recently, Mohit et al. have proposed an authentication protocol for WSN-based smart vehicular system. Their protocol consists of three main entities namely vehicle sensor, sink node and user. Vehicle sensors collected traffic data and send it to a sink node of WSN. User used traffic data from sink node in off-line mode for the traffic management. Mohit et al. claimed that the proposed protocol is secure against various attacks such as untraceable, impersonation and password guessing attacks. However, their proposed protocol still has some vulnerabilities such as absence of session key, suffering user duplication and sink node impersonation attacks. Thus their protocol cannot guarantee complete security. In this paper, we aim to propose an improved protocol based on their work which overcomes these security loopholes in their protocol. The informal security analysis shows that our proposed protocol is cable to defend the security weaknesses found in Mohit et al.'s authentication protocol.

Keywords: Authentication · Internet of things · Session key
Smart vehicular system · Wireless sensor network

© Springer Nature Switzerland AG 2018
A. M. J. Skulimowski et al. (Eds.): IOV 2018, LNCS 11253, pp. 278–288, 2018.
https://doi.org/10.1007/978-3-030-05081-8_20

1   Introduction

With the development of technological advances in Internet of Things (IoTs), the wireless sensor networks (WSNs) have been widely applied in many domains [4,9–11], such as health care, military, industry, home safety and traffic etc., due to their ease of deployment in the intended field. The vehicular system [3,5,7,8] is playing a critical role in the traffic management such as traffic controlling, speed monitoring and setting of traffic signal. Figure 1 demonstrates a typical architecture of the smart vehicular system using WSN. Two types of communications exist in the system, which include: (1) vehicle-to-roadside sink node; (2) user-to-roadside sink node. First, the vehicle sensors are placed on a vehicle and vehicles are deployed in the intended field. After deployment, those sensors collect real-time traffic data of road and send it to the nearby roadside sink node. Then, the roadside sink nodes send traffic data to the user. After that, the user can analysis traffic data and forward data to roadside sink node for traffic management.

In the past years, a number of authentication protocols for WSNs have been proposed in the literature. In 2009, Das first proposed a hash-based authentication protocol [2] for WSNs. However, Das's protocol does not provide mutual authentication [1] and has some security flaws such as sensor node compromising attack [15] and privileged insider attack [6]. The smart vehicular system is a class of mobile ad hoc network (MANET) an it is vulnerable to security attacks when compared to MANET because of its unique features such as high mobility and dynamic network topology [12,14]. In order to ensure security in smart vehicular system, the authentication is a vital step to prevent insecure access from the illegal users and it can be classified as two parts: node authentication and message authentication. Recently, Mohit et al. propose an authentication protocol [13] for smart vehicular system using WSN and the performance of their authentication protocol is efficient because it only uses lightweight one-way hash functions and bitwise XOR operations. Moreover, Mohit et al. presents that it is secure against various known security attacks and provides important functionality features. However, in this paper, we demonstrated that Mohit et al.'s authentication protocol cannot withstand user duplication attack and sink node impersonation attack. Besides, we also found that Mohit et al.'s authentication cannot provide the feature of session key agreement. To enhance the security of their authentication protocol, we propose a new authentication protocol for WSN-based smart vehicular system.

The remainder of the paper is organized as follows. Section 2 reviews Mohit et al.'s authentication protocol and Sect. 3 presents our cryptanalysis on Mohit et al.'s authentication protocol. A new lightweight authenticated key agreement protocol for WSN-based smart vehicular system is presented in Sect. 4. Section 5 presents informal security analyzation of the proposed protocol. Finally, we make some conclusions in Sect. 6.

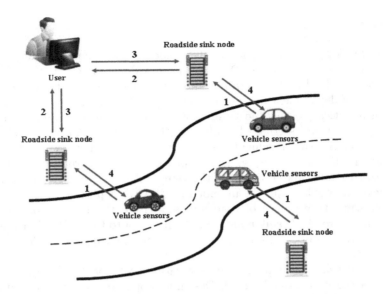

Fig. 1. Architecture for smart vehicle system

2   Review of Mohit et al.'s Authentication Protocol

In this section, Mohit et al. proposed an authentication protocol for WSN-based smart vehicular system. There are four entities, including: registration authority (RA), vehicle sensor, sink node and user. In addition, their authentication protocol consists of five different phases, including: system setup, user registration, user login, authentication and password change. Table 1 describes the symbols used in this paper and the details of each phase are briefly illustrated in the following subsections.

2.1   System Setup Phase

In this phase, the registration authority registers all the vehicle sensors available in WSN during the time of purchase and maintains all the relevant data of each vehicle sensor such as its battery capacity, engine number and insurance expire date etc.

2.2   User Registration Phase

To access the data from the vehicle sensor, each user needs to complete registration with the nearby sink node by performing the following steps.

Step 1. The user U_i chooses his/her identity and password (ID_i, PW_i) and computes a masked identity $HID_i = h(ID_i \| RN_i)$ and a masked password $HPW_i = h(PW_i \| RN_i)$, where RN_i is a random nonce selected by U_i. Then U_i sends (HID_i, HPW_i) to sink node S_j via a secure channel.

Table 1. Symbols used in the paper

Symbol	Description
ID_i, PW_i	The identity and password of ith user
ID_j	The identity of jth sink node
ID_k	The identity of kth vehicle sensor
RA	Registration authority
KS	The secret key of sink node
NU_i	Random nonce generated by ith user
NS_j	Random nonce generated by jth sink node
NV_k	Random nonce generated by kth vehicle sensor
$h(.)$	One-way cryptographic hash function
$\|\|$	Message concatenation
$\oplus$	A bitwise exclusive OR operation
SK_{ijk}	Session key negotiated between ith user, jth sink node and kth vehicle sensor
$A \overset{?}{=} B$	Check whether A equal to B or not

Step 2. Upon receiving the registration request from U_i, S_j chooses a nonce RG_i and a random number q_i and computes $A_i = h(HID_i\|\|RG_i)$, $B_i = h(HID_i\|\|HPW_i\|\|RG_i)$, $C_i = q_i \oplus HPW_i$ and $D_i = C_i \oplus h(K_S)$, where K_S is the secret key of sink node. Then S_j stores $(A_i, B_i, C_i, D_i, RG_i)$ in the memory of smart card and sends smart card to U_i via a secure channel.

Step 3. After receiving the smart card from the sink node, U_i computes $HN_i = h(ID_i\|\|PW_i) \oplus RN_i$ and stores HN_i in the memory of smart card. Finally, the parameters $(A_i, B_i, C_i, D_i, RG_i, HN_i)$ are stored in the smart card.

2.3   User Login Phase

In this phase, U_i logins into the smart vehicular system with his/her identity and password using smart card. Then the smart card checks the correctness of the entered parameters and sends login request to sink node by performing the following steps.

Step 1. The user U_i enters his/her identity and password (ID_i^*, PW_i^*) into the terminal of smart card and the smart card computes $RN_i = h(ID_i^*\|\|PW_i^*) \oplus HN_i$, $HID_i^* = h(ID_i^*\|\|RN_i^*)$, $HPW_i^* = h(PW_i^*\|\|RN_i^*)$ and $B_i^* = h(HID_i^*\|\| HPW_i^*\|\|RG_i)$ Then the smart card checks whether $B_i^* \overset{?}{=} h(HID_i^*\|\|HPW_i^*\|\|RG_i)$ holds or not. If it is valid, it goes to step 2, otherwise rejects the smart card.

Step 2. The smart card chooses a nonce NU_i and computes $q_i = C_i \oplus HPW_i^*$, $M_{TS} = h(q_i\|\|B_i\|\|NU_i)$, $p_1 = NU_i \oplus q_i$, $p_2 = ID_j \oplus h(p_1\|\|q_i)$ and $E_i = D_i \oplus HPW_i^*$.

Step 3. Finally, the smart card sends the login request message (M_{TS}, p_1, p_2, E_i) to the sink node S_j via a public channel.

2.4 Authentication Phase

In this phase, it is initiated by U_i after successfully login phase. The aim of this phase is to negotiate a secret session key between the user, sink node and vehicle sensor. Then all parties can use it to securely communicate in smart vehicular system. The execution steps of authentication phases are performed as follows.

Step 1. After receiving the login request message from U_i, the sink node S_j computes $q_i^* = E_i \oplus h(K_S)$, $NU_i^* = p_1 \oplus q_i^*$, $ID_j = p_2 \oplus h(p_1||q_i^*)$ and $M_{TS}^* = h(q_i^*||B_i||NU_i^*)$ and checks the freshness of NU_i^* and the validity of M_{TS}^*. If above verifications failed, S_j rejects U_i's login request. Otherwise, S_j computes $X_k = h(ID_k||K_S)$, $M_{SV} = h(ID_k||NS_j||X_k||ID_j)$, $d_1 = NS_j \oplus h(ID_k)$ and $d_2 = ID_j \oplus ID_k$ and sends (M_{SV}, d_1, d_2) to the vehicle sensor V_k via a public channel.

Step 2. Upon receiving the message from S_j, the vehicle sensor V_k computes $NS_j^* = d_1 \oplus h(ID_k)$ and $ID_j = d_2 \oplus ID_k$ and checks the freshness of NS_j^*. If it is not valid, V_k rejects the request. Otherwise, V_k request X_k from registration authority by sending ID_k. In response RA sends X_k to V_k via a secure channel. Then V_k computes $M_{SV}^* = h(ID_k||NS_j^*||X_k||ID_j)$ and checks whether $M_{SV}^* \overset{?}{=} M_{SV}$ holds or not. If it is not valid, V_k rejects the request. Otherwise, V_k computes $v = h(ID_k||NV_k||NS_j^*)$, $M_{VS} = h(X_k||NS_k||v)$ and $t = NV_k \oplus NS_j$ and sends (M_{VS}, t) to S_j via a public channel, where NV_k is a nonce randomly selected by V_k.

Step 3. After receiving the reply message from V_k, the sink node S_j computes $NV_k^* = t \oplus NS_j$ and checks the freshness of NV_k^*. If it is valid, S_j computes $v^* = h(ID_k||NV_k^*||NS_j)$ and $M_{VS}^* = h(X_k||NV_k^*||v^*)$ and checks whether $M_{VS}^* \overset{?}{=} M_{VS}$ holds or not. If it is nod valid, S_j terminates the session. Otherwise, S_j computes $w = NS_j \oplus NU_i^*$ and $M_{ST} = h(q_i^*||NU_i^*||NS_j||ID_j||ID_k)$ and sends (M_{ST}, w) to U_i via a public channel.

Step 4. After receiving the reply message from S_j, U_i computes $NS_j^* = w \oplus NU_i$ and $M_{ST}^* = h(q_i||NU_i||NS_j^*||ID_j||ID_k)$ and checks whether $M_{ST}^* \overset{?}{=} M_{ST}$ holds or not. If it is valid, U_i accepts it. Otherwise, U_i rejects the session.

2.5 Password Change Phase

In this phase, the user U_i could change his/her current password PW_i to a new password PW_i^{new} without notifying the sink node and the smart card will examine the correctness of the current ID_i and PW_i. If they are correct, the smart card will ask U_i to enter a new password PW_i^{new} and complete the password update through the following steps.

Step 1. The user U_i inserts the smart card into card reader and enters original identity and password (ID_i^*, PW_i^*) to card reader.

Step 2. The smart card computes $RN_i = HN_i \oplus h(ID_i^*||PW_i^*)$, $HID_i^* = h(ID_i^*||RN_i)$, $HPW_i^* = h(PW_i^*||RN_i)$ and $B_i^* = h(HID_i^*||HPW_i||RG_i)$ and checks whether $B_i^* \overset{?}{=} B_i$ holds or not. If it is not valid, the smart card rejects the request. Otherwise, U_i enters the new password PW_i^{new}.

Step 3. The smart card computes $HPW_i^{new} = h(PW_i^{new}||RN_i)$, $HN_i^{new} = RN_i \oplus h(ID_i^*||PW_i^{new})$, $B_i^{new} = h(HID_i^*||HPW_i^{new}||RG_i)$, $C_i^{new} = q_i \oplus HPW_i^{new}$ and $D_i^{new} = D_i \oplus C_i \oplus C_i^{new}$. Finally, the smart card replaces (HN_i, B_i, C_i, D_i) with $(HN_i^{new}, B_i^{new}, C_i^{new}, D_i^{new})$.

3 Cryptanalysis of Mohit Et Al.'s Authentication Protocol

In this section, the listing and the discussion of various security problems of Mohit et al.'s protocol are given below.

3.1 User Duplication Attack

In Mohit et al.'s protocol, we observed that a legal user U_i can intentionally duplicate multiple non-registered accounts by using the system parameter $h(K_S)$ with different identities and passwords. A more detailed cryptanalysis is described below.

Step 1. After registration, the parameters $(A_i, B_i, C_i, D_i, RG_i, HN_i)$ are stored in the memory of U_i's smart card. We assume that U_i can extract all the stored parameters from smart card.

Step 2. U_i uses its own parameters C_i and D_i from the smart card to derive $h(K_S) = D_i \oplus C_i$. Then U_i randomly chooses (ID_i', PW_i', RN_i') and duplicates a masked identity $HID_i' = h(ID_i'||RN_i')$ and a masked password $HPW_i' = h(PW_i'||RN_i')$.

Step 3. U_i further chooses (q_i', RG_i') and computes $A_i' = h(HID_i'||RG_i')$, $B_i' = h(HID_i'||HPW_i'||RG_i')$, $C_i' = q_i' \oplus HPW_i'$, $D_i' = C_i' \oplus h(K_S)$ and $HN_i' = H(ID_i'||PW_i') \oplus RN_i'$, where $h(K_S)$ is derived from Step 1.

Step 4. Finally, U_i stores $(A_i', B_i', C_i', D_i', RG_i', HN_i')$ in the memory of a new smart card for other non-registered user.

Therefore, Mohit et al.'s authentication protocol cannot resist user duplication attack.

3.2 Sink Node Impersonation Attack

Continued to the Sect. 3.1, once a malicious user U_a has learned the parameter $h(K_S)$, he/she can impersonate the sink node to communicate with a victim user U_i". A more detailed cryptanalysis is described below.

Step 1. After successfully login phase, the login request message $(M_{TS}", p_1", p_2", E_i")$ of U_i" will send to the sink node via a public channel, where $M_{TS}" = h(q_i"||B_i"||NU_i")$, $p_1" = NU_i" \oplus q_i"$, $p_2" = ID_j \oplus h(p_1"||q_i")$, $E_i" = D_i" \oplus HPW_i"$ and $NU_i"$ is a nonce chosen by $U_i"$. Suppose the malicious user U_a intercepts this login request message and tries to impersonate as the sink node by forging a valid response message.

Step 2. U_a uses the parameter $h(K_S)$ to derive $q_i" = E_i" \oplus h(K_S)$, $NU_i" = p_1" \oplus q_i"$ and $ID_j = p_2" \oplus h(p_1"||q_i")$.

Step 3. To impersonate the sink node during the authentication phase, U_a needs to create a valid response message $(M_{ST}", w")$. To do so, U_a chooses its own nonce NS_a and uses it to compute $w" = NS_a \oplus NU_i"$ and $M_{ST}" = h(q_i"||NU_i"||NS_a||ID_j||ID_k)$. Then U_a sends $(M_{ST}", w")$ to the victim user U_i.

Step 4. Finally, U_i computes $NS_a = w" \oplus NU_i"$ and checks if $h(q_i"||NU_i"||NS_a||ID_j||ID_k)$ is equal to $M_{ST}"$ which would obviously be correct. As a result, U_i believes that the response message is from S_j and feels to be connected with the legal sink node.

Hence, Mohit et al.'s authentication is insecure against sink node impersonation attack.

3.3   Absence of B_i Recording in S_j Side

It is observable that during the authentication phase of Mohit et al.'s authentication protocol, the sink node S_j is unable to check the validity of M_{TS}. In Step 1 of the authentication phase, S_j needs to compute $M_{TS}^* = h(q_i^*||B_i||NU_i^*)$ and uses M_{TS}^* to verify the validity of U_i's M_{TS}. However, due to the lack of B_i recording in S_j side, S_j is unable to compute M_{TS}^*. This problem clearly indicates that Mohit et al.'s authentication cannot preserve the property of mutual authentication between U_i and S_j.

3.4   Absence of Session Key Agreement

In Mohit et al.'s authentication protocol, they claimed that their protocol can negotiate a secret session key between U_i, S_j and V_k for securing future communications. However, it is observable that during the above described phases of their authentication protocol, the property of session key negotiation is not proposed between all parties in smart vehicular system.

4   The Proposed Authentication Protocol

In this section, we propose a refined version of the authentication protocol to provide strong security by resolving the vulnerabilities of Mohit et al.'s protocol. In the proposed protocol, we integrate a hashed key parameter and a session key verification into the authentication process to prevent user duplication and sink node impersonation attacks. The description of each phase is described as follows.

4.1   System Setup Phase

In this phase, the executed steps are the same as in Mohit et al.'s authentication protocol.

4.2 User Registration Phase

This phase is about the registration of U_i with S_j and the execution steps of user registration phase is performed as follows.

Step 1. The user U_i chooses his/her identity and password (ID_i, PW_i) and computes a masked identity $HID_i = h(ID_i \| RN_i)$ and a masked password $HPW_i = h(PW_i \| RN_i)$, where RN_i is a random nonce selected by U_i. Then U_i sends (ID_i, HID_i, HPW_i) to sink node S_j via a secure channel.

Step 2. Upon receiving the registration request from U_i, S_j chooses a nonce RG_i and a random number q_i and computes $A_i = h(HID_i \| RG_i)$, $B_i = h(HID_i \| HPW_i \| RG_i)$, $C_i = q_i \oplus HPW_i$ and $D_i = C_i \oplus h(ID_i \| K_S)$, where U_i's identity is integrated into $h(ID_i \| K_S)$. Then S_j stores $(A_i, B_i, C_i, D_i, RG_i)$ in the memory of smart card and sends smart card to U_i via a secure channel.

Step 3. After receiving the smart card from the sink node, U_i computes $HN_i = h(ID_i \| PW_i) \oplus RN_i$ and stores HN_i in the memory of smart card. Finally, the parameters $(A_i, B_i, C_i, D_i, RG_i, HN_i)$ are stored in the smart card.

4.3 User Login Phase

To access the service from smart vehicular system, U_i creates his/her login request and sends it to S_j. The detailed steps of this phase are as follows.

Step 1. The user U_i enters his/her identity and password (ID_i^*, PW_i^*) into the terminal of smart card and the smart card computes $RN_i = h(ID_i^* \| PW_i^*) \oplus HN_i$, $HID_i^* = h(ID_i^* \| RN_i^*)$, $HPW_i^* = h(PW_i^* \| RN_i^*)$ and $B_i^* = h(HID_i^* \| HPW_i^* \| RG_i)$ Then the smart card checks whether $B_i^* \overset{?}{=} h(HID_i^* \| HPW_i^* \| RG_i)$ holds or not. If it is valid, it goes to step 2, otherwise rejects the smart card.

Step 2. The smart card chooses a nonce NU_i and computes $q_i = C_i \oplus HPW_i^*$, $M_{TS} = h(ID_i \| ID_j \| q_i \| NU_i)$, $p_1 = NU_i \oplus q_i$, $p_2 = ID_j \oplus h(p_1 \| q_i)$ and $E_i = D_i \oplus HPW_i^*$.

Step 3. Finally, the smart card sends the login request message $(ID_i, M_{TS}, p_1, p_2, E_i)$ to the sink node S_j via a public channel.

4.4 Authentication Phase

In this phase, it is initiated by U_i after successfully login phase. The aim of this phase is to negotiate a secret session key between the user, sink node and vehicle sensor. Then all parties can use it to securely communicate in smart vehicular system. The execution steps of authentication phases are performed as follows.

Step 1. After receiving the login request message from U_i, the sink node S_j computes $q_i^* = E_i \oplus h(ID_i \| K_S)$, $NU_i^* = p_1 \oplus q_i^*$, $ID_j = p_2 \oplus h(p_1 \| q_i^*)$ and $M_{TS}^* = h(ID_i \| ID_j \| q_i^* \| NU_i^*)$ and checks the freshness of NU_i^* and the validity of M_{TS}^*. If above verifications failed, S_j rejects U_i's login request.

Otherwise, U_i is authenticated by S_j. Next S_j chooses a nonce NS_j and computes $X_k = h(ID_j||ID_k||K_S)$, $M_{SV} = h(ID_k||X_k||ID_j||NU_i^* \oplus NS_j)$, $d_1 = NU_i^* \oplus NS_j \oplus h(X_k)$ and $d_2 = ID_j \oplus ID_k$. S_j sends (M_{SV}, d_1, d_2) to the vehicle sensor V_k via a public channel.

Step 2. Upon receiving the message from S_j, the vehicle sensor V_k computes $ID_j^* = d_2 \oplus ID_k$ and request X_k from registration authority by sending (ID_j^*, ID_k). In response RA sends X_k to V_k via a secure channel. V_k computes $NU_i^* \oplus NS_j = d_1 \oplus h(X_k)$ and checks the freshness of $NU_i^* \oplus NS_j$. If it is not valid, V_k rejects the request. Otherwise, V_k further computes $M_{SV}^* = h(ID_k||X_k||ID_j^*||NU_i^* \oplus NS_j)$ and checks whether $M_{SV}^* \overset{?}{=} M_{SV}$ holds or not. If it is not valid, V_k rejects the request. Otherwise, S_j is authenticated by V_k and V_k computes the session key $SK_{ijk} = h(NU_i^* \oplus NS_j \oplus NV_k)$, $M_{VS} = h(X_k||NV_k||SK_{ijk})$ and $t = NV_k \oplus h(NU_i^* \oplus NS_j)$, where NV_k is a nonce randomly selected by V_k. Then V_k sends (M_{VS}, t) to S_j via a public channel.

Step 3. After receiving the reply message from V_k, the sink node S_j computes $NV_k^* = t \oplus h(NU_i^* \oplus NS_j)$ and checks the freshness of NV_k^*. If it is valid, S_j computes the session key $SK_{ijk} = h(NU_i^* \oplus NS_j \oplus NV_k)$ and $M_{VS}^* = h(X_k||NV_k^*||SK_{ijk})$ and checks whether $M_{VS}^* \overset{?}{=} M_{VS}$ holds or not. If it is nod valid, S_j terminates the session. Otherwise, V_k is authenticated by S_j. S_j further computes $w = NS_j \oplus NV_k^* \oplus h(h(ID_i||K_S)||q_i^*)$ and $M_{ST} = h(q_i^*||NU_i^*||SK_{ijk})$ and sends (M_{ST}, w) to U_i via a public channel.

Step 4. After receiving the reply message from S_j, U_i computes $NS_j \oplus NV_k^* = w \oplus h(h(ID_i||K_S)||q_i)$, the session key $SK_{ijk} = h(NU_i \oplus NS_j \oplus NV_k^*)$ and $M_{ST}^* = h(q_i||NU_i||SK_{ijk})$ and checks whether $M_{ST}^* \overset{?}{=} M_{ST}$ holds or not. If it is valid, U_i accepts it. Otherwise, U_i rejects the session. Finally, the session key SK_{ijk} can be used for the following secret communications between U_i, S_j and V_k in smart vehicular system.

4.5 Password Change Phase

In this phase, the executed steps are the same as in Mohit et al.'s authentication protocol.

5 Security Analysis of the Proposed Authentication Protocol

In this section, we analyze the security of the proposed authentication protocol informally and demonstrate that our proposed protocol has the ability to resist the security weaknesses mentioned in Sect. 3.

Remark 1. *In order to put emphasis on describing the security of our proposed protocol, we assume that sink node's secret key K_S and each party's nonce have been well-protected by themselves.*

Remark 2. *Assume that a malicious attacker U_a has the capacity to eavesdrop and intercept the transmission messages over the public channel between the user, sink node and vehicle sensor.*

5.1 Resistance to User Duplication Attack

According to the threat model mentioned in Sect. 3.1, U_i can extract all the stored parameters $(A_i, B_i, C_i, D_i, RG_i, HN_i)$ from his/her smart card. U_i may try to derive $h(ID_i \| K_S)$ by computing $D_i \oplus C_i$. With the protection of one-way cryptographic hash function, it is computationally difficult for U_i to derive K_S from $h(ID_i \| K_S)$. Thus, without the knowledge of K_S, it is difficult job for U_i to duplicate a legal account for a non-registered user. Moreover, the parameter $h(ID_i \| K_S)$ is only used for U_i to access system after successfully verification by sink node. This clearly indicates that the proposed authentication protocol is secure against user duplication attack.

5.2 Resistance to Sink Node Impersonation Attack

To impersonate the sink node during the authentication phase, a malicious attacker U_a needs to create a valid response message (M_{ST}, w), where $M_{ST} = h(q_i^* \| NU_i^* \| SK_{ijk})$, $w = NS_j \oplus NV_k^* \oplus h(h(ID_i \| K_S) \| q_i^*)$ and $SK_{ijk} = h(NU_i^* \oplus NS_j \oplus NV_k)$. For this purpose, U_a requires q_i^*, $h(ID_i \| K_S)$ and SK_{ijk}. Without knowing the knowledge of above-mentioned parameters, U_a cannot create a valid response message to impersonate the sink node during authentication phase. Therefore, the proposed authentication protocol resists sink node impersonation attack.

5.3 Security of Session Key

After the successfully authentication process in the proposed protocol, U_i, S_j and V_k negotiate a common session key $SK_{ijk} = h(NU_i \oplus NS_j \oplus NV_k)$ for securing future communications between them in smart vehicular system. Since U_a has no knowledge of q_i, the nonce NU_i cannot be derived from eavesdropped p_1, where $p_1 = NU_i \oplus q_i$. Similarly, as mentioned in previous subsection, the parameter $NS_j \oplus NV_k$ cannot be directly derived, as SK_{ijk} is protected by the one-way feature of cryptographic hash function. As a result, the security of session key can be guaranteed in the proposed authentication protocol.

6 Conclusions

In this paper, we have analyzed Mohit et al.'s authentication protocol designed for a smart vehicular system using wireless sensor network is vulnerable to user duplication and sink node impersonation attacks. Moreover, we also found that their protocol cannot provide a session key establishment for securing communications between the user, the sink node and the vehicle sensor. Therefore, we suggested a new authentication and session key establishment protocol for the same, which prevented the above-mentioned security problems.

Acknowledgements. The authors would like to thank the anonymous reviewers for their valuable comments and suggestions. This research was partially supported by the Ministry of Science and Technology, Taiwan, R.O.C., under contract no.: MOST 107-2410-H-165-001.

References

1. Chen, T.H., Shih, W.K.: A robust mutual authentication protocol for wireless sensor networks. ETRI J. **32**(5), 704–712 (2010)
2. Das, M.L.: Two-factor user authentication in wireless sensor networks. IEEE Trans. Wirel. Commun. **8**(3), 1086–1090 (2009)
3. Förster, D., Kargl, F., Löhr, H.: PUCA: a pseudonym scheme with strong privacy guarantees for vehicular ad-hoc networks. Ad Hoc Netw. **37**(1), 122–132 (2016)
4. He, D., Kumar, N., Chen, J., Lee, C.C., Chilamkurti, N., Yeo, S.S.: Robust anonymous authentication protocol for health-care applications using wireless medical sensor networks. Multimed. Syst. **21**(1), 49–60 (2015)
5. Kang, Q., Liu, X., Yao, Y., Wang, Z., Li, Y.: Efficient authentication and access control of message dissemination over vehicular ad hoc network. Neurocomputing **181**, 132–138 (2016)
6. Khan, M.K., Alghathbar, K.: Cryptanalysis and security improvements of two-factor user authentication in wireless sensor networks. Sensors **10**(3), 2450–2459 (2010)
7. Lee, C.C., Lai, Y.M., Cheng, P.J.: An efficient multiple session key establishment scheme for VANET group integration. IEEE Intell. Syst. **31**(6), 35–43 (2016)
8. Li, C.T., Hwang, M.S., Chu, Y.P.: A secure and efficient communication scheme with authenticated key establishment and privacy preservation for vehicular ad hoc networks. Comput. Commun. **31**(12), 2803–2814 (2008)
9. Li, C.T., Wu, T.Y., Chen, C.L., Lee, C.C., Chen, C.M.: An efficient user authentication and user anonymity scheme with provably security for IoT-based medical care system. Sensors **17**(7), 1–18 (2017). Article no. 1482
10. Li, C.T., Lee, C.C., Weng, C.Y., Chen, C.M.: A secure three party node authentication and key establishment scheme for the Internet of things environment. J. Internet Technol. **19**(1), 147–155 (2018)
11. Li, C.T., Lee, C.C., Weng, C.Y., Chen, C.M.: Towards secure authenticating of cache in the reader for RFID-based IoT systems. Peer-to-Peer Netw. Appl. **11**(1), 198–208 (2018)
12. Manvi, S.S., Tangade, S.: A survey on authentication schemes in VANETs for secured communication. Veh. Commun. **9**, 19–30 (2017)
13. Mohit, P., Amin, R., Biswas, G.P.: Design of authentication protocol for wireless sensor network-based smart vehicular system. Veh. Commun. **9**, 64–71 (2017)
14. Mokhtar, B., Azab, M.: Suvery on security issues in vehicular ad hoc networks. Alexandria Eng. J. **54**(4), 1115–1126 (2015)
15. Nyang, D., Lee, M.K.: Improvement of Das's two-factor authentication protocol in wireless sensor networks. IACR Cryptology ePrint Archive, 2009:630 (2009)

An Acceleration Method for Similar Time-Series Finding

Yuan Yuan[(✉)], Qibo Sun, Ao Zhou, Siyi Gao, and Shangguang Wang

The State Key Laboratory of Networking and Switching Technology,
Beijing University of Posts and Telecommunications,
Beijing, China
2012213132@bupt.edu.cn

Abstract. Finding a time series subsequence that is similar to a specific time series is an important problem in trajectory data of vehicles analysis. The problem is made significantly harder for the massive and high-dimensional features of time series. The existing methods for finding the similar subsequences in time series have high time complexity and poor applicability to similar subsequence finding of different lengths. In this paper, we propose an acceleration method for similar time-series finding to address this issue. Firstly, our method defines and extracts the feature of the query sequence. Then, we use the feature as the key to search sequence with the same feature to form a candidate set. After that, in each sequence in candidate set, we filter the important points and add it into feature points list to hold the shape characteristics of original sequence better. Finally, Dynamic time warping (DTW) is used to find the similar time-series. Experiment results illustrate that the proposed method can improve the search efficiency and accuracy.

Keywords: Time series · Similarity searching · Dimensions reduction
Acceleration method

1 Introduction

With the development of science and technology, a large amount of data, such as communication data and trajectory data of vehicles, are generated every day [1]. Not only in the Internet, but also in daily life, data is generated everywhere. Time series data are a set of data arranged in chronological order, such as traffic at an intersection [2] and stock price changes [3, 4]. Analysis of time series data can help us to better understand the development law of things. For example, analysis of trajectory data of vehicles can help to find road traffic anomalies, and analysis of traffic flow data can help do route planning for vehicles.

Similar time series is defined as similar in shape. Time series similarity evaluation is the premise of other data mining tasks, such as classification [5], clustering [6], anomaly detection [7] and pattern recognition [8]. Therefore, from a certain point of view, the performance of time series similarity finding determines the efficiency of time series mining algorithm [9].

A. M. J. Skulimowski et al. (Eds.): IOV 2018, LNCS 11253, pp. 289–301, 2018.
https://doi.org/10.1007/978-3-030-05081-8_21

Traditionally, finding the time series subsequence that is similar to a specific time series consists of three steps. Firstly, do dimension reduction on time series, secondly, a similarity measurement method is employed to calculate the similarity between two time-series. Finally, similar time-series can be found if the similarity between the query time series and a time series subsequence is smaller than the user defined parameter.

Euclidean distance [10] is a traditional time-series similarity evaluation method. However, similar subsequence finding based on Euclidean distance [11, 12] is not suitable. That's because Euclidean distance can only be applied to the comparison of time series with equal length. For example, if there are two time-series with similar M-shaped trends but different length, it is hard to detect the similarity using Euclidean distance.

Dynamic time warping (DTW) is another similarity evaluation method [13–15]. Compared with Euclidean distance, DTW has better robustness. Although DTW [16] is a good solution to the problem of horizontal drift of time series, how to index time-series has always been a difficult problem to solve [17]. Comparing all sub-sequences with the query sequence is time-consuming. Using the DTW to calculate the distance between sequences directly is also inefficient, due to the high time complexity of the algorithm.

To address this issue, we propose an acceleration method for similar time-series finding in this paper. Our method mainly consists of four steps. Firstly, we use Adaptive Piecewise Constant Approximation (APCA) method and extreme point method [18] to get the local maximum and minimum points as feature points, arrange them in chronological order forming a feature point sequence. Currently, there are still many small fluctuations that will disturb the similar sub-sequence finding. Then, we calculate trend of the sequence. By applying a trend extraction algorithm to all time series in the database, we get trends of all series. Searching similar time series becomes searching the same trends. Thirdly, we get the trends start time and end time and cut it from the original series to form the candidate set. Then, we add several important points into the feature point list to form an important point list. Finally, we, calculate DTW of the processed series to find similar time-series. Experiment results illustrate the effectiveness of our method.

This paper is organized as follows. Section 2 introduces related works. The technical details of our method are presented in Sect. 3. Section 4 shows the experimental results. Section 5 concludes this paper.

2   Related Works

2.1   DTW

In order to solve the problems caused by Euclidean distance [19], dynamic time warping (DTW) was proposed [20]. The algorithm uses the dynamic programming method to align the time axis dynamically [21]. There are two time series $X^Q(v^Q, t^Q) = [(v_1^Q, t_1^Q), (v_2^Q, t_2^Q), (v_3^Q, t_3^Q)....(v_m^Q, t_m^Q)]$ and $X^C(v^C, t^C) = [(v_1^C, t_1^C), (v_2^C, t_2^C), (v_3^C, t_3^C)....(v_n^C, t_n^C)]$, X^Q and X^C are respectively placed on two axes of two-dimensional coordinate system. The warping path of X^Q and X^C is the regular path of DTW [22], which achieves the shortest distance between warped X^Q and X^C. With the warping of time series, the DTW distance is the minimum value of the sum of the point-to-point distances, the corresponding normalized path is the best path. Therefore, the definition of the DTW distance between Q and C is as follows

$$D_{dtw}(X^Q,\ X^C) = f(m,\ n,\ X^Q,\ X^C) \tag{1}$$

$$f(m,\ n,\ X^Q,\ X^C) = D_{dtw}(c_i,\ q_i,\ X^Q,\ X^C) + \min\{d(i,\ j-1),\ d(i-1,\ j),\ d(i,\ j)\} \tag{2}$$

$$d(0,\ 0) = 0, d(i,\ 0) = d(0,\ i) = \infty \tag{3}$$

where $(1 \le i \le m,\ 1 \le j \le n)$, c_i and q_i represent the ith point in X^C and X^Q respectively, $d(i,\ j)$ is the distance between the ith point of X^C and j^{th} point of X^Q, $f(m,\ n,\ X^Q,\ X^C)$ is the accumulative distance. To find the best path, we need to construct an $m * n$ cost matrix W_{m*n}. $W(i,\ j)$ is an element in W_{m*n}. In general, the DTW distance can be computed by dynamic programming. When calculating the DTW distances of above two time series, the algorithm complexity is $O(mn)$ [23].

2.2   DTW with Range

Suppose the length of the query sequence is L, we intercept all sub-sequence of sequence in database from index α (lower boundary) to index β (upper boundary) and compare them to query sequence find similar subsequence. The method traverses all the sub-sequence within this ranges, and calculates the DTW distance between the query sequence and the sub-sequence. If the DTW distance is smaller than the user-defined threshold, we find a similar sub-sequence. The start point and the end point are marked.

2.3   DTW with Lower Boundary

This method extracts the upper and lower boundary of the query sequence as query features and then constructs a DTW lower bound distance [23]. Suppose the maximum range is r. The upper and lower boundary sequences U and L are defined as follows:

$$U_i = \max(q_{i-r} : q_{i+r}),\ L_i = \min(q_{i-r} : q_{i+r}) \tag{4}$$

$$LB\_keogh(Q, C) = \begin{cases} \sqrt{(c_i - U_i)^2}, & c_i > U_i \\ \sqrt{(L_i - c_i)^2}, & c_i < L_i \\ 0 & , \text{ otherwise} \end{cases} \tag{5}$$

By defining the lower bound of DTW, we can filter out some sub-sequences to accelerate the searching process. However, for the time series with different values but similar trends, the method do not work well.

2.4   Non-DTW-Based Similarity Finding Methods

Although DTW has its advantages, there are still many complicated situations where DTW may not be the perfect choice, such as protein motif discovery, which needs efficient mining of contiguous approximate patterns. Non-DTW-based similarity finding methods is more suitable in this condition. A new algorithm called FLAME (FLexible and Accurate Motif DEtector) [24] is proposed to find frequent patterns with a variety of definitions of motif models. Based on the monotonic aggregation transform, a novel method is proposed in [25] to improve the quality of forecasts for long-memory time series.

3   Acceleration Method for Similar Time-Series Finding

Our method consists of four steps: (1) feature extraction; (2) candidate set construction; (3) dimension reduction; (4) similar time-series finding based on DTW. In this section we describe the technical details of those steps. All notation used in this paper are summarized in Table 1.

Table 1. A summarization of the notations

Symbol	Meaning
$X(v, t)$	Time series
λ	Tolerance of dimension reduction, its optimal value can be obtained after training on the dataset [26].
L	Length of window
$F[]$	Features of the query series
$APCA()$	APCA dimension reduction method
$X'(v, t)$	Time series after APCA is applied
$Extreme()$	Extreme dimension reduction method
$X''(v, t)$	Time series after extreme dimension reduction is applied
$head$	The start time of a time interval
$tail$	The end time of a time interval
$query$	Query time sequence after APCA is applied
∂	User defined threshold of importance (0–1)
DR	Dimension reduced candidate set
$slope$	Slope list of time series in candidate set
$slopeD$	The first derivative of $slope$
$expS$	A time series after all dimension reduction steps are applied

3.1 Feature Extraction

The process is illustrated in Algorithm 1. First, we employ APCA [26] and extreme point extraction [23] to eliminate small peaks and valleys. APCA has two parameters λ and L. We add point into the window when the length of the window is less than L and the sum of error between real value and mean value is less than λ. When one of the laws is broken, we remove the latest point in the window.

Then, the trend of the time series is determined by comparing the relationship between two adjacent points of the time series after dimension reduction. When the current point is greater than the latter point, the slope is negative, and the feature of current point is 0. When the current point is smaller than the next point, the slope is positive and the feature of current point is 1. The time complexity of this algorithm is $O(n^3)$ where n is the length of input time series. The feature need to be extracted when a new time series is added.

Algorithm 1 Feature extraction

Input: $X(v,t)$--- input time series
λ ---the tolerance of dimension reduction
L ---the length of window
Output: F [ ]--- feature of the series

Begin:
1. $X'(v,t)$=APCA($X(v,t)$)
2. $X''(v,t)$=extreme($X'(v,t)$)
3. F []=$\varnothing$
4. **for** point in $X''(v,t)$:
5.   **if** $v_{i+1} > v_i$:
6. F .add(1)
7.   **else**
8. F .add(0)
9. **return** F

3.2 Candidate Set Construction

The process is illustrated in Algorithm 2. The algorithm takes the feature array of query time series as input and traverses all time-series in the database to find the candidate series. We first traverse all the time series in the database, and obtain the feature of current traversed time series by employing Algorithm 1. Then we compare the subsequences of feature series of current traversed time series and the feature array of the query sequence. If the sub-sequences of feature series of current traversed time series are the same to the feature series of the query sequence, we get the sub-sequence by mapping start point and end point back to original time series. After employing APCA to eliminate small peaks and valleys of the original time series, the sub-sequence is added to the candidate set. The time complexity of Algorithm 2 is $O(n)$, where n is the length of feature array.

Algorithm 2 Candidate set construction

    Input: F --- feature of query sequence
    Output: *result* --- similar sequence list

    Begin:
1.   **for** each time series in database:
2.   get feature of this time series
3.   **for** *ele* in *TimeSeries.F* :
4. $i = ele.index$
5.   **if** $F = TimeSeries.F[i, i + F.length]$
6. $head$, $tail$ =Get time interval of $TimeSeries.F[i, i + F.length]$
7.   //get APCA series
8. $series$ = APCA ($head$, $tail$)
9. $result$ .add($series$)
10. **return** *result*

3.3   Important Point Insertion

Because there are also important points that are not extreme points, we add the additional point into candidate time series. The process is illustrated in Algorithm 3. We connect every two adjacent points, and calculate the slope of the segment. After traversing all the segment, we calculate the first derivative of the slope list. The first derivative of the slope list shows the changing altitude of the slope. If the first derivative is larger than ∂, we think that there is an important point need to be added. We locate the important point through indexing, and add it into the candidate time series.

Algorithm 3 Important point insertion

Input: *result* []---candidate time series after APCA

   query —query time sequence after APCA

   ∂ --- User defined threshold of importance

Output: *DR* --- dimension reduced candidate set

Begin:
1. $DR = []$
2. $slope = []$
3. $slopeD = []$
4. **for** a_series in *result* :
5. $\exp S = []$
6.   **for** a_p in a_series :
7.   **if** a_p is not last:
8. $slope \leftarrow a\_slope = \Delta value / \Delta time$
9.   **for** a_SlopeP in $slope$:
10.   **if** a_SlopeP is not last:
11. $slopeD \leftarrow a\_slopeD = \Delta value / \Delta time$
12.   **for** a_sD in $slopeD$:
13.   **if** $a\_sD > \partial$:
14. imp_p // map back the point in a_series
15. $\exp S \leftarrow imp\_p$
16. DR .add($\exp S$)
17. **return** DR .

3.4   Similar Time-Series Finding Based on DTW

We obtain the feature series of the query time series by employing Algorithm 1. Then the DTW distance between the feature series of the query time series and each candidate series is calculated. If the DTW distance is smaller than the user-set parameter ε, the candidate series is defined to be similar to query sequence.

4   Performance Evaluation

4.1   Experiment Setup

We experiment on two datasets:

(1) The traffic flow data in Beijing. The dataset can be found in http://traflow.fudan.edu. cn/index.html. The dataset consists of the traffic flow of 12 crossroads for 61 days.
(2) 300 stocks from Shanghai-Shenzhen (CSI) 300 Index. Our method is also effective in some nonlinear time series. In order to prove it, we experiment on

financial dataset. The stock market data can be found in wind financial analyze software in http://www.wind.com.cn/. The dataset consists of price of 300 stocks in Shanghai and Shenzhen stock market.

We have realized the methods using Python language. Experiments are conducted on a computer with Intel (R) i7-7660U CPU 4.0 GHz, 8 GB of RAM and Windows 10.0 operating system professional version. We compare our methods with three other methods: (1) DTW with Equal Length: (2) DTW with Range: (3) DTW with Lowerbound. In this experiment, we define $\alpha = 1/2$, β as $3/2$. λ is set as 0.5 in experiment on stock price, and as 1800 in experiment on traffic flow data, L as 4 and ∂ as 0.5. We employ the missing rate, the error rate and the execution time to evaluate all method. Error rate and missing rate are defined as follows:

$$\text{Error rate} = \frac{\text{total number of incorrectly detected sub-sequence}}{\text{total number of similar sub-sequence}} \qquad (6)$$

$$\text{Missing rate} = \frac{\text{total number of sub-sequence failed to be detected}}{\text{total number of similar sub-sequence}} \qquad (7)$$

4.2   Experiment Results on Traffic Flow Dataset

The experiment results on traffic flow dataset are shown in Tables 2 and Figs. 3, 4, 5 and 6. The corresponding DTW distances of the five similar sub-series are shown in Table 3. All similar sub-sequences are marked in different colors. The query sequence is shown in Fig. 1. We take flow data in West Xueyuanlu Bridge (in Beijing) as an example. As shown in Fig. 2 there are five similar sub-sequences. DTW with Equal Length only find one similar sub-sequence. DTW with Range and DTW with Lowerbound find three similar sub-sequences, but one of them is false positive. DTW with acceleration detects four similar sub-sequence. Error rate and missing rate are shown in Table 2.

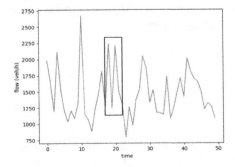

Fig. 1. Query series and its dimension reduction result

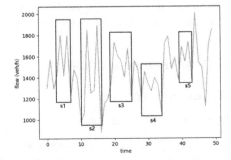

Fig. 2. The actual sub-sequences that are similar to the query sequence

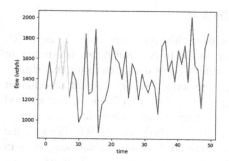

Fig. 3. Result of DTW with Equal Length

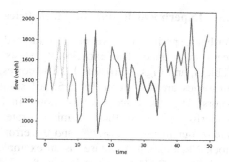

Fig. 4. Result of DTW with Range

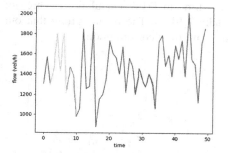

Fig. 5. Result of DTW with Lower-bound

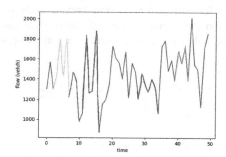

Fig. 6. Result of DTW with Acceleration

Table 2. Experiment results in traffic flow dataset

	Missing rate	Error rate	Time(s)
DTW with Equal Length	73.1%	97.7%	133.535
DTW with Range	37.4%	59.8%	9559.534
DTW with Lower-bound	36.9%	59.6%	27.728
DTW with Acceleration	**22.1%**	**46.9%**	**4.791**

Table 3. DTW distance in traffic flow dataset

	S1	S2	S3	S4	S5
DTW with Equal Length	0.426	0.692	0.853	0.795	0.701
DTW with Range	0.403	0.581	0.722	0.454	0.562
DTW with Lower-bound	0.403	0.581	0.722	0.454	0.562
DTW with Acceleration	**0.338**	**0.46**	**0.635**	**0.425**	**0.473**

4.3   Experiment Results on Stock Price Dataset

Further experiments have been conducted with highly nonlinear time series which occur in finance. The experiment results on stock price dataset are illustrated in Table 4, and Figs. 9, 10, 11, 12. The corresponding DTW distances of the five similar sub-series are shown in Table 5. All similar sub-sequences are marked in different colors. The query sequence is shown in Fig. 7. As shown in Table 4, our method outperforms other methods in missing rate, error rate and execution time. The correct rate of our method is 78.7%, and the error rate of our method is 48.9%. We take the stock No. 002074 in dataset as an example. There are four similar sub-sequences in stock No. 002074 as shown in Fig. 8. DTW with Equal Length only find one similar sub-sequence. DTW with Range and DTW with Lower-bound find two similar sub-sequence. DTW with Lower-bound uses the upper and lower bounds eliminates non-conforming sub-sequences, and avoids wasting time in DTW calculations. Three of them are found by us and the process only take 0.147 s. The results prove that our algorithm has a great improvement in accuracy and time consumption.

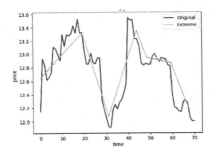

Fig. 7. Query series and its dimension reduction result

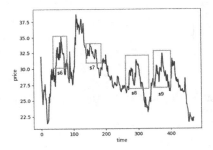

Fig. 8. The actual sub-sequences that are similar to the query sequence

Table 4. Experiment results in stock price dataset

	Missing rate	Error rate	Time(s)
DTW with Equal Length	76.6%	104.2%	102.857
DTW with Range	36.2%	63.8%	7302.85
DTW with Lower-bound	31.9%	59.6%	21.183
DTW with Acceleration	**21.3%**	**48.9%**	**3.797**

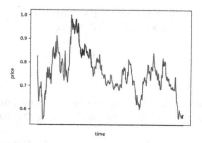

Fig. 9. Result of DTW with Equal Length

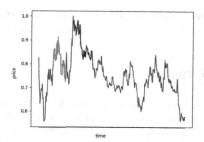

Fig. 10. Result of DTW with Range

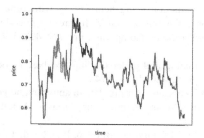

Fig. 11. Result of DTW with Lower-bound

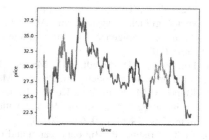

Fig. 12. Result of DTW with Acceleration

Table 5. DTW distance in stock price dataset

DTW distance of different methods	S6	S7	S8	S9
DTW with Equal Length	0.614	0.348	0.683	0.627
DTW with Range	0.323	0.471	0.567	0.503
DTW with Lower-bound	0.323	0.471	0.567	0.503
DTW with Acceleration	**0.237**	**0.465**	**0.439**	**0.419**

5 Conclusion

Similar time-series finding is significant in decision-making for vehicles. For example, finding similar time-series in traffic flow data can help to path planning for vehicles, and finding similar time-series in vehicle login data can help to recommendation parking lot for vehicles. In this paper, we present an acceleration method for similar time-series finding. First, we use APCA and extreme point to reduce dimension, and calculate the relationship between two adjacent feature points as the trend. Secondly, we get the candidate set and add important points to the candidate set. Finally, we search for similar sub-sequences by calculating DTW on processed query series and candidate series. By experimenting with real-world data, we find that our method outperforms other DTW-based methods in accuracy and execution time. We will conduct experiments on other types of datasets in the future.

Acknowledgment. This research is supported in part by NSFC (61571066, 61602054), and Beijing Natural Science Foundation under Grant No. 4174100 (BNSF, 4174100).

References

1. Agrawal, D., Das, S., Abbadi, A.: Big data and cloud computing: current state and future opportunities. In: Proceeding of the 14th International Conference on Extending Database Technology, pp. 530–533. ACM (2011)
2. Basu, S., Mukherjee, A., Klivansky, S.: Time series models for internet traffic. In: Fifteenth Joint Conference of the IEEE Computer Societies. NETWORKING the Next Generation, pp. 611–620. IEEE (1996)
3. Meesad, P., Tong, S.: Stock price time series prediction using neuro-fuzzy with support vector guideline system. In: ACIS International Conference on Software Engineering, Artificial Intelligence, Networking, and Parallel/distributed Computing, pp. 422–427. IEEE Press (2008)
4. Fortuny, E.T.D., Smedt, T.D., Martens, D.: Evaluating and understanding text-based stock price prediction models. Inf. Process. Manage. **50**(2), 426–441 (2014)
5. Ramos, C.M., Brito, Z.P., Kostov, B.: Google driven search for big data in autoimmune geo epidemiology: Analysis of 394,827 patients with systemic autoimmune diseases. Autoimmun. Rev. **14**(8), 670–679 (2015)
6. Radha Krishna, P.: Big data search and mining. In: Mohanty, H., Bhuyan, P., Chenthati, D. (eds.) Big Data. SBD, vol. 11, pp. 93–120. Springer, New Delhi (2015). https://doi.org/10.1007/978-81-322-2494-5_4
7. Leung, K.S., Mackinnon, R.K., Jiang, F.: Reducing the search space for big data mining for interesting patterns from uncertain data. In: IEEE International Congress on Big Data, Anchorage, pp. 315–322. IEEE Press (2014)
8. Pez, Y., Ez, I., Sheremetov, L.: A novel associative model for time series data mining. Pattern Recogn. Lett. **41**(1), 23–33 (2014)
9. Hu, B., Chen, Y., Zakaria, J.: Classification of multi-dimensional streaming time series by weighting each classifier's track record. In: 2013 IEEE 13th International Conference on Data Mining, Texas, pp. 281–290. IEEE Press (2013)
10. Tataw, O.M., Rakthanmanon, T., Keogh, E.J.: Clustering of symbols using minimal description length. In: 12th International Conference on Document Analysis and Recognition, Washington, pp. 180–184, IEEE Press (2013)
11. Mennitt, D.J., Fristrup, K.: Anomaly detection and other practical considerations for estimating acoustical metrics from time series data. J. Acoust. Soc. Am. **140**(4), 3424 (2016)
12. Gharehbaghi, A., Ask, P., Babic, A.: A pattern recognition framework for detecting dynamic changes on cyclic time series. Pattern Recognit. **48**(3), 696–708 (2015)
13. Esling, P., Agon, C.: Time-scales data mining. ACM Computing Surveys (CSUR), **45**(1), 1–34, ACM (2015)
14. Goldin, D.Q., Kanellakis, P.C.: On similarity queries for time-series data: Constraint specification and implementation. In: Montanari, U., Rossi, F. (eds.) CP 1995. LNCS, vol. 976, pp. 137–153. Springer, Heidelberg (1995). https://doi.org/10.1007/3-540-60299-2_9
15. Hailin, L., Huichong, G.: Feature representing in data mining and similar distance measure in time series. Res. Comput. Appl. **30**(5), 1285–1291 (2013)
16. Junkui, L.: Research in time series similarity, Doctoral Dissertation, Huazhong University of Science and Technology (2008)

17. Agrawal, R., Faloutsos, C., Swami, A.: Efficient similarity search in sequence databases. In: Lomet, David B. (ed.) FODO 1993. LNCS, vol. 730, pp. 69–84. Springer, Heidelberg (1993). https://doi.org/10.1007/3-540-57301-1_5
18. Hongbao, M., Fengming, Z.: Time series symbolization method based on feature point conversion. Comput. Eng., China Electron. Technol. Group Corporation. **34**(12), 61–63 (2008)
19. Fu, W.C., Keogh, E., Lau, L.Y.: Scaling and time warping in time series querying. VLDB J. **17**(4), 899–921 (2008)
20. Bankó, Z., Abonyi, J.: Correlation based dynamic time warping of multivariate time series. Expert Syst. Appl. **39**(17), 12814–12823 (2012)
21. Kremer, H., Günnemann, S., Ivanescu, A.-M., Assent, I., Seidl, T.: Efficient processing of multiple DTW queries in time series databases. In: Bayard Cushing, J., French, J., Bowers, S. (eds.) SSDBM 2011. LNCS, vol. 6809, pp. 150–167. Springer, Heidelberg (2011). https://doi.org/10.1007/978-3-642-22351-8_9
22. Faloutsos, C., Ranganathan, M., Anolopoulos, Y.: Fast subsequence matching in time-series database. In: Proceedings of the 1994 ACM SIGMOD international conference on Management of data, pp. 419–429. ACM Press (1994)
23. Yi, B.K., Jagadishg, H.V., Faloutsos, C.: Efficient retrieval of similar time sequences under time warping. In: Data Engineering, 1998. Proceedings, 14th International Conference on Data Engineering, pp. 201–208, IEEE (1998)
24. Floratou, A., Tata, S., Patel, J.M.: Efficient and accurate discovery of patterns in sequence data sets. In: 2010 IEEE 26th International Conference on Data Engineering, pp. 1154–1168. IEEE (2011)
25. Skulimowski, A.M.J.: Reveiling complexity-related time-series features with the monotonic aggregation transform. In: IEEE, International Conference on TOOLS with Artificial Intelligence, pp. 694–700. IEEE (2014)
26. Berndt, D.J., Clifford, J.: Using dynamic time warping to find patterns in time series. In: KDD workshop, Washington, pp. 359–370. KDD Press (1994)

Author Index